Inside the Jazzomat

Martin Pfleiderer, Klaus Frieler, Jakob Abeßer,
Wolf-Georg Zaddach, Benjamin Burkhart (Eds.)

Inside the Jazzomat

New Perspectives for Jazz Research

The book was funded by the German Research Foundation

(research project „Melodisch-rhythmische Gestaltung von Jazzimprovisationen. Rechnerbasierte Musikanalyse einstimmiger Jazzsoli")

Bibliografische Information der Deutschen Nationalbibliothek

Die Deutsche Nationalbibliothek verzeichnet diese Publikation in der Deutschen Nationalbibliografie; detaillierte bibliografische Daten sind im Internet über http://dnb.d-nb.de abrufbar.

978-3-95983-124-6 (Paperback)
978-3-95983-125-3 (Hardcover)

© 2017 Schott Music GmbH & Co. KG, Mainz
www.schott-campus.com

Alle Rechte vorbehalten
Nachdruck in jeder Form sowie die Wiedergabe durch Fernsehen, Rundfunk, Film, Bild- und Tonträger oder Benutzung für Vorträge, auch auszugsweise, nur mit Genehmigung des Verlags.

Cover: Portrait of Fats Navarro, Charlie Rouse, Ernie Henry and
Tadd Dameron, New York, N.Y., between 1946 and 1948 (detail)
© William P. Gottlieb (Library of Congress)

Printed in Germany

Contents

Acknowledgements   1

Intro

Introduction   5
   Martin Pfleiderer

Head: Data and concepts

The Weimar Jazz Database   19
   Martin Pfleiderer

Computational melody analysis   41
   Klaus Frieler

Statistical feature selection: searching for musical style   85
   Martin Pfleiderer and Jakob Abeßer

Score-informed audio analysis of jazz improvisation   97
   Jakob Abeßer and Klaus Frieler

Solos: Case studies

Don Byas's "Body and Soul"   133
   Martin Pfleiderer

Mellow Miles? On the dramaturgy of Miles Davis's "Airegin"   151
   Benjamin Burkhart

West Coast lyricists: Paul Desmond and Chet Baker *Benjamin Burkhart*	175
Trumpet giants: Freddie Hubbard and Woody Shaw *Benjamin Burkhart*	197
Michael Brecker's "I Mean You" *Wolf-Georg Zaddach*	211
Right into the heart. Branford Marsalis and the blues "Housed from Edward" *Wolf-Georg Zaddach*	227
Bob Berg's solo on "Angles" *Klaus Frieler*	243
Steve Coleman—Balanced improvisation *Friederike Bartel*	273
Following the red line: Chris Potter's solo on "Pop Tune #1" *Wolf-Georg Zaddach*	291

Head out

Conclusion and outlook *Martin Pfleiderer*	305

Outro: Appendix

JazzTube: Linking the Weimar Jazz Database with YouTube *Stefan Balke and Meinard Müller*	315
The FlexQ algorithm *Klaus Frieler*	319
Brief introduction to circular statistics *Klaus Frieler*	323
Glossary	327
References	335

Acknowledgements

During the project runtime, a close and inspiring collaboration with several persons and institutions arose: The International Audio Laboratories Erlangen, in particular Meinard Müller, Stefan Balke, and Christian Dittmar, the Semantic Music Technologies group at Fraunhofer IDMT Ilmenau, namely Estefanía Cano, and the Center of Jazz Studies and its J-DISC group, namely Tad Shull. Moreover, we would like to thank Andreas Kissenbeck, Munich, for inspiring exchanges about jazz theory, Wolfram Knauer, Jazz Institute Darmstadt, for his continuous interest in our project, and Simon Dixon, Queen Mary University London, who initiated a successful application for an international two-year follow-up research project focused on pattern usage in jazz.

Most of the aforementioned persons came to Weimar to participate in one or both of our International Jazzomat Research Workshops in September 2014 and September 2016. We would like to thank all the participants, speakers and audience, of these workshops for sharing their time and taking part in discussions about computational perspectives of jazz research with us.

Moreover, we extend our thanks to the Jazzomat community who tested preliminary versions of our software and our database and gave invaluable feedback, and to all the people who helped the project find a broader public.

A heartfelt thank you goes out to Christiane Kraft and Kerstin Höhn from the administration of the Music University Weimar, who helped manage the project. We would also like to thank the German Research Foundation for the two grants which enabled both the existence of the project during 2012–2017 and this publication in the first place and Nicola Heine for proofreading and revising the manuscript.

Last but not least, cheers to all jazz musicians who provided us with this wonderful music.

Weimar, June 2017
Martin Pfleiderer, Klaus Frieler, Jakob Abeßer,
Wolf-Georg Zaddach, and Benjamin Burkhart

Intro

Introduction

Martin Pfleiderer

The Jazzomat Research Project is situated at the intersection between jazz research, music psychology and computational musicology. It aims at developing new perspectives for jazz analysis as well as for the psychology of improvisation and, last but not least, for computational music research and music information retrieval (MIR). Up to now, the ongoing research project's main contributions have been a database of 456 transcriptions of monophonic jazz improvisations (the Weimar Jazz Database) and a standalone software toolkit (MeloSpySuite/GUI) for the analysis of monophonic music; both of these, the database and software toolkit, are freely available and open to further additions and adjustments by users. Several studies and new approaches have been devised within the project both in the areas of jazz research and music psychology, e. g., the concept of midlevel units for analyzing jazz improvisations, resulting in a new model of improvisation, as well as in music information retrieval, e. g., approaches involving score-informed automated feature annotations of music recordings. The database and the software as well as the project's contributions to music information retrieval are introduced within the four chapters in the first part of this publication. The subsequent chapters within the second part of the book are devoted to nine analytical case studies using the Weimar Jazz Database and MeloSpyGUI. In this introductory chapter, the project's background both in jazz research, mainly jazz analysis, and in the computer-aided analysis of music is outlined. Then, a brief overview over the book's contents is given.

Jazz research: studying the infinite art of improvisation

The Jazzomat Research Project ties in with a long tradition of jazz research which focuses on musicians and their performances, on creative processes and their cultural contexts. By introducing computational methods for the analysis of recorded jazz improvisations the project aims at contributing to this multifaceted research tradition with new analytical methods, a comprehensive database and corresponding software tools.

Jazz is a musical performance practice which now spans over more than a century. The origins of jazz extend back to musical practices of African Americans living in New Orleans around 1900. In the 1920s, jazz increasingly gained recognition all over the United States and worldwide, culminating in the swing craze of the late 1930s and early 1940s. In these times, jazz was often viewed as a very popular musical practice for entertainment and dancing. However, since its beginnings, jazz has also striven for recognition as an art form. During the 1940s, 1950s, and 1960s, both jazz musicians and jazz critics strove for a cultural recognition of jazz. Modern jazz was increasingly appreciated in concerts and festivals as music one has to primarily listen to 'seriously', and jazz critics such as André Hodeir (1956) or Gunther Schuller (1958) started to write about the artistic value of jazz music. This critical writing involved an analytical approach to the music, relying strongly on recordings and transcriptions. In particular, Schuller (1958) intended to use methods of music analysis to prove that a jazz musician, in this case Sonny Rollins with his improvisation on "Blue Seven" (1956), is at a similar artistic level to European composers. Later, Schuller wrote two extensive historical studies of traditional jazz and swing (Schuller, 1968, 1989) featuring comprehensive analytical style portraits of leading musicians.

Since the late 1960s, the project of writing a history of jazz that is founded in analytical scrutiny was pursued by jazz critics and musicologists with analytical studies on jazz musicians such as Charlie Parker (Owens, 1974), Miles Davis (Kerschbaumer, 1978), Lester Young (Porter, 1985), or John Coltrane (Putschögl, 1993; Porter, 1998). Moreover, Thomas Owens (1995) adopted Schuller's approach of an analytical style history with regard to modern jazz styles (bebop, cool jazz, hardbop). His rather sketchy style portraits were complemented by many other studies, e. g., Bickl's study of several bebop musicians (Bickl, 2000). Ekkehard Jost (1975) presented an extensive study of the creative principles guiding free jazz or avant-garde jazz musicians of the 1960s by analyzing the music of, among others, Ornette Coleman, Cecil Taylor, and the late John Coltrane.

In general, the analysis of the creative principles that guide jazz improvisation relies strongly on recordings. However, it is questionable to study a recorded improvisation as a final musical work even if it results from a longer chain of rehearsals and preliminary recordings which could be conceived as draft versions (Tirro, 1974). On the contrary, the art of jazz could be termed an "infinite art of improvisation", as the subtitle of Paul Berliner's seminal study states (Berliner, 1994), one that does not find its objective in an ultimate performance or recording of a piece. Ekkehard Jost argues for a methodology of jazz analysis that aims at describing the prevailing creative principles of an individual style of improvisation rather than certain musical artifacts:

> How relevant is an analysis of recorded improvisations made on a certain date and under certain circumstances (the group involved, the improviser's physical and mental disposition, the conditions imposed by the producer, etc.)? This will depend on the extent to which those improvisations can be taken, beyond the immediate musical facts, as indicative of the specific musicians' and groups' creative principles. (...) analysing and interpreting the features of a given improvisation demands that the analyst take (sic!) into account everything he has learned from other improvisations by the same musician. The significance of general pronouncements on the stylistic features of an improviser, from whom one has just a single solo at hand, is minimal, while the likelihood of drawing false conclusions is very great (Jost, 1975, p. 13f.).

This suggests a two-step methodology of jazz analysis: First, listen to the available recordings of a musician or a group. Then, choose the pieces that seems to be typical for the creative principles of the respective musician and analyze them in detail in order to pinpoint and depict those principles.

John Brownell (1994) emphasizes that jazz unfolds dynamically within a performance process which involves instantaneous improvisation as well as interaction between the musicians. Therefore, he differentiates between the analysis of those unfolding processes and an analysis of the results, such as commercial recordings. Focusing on improvisation as a process opens up an interdisciplinary field of investigation involving approaches and methodologies taken from ethnomusicology, sociology and music psychology. This involves interviews with musicians (Berliner, 1994; Monson, 1996; Norgaard, 2008; C. Müller, 2017), participatory observation in the recording studios and at club stages (Jackson, 2012), and introspection (Sudnow, 1999). Notably, many of these scientific approaches to jazz improvisation also involve an analytical study of recordings and their transcriptions. For instance, at least one third of Berliner's ethnographic study *Thinking in Jazz* (1994) is devoted to music examples transcribed from jazz recordings and to their analytical exploration.

Following the ideas put forth by André Hodeir and Gunther Schuller, Barry Kernfeld (Kernfeld, 2002b, 1995, p. 119-158) proposes different types of improvisation. In paraphrase improvisation, prevalent in jazz of the 1920s and 1930s, a musician refers closely to the original melody of a piece, ornamenting, varying or reworking it. By contrast, in so-called chorus phrase improvisation, jazz musicians improvise without much reference to a tune's theme, instead inventing new lines that fit the harmonies of the original composition. Often, this strategy relies on a vocabulary of formulas, patterns or 'licks' which are artfully woven into ever-changing melodic lines (formulaic improvisation). The usage of repeated patterns during improvisation has become one of the main issues in the study of jazz improvisation and is thoroughly discussed by Owens (1974, 1995), Smith (1991), Berliner (1994), and Finkelman (1997). In motivic improvisation, the musicians vary one or several motives, sometimes taken from the theme of a piece, but more often drawn from the ongoing stream of improvisational ideas, with strategies such as ornamentation, transposition, rhythmic displacement, expansion, compression etc. In particular, this type of improvisation flourished within modal jazz, avant-garde jazz and fusion music, since in those styles the musician is for the most part free from rapidly changing chords.

Besides these improvisation strategies identified by Kernfeld, there are several further dimensions and creative principles to be investigated in improvised jazz music. These are, first of all, the tonal and harmonic implications of improvised melodic lines as well as their relation to the original melody and the chords they are based on and, secondly, the rhythmic features of the improvised lines, including particular features such as cross rhythms or micro-rhythmic play that contribute to the overall 'feel', 'swing' or 'drive' of a solo (see e. g., Friberg & Sundström, 2002). While for a long time analytical jazz studies focused on the improvising soloists alone, Berliner (1994) and Monson (1996) presented transcriptions and analyses of a whole jazz group playing together. This, thirdly, opens up perspectives on the interactive processes between musicians. Robert Hodson (2007) and Benjamin Givan (2016) continued to systematically explore the interplay both between the soloist and rhythm section and within the rhythm section. Last but not least, the individual instrumental or vocal 'sound' characterizes the style of a jazz musician. All of these features contribute to the overall dramaturgy of a jazz improvisation, often described by metaphors such as "telling a story", "making a journey" or "doing a conversation" (see Berliner, 1994; Bjerstedt, 2014), its aesthetic coherence and complexity or simplicity, as well as to the stylistic conciseness and recognizability of a musician or style.

While there are countless studies on the leading jazz musicians of the 1940s and 1950s, approaches to postbop avant-garde and fusion music are still rather scarce. Besides Jost's seminal research on free jazz both in the United States and in Europe (Jost, 1975, 1987), e. g., Keith Waters (2011) examined the recordings of Miles Davis' 1960s quintet, and Andrew Sugg compared improvisational strategies of saxophone players John Coltrane, Dave Liebman, and Jerry Bergonzi (Sugg, 2014).

Since the late 1960s, the growth of jazz studies was paralleled by a growing demand for jazz education and jazz theory, both in the United States and in Europe, and resulted in a consolidation or even canonization of jazz history for students' textbooks. However, since the 1990s, a critique of that canon and new approaches to jazz studies have been promoted by several researchers from various disciplines, namely by film scholar Krin Gabbard (1995a, 1995b, 1996) and literary scholar Robert O'Meally (2004; 2007). Both of them looked for relationships between jazz and American cultural history, e. g., by inquiring into the contribution made by jazz critics to the history of jazz, or the intersections between jazz music and other art forms such as literature, film, photography, and painting. This approach was labeled "new jazz studies" (cf. O'Meally et al., 2004) to set it apart from the 'old' jazz studies pursued by jazz critics and musicologists, who investigated jazz primarily as an art form and sometimes detached from its cultural meanings and the social conditions of production and reception. However, in 'new jazz studies', the music itself often tends to be faded out altogether and in this regard its approach often falls behind the efforts of jazz analysis to appreciate the sounding dimensions of jazz performances. Surprisingly, many studies in the anthologies edited by Gabbard and O'Meally are dedicated to the American jazz canon from 1940s bebop to 1960s avant-garde jazz, while minor figures as well as the somewhat confusing varieties of both jazz after 1980 and jazz outside the United States tend to be neglected.

To sum up, there are several approaches to studying jazz improvisation, all of which complement each other and in doing so, deepen and enrich the understanding, aesthetic pleasure and appreciation of the music as well as an interpretation of its meaning within its cultural and social context. The Jazzomat Research Project aims at contributing to these approaches with both a repository of several hundreds of high-quality transcriptions and computer-based methods. The transcriptions were manually annotated by jazz experts with the aid of computer software using a newly developed data format. Furthermore, a software toolkit was developed to meet the manifold requirements of an analytical approach to monophonic lines, e. g., the examination of pitches and their harmonic implications, duration, rhythm and micro-rhythm, as well as the usage of patterns. These achievements were possible thanks to the close collaboration of software engineers with both an interest in music research and an understanding of jazz on the one hand, and jazz researchers open to concepts and procedures from computational music anaylsis and music information retrieval on the other.

Computational music analysis

The Jazzomat Research Project is rooted in a longer tradition of computational musicology and aims to contribute to that growing field of research—within and beyond jazz music. Computational musicology started within ethnomusicology where researchers often collected, annotated and examined large repositories of music recordings and manual transcriptions. Computers helped to handle these collections, e. g., by systematically managing the metadata and manual annotations (Bronson, 1949; Lomax, 1976) and enabling automated inquiries into those data. An important step towards computational music analysis was the introduction of machine-readable formats for sheet music. Besides widespread music formats such as MIDI (since 1982), several formats were developed for scientific purposes, e. g., the Essen Associative Code (EsAC), designed for building and analyzing the Essen Folk Song Collection, and the **kern-format. Since the 1990s, David Huron and others have encoded large amounts of sheet music in the **kern-format (Huron, 1999; Cook, 2004), including the Essen Folk Song Collection and many scores of classical European as well as non-Western music. Recently, Temperley and de Clerq designed a new format for their transcriptions of rock songs (Temperley & DeClercq, 2013; DeClercq & Temperley, 2011). According to Nicholas Cook, these new music databases

> present a significant opportunity for disciplinary renewal: [...] there is potential for musicology to be pursued as a more data-rich discipline than has generally been the case up to now, and this in turn entails a re-evaluation of the comparative method (Cook, 2004, p. 103).

Huron and collaborators developed a modular software toolkit, the Humdrum Toolkit, which enables a flexible analysis of various features encoded in **kern-format. Further modular analysis toolkits are the MIDI-Toolbox (Eerola & Toiviainen, 2004), which works within the MATLAB environment, and the music21 library for Python (Cuthbert & Ariza, 2010). All of these software tools have their merits and downsides of course; their helpfulness for jazz research appears to be rather limited. By contrast, the software toolkit MeloSpySuite/GUI for Windows and OS X was designed especially for the analysis of monophonic melodic lines and has several specific functionalities for jazz improvisations.

In general, computer-aided music analysis has many advantages. Computers are able to extract musical features quickly, accurately and automatically from large amounts of data, such as an improvisation encompassing hundreds or thousands of tone events, and repositories of thousands of folk songs or jazz improvisations. The feature extraction results in representations (e. g., tables, graphs, statistical values) of the music in regard to various musical dimensions and creative principles, e. g., histograms of pitch class occurrence throughout a music piece or statistical values concerning its degree of syncopicity or chromaticity. As Cook puts it,

> [t]he value of objective representations of music, in short, lies principally in the possibility of comparing them and so identifying significant features, and of using computational techniques to carry out such comparisons speedily and accurately (Cook, 2004, p. 109).

Comparison is a central capacity of the human mind and an important operation in science. To compare two or more objects, one has to identify some common feature dimensions; if they had nothing in common, one would be comparing apples and oranges. Several objects can then be compared in regard to their similarities along these feature dimensions. The researcher's task is to choose suitable feature dimensions based on research objectives. The computer algorithms can then be used in order to extract the chosen features objectively and, in many cases, also more quickly and reliably. In any case, clear and explicit analytical terminology that can be unambiguously transformed into algorithms and data structures is a prerequisite of computer-aided analysis routines. At times, this can help clarify fuzzy 'traditional' terminology, which is a welcome side-effect.

Besides comparing pieces and identifying their significant features, computer-generated representations could also be used in a more explorative manner—as a kind of guidance leading the researcher to listen to particular features that had hitherto passed unnoticed. However, it is important to emphasize that these computational tools and facilities are not meant to (and are hardly able to) replace human researchers, but are for the most part designed for the purpose of enriching traditional methodologies. Since music analysis always involves individual processes of learning and understanding, a researcher has to listen closely to the music in the first place and then identify its typical and idiosyncratic features (cf. Cook, 2004, p. 107). However, this process of 'close listening' to certain pieces could be enhanced and stimulated by a kind of 'distant listening' enabled by algorithms and software tools. One main intention of the analytical case studies presented in the second part of this book is to demonstrate how the analysis of certain typical or particular examples can be fruitfully combined with computer-aided 'distant listening' to larger repertoires and how these latter routines could support and extend an understanding of the music.

Inside the Jazzomat: an overview

This book is an interim report on the ongoing Jazzomat Research Project, focusing mainly on its contributions to jazz research and jazz analysis. In its first part, several basic assumptions and concepts of the project are introduced. In the following chapter the Weimar Jazz Database is introduced, including the transcription process, the assets and drawbacks of the data format as well as the criteria for data selection. Additionally, the contents of the Weimar Jazz Database (release version 2.0) and some of its features and peculiarities are outlined.

Then, the basics of computational melody analysis are discussed—which are at the core of the MeloSpySuite/GUI software. With the aid of this stand-alone software, various musical features of several musical dimensions can be extracted from the transcription data. The mathematical concepts of music representation, segmentation and annotation, feature extraction and pattern mining are introduced along with several examples. Included are short introductions into the approach to a metrical quantification of the data, the concept of midlevel annotation, descriptions of the most important of those features available in MeloSpySuite/GUI as well as the approach to pattern search with regular expressions.

In the subsequent chapter, a statistical approach to the characterization and analysis of musical style is depicted. By using a subset of the musical features extracted by MeloSpySuite/GUI as well as subsets of the Weimar Jazz Database, one can explore which musical features distinguish a certain subset of improvisations, e. g., all improvisations by a certain musician or in a certain jazz style, from the remaining improvisations of the database. The potentials of this powerful and promising statistical approach are exemplified in regard to several subsets and research issues.

While the Jazzomat Research Project focuses on symbolic data, i.e., transcriptions of recorded jazz improvisations, there are several additional aspects concerning an exploration of the audio recordings. Therefore, in the last chapter of the first part, several approaches to linking symbolic and audio data using state-of-the-art algorithms are introduced. At first, approaches based on a score-informed source separation between soloing and accompanying instruments are depicted. This approach leads to an automatic assessment of instrument tuning, tone intensity and tone-wise pitch contour tracking. Furthermore, approaches to an analysis of instrument timbre (as a central aspect within the personal sound of a jazz musician) and an approach to an automatic beat-wise transcription of walking bass lines with deep neural networks are introduced. Additionally, several findings that rely on these new approaches and the data of the Weimar Jazz Database are depicted.

Introduction

The second part of the book encompasses nine analytical case studies which can also be read as examples of how to research on jazz improvisation either with statistical methods and computational analysis tools or with more conventional analytical methods—or with a combination of both approaches. By demonstrating some of these possibilities, the case studies aim at stimulating further analytical research with both the transcriptions included within the Weimar Jazz Database and the MeloSpySuite/GUI software. The main challenge is to meaningfully relate insights gained from closely listening to the music and from its close description with more abstract musical features and representations that can be generated automatically by the software. Each chapter focuses on certain issues exemplified by the analysis of one or more particular improvisations. In most cases, these analytical findings are contextualized within a larger stylistic context—be it within the context of other improvisations by the same musicians or other musicians, or within a larger repertoire of recordings. The comprehensive aim of these analytical case studies is to open up new perspectives for analytical jazz research by combining the advantages of old-school jazz analysis with an analysis supplemented by computer-based methods and comparative approaches.

The first case study is dedicated to two improvisations on "Body and Soul"—one of the jazz standards most favored by jazz musicians. While Coleman Hawkins's recording of "Body and Soul" (1939) is widely appreciated as an important and influential milestone in the history of jazz improvisation, the focus is at first placed on the improvisation by a minor figure in jazz history, Don Byas, who recorded "Body and Soul" in 1944. Then, features of the improvisations by Byas and Hawkins are compared with each other and, in doing so, Gunther Schuller's characterization of an overall intensification process within Hawkins's solo (Schuller, 1989, p. 444) is re-examined by statistical means.

Trumpet player Miles Davis is said to have established a less formulaic and instead more melodic and motivic style of improvisation. In the case study on Davis's improvisation on "Airegin" (1954), presumably one of the first hardbop recordings, several features of Davis's 'mellow' style are characterized, especially in regard to both the usage of different categories of midlevel units and the overall dramaturgy of the improvisation. Additionally, Davis's solo is compared with both improvisations by several bebop trumpeters and other improvisations by Davis.

While Davis is a pivotal figure within the history of modern jazz and has been discussed in many books and articles, there are legions of jazz musicians who have been rather neglected by jazz analysis so far. Moreover, jazz styles such as West Coast jazz or postbop have only been tentatively explored by jazz research up until today. In *West Coast lyricists* the styles of trumpeter Chet Baker and alto saxophonist Paul Desmond, which are often described as 'lyrical', are characterized and compared with those of other cool jazz and West Coast jazz musicians included in the Weimar Jazz Database. The case study aims both at exploring characteristics associated with Baker and Desmond as well as with West Coast jazz in general and at providing a foundation for further analytical research.

The remaining six case studies are dedicated to important musicians who are usually attributed to postbop style. Postbop musicians seem to be very influential for young jazz musicians and improvisation techniques developed by them are at the very core of more recent trends in jazz education (Kissenbeck, 2007). However, there is still a gap concerning an analytical, comprehensive characterization of improvisation strategies in postbop. The case studies aim at contributing to fill this gap. At first, two influential postbop trumpeters, Freddie Hubbard and Woody Shaw, are examined in regard to two aspects which seem to be characteristic for their personal style of improvisation: the usage of uncommon interval leaps within the fast lines played by both of them and the usage of recurring patterns, especially within Hubbard's solo on "Maiden Voyage" (1965) and Shaw's solo on "In a Capricornian Way" (1978).

Tenor saxophonist Michael Brecker is one of the most influential postbop musicians. His playing style could be characterized as a virtuosic exploration of several improvisation techniques, including temporarily playing 'outside' the chord changes or tonality. As is shown in the analytical case study of his improvisation on Thelonious Monk's "I Mean You" (1995), however, his inventive personal style is rooted in the jazz tradition and alludes to several more conventional strategies of improvisation. The relation between postbop playing and the jazz tradition is analyzed in an analytical case study of a solo played by tenor saxophonist Branford Marsalis in the trio recording "House from Edward" (1988). Again, the question of how different strategies of improvisation contribute to the overall dramaturgy of the piece is discussed.

While the case studies on Brecker and Marsalis are conceived as both a close analytical description of the particularities of a certain improvisation and a questioning and contextualizing of more conventional analytical tools based on jazz theory, the case study on tenor saxophonist Bob Berg's solo on "Angles" (1993) takes a slightly different approach. The dramaturgy of the solo is exhaustively explored in regard to many of the features that could be extracted by the MeloSpyGUI software, including midlevel units and pattern usage, and then contextualized within the repertoire of the whole Weimar Jazz Database. This statistical contextualization aims at answering one central question of jazz analysis: Which musical aspects and which creative strategies differentiate a certain improvisation from other improvisations?

Steve Coleman stands out from various other postbop saxophonists in regard to his idiosyncratic concept of tonality which he has described as "symmetrical movement". Taking his solo in "Pass It On" (1991), it is asked which traces of this guiding principle can be found within Coleman's improvisations and how the tonal and rhythmical dimension of his playing style might be characterized in general. This includes a comparison with another solo by Coleman as well as with two solos on "Pass It On" played by other musicians.

The analytical part of the book is concluded by a case study of a solo by saxophone player Chris Potter, who is one of the most widely appreciated jazz musicians of a younger generation born after 1970. His solo on "Pop Tune #1", recorded live in 2007, is a striking example of his distinctive personal style, which both emphasizes rhythmical improvisation orientated towards groove-based popular music and includes advanced strategies of 'outside' playing.

The book closes with a summary and a critical discussion of the findings, and leads to conclusions in regard to new perspectives and possibilities as well as challenges and tasks opened up for jazz research, both by transcriptions in a data format readable by computer and by software tools for music analysis, such as the MeloSpyGUI. In the appendix, there are condensed introductions into the the concept of JazzTube, the FlexQ algorithm and circular statistics, a glossary of technical terms from jazz theory, music analysis, statistics and music information retrieval as well as a bibliography of cited works. Discographical information in regard to the analysed recordings as well as a comprehensive documentation and tutorials of both the Weimar Jazz Database and MeloSpyGUI are available at the website of the Jazzomat Research Project.[1]

---

[1] http://jazzomat.hfm-weimar.de

Head: Data and concepts

The Weimar Jazz Database

Martin Pfleiderer

In this chapter, the Weimar Jazz Database is described. Concepts and purposes of the transcriptions and the data format are presented in detail and the transcription process is outlined. Furthermore, the criteria for the selection of jazz solos are discussed. Finally, the database content and some of its peculiarities are portrayed.

Transcription and data format

The art of jazz improvisation is elusive and hard to grasp. However, audio recordings offer an opportunity to reproduce the sounding dimension of improvised performances, to listen to them repeatedly and to study them in detail. Transcriptions, i. e., visual representations of what one hears and comprehends while listening to music, are of great help for musical analysis. They allow for comparisons both between temporally distant passages within a performance and between different improvisations by one musician or many musicians.

Therefore, it is not surprising that the use of transcriptions of audio recordings is widespread in jazz research as well as in jazz education. While transcribing musical details, the listener becomes more familiar or even intimate with the music—leading to a deepening of his or her knowledge and understanding of the music (cf. Winkler, 1997). Many transcriptions of jazz solos can serve both as an analytical description of music structures and processes as well as a prescription—or used less rigidly, as inspiration—for performance and improvisation and therefore lie somewhere on a continuum between descriptive and prescriptive music notation (cf. Seeger, 1958; Rusch, Salley, & Stover, 2016). On the one hand, there are countless prescriptive transcriptions of jazz solos that serve as the basis for a re-performance by younger musicians.

This is a common learning strategy for enhancing and enlarging one's own improvising skills and for learning about the improvisational strategies of the older generation (see Berliner, 1994). Therefore, building on a set of handy conventions within the jazz community, e. g., in regard to the notation of swinging eighths, prescriptive transcriptions should be easy to read. Descriptive transcriptions, on the other hand, are made by scholars in order to analyze certain stylistic features or aesthetic peculiarities of a performance. While these analytical transcriptions tend to be more detailed, every transcription is a compromise situated between the poles of easy readability and a precise representation of musical details.

Within the field of jazz research, there are various analytical strategies. One could be interested, e. g., in the examination of and comparison between melodic dramaturgies, harmonic strategies, pattern usage, interaction processes, micro-rhythmic peculiarities or expressive qualities. The notational system used in a transcription can vary substantially with regard to style and the amount of detail, depending on these various analytical objectives. Thus, descriptive music transcription in general is hardly separable from both the analytical issues at stake and from an interpretation of analytical findings (Owens, 2002; Rusch et al., 2016, p. 293).

The aim of the Weimar Jazz Database is to meet the requirements for as many analytical issues as possible. What is actually annotated manually are pitches and their durations (onset and offset time), chord changes, beat and meter, form sections, phrase boundaries as well as some expressive features. Additionally, information regarding the dynamics and the intonation of the tones played is extracted automatically, as are accompanying bass lines. Last but not least, annotations of so-called midlevel units are included for all solos (cf. Chapter *Computational melody analysis*). The annotation of midlevel units follows a new qualitative approach introduced by Frieler et al. (2016a) to examine improvisational processes. Therefore, scholars interested in creative processes, jazz theorists interested in harmonic strategies and jazz historians who follow stylistic differences in regard to dramaturgy, melody or rhythm and micro-rhythm can all benefit from the transcriptions within the Weimar Jazz Database.

Unfortunately, due to temporal resources, it was not possible to transcribe all the information in a recorded solo. First of all, the database is restricted to monophonic improvisations. Although it would be desirable to include polyphonic solos played, e. g., on the piano, guitar or vibraphone, these transcriptions would be quite laborious to produce. However, a few single-line solos played on the piano, guitar and vibraphone are included. Secondly, each transcription includes only the melodic line of one improvising soloist and does not refer to the full accompaniment of the rhythm section or the interplay between several musicians. The transcription of a whole group (cf. Berliner, 1994; Hodson, 2007; Waters, 2011; Givan, 2016) was beyond the scope of our project. However, the melodic lines were placed within the metric and harmonic framework of the performance and beat-wise pitch estimates of the accompanying bass lines were added. Thirdly, features of the sounds actually played by a musician, their timbre, dynamics and intonation as well as expressive features such as ghosted notes, vibrato etc. are crucial for the particular rendition of a melodic line and for the overall style of a jazz musician. However, it is hard to transcribe these features reliably. Therefore, vibrato, slides etc. are only roughly described using verbal tags, while dynamics and intonation are extracted automatically by advanced audio algorithms.

The improvised solos were transcribed manually by a team of students and supervised by one of the editors (Wolf-Georg Zaddach). While there are several automatic transcription programs available today (e. g., Songs2see, Tony), none of them met our purposes. The results of these automatic transcription software are quite inaccurate, so that a correction of the faulty output appeared to be more laborious than transcribing from scratch. However, the Sonic Visualiser[2] software proved to be a helpful tool for the transcription process. Sonic Visualiser is a powerful and easy-to-handle tool for the visualization of various aspects of an audio-file. Its main concept is the non-destructive superposition of annotation or visualization layers or panes. Sonic Visualiser allows for

- transcribing notes in a piano-roll-like notation that is easily generated in a note layer;
- tapping along with the recording in order to generate a beat grid in a time-instant layer;
- adding chords and section names (e. g., chorus 1 or secetion A, B etc.) to the beats in an editor window;
- adding further region and text layers in which phrases and expressive characteristics (slides, vibrato, bends etc.) can be captured;
- monitoring the transcription in parallel with listening to the recording;
- slowing down the recording speed while listening to it in order to identify details;

---

[2] http://www.sonicvisualiser.org/

- visual support during the transcription process with a spectrogram layer.

The staff members involved in the transcription process relied heavily on these features. For each solo, they used a note layer to notate the pitch, onset, and offset of the tones. They did not have to assign metric starting points or note values to the tones—one of the more intriguing aspects of transcription which is often open to a certain amount of ambiguity and interpretation (see Rusch et al., 2016). Since automatic beat and bar detection algorithms—which were integrated in the Sonic Visualiser software via Vamp Plugins—proved to be not very reliable in the case of jazz, we settled on manual tapping in a time-instant layer for beat annotation. To this beat track, metric information, chords and form sections were added manually. In general, annotated chords were taken from available lead sheets (mainly various issues of Realbooks and Aebersold recordings) and were added in the same manner throughout all the choruses during a solo. In some cases, chords taken from lead sheets were modified to correspond to the chords actually played by the rhythm section. Musical phrases were annotated in a region layer according to the perception and judgment of the transcriber. Additionally, bass pitches per beats, e. g., the pitch of the walking bass line, dynamics of the solo tones as well as aspects of intonation were added automatically to the transcriptions.

The structure of the transcription process and the resulting transcription data is depicted in Figure 1. The annotations can be exported in Sonic Visualiser project files (with the file extension .sv), which are the basis for the database. Additionally, various metadata concerning the solo, the recording, and the transcription were collected in an Excel spreadsheet, the so-called master table. The metadata can be partially inspected and exported for analytical purposes with MeloSpyGUI. A short introduction into the database format and into some manually annotated metadata categories (such as style, genre, rhythmic feel and tonality type), as well as a complete list of the solos and short descriptions of each solo including graphs and statistical values are available online.[3] The data format allows for a seamless addition of new solos transcribed by the user as well as other transcriptions, following the given data syntax (see online tutorial[4]). Additionally, one can build up a new database by compiling several new transcriptions and including their metadata in a new database.

---

[3] http://jazzomat.hfm-weimar.de/dbformat/dboverview.html
[4] http://jazzomat.hfm-weimar.de/tutorials/sv/sv_tutorial.html

The Weimar Jazz Database

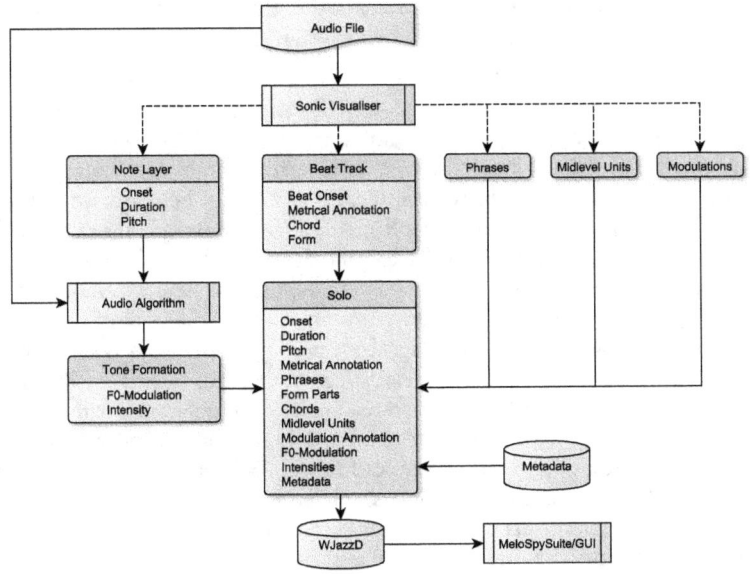

Figure 1: Transcription process and data structures for the Weimar Jazz Database. Dashed lines denote human/manual processes.

The transcription: process and challenges

The twelve staff members involved in the transcription and annotation process were students of either musicology, music education or the jazz program at the Music University 'Franz Liszt' Weimar. They had various musical backgrounds but were in general familiar with jazz, mostly by both listening to and playing jazz. Despite a high level of expertise, the quality of the transcriptions inevitably varied according to the respective solos, transcribers and their form on the day. To guarantee a consistently high quality of data, a multi-level quality improvement procedure was installed. In a first step, a specialized software tool which checks for syntactical errors and omissions in the data structure of sv-files as well as for suspicious data such as beat outliers was developed. After these issues had been dealt with, the files were cross-checked by a single supervisor (Wolf-Georg Zaddach), who is at the same time a postgraduate student of musicology and an experienced jazz guitarist. Sometimes, chord changes had to be adjusted or the beat layer had to be tapped again due to irregularities. Midlevel units were annotated exclusively by Benjamin Burkhart, Friederike Bartel and, initially, by Martin Breternitz. These midlevel annotations were cross-checked by Klaus Frieler to get a consistent coding.

The resulting data can be converted to MIDI and conventional music notation using MeloSpySuite/GUI; the software allows for transpositions, too. Although these scores could be used as a starting point for analyzing or re-performing a given improvisation, they should not be confused with a conventional prescriptive transcription, e. g., jazz transcriptions published for educational purposes. In order to generate readable music scores, however, and also for analytical purposes, metrical positions have to be annotated during post-processing. This is done automatically on the basis of the annotated beat track and the event onsets by a new specially devised algorithm called FlexQ (see Appendix *The FlexQ algorithm*). Since there are still some uncommon note values and hard-to-read metric irregularities, it might be necessary to 'smooth' this score with Lilypond notation software in order to obtain a prescriptive score that could easily be examined by a scholar or performed by a musician. One has to keep in mind that all these scores are only approximations of the transcription data stored within the Sonic Visualiser files and the database.

The transcriptions provided by the Weimar Jazz Database have several advantages. One advantage is the exact annotation of tone onsets regardless of metric positions and duration values which allows for a detailed analysis of micro-rhythmic playing. Since there are many micro-rhythmic subtleties that can be examined only if a precise notation of tone onsets and durations is available, we prefer to provide our data in a raw, unquantified version, albeit accompanied by metrical annotation. Moreover, the transcribed pitches are highly accurate since they are cross-checked several times by several persons. Nevertheless, the transcriptions still involve a moment of fuzziness due to several subjective factors and algorithmic short-comings in regard to the metrical beat grid, pitch notation and the annotation of phrases and midlevel units. One has to keep these aspects in mind whenever one explores the data.

Beat and rhythm transcription

In many jazz performances, the tempo changes subtly and more or less continuously. Therefore, it is very important to have a beat grid that follows these subtle modulations. Since automatic beat trackers were not able to reliably follow the beat in most jazz recordings, the manual tapping of a beat track was a central task for the music transcribers. As it turned out, there are several problems with beat-tapping. First of all, the common concept of beats as definite time points is questionable *per se*. Is it the soloist, the drummer or the bass player with his walking bass line who provides the metric beat grid for the whole ensemble? What about those cases when the soloist plays behind or before the beat played by the rhythm section while, additionally, the beats of the drummer and the bass player constantly shift in relation to each other? Since the transcribers could however only tap definite time points, they were advised to focus on the probably most reliable beat reference, i. e., the drummers' ride cymbal and hi-hat. Although the drums are sometimes hard to perceive in older recordings, this turned out to be a practicable solution. Nonetheless, beat tapping remains an interpretation on the part of the transcriber—similar to the beat interpretation amongst musicians of the band, which may differ sometimes, too.

A second uncertainty was introduced by the differing cognitive and motoric abilities of the staff members in tapping a beat constantly over a whole solo, which sometimes goes on for several minutes. Therefore, in some of the more difficult cases (high tempo, complex playing by the drummer), a jazz drummer was recruited to tap the whole beat track. In other cases, the playback speed was slowed down while tapping, or the transcriber chose to tap in half tempo first. Additionally, it turned out that different computer keyboards used for tapping had different latency times, posing another source of challenge and error. Despite these problems, the beat tracks of most transcriptions seem to be sufficiently exact and appropriate. Nevertheless, in the future, the beat tracks will be checked and compared with state-of-the-art beat detection algorithms.

In some cases, the offsets of tones are not clear-cut but rather vague, in particular when the tones are very short, very low or within fast lines. Additionally, due to the acoustics of the recording room as well as studio post-production techniques such as reverb, it is sometimes hard to detect the exact offsets in terms of milliseconds. Although these offsets have also been cross-checked, some tone durations and offsets are still disputable.

Pitch transcription

In regard to pitches, uncertainties were rather scarce. At the most, it sometimes turned out to be difficult to determine a definite pitch within fast lines, very low tones and glissandi, as well as in the case of slides, ambiguously intoned tones and appoggiaturas or grace notes. While the cross-checked pitch notation is, in general, very precise, one has to keep in mind that every tone—even a very short appoggiatura or the many tones within a longer glissando—is notated in the same way an as, e. g., a long tone played over a whole bar. Slides at the beginning of a tone, 'bends' (raising or lowering the pitch within a tone) and 'fall-offs' at its ending were either notated as two (or more) separate tones or as one tone with an additional note ('slide', 'bend', 'fall-off') in the annotation text layer (see the glossary for further explanation).

Metadata

For each improvisation, a large variety of metadata was collected and included in the Weimar Jazz Database. These metadata can be used for filtering within the software, e. g., choosing or excluding certain solos for a comparative exploration. Most of the metadata values can also be exported and serve for further statistical analysis. An overview of the most important metadata fields can be found in Table 1.

Table 1: The most important metadata fields

Field name	Description
filename_sv	Name of the originating SV file.
filename_solo	Name of the solo cut from the original track.
filename_track	Name of the original track.
solotime	Start/Endtime of the solo in the original track. Format mm:ss-mm:ss.
performer	Performer.
title	Title of tune.
instrument	Instrument used in the solo.
style	Style of the solo. Possible values: TRADITIONAL, SWING, BEBOP, COOL, HARDBOP, POSTBOP, FREE, FUSION, OTHER, MIX.
avgtempo	Avg. tempo (beats per minute, bpm) of the solo as determined by the SV project file.
tempoclass	Rough classification of tempo of the solo. Possible values: SLOW, MEDIUM SLOW, MEDIUM, MEDIUM UP, UP.
rhythmfeel	Basic rhythmic groove of the solo. Possible values: TWOBEAT, SWING, BALLAD, LATIN, FUNK.
key	Key of the solo (if applicable) or tonal center.
signature	Signature(s) of the solo.
chord_changes	Chord changes of solo (as a compact string, as defined by one chorus).
chorus_count	Number of choruses played.
composer	Composer(s) of the underlying tune.

Field name	Description
form	Basic form of the song (e. g., AABA), including labels and length (in bars).
tonalitytype	Tonality type of the song. Possible values: FUNCTIONAL, BLUES, JAZZ-BLUES, MODAL, COLOR, FREE.
genre	Genre of the composition. Possible values: TRADITIONAL, BLUES, GREAT AMERICAN SONGBOOK, WORMS, ORIGINAL, RIFF.
artist	Name of the artist of the record containing the track with the solo.
recordtitle	Title of the record containing the track with the solo.
lineup	Line up of the track containing the solo.
label	Record label.
record	Discographic entry for the record.
mbzid	MusicBrainz identifier for the track containing the solo.
trackno	Number of the track containing the solo on the record.
releasedate	Release date of the record.
recordingdate	Recording dates of the record.

Besides the recording year and line-up, key, meter and tonality type, the rhythmic feel and style of a recording was also attributed. The style categories will be discussed later in this chapter. The 'key' annotation encompasses the tonal center as well as the mode, i. e., major, minor or one of the modal scales. If the tonal center or mode is ambiguous or non-existent, the entry is missing (i. e., 'not available') or if there is a clear tonal center but no discernible mode, the label '-chrom' (for 'chromatic') is used. Additionally, we introduced the variable 'tonality type' to distinguish categories indicating chord changes with a more traditional, functional harmony (FUNCTIONAL), chord changes implying a blues tonality (BLUES), chord changes with a mixture of functional and more modal harmony (COLOR), improvisation based on scales with few or no chord changes (MODAL) and free playing with no definite harmonic framework (FREE). Meter is, in the overwhelming majority, common time ($\frac{4}{4}$), with only few exceptions. The prevailing meter is annotated. However, if no clear meter is discernible (as with some recordings of Ornette Coleman), the respective improvisation is labeled $\frac{1}{4}$, i. e., each beat has the same metric value ('pulse'). The rhythmic feel is in most cases SWING—even if there is a ride cymbal figure with straight eighths. Further categories are TWOBEAT for recordings of traditional jazz, LATIN including bossa nova, FUNK including many fusion recordings (even if they are played with more rock-like patterns), and BALLAD for improvisations which have no ride cymbal accompaniment and are often played in half time. As with any classification system, the categories themselves as well as the attributions are at times debatable, not least because we did not allow multi-class membership. In uncertain cases, we generally took a majority vote among the staff members. In this regard, all class labels can be viewed as most likely labels, not as a unique one. The philosophy behind our various categories is that any classification is better than no classification. In particular when dealing with large amounts of data, categories give some orientation and allow for easy filtering and navigation. Besides these content-based metadata, we also included standard discographic data such as record label, record title, recording and release date, lineup and MusicBrainz-ID (if available).

The original audio recordings of the Weimar Jazz Database are not available at the website of the Jazzomat Research Project due to copyright restrictions. Fortunately, however, Stefan Balke and Meinard Müller designed an internet application called JazzTube which is automatically linked to freely available YouTube clips of most of the recordings.[5] Additionally, statistical information of the solos are given as well as piano roll representations which moves along on the screen while listening to the YouTube recording. The conception of the online application is sketched in Appendix *JazzTube: Linking the Weimar Jazz Database with YouTube*.

The Weimar Jazz Database: within and beyond the canon

The Weimar Jazz Database v2.0 contains 456 transcriptions of improvised jazz solos. It is clear that some sort of selection process had to take place during the development. The final selection of musicians and solos does not automatically imply that these musicians and recordings are deemed more important or more valuable than those left out. A pragmatic stance was often taken and recordings were included that were easily available in the university library or the private collections of staff members. Nonetheless, several selection criteria were devised. These include criteria according to style, the number of solos by one musician, as well as the distribution of instruments and compositions. All criteria and all decisions are, of course, negotiable and open for revision.

In general, when building databases of musical works, two principles can be adopted: 'depth first' or 'breadth first'. Since our goals were rather general and designed to serve a variety of analytical and scientific needs, we chose a 'breadth first' approach, i. e., we decided to cover a broad range of jazz styles rather than focusing exclusively on a very narrow range of (eminent) players.

---

[5] http://mir.audiolabs.uni-erlangen.de/jazztube/

We nevertheless decided to represent some players more strongly than others (e. g., Charlie Parker, Miles Davis, or John Coltrane) because for some analyses (e. g., of personal style), a certain depth is necessary. Likewise, due to our rather broad goals, we decided to start from a core of players and solos, guided by the established jazz canon, and then to further supplement this core with lesser-known players to serve as a context for analytical applications

Jazz is a global music practice. Since its beginnings in the early 20th century, jazz music has been performed not only in the United States, but also in Europe, Australia, Canada, and all over the world (Atkins, 2003; Bohlman & Plastino, 2016). This is one of the reasons why the US jazz canon—as documented in the Smithsonian Collection of Classical Jazz (Williams, 1973) or in several jazz history textbooks (Tirro, 1977; Gridley, 1978; Porter, Ullman, & Hazell, 1993)—was questioned by authors such as Scott DeVeaux (1991), Gary Tomlinson (1991), or Krin Gabbard (1995a, 1995b). However, there is a need for a jazz canon for teaching purposes, e. g., in jazz history courses at colleges and universities. As Kenneth E. Prouty puts it:

> It is one thing to point out what is missing or what is wrong with a particular historical narrative. Suggesting an alternative, however, is more difficult. Perhaps this is why we have yet to see a jazz history text that truly departs from the canon, one that represents a clear break from the 'consensus view' of Marshall Stearnes, or of Scott DeVeaux's 'official history' (Prouty, 2010, p. 43).

Significantly, and despite his own critique of the canon, Scott DeVeaux's account of jazz history—published in cooperation with Gary Giddins in 2009 (DeVeaux & Giddins, 2009)—predominantly follows the well-trodden paths of established jazz historiography. Moreover, many jazz musicians worldwide refer profoundly to the US-American—predominantly Afro-American—jazz tradition. This has practical reasons, too. Following the stylistic paths of swing, bebop, cool jazz, and hardbop as well as relying on a common repertoire of jazz standards (compositions from the Great American Songbook and well-known original compositions by jazz musicians) allows for spontaneous playing and jamming together—regardless of the jazz musicians' provenience. In regard to this repertoire and common strategies for improvising with its functional harmony, one might speak of a 'common practice jazz' which relies mainly on role models from US-jazz of the 1940s, 1950s and 1960s. Investigations of more recent directions in jazz after 1970 have to deal with this tradition in a comparative manner, too. Therefore, it is important to start with a corpus which encompasses the 'American jazz canon'—ranging from the first jazz recordings of the 1920s over the great improvisers of the 1930s, 1940s and 1950s until the avant-garde, e. g., the 1960s recordings of Ornette Coleman, John Coltrane, or Miles Davis.

While the history of jazz until the 1960s and to some parts of the 1970s is well examined and documented, there are still debates going on concerning jazz after 1980 and jazz outside the United States (Nicholson, 2005, 2014). It is the intention of the Jazzomat Research Project to contribute to the debate on canonization by including jazz musicians beyond the established canon—minor figures such as Don Byas, Pepper Adams and Don Ellis, as well as musicians of the younger generation such as Chris Potter, Steve Coleman or Pat Metheny. However, the current version of the Weimar Jazz Database focuses strongly on jazz musicians from the United States—with only a few exceptions, e. g., Canadian trumpet player Kenny Wheeler, who lived in Great Britain from the 1950s onwards. The history of jazz improvisation in Europe, Canada, Australia, Latin America, Africa and Asia will have to be examined in follow-up research projects. Nonetheless, it is necessary for those further studies to be able to draw on a repository of the established US jazz canon for comparison.

The corpus

The Weimar Jazz Database focuses on monophonic instruments, mostly saxophone (alto, tenor, soprano and baritone), trumpet, trombone, and clarinet (see Table 2). Additionally, there are several monophonic improvisations on the vibraphone (Lionel Hampton and Milt Jackson), guitar (Pat Metheny, John Abercrombie, and Pat Martino) and piano (single-line improvisations by Red Garland and Herbie Hancock). Unfortunately, piano, guitar and vibraphone solos had to be excluded if chords or polyphonic lines were played. Transcriptions of bass solos and drum solos were also excluded.

There is a large variety of tempo, ranging from 50 bpm to over 300 bpm (Figure 2), but with a certain preference for fast tempos (the median of tempos is 170.5 bpm). Most of the solos are rather short (Table 3, Figure 3), with a median of two choruses and a median duration of 87 s (1 min 27 s). The rhythmic feel of about 80 % of the solos is SWING, but LATIN, FUNK, and others can be found, too (Table 4).

The selection of musicians and pieces for the Weimar Jazz Database follows the historical occurrence of jazz styles—from traditional jazz and swing, via bebop, cool jazz and west coast jazz, to hardbop, modal jazz and new concepts of improvisation that are often summarized under the umbrella term 'postbop'. Additionally, a few recordings of free jazz (Ornette Coleman)

Table 2: Distribution of instruments in the Weimar Jazz Database.

Instrument	Count	Percentage
ts	158	34.6
tp	101	22.1
as	80	17.5
tb	26	5.7
ss	23	5.0
cl	15	3.3
cor	15	3.3
vib	12	2.6
bs	11	2.4
g	6	1.3
p	6	1.3
bcl	2	0.4
ts-c	1	0.2
Total	456	100.0

Table 3: Number of choruses in the Weimar Jazz Database.

Choruses	Count	Percentage
1	173	37.9
2	128	28.1
3	55	12.1
4	28	6.1
5	21	4.6
6	13	2.9
7	10	2.2
8	9	2.0
More than 8	19	4.2
Total	456	100.0

and fusion jazz are also included. Most of the musicians included in the Weimar Jazz Database are represented by five or six solos each (see Table 6; the complete list is available online[6]). This number allows for the comparison

---

[6] http://jazzomat.hfm-weimar.de/dbformat/dbcontent.html

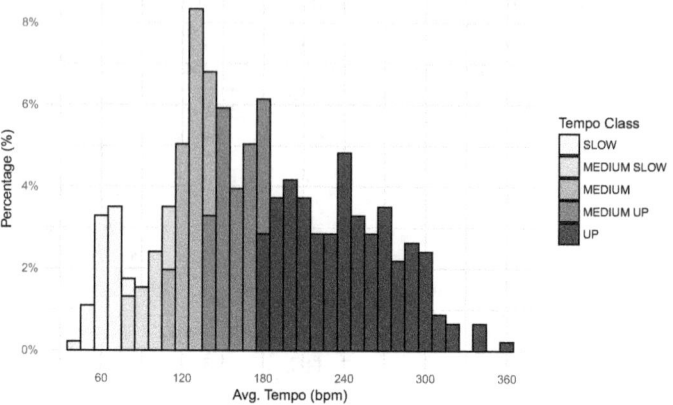

Figure 2: Distribution of tempos in the Weimar Jazz Database, colored by tempo class.

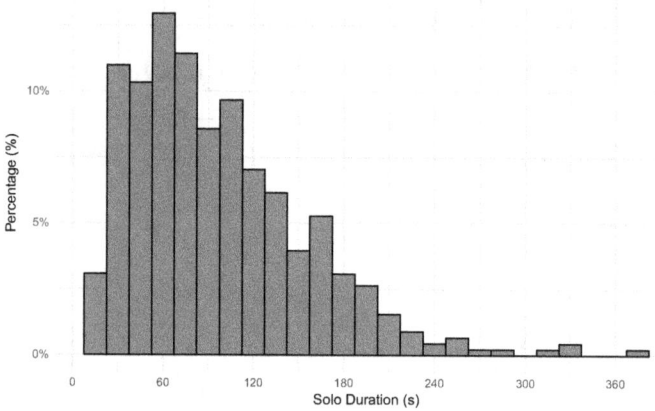

Figure 3: Distribution of solo durations in the Weimar Jazz Database.

between different improvisations by each musician, mostly with different tempos and chord changes, and for tentative conclusions about personal style. If a musician has played two or more solos within one recording of a certain piece, e. g., at the start and the end, all solos are included as separate items in order to allow for comparison. Some seminal musicians are represented with ten or more improvisations—Sonny Rollins with 17 solos, Charlie Parker and

Table 4: Distribution of rhythm feels in the Weimar Jazz Database.

Rhythm Feel	Count	Percentage
SWING	361	79.2
TWOBEAT	32	7.0
LATIN	27	5.9
FUNK	20	4.4
BALLAD	10	2.2
MIX	6	1.3
Total	456	100.0

Table 5: Distribution of harmonic templates in the Weimar Jazz Database.

Harmonic Template	Count	Percentage
None	329	72.1
Blues	97	21.3
I Got Rhythm	19	4.2
So What	5	1.1
All the Things You Are	1	0.2
Cherokee	1	0.2
Confirmation	1	0.2
How High the Moon	1	0.2
Tune Up	1	0.2
What Is this Thing Called Love	1	0.2
Total	456	100.0

Miles Davis with 19 solos each, and John Coltrane with 21 solos —in order to enable a more thorough examination of their improvisation strategies, their personal style or their stylistic development over time. In most cases, several improvisations by different musicians over the same piece are included; therefore, these solos allow not only for a reliable depiction of their personal style but also enable comparison between different musicians improvising during the same recording session over the same piece. On the other hand, this is the reason why some musicians are represented by only one or two solos: they had participated in only one of those recordings and their solos were included for comparison. In some cases, there are two alternate takes of an improvisation, coming from two recordings of the same piece made during the same recording session. Moreover, there are many solos improvised to the same chord changes, e. g., 12-bar-blues, rhythm changes, or standards such as "Body and Soul", in order to enable comparisons between improvisational strategies and solutions (Table 5). Additionally, a number of special research interests led to the inclusion of certain musicians or pieces (see below), e. g., musicians after 1980. Again: Extensions of the repository are absolutely desirable for the future.

We were faced with several restrictions regarding the inclusion of certain pieces and musicians. Many pieces for which no reliable source for chord changes was available had to be excluded. In a few cases, we transcribed some chord changes, but for the most part, determining chord changes turned out to be very difficult and time-consuming, not least due to harmonic ambiguities. Unfortunately, the lack of available lead-sheets resulted in gaps with regard to jazz after 1960. As a small remedy, we included several solos over a modal framework, marked by a bass pedal point or ostinato pattern, or solos with no recurring chord changes at all. Moreover, solos within a big band arrangement and with brass or reed section backings seemed to be a special case and are, for reasons of comparability, excluded from the repository. The omission of these recordings does not imply that they have less aesthetic or historic value.

A chronological run-through

In the Weimar Jazz Database, there are 31 solos of TRADITIONAL jazz recorded between 1925 and 1941 with a rhythmic feel labeled as TWOBEAT. These are solos by members of the Louis Armstrong Hot Five and Hot Seven: Armstrong (8 solos), Johnny Dodds (6) and Kid Ory (5), by Sidney Bechet (5) and by Bix Beiderbecke (5), as well as one solo each by J.C. Higginbotham, Charlie Shavers and Henry Allen. Due to the restrictions imposed by the shellac format, these solos are rather short, lasting one or two choruses of a maximum of one to two minutes duration. This also holds true for solos of the swing era as well as most of the bebop musicians.

There are 68 solos by musicians of the swing era: tenor saxophonists Don Byas (7), Coleman Hawkins (6), Lester Young (7) and Ben Webster (5), as well as Chu Berry with his two solos over "Body and Soul", alto sax player Benny Carter (7), trumpet players Roy Eldridge (6) and Buck Clayton (3), plus one solo each by Rex Stewart and Harry Edison, trombone player Dickie Wells (6) as well as the "King of Swing", clarinetist Benny Goodman (7), and Lionel Hampton (6), vibraphone, a member of the Goodman combo. Unfortunately, seminal alto player Johnny Hodges is represented by only two solos since most of his available solos are rather short or interwoven with band backings. Don Byas is a special case since many of his recordings are situated at the transition between swing and bebop. Therefore, one of his solos (entitled "Be-Bop") is labeled BEBOP, while all solos by Coleman Hawkins, another border crosser between the styles, are unambiguously performed within the swing idiom.

Similarly, it is sometimes hard to draw a clear distinction between bebop and hardbop (as well as between hardbop and postbop, see below) and there are also intersections between bebop and cool jazz, e. g., vibraphone player Milt Jackson was an integral member of bebop pioneer Dizzy Gillespie's big band before joining the Modern Jazz Quartet, one of the most famous cool jazz ensembles. Therefore, deciding whether a musician can be attributed to bebop, hardbop or cool jazz (or postbop) was often a question of what year the recording was made. There are 61 improvisations labeled BEBOP, among them solos by trumpet players Dizzy Gillespie (6) and Fats Navarro (6) as well as one early solo each by Kenny Dorham and Miles Davis on trumpet. The Weimar Jazz Database includes 17 solos by alto saxophonist Charlie Parker. Other saxophonists are Sonny Stitt (with three alto and three tenor solos), Phil Woods (6) and one early solo by Dexter Gordon. Moreover, trombone players J. J. Johnson (7) and Kai Winding (one solo) are included, as well as three early solos by vibraphonist Milt Jackson. Most of the bebop solos are performed with a swing feel and most of the solos were recorded between 1945 and 1952—except for some later solos by J. J. Johnson (1957) and Phil Woods (1961).

There are 53 cool jazz and West Coast jazz solos which are labeled COOL throughout since there is no clear musical distinction between the two styles. These are mostly solos by saxophone players: Lee Konitz (8), Warne Marsh (3), Zoot Sims (6), Gerry Mulligan (6), Stan Getz (6), Paul Desmond (8) and Art Pepper (6). Moreover, trumpet player Chet Baker (8 solos) and three solos by Milt Jackson performing with the Modern Jazz Quartet are also included. While most of the solos are situated in a swing feeling, there are some latin—bossa nova, to be precise—recordings, too. Most of the solos were recorded in the 1950s, but some early recordings from 1949 (Lee Konitz, Warne Marsh) and 1950 (Zoot Sims), as well as recordings from the 1970s (Chet Baker and Art Pepper) are also included. While Chet Baker clearly follows his early cool style throughout his career, it is disputable whether Art Pepper's style after his comeback in the 1970s is still West Coast jazz in the sense of the 1950s or if he changed his style of improvising. However, his 1979 recordings were marked as COOL.

There are 68 solos labeled HARDBOP: solos by trumpet players Clifford Brown (9), Miles Davis (8) and Lee Morgan (3), as well as two solos each by Kenny Dorham, Freddie Hubbard and Nat Adderley. The saxophone players included are Steve Lacy on soprano (6), Cannonball Adderley on alto (4), Pepper Adams on baritone (5) and John Coltrane (11), Sonny Rollins (9), Dexter Gordon (5) and Hank Mobley (4) on tenor, as well as an early solo by Wayne Shorter. Moreover, there are two solos by trombonist Curtis Fuller and one trombone solo by J.J. Johnson ("Walking" with Miles Davis), as well as one single-line piano improvisation by Red Garland. Of course, there are several musicians whose career spans over several decades and several jazz styles—first of all Miles Davis, who is included as a soloist within BEBOP (1), HARDBOP (8), POSTBOP (6) and FUSION (4), but unfortunately not with solos from his short cool jazz period. Besides Miles Davis, many other musicians played several jazz styles, e.g., Kenny Dorham who started to play in the bebop era and continued to play in the 1960s with Joe Henderson, or John Coltrane who passed from hardbop to a modal jazz and, finally, a free jazz period (the latter not included in the database). It is not easy to decide where exactly hardbop ends and postbop starts. The term 'postbop' seems to function as an umbrella term for all kinds of jazz that depart from hardbop with more advanced strategies of improvisation, e.g., in regard to harmonies (modal or non-functional harmonies) or rhythm (more groove-based pieces, in particular in 1960s recordings with Blue Note Records). We decided to start with Miles Davis' "Kind of Blue" (1959) as the first postbop album—since it was the first album with prevailingly modal compositions and improvisations. By contrast, Coltrane's solos over "Giant Steps" and related chord changes with circles of (major) thirds, e.g., "26-2" or "Countdown", are labeled HARDBOP because of their functional harmony—and in spite of their harmonically inspiring impact on postbop players. Therefore, there are some hardbop solos as well as, then, many postbop solos by quite a lot of musicians in the database, e.g., trumpet players Freddie Hubbard (four postbop solos, two hardbop), Kenny Dorham (three postbop solos, two hardbop) and Lee Morgan (one postbop solo, three hardbop), as well as saxophone players Wayne Shorter (9 postbop, one hardbop) or John Coltrane (9 postbop solos including two long improvisations on performances of "Impressions" and his two solos in "My Favourite Things").

Exclusively postbop musicians include both musicians with recordings from the early 1960s, e.g., Eric Dolphy (6 solos) and Don Ellis (6)—both of whom are situated at the transition to avant-garde or free jazz—as well as many musicians who continued to record in the 1970s, 1980s and 1990s: tenor sax players David Liebman (11), Michael Brecker (10), Joe Henderson (9), Joe Lovano (8), Bob Berg (6) and Branford Marsalis (6), as well as alto sax player Steve Coleman (7). Along with Freddie Hubbard, Miles Davis, Kenny Dorham and Lee Morgan (see above), there are trumpet solos by Woody Shaw (8) and Kenny Wheeler (2), as well as three trombone solos by Steve Turre, performing with Woody Shaw. Moreover, there are five single-line piano solos by Herbie Hancock (with the Miles Davis Quintet), four single-line guitar solos by Pat Metheny, and one solo each by tenorist George Coleman and guitarists John Abercrombie and Pat Martino.

In addition, there are two special cases: Both the solos by trumpeter Wynton Marsalis (7 solos) and tenor saxophonist David Murray (6) are labelled as POSTBOP, even though Marsalis situates himself as a traditionalist with many stylistic references to jazz styles from the 1920s to the 1960s, and Murray clearly has his origins in the late 1970s avant-garde scene. However, in the improvisations selected for the database, Marsalis tends to improvise in a more contemporary fashion, while David Murray improvises around blues and jazz standards in a more conventional manner (without ignoring his personal style coined by his earlier avant-garde jazz performances).

Regarding free or avant-garde jazz, only five Ornette Coleman solos from Coleman's early quartet recordings are included (labeled FREE). Playing with sound rather than definite pitches and without a constant beat is widespread among avant-garde players. However, the computer-based analysis tools used in our project can only handle lines with pitches and onsets related to a metrical grid. Developing computer coding for these free improvisations that also enables their computational exploration is a challenge for the future.

Again, the dividing lines between postbop and fusion music are blurred. Therefore, several musicians are represented with solos both within a more straight-ahead or swing feel (POSTBOP) and with more of a funk or rock accompaniment, then labeled FUSION. This applies to saxophone player Bob Berg (six POSTBOP solos, one FUSION), Joshua Redman (three POSTBOP, two FUSION), Chris Potter (two POSTBOP, four FUSION), Steve Coleman (two POSTBOP solos with the Dave Holland group and three FUSION solos with his own groups), as well as hardbop tenorist Sonny Rollins (2) who played calypso-jazz-fusion since the 1970s and, of course, Miles Davis (with four solos from his seminal album *Bitches Brew*). Moreover, there are two fusion solos by Kenny Garrett and one solo each by Kenny Wheeler and tenorist Van Freeman, both playing with Steve Coleman.

Of course, this selection is open to question and there are probably both several gaps as well as many musicians that could have been included in the database, too. However, there is a kind of balance between musicians from the established jazz canon as well as musicians who further developed the infinite art of jazz improvisation after the 1960s with their achievements in modal, free and fusion playing. Unfortunately, it passed unnoticed during project runtime that there are no women musicians included within the database. This deplorable gap will be filled up in a future version of the database.

Table 6: Performers, styles, and solos in the Weimar Jazz Database.

Performer	Solos	Styles
Art Pepper	6	COOL (6)
Ben Webster	5	SWING (5)
Benny Carter	7	SWING (7)
Benny Goodman	7	SWING (7)
Bix Beiderbecke	5	TRADITIONAL (5)
Bob Berg	7	POSTBOP (6), FUSION (1)
Branford Marsalis	6	POSTBOP (6)
Buck Clayton	3	SWING (3)
Cannonball Adderley	5	HARDBOP (4), POSTBOP (1)
Charlie Parker	17	BEBOP (17)
Charlie Shavers	1	TRADITIONAL (1)
Chet Baker	8	COOL (8)
Chris Potter	7	FUSION (4), POSTBOP (3)
Chu Berry	2	SWING (2)
Clifford Brown	9	HARDBOP (9)
Coleman Hawkins	6	SWING (6)
Curtis Fuller	2	HARDBOP (2)
David Liebman	11	POSTBOP (11)
David Murray	6	POSTBOP (6)
Dexter Gordon	6	HARDBOP (5), BEBOP (1)
Dickie Wells	6	SWING (6)
Dizzy Gillespie	6	BEBOP (6)
Don Byas	8	SWING (7), BEBOP (1)
Don Ellis	6	POSTBOP (6)
Eric Dolphy	6	POSTBOP (6)
Fats Navarro	6	BEBOP (6)
Freddie Hubbard	6	POSTBOP (4), HARDBOP (2)
George Coleman	1	POSTBOP (1)
Gerry Mulligan	6	COOL (6)
Hank Mobley	4	HARDBOP (4)
Harry Edison	1	SWING (1)
Henry Allen	1	TRADITIONAL (1)

Herbie Hancock	5	POSTBOP (5)
J. C. Higginbotham	1	TRADITIONAL (1)
J. J. Johnson	8	BEBOP (7), HARDBOP (1)
Joe Henderson	8	POSTBOP (8)
Joe Lovano	8	POSTBOP (8)
John Abercrombie	1	POSTBOP (1)
John Coltrane	20	POSTBOP (9), HARDBOP (11)
Johnny Dodds	6	TRADITIONAL (6)
Johnny Hodges	2	SWING (2)
Joshua Redman	5	POSTBOP (3), FUSION (2)
Kai Winding	1	BEBOP (1)
Kenny Dorham	7	HARDBOP (3), POSTBOP (3), BEBOP (1)
Kenny Garrett	2	FUSION (2)
Kenny Wheeler	3	POSTBOP (2), FUSION (1)
Kid Ory	5	TRADITIONAL (5)
Lee Konitz	8	COOL (8)
Lee Morgan	4	HARDBOP (3), POSTBOP (1)
Lester Young	7	SWING (7)
Lionel Hampton	6	SWING (6)
Louis Armstrong	8	TRADITIONAL (8)
Michael Brecker	10	POSTBOP (10)
Miles Davis	19	HARDBOP (8), POSTBOP (6), FUSION (4), BEBOP (1)
Milt Jackson	6	BEBOP (3), COOL (3)
Nat Adderley	2	HARDBOP (2)
Ornette Coleman	5	FREE (5)
Pat Martino	1	POSTBOP (1)
Pat Metheny	4	POSTBOP (4)
Paul Desmond	8	COOL (8)
Pepper Adams	5	HARDBOP (5)
Phil Woods	6	BEBOP (6)
Red Garland	1	HARDBOP (1)
Rex Stewart	1	SWING (1)
Roy Eldridge	6	SWING (6)
Sidney Bechet	5	TRADITIONAL (5)
Sonny Rollins	13	HARDBOP (9), FUSION (2), POSTBOP (2)
Sonny Stitt	6	BEBOP (6)
Stan Getz	6	COOL (6)
Steve Coleman	10	POSTBOP (7), FUSION (3)

Steve Lacy	6	HARDBOP (6)
Steve Turre	3	POSTBOP (3)
Von Freeman	1	FUSION (1)
Warne Marsh	3	COOL (3)
Wayne Shorter	10	POSTBOP (9), HARDBOP (1)
Woody Shaw	8	POSTBOP (8)
Wynton Marsalis	7	POSTBOP (7)
Zoot Sims	6	COOL (6)

Computational melody analysis

Klaus Frieler

Introduction

This chapter provides an introduction into both the basic principles of computational melody analysis and their application and implementation in MeloSpySuite/GUI as developed and applied within the Jazzomat Research Project, especially within the case studies in the second part of this volume. The chapter addresses at a wide and diverse audience ranging from jazz researchers and musicologists seeking for an understanding of MeloSpyGUI, its possibilities and functionalities, to computer scientists who wishes to comprehend or build on the concepts used within the software. Of course, both groups have different needs and different sets of previous knowledge. We tried to accommodate as many of these needs as possible and decided on a dual strategy of using exact mathematical notations on the one hand and verbal descriptions and concrete examples on the other. Mathematical notation might be hard to read or even off-putting for non-experts, but in the spirit of reproducibility and transparency it is inevitable if one wishes to be as precise as possible for those who want to know or to recreate the details of an algorithm. Some mathematical basics as well as details regarding the implementation of features and categories are included in 'info boxes' along the main text. Additionally, there are short introductions to the FlexQ quantization algorithm and into circular mathematics in the appendix. We think that those readers who are more interested in the applications and the functionality of the software for jazz research as well as music research in general can safely skip the formulas and stick to the verbal contexts and particularly the examples. Nevertheless, a minimum openness to the math might be necessary for a more comprehensive picture.

This chapter focuses on three main topics: Firstly, the basic mathematical concepts for the computational representation of music used within the Weimar Jazz Database as well as the main annotation categories (segmentation, chords, meter and midlevel units) are explained. Secondly, both the general concepts of feature extraction and the most important musical features that can be extracted with our software are discussed. The features are grouped into the main types in alphabetical order: accents, auxiliary, melodic contour, intervals, metadata, meter, pitch, rhythm, sequences of intervals pitch or rhythm, structure, and tone formation (including dynamics, articulation, and intonation). The last section is dedicated to the concepts of pattern search and pattern mining which is a powerful tool within the MeloSpy software.

Music representation and annotation

Computational musicology aims to extract useful information from music by using suitable (digital) representations of music. This is a very general task with many different approaches, depending on the concrete goals at hand. It is very unlikely that any representational system will fulfill all possible needs. In fact, quite a few representational systems have already been proposed, implemented, and used. The best-known approach is common Western musical notation, which was originally developed for practical purposes. But since it features rather good mapping between scores and musical objects, musicologists and music theoreticians have used common Western musical notation for many centuries and are still using it today. In fact, it is still the most commonly used analytical representation. Many musical representation systems aim towards a digital version of common Western musical notation, e. g., MusicXML, MEI, MuseScore and Lilypond. But since common Western musical notation is basically a prescriptive system fraught with a lot of historic conventions, idiosyncrasies, and implicit assumptions, it is not always well-suited for analytical tasks, e. g., for performance research where information on micro-timing, loudness, and timbre is needed.

Moreover, since common Western musical notation is basically a graphical (two-dimensional) representation, encoding it to a digital format is not always straight-forward and the results might not be well suited for analytical purposes due to of many purely graphical elements. Hence, computational analysis very often relies on more task-compatible encoding formats, e. g., **kern, ABC, EsAC or MIDI, all of which have all their own advantages and disadvantages. They are all based on certain (simplifying) assumptions, which reduce the expressiveness of the encoding, i. e., the amount of available information.

In regard to expressiveness, audio files contain maximal information in the sense that they facilitate a re-creation of the sounding music with the aid of a suitable audio player. However, this maximal expressiveness comes at a high analytical cost, since a large amount of effort is necessary to extract the analytically relevant information. This poses technological problems that can not be deemed fully solved today, though impressive progress has been made in this regard in the field of music information retrieval (MIR) in the last two decades. Music is ultimately a psychological phenomenon and the human cognitive system acts as a very powerful and specific filter system which, for example, can easily extract the main melody from a complex polyphonic track, a task that modern algorithms are still struggling with. Also, musically very important phenomena such as beat induction and meter or tonality perception are not easily defined and extracted from complex audio files, although these are often the focus of analytical endeavors.

In a more formal sense, a musical performance[7] can be viewed (physically) as a sound-wave $p(t)$ over a bounded time interval T. This sound wave is then transformed into a psychological representation $p'(t)$ during listening. We further assume that music differentiates into streams of (sonic, musical) event series. This assumption is strongly supported by research on auditory scene analysis (Bregman, 1990). Events in this context have a defined beginning (onset) and end (offset). The content of a musical event, however, cannot be described easily in full generality, particularly not in psychological terms. But very often it can be agreed upon that musical events have certain qualities (*qualias*) such as pitch, loudness, and timbre as well as modulations of these qualities.

Infobox 1: Mathematical basics: sets, maps, and sequences

The math used here deals mostly with 'sets', 'maps', and 'sequences'. A set is basically a collection of items, each counted only once and in no particular order. Sets are notated using curly brackets which embrace either a list of elements or some sort of condition that defines the elements in the set. For example, $A = \{1, \ldots, N\}$ is the set of the first N natural numbers. Standard sets often used in the context of computational musicology are the natural numbers (symbol $\mathbb{N}$), the integer numbers (symbol $\mathbb{Z}$), and the real numbers (symbol $\mathbb{R}$). To indicate that x is contained in a set A, one writes $x \in A$. For example, $17 \in \mathbb{N}$. The empty set with no elements is notated $\emptyset$. The numbers of elements in a set A is written as $|A|$. Sets can have infinitely or finitely many elements. Sets can also have subsets, notated $A \subset B$. Sets of consecutive numbers are

---

[7] We do not wish to go into the complicated discussion of what music actually *is* here, but simply take this as an externally given label. However, in certain audio engineering applications, it is an important to classify chunks of audio files into music or non-music, e.g., speech, environmental noise, or bird song.

> very important in the context of computational musicology and are written as $[N:M] = \{N, N+1, \ldots, M\}$, which means all integers between N and M including M. It holds $[N:M] \subset \mathbb{N}$. Intervals of real numbers are written with a comma instead of a colon, e. g., $[x, y]$ is the interval of all real numbers between and including x and y. Sets have intersections $A \cap B$, i. e., the set of all elements both in A and B, and unions $A \cup B$, i. e., the set of elements either in A or B. Large symbols are used to indicate intersections and unions of more than one set, e. g., $\bigcup_{1 \leq i \leq N} A_i$ is a shorthand notation for $A_1 \cup A_2 \cup \cdots \cup A_N$. Another important construction is the so-called Cartesian product. For two sets A and B the Cartesian product $A \times B$ is the set of pairs (x, y) where $x \in A$ and $y \in B$. This also works for more than two sets, and the elements are then called N-tuples for a Cartesian product of N sets. The order is important, i. e., $A \times B \neq B \times A$. Maps are collections of arrows between two sets, starting in a domain set, say A, and ending in a image set (or co-domain), say B. A map from A to B is written as $M : A \to B$. If one wants to express the mapping of a concrete element in the domain to an element in the image of M, one writes $x \mapsto y = M(x)$. Not all elements in B have to be the endpoint of an arrow. Likewise, not all elements in A need to be a starting point, but in most cases we will assume this to be the case. We also assume that at most one arrow points from each element in the domain to an element in the image set. Maps can also be defined between maps, which will be encountered quite often in computational musicology, e. g., in the case of transformations or vector features. This comes from the fact that sequences play an important role.
>
> A sequence is simply a collection of elements with an order; thus, one can say such things as "element x appears earlier than element y in the sequence". Since the integer numbers have a natural order of this kind, they can be used to define sequences as maps from integer intervals onto a certain image set X. For example, $x : [1 : N] \to X$, with $i \mapsto x(i) \in X$. Very often, index notation is used for this, i. e., $i \mapsto x_i$. Another compact notation for this is with simple parentheses $(x_i)_{1 \leq i \leq N}$, or, even lazier, just x_i. An explicit listing of elements in parentheses means that it is a sequence or a tuple and not just a set.

In some cases, e. g., for percussive events, a simple (task-relative) categorization might be sufficient, e. g., naming the percussive instrument that has produced the event. In other cases, a justifiable simplification is to use a constant single pitch as a sole descriptor, whereby pitch is represented with a symbol (e. g., a note name) or a number as a proxy derived from the fundamental frequency (f_0) of the event. These events are called tone events. Chords can then be represented as collections of pitches (and further abstracted into chord symbols).

In the context of the Jazzomat Research Project, we are dealing exclusively with monophonic solos and therefore use exactly this simplified representation as a core, complemented by various annotations. Formally, thus, a melody is a discrete times series

$$t_i \mapsto e_i = (t_i, d_i, p_i),$$

where an event e_i is described by a triple (t_i, d_i, p_i) of numbers which represent

- onset t_i (seconds),
- duration d_i (seconds),
- and a (constant) pitch value p_i (MIDI number),

of a tone event.

Pitch values are represented by indices in the 12-tone equal tempered system, using the well-known and common MIDI indexing scheme (Selfridge-Field, 1997), which represents an associated f_0 value via the formula[8]

$$p = 12 \left\lfloor \log_2 \frac{f_0}{440\,\text{Hz}} \right\rfloor + 69,$$

where the square brackets mean taking only the integer part. The note $A4 = 440\,\text{Hz}$ is mapped to MIDI index 69 and every octave equals 12 semi-tone steps, e.g.,

$$A3\,(220\,\text{Hz}) \mapsto 12\log_2 \frac{1}{2} + 69 = -12 + 69 = 57,$$

or

$$A5\,(880\,\text{Hz}) \mapsto 12\log_2 2 + 69 = 12 + 69 = 81.$$

The number of events in a melody is called its length, whereas the duration of a melody is defined as the difference between the onset of its first element and the offset of its last event. For the following, we will use the convention that the first element in an event series is indexed by 0 (zero-indexing). Hence, a melody of length N is indexed with $0 \ldots N-1$. For intervals of integer numbers we will adopt the notation $[N:M]$ for the set of integers between and including N and M (with $M \geq N$). Formally, a melody of length N is then a map $e : [0:N-1] \to \mathbb{R} \times \mathbb{R}^+ \times [0:127]$.

---

[8] The actual transcription process for the Weimar Jazz Database was performed by human transcribers who assigned the most fitting pitch to a tone event. See Chapter *Score-informed audio analysis of jazz improvisation* for measuring the exact intonation of the played tones.

A melody is defined as monophonic, which means that its onsets should be strictly ordered ($t_i < t_{i+1}$, for all i). In a strictly monophonic melody, events do not overlap, i.e., the offset $t_i + d_i$ of an event should be smaller than or at most equal to the onset of the following event, $t_i + d_i \leq t_{i+1}$ for all i. The inter-onset intervals (IOI) are then defined as the differences of onsets between consecutive events, $IOI_i = t_{i+1} - t_i$. Note that there are one fewer IOI than there are events. Semitone intervals are defined as differences of pitches between consecutive events, $\Delta p_i = p_{i+1} - p_i$. An elementary set of operations that can be applied to melodies or series is a projection, which is a formal term for 'forgetting information'. A projection means to only use a subset of the information, e. g., onsets, durations, or pitches or combinations thereof. For example, the sequence (t_i) is the list of onsets, the sequence (p_i) is the pitch sequence derived from a melody, and so on. Using only part of the information in a melody (or annotated melody, see below) is a very common technique for constructing features and defining patterns.

Figure 1: Beginning of Chet Baker's solo on "Let's Get Lost", also known as the "The Lick".

Example. The core representation and some derived values of the melody depicted in Figure 1 (in common Western musical notation) can be found in Table 1. In output files of the MeloSpyGUI the value NA (not available) is mostly used for this. Note that the difference values IOI and interval are attached to the first interval here, which is the convention used in the Jazzomat Research Project; other authors prefer to attach it to the second value. However, attaching difference values to the first element often simplifies subsequent computations.

Annotations

Obviously, this core representation of a melody is rather bare-bone and of only limited analytical value (although it already allows for the derivation of pitch and interval features as well as Markov models and very basic rhythm analysis). Thus, it is desirable to 'thicken' this description of tone events with a flexible annotation system, which allows the 'tagging' of additional information to an event or a series of events. Most annotations are generated externally, mostly by humans, and are not directly derivable from the basic

Table 1: Core representation and some derived values of the beginning of Chet Baker's solo on "Let's Get Lost".

Note	Core representation			Derived values		
	Onset (s)	Duration (s)	Pitch	Offset (s)	IOI (s)	Interval
1	2.667	0.195	71	2.862	0.395	0
2	3.062	0.087	71	3.150	0.166	-2
3	3.228	0.194	69	3.422	0.221	2
4	3.448	0.190	71	3.638	0.192	1
5	3.640	0.190	72	3.830	0.200	2
6	3.840	0.161	74	4.001	0.200	-3
7	4.040	0.280	71	4.310	0.360	-4
8	4.400	0.155	67	4.555	0.244	2
9	4.644	0.673	69	5.317	n. d.	n. d.

Note. n. d. = not defined.

representation. Most annotations are generated only once and then stored along with the basic presentations. Hence, the term annotation expresses a more practical distinction to transformations and features, as described below in p. 60.

One has to differentiate two types of annotations: local and contextual. Local annotations pertain to the event itself and are directly derived from it. Important examples are acoustical features such as f_0 modulations (vibrato, slides etc.), intensities/loudness or timbre (cf. Chapter *Score-informed audio analysis of jazz improvisation*). Contextual annotations are only derivable with respect to a certain context of an event, e. g., segmentations (cf. Infobox 2). However, contextual annotation can always be represented (and stored) as local annotations to certain events, e. g., a phrase segmentation can be expressed by annotating phrase IDs. The contextuality must then be reflected by certain consistency conditions, e. g., the phrase IDs of two adjacent events must be equal or the second must be greater than that of the first.

Formally, we define an annotated melody as the map

$$t_i \mapsto (e_i, a_i),$$

where e_i is the core representation (t_i, d_i, p_i) and the annotations

$$a_i = (a_{i1}, a_{i2}, \ldots, a_{iM})$$

are M-dimensional tuples of values (i. e., vectors of M values for each event).

The only condition imposed on an annotation is applicability to each event in a series (which can always be fulfilled trivially by allowing the empty set or a similar special symbol as a valid annotation value). We will encounter several important annotations (e. g., metrical and chord annotations) in the following sections.

Segmentations

Segmentations play an important role in computational musicology. They occur naturally, e. g., in the form of melodic phrases, during melody perception (Lerdahl & Jackendoff, 1983). Segmentation simply refers to sets of subsequences or segments. A subsequence is any consecutive patch of a series, i. e., without 'holes'. Formally, a subsequence of a melody $e : [0 : N-1] \to e_i$ is a restriction on $[k : l]$ with $0 \leq k \leq l \leq N-1$. We will notate such a subsequence as $e_{k:l}$.

Two main kinds of segmentations can be differentiated: overlapping and non-overlapping. Overlapping segmentations contain segments that can share common events, whereas in non-overlapping segmentations segments are disjunctive. Exhaustive segmentations are those for which every event is contained in at least one segment. Pattern partitions (s. p. 82) are an important example of non-exhaustive overlapping segmentations, whereas phrase and chord annotations are an example for exhaustive non-overlapping segmentations. Very often, segmentations are themselves equipped with some kind of annotation, e. g., an ID or a value of arbitrary type, cf. Infobox 2 for examples. In the following, we will briefly discuss three important segmentation types—form parts, chord and midlevel annotation—which are specific to the jazz solos in the Weimar Jazz Database.

Infobox 2: Segmentations in the Weimar Jazz Database

Several important segmentations are included in the Weimar Jazz Database and accessible via different mechanisms in the MeloSpyGUI. On the database level, the following (exhaustive, non-overlapping) segmentations are available.

- *Phrase IDs* These are integer IDs, starting with phrase 1, for each phrase annotated by the transcriber.
- *Chord annotations.* These contain chord symbols for each event under the scope of this chord, which were manually annotated to the beat track. See Infobox 3 and Chapter *The Weimar Jazz Database*.
- *Form parts.* Annotated according to the lead sheet. Each event is also

> part of a form part which is represented by specific form part symbols (e. g., A1, B2).
> - *Chorus IDs.* Each solo consists of one or more choruses, i. e., cycles of the underlying form as embodied in the chord sequences. Chorus IDs are integers, starting from chorus 1. However, sometimes there are pick-up bars, i. e., a solo starting slightly before the beginning of a new form cycle. These pick-ups are notated as chorus ID -1.
> - Midlevel Units (MLU) → p. 54.
>
> Segmentations are stored in the Weimar Jazz Database in the SECTIONS table using the IDs of the first and last element index of the segmentation in the annotated melody plus the annotated value/ID. All these segmentations can be used in the MeloSpyGUI during feature extraction to chop a melody into segments for which features are calculated. There are also auxiliary features which add the values/IDs for direct event-wise annotations. Additionally, segmentations with bar chunks can be chosen, which will segment the melodies/solos into consecutive patches of bars of arbitrary length with user-definable overlap (i. e., these are overlapping, exhaustive segmentations if the overlap is not empty).

Chord symbols

Chords play a major role in jazz improvisation, thus a comprehensive representation of chords is vital for the computational analysis of jazz solos. Consequently, the beat tracks in the Sonic Visualiser project files of the solo transcriptions have been annotated with chord symbols taken from lead sheets. Chord annotations are included in the Weimar Jazz Database and are, for instance, used for chord-related pitch representations (s. p. 63).

A chord is basically a pitch class set with a certain structure, in which the root is the most important tone. Chords are represented by chord labels, which hold all relevant information and follow a certain syntax. The MeloSpyGUI chord syntax is designed to match the chord symbols that are in practical (jazz) use as closely as possible. Internally, a CHORD object consists of a root note, a triad type (major, minor, diminished, augmented, half-diminished/7b5) and an optional bass note (for slash chords and inversions). Sevenths (major, minor, or diminished), ninths (natural, flat, or sharp), elevenths (natural or sharp), and thirteenths (natural or flat) are optional.

Instead of using existing chord syntax (e. g., Harte, Christopher, Sandler, Samer, & Gómez, 2005), we decided to devise our own, closer to traditional chord symbols, in order to facilitate annotation and readability. However, very often users will not have to deal with the low-level chord annotations, since during exporting, internal chord symbols are translated back to standard notation. For sake of completeness, and for those users who would like to produce their own Sonic Visualiser project files in our format, the syntax can be found in Infobox 3.

Infobox 3: Chord syntax

Chords are expressed using the following grammar. The grammar should be read as follows: Each line contains a definition of an expression, indicated by the ::= sign, where small letter names represent other expressions and quoted strings are the terminal symbols. For example, a chord can either be the 'no chord' expression, which is the string NC, or a normal chord, defined on the third line, or a special chord, defined on the fourth line. Vertical bars denote alternatives and square brackets denote optional elements. For example, an accidental can be either a sharp (♯) or a flat (♭) and a 'generic note name' is note letter ('A' to 'G') optionally followed by an accidental.

Note that some conveniences and optional expressions are included to facilitate annotation. The main difference to standard notation (e. g., in the Realbook) is that accidentals of chord tensions are placed after the number. For instance, a $C^{7\sharp 9\sharp 11\flat 13}$ chord is translated to C79♯11♯13b. The usual implications of lower tension in the presence of a higher tension also apply. Hence, a Cm^{11} notated as C-11 or Cm11 automatically includes the sevenths and the ninth as well and is therefore equivalent to C-7/9/11. Currently, no mechanism is included for 'adding' single tension without implications. For example, a C^{add9} with added ninth but without the seventh is not expressible in our chord syntax.

```
chord        ::= no_chord | normal_chord | special_chord
no_chord     ::= "NC"
normal_chord ::= generic_note_name triad_type
                 [seventh] [ninth] [eleventh] [thirteenth]
                 [slash_expr]
special_chord ::= generic_note_name exception [slash_expr]
generic_note_name ::= note_letter [accidental]
note_letter  ::= "A"-"G"
accidental   ::= sharp | flat
sharp        ::= "#"
flat         ::= "b"
triad_type   ::= major | minor | augmented |
                 diminished  | suspended
major        ::= "maj" | ""
minor        ::= "min" | "m" | "-"
augmented    ::= "aug" | "+"
diminished   ::= "dim" | "o"
```

```
        suspended  ::= "sus"
        seventh    ::= ["j"]"7"
        ninth      ::= "9" accidental
        eleventh   ::= "11" [sharp]
        thirteenth ::= "13" [flat]
        slash_expr ::= "/" generic_note_name
        exception  ::= "7b5"  | "alt"    | "7#9"  |
                       "m7b5" | "7sus4"  | "maj7"
```

Metrical annotation

Metrical frameworks are very important for the perception and production of music around the world. The perception and induction of a beat is a precondition for the occurrence of the phenomenon of meter. For our representation of the musical surface, we adopted a very general framework which works with minimal assumptions, e. g., without presupposing a deeply nested metrical hierarchy.

The basic conception puts the beat level in the center, with beats not being assumed to be isochronous, or even regular, but are essentially just a series of time points. Internally, a beat is stored as an onset with a duration, which is the interval between consecutive beats, i. e., the inter-beat interval (IBI).

In our metrical framework, there are only three hierarchical levels: Beats are grouped into units ('measures') of certain length (called 'period') on one hand, and divided into sub-beat levels ('tatums') on the other; no regularity assumptions are made for either. A sequence of measures with constantly varying periods can be represented as well as beat-wise changing subdivisions, which are not required to be of equal length although this is common. A metrical framework has to be differentiated from a concrete realization of this framework. For transcriptions, the task is often to infer an underlying metrical framework to a certain realization of a musical rhythm, which might not be unequivocal. For the transcriptions in the Weimar Jazz Database, the core part is implemented via human annotations, i. e., based on manual beat tracks with annotated time signatures. To accelerate and facilitate the transcription process, the annotation of musical tones to metrical position is done algorithmically based on the beat track and the tone onsets. This algorithm, called 'FlexQ', was specifically devised in the context of the Jazzomat Research Project and is described in more detail in Appendix *The FlexQ algorithm* (see also Frieler and Pfleiderer (2017) for a discussion of general issues with respect to metrical annotations).

First, we will introduce some notations and concepts. A beat track is a sequence of time points t_i, with inter-beat intervals $\Delta t_i := t_{i+1} - t_i$. The inverse $\frac{1}{\Delta t_i}$ of the inter-beat interval is the (instantaneous) tempo of the beat track.

A metrical annotation of the beat track is a mapping of beat times to pairs of integer values $t_i \to (p_j(i), b_{k_j}(i))$ subject to the following conditions: $p_j \geq 1$ and $1 \leq k_j \leq p_j$ for all j. The numbers j are the bar numbers, the p_j are the periods (number of beats in a bar j) and the b_{k_j} are the beat indices in the j-th bar, running from 1 to p_j. A shorthand notation for the metrical annotation is $m_i = (j(i), p_j(i), b_{k_j}(i))$.

Example. Assume an (isochronous) series of six beats (cf. Figure 2). A 2-period metrical annotation, using the shorthand notation, would then be given by

$$(1,2,1),(1,2,2),(2,2,1),(2,2,2),(3,2,1),(3,2,2),$$

and a 3-period one by

$$(1,3,1),(1,3,2),(1,3,3),(2,3,1),(2,3,2),(2,3,3).$$

A mixed 4-period/2-period annotation is also feasible:

$$(1,4,1),(1,4,2),(1,4,3),(1,4,4),(2,2,1),(2,2,2).$$

Since the numbers are only a function of the beat indices i, but not of the actual beat times t_i, this representation is purely abstract. Consequently, given such a metric representation, any series of beat onsets can be viewed as a realization of such a metric framework.

To establish a connection to an actual perceived meter, the beat times should fulfill certain criteria, e.g., approximate isochrony. Note that, in contrast to common Western musical notation's time signatures, only the number of beats per group (periods) are provided. No distinction is made between $\frac{2}{4}$ or $\frac{2}{2}$, or $\frac{6}{8}$, all of which have two beats grouped into a bar. The difference between $\frac{2}{4}$ and $\frac{6}{8}$ is that in the former one beats are more likely to be subdivided binarily, whereas in the latter the prevalent subdivision is ternary. Note, that binary or ternary subdivisions are not a fixed rule, but only prevalences, e.g., triplets occur less often in $\frac{2}{4}$ and duplets (dotted eighths notes) in $\frac{6}{8}$. The system proposed here leaves this mostly to the user and simply provides a system for annotating arbitrary subdivisions for each beat. This brings us to the general definition of a metrical annotation.

Computational melody analysis

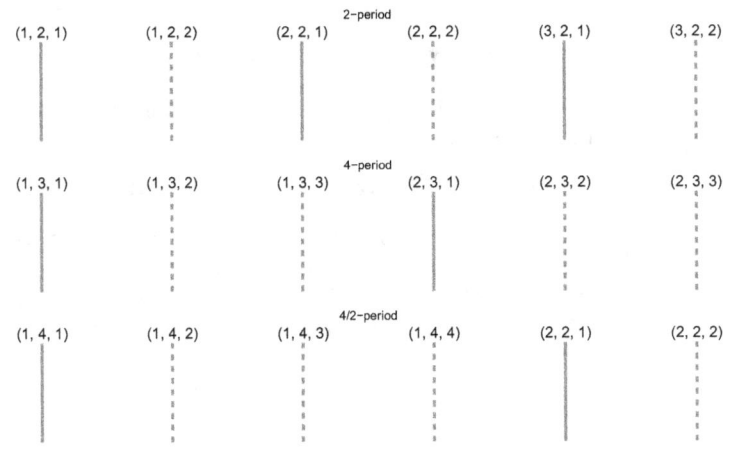

Figure 2: Three different sample metrical annotations of a six beat sequence. Solid lines: first beat of a bar; dashed lines: all other beats. Annotations are given in the format (bar number, period, beat index).

Consider an arbitrary rhythm, i.e., a series of time-points t_i. A metrical annotation for this rhythm is then a map onto tuples of five integers

$$(j, p_j, b_{k_j}, d_{k_j}, s_m),$$

where (j, p_j, b_{k_j}) is a beat annotation as defined above, $d_{k_j} \in \mathbb{N}$ is the division of the beat b_{k_j}, and $1 \leq s_m \leq d_{k_j}$ is the tatum position below the beat b_{k_j}, which runs between 1 and the division of the beat.

Example. Consider the rhythm of the 'The Lick' in Figure 1. The metrical annotation consists of two bars (mm. 1 and 2), both of period 4. The first two notes are each placed on the second tatums of beat 1 and 2. The following four eighth notes are on tatum 1 or 2 of the binary subdivided beats 3 and 4. The next note is on tatum 1 of the undivided first beat of the second bar, while the last two notes are on tatum positions 2 and 4 of beat 2 with a 4-subdivision (sixteenth notes). Rests are not considered here. The resulting metrical annotations can be found in Table 2 and Figure 3.

> **Infobox 4: Metrical position notation**
>
> For output purposes, the MeloSpyGUI uses a special dot-notation for metrical positions. The format is
>
> ```
> period.division.bar_number.beat_number.tatum_position
> ```
>
> period is the number of beats in a bar. If beat_proportions are set (for non-isochronous beats), beat_proportions will be used instead of period in an 'additive' notation, e. g., (3+2+2). division is the number of tatums in the current beat. The other fields are bar number, beat number, and tatum position.

Midlevel annotation

Midlevel analysis (MLA) can be regarded as a short and compact system to segment the musical surfaces into sections of sufficiently distinct character. These units are called midlevel units (MLU). It was developed in an attempt to identify underlying playing ideas of jazz improvisations. The approach was first developed for piano solos (Frieler & Lothwesen, 2012; Schütz, 2015) and then adapted for monophonic solos (Frieler et al., 2016a).

MLA is based on the hypothesis that jazz players are more likely to make decisions on a middle level (with regard to playing details), comprising times spans of a few seconds, which are then actualized using preconceived or spontaneous material from motor memory. This guiding principle led to the identification of several distinct types of ideas by analyzing a large sample of solos. First, solos were segmented into parts of discernibly different character, which were tentatively named. In a second step, these types were condensed and re-ordered by simultaneously establishing a comprehensive system of sub- and sub-subtypes. In principle, this typology of playing ideas is not closed, but can be considered saturated for the Weimar Jazz Database, in the sense that it is possible to typify all playing ideas into one of the devised types. However, with new data or data of a different kind, it might be desirable to add new types if enough ideas are encountered that cannot be reasonably well fitted into one of the existing categories. For example, due to instrument specifics, playing ideas for piano solos and monophonic solos are not identical, although a large overlap exists. There is evidence that piano players, when

Table 2: Metrical annotation of the rhythm of 'The Lick'.

Note	TAS	Metrical annotation $(j, p_j, b_{k_j}, d_{k_j}, s_m)$	Dot notation $(p_j, d_{k_j}, j, b_{k_j}, s_m)$
1	1+	(1, 4, 1, 2, 2)	4.2.1.1.2
2	2+	(1, 4, 2, 2, 2)	4.2.1.2.2
3	3	(1, 4, 3, 2, 1)	4.2.1.3.1
4	3+	(1, 4, 3, 2, 2)	4.2.1.3.2
5	4	(1, 4, 4, 2, 1)	4.2.1.4.1
6	4+	(1, 4, 4, 2, 2)	4.2.1.4.2
7	1	(2, 4, 1, 1, 1)	4.1.2.1.1
8	2e	(2, 4, 2, 4, 2)	4.4.2.2.2
9	2a	(2, 4, 2, 4, 4)	4.4.2.2.4

Note. Note = note number in the example from Figure 1 and Table 1; TAS = traditional American system for counting metrical positions (second sixteenth = e, eighth = +, fourth sixteenth = a); metrical annotation as defined in the text; dot notation = metrical dot notation used in the MeloSpyGUI, see Infobox 4.

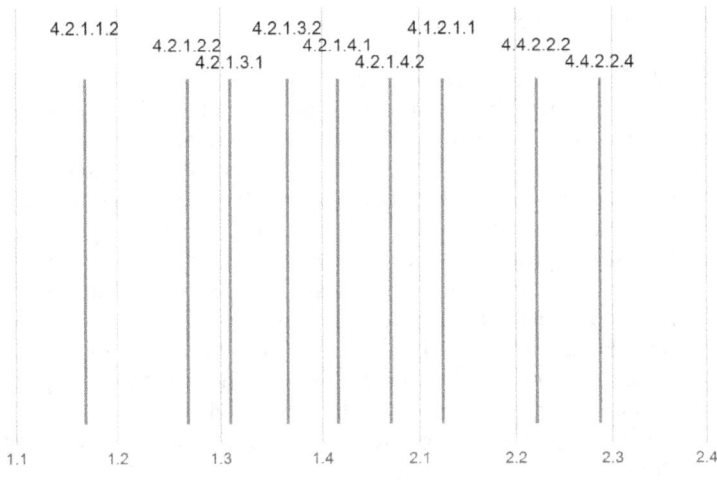

Figure 3: Metrical annotation for 'The Lick'. Thick vertical lines correspond to the onsets, thin lines to annotated beats. Labels are given in metrical dot notation for the onsets and in the format (bar number, beat index) for the beats.

confronted with the system, find the concept at least partly adequate for internal improvisation processes, though possibly not with regard to all details of the typology (Schütz, 2015). However, the exact connection to actual playing ideas is still an open research question. Besides identifying distinct MLUs, the system also incorporates an easy way to encode musical relationships and similarities between MLUs, e. g., variations, which permit interesting insights into the process of improvisation and an examination of dramaturgy and form.

1. *line*:[9] A line is a series of tones for the most part proceeding in small, step-sized intervals with high rhythmical uniformity and a salient trajectory in pitch space. Depending on the trajectory, there are several sub- and sub-subcategories. The main subcategories are simple (default), tick, interwoven, and wavy lines. The main shapes are 'horizontal', 'ascending', 'descending', 'concave', and 'convex'. Tick lines are lines of exclusively convex and concave shapes but with asymmetric arms, i. e., a longer or shorter descent or ascent combined with an accordingly longer or shorter ascent or descent. Simple lines show a straight direction, i. e., without too many twist and turns, which are characteristic of wavy lines. Wavy lines tend to be rather long and may have an overall direction besides 'wiggling around'. Interwoven lines consist of two independent horizontal ascending or descending lines that are played in tone-wise alternation.

2. *licks*: In the context of MLA, a lick is a rather short and concise melodic figure that often includes rhythmical and intervallic salience. Licks have a clear gestalt-like quality, which distinguishes them from fragments. They comprise mostly short tones and sometimes large intervals and chromaticism, which distinguishes them from melodies. Shortness, rhythmic diversity, or both qualities together separate licks from lines. We have two proper subtypes in this category: *lick_bebop* and *lick_blues*. All other licks are grouped into a residual subclass *lick*. Blues licks are defined by tonal features such as blue notes as well as typical constructions. Historically, the blues played (and still plays) a special role in jazz improvisation (Schuller, 1958), so it seemed worth defining a special subcategory. Bebop licks on the other hand use certain techniques which are typical for bebop lines, such as approach notes and chromatic passing tones.

---

[9] The following description of the nine main MLU types is a slightly edited version taken from Frieler et al. (2016a).

3. *melody*: A melodic figure that is not derived from the theme of the song and embodies some kind of song-like, lyrical, cantabile character. A rule of thumb may be: If an MLU sounds more like scatting (if sung), it should be termed a lick or a line; if it sounds more like a Broadway tune, a pop song or a folk tune, it should be labeled as *melody*.

4. *rhythm*: This category describes units in which the rhythmical expression is the single most prominent feature. There are four subtypes that differ according to the number of pitches (single or multiple) and basic rhythm quality (regular or irregular). The most important subtypes are single tone repetitions, predominantly regular and isochronous, and oscillations with multiple tone repetitions, predominantly regular.

5. *theme*: Denotes material taken directly from the theme of the tune, possibly with variations. The characteristics of a *theme* MLU are often similar to those of melody, but because of its relationship to the tune, it is a distinct playing idea.

6. *quote*: These are direct quotes from another piece of music (jazz tune, classical tune etc.), which might resemble a melody or a theme. Playing a pattern taken from another jazz musician as part of a longer line or a lick does not count as a quote if it is not clearly recognizable as such.

7. *fragment*: A small set of tones which neither form a clear contour-based succession or motivic/thematic figure nor are very expressive. Fragments are most often single tones or very short segments which can even sound like 'mistakes'.

8. *expressive*: These are figures or single tones with a sound- or gesture-like character in which aspects of expressivity are clearly focused, e. g., scream-like sounds.

9. *void*: This category refers to moments of 'actively playing nothing'. Generally, jazz soloists add short breaks between phrases, e. g., just for breathing, which do not belong to this category. The length of the break in the flow of a solo should clearly exceed these usual gaps between phrases.

All solos in the Weimar Jazz Database were manually annotated with MLUs by three annotators. Special care has been taken to ensure that the MLU types are consistently annotated. One annotator double-checked all other annotations. As this is basically a qualitative system with categories that cannot be defined unequivocally and which have continuous and overlapping boundaries, there is some leeway for the annotators. However, when comparing annotations of three to four different coders using a small subset of solos, high agreement (Fleiss's $\varkappa = .81$) for assignment of MLU boundaries was found, whereas the agreement for MLU types was lower (Fleiss's $\varkappa = .60$), but still sufficiently good. The main disagreement was between *line* and *lick* as well as between *melody* and *lick*. For specific MLUs, disagreements between different coders might come about due to the fact that several equally adequate solutions exist, but each MLU has to be assigned to exactly one type. Even when annotations might disagree, they can often still be considered as 'correct' (or 'not wrong'). Hence it can be safely assumed that for statistical analyses the disagreements level each other out and that the resulting statistics are sufficiently valid. The most common MLU type is, not surprisingly, *lick* with about 45 % followed by *lines* 30 %. However, since *lick*s are much shorter than *line*s, they only account for about 37 % of the duration of all solos, whereas *line*s account for about 40 %. For more details about MLU statistics and distributions in the Weimar Jazz Database, we refer to Frieler et al. (2016a).

Infobox 5: MLU syntax

For the MLA annotation in Sonic Visualiser, a specific short mnemonic code was devised (see Online Supplementary Material S2 of Frieler et al., 2016a). The basic rule is that a musical phrase starts an MLU, but that more than one MLU can be contained in one musical phrase, which is called 'glueing'. Each MLU contains information about its type (full type with all possible sub-subtypes), whether the MLU is glued on, possible reference or relationship to a foregoing MLU (called 'back reference'), some additional information about this relationship, and finally comments of further specification.
The basic syntax is:

```
[~][#[N][*+-=]]cat-label[:specifier]
```

where square brackets denote optional elements. The first element, the tilde ~, if present, indicates a glued MLU. The hash #, followed by an optional integer number N indicates a back reference to the MLU N MLUs before. If N is missing, a value of one is assumed, i.e., a relationship to the immediately preceding MLU. Equivalently, this can also be expressed by sequences of N hashes. The following symbols *+-= indicate the type of relationship, if clearly identifiable. The asterisk * indicates an unspecified variant and can be omitted. The plus and minus signs denote transpositions up + or down - in pitch space, whereby the transposition does not need to be exact (hence an asterisk is implied). For exact (possibly transposed) repetitions, the equal sign = can be used.
The cat-label has to be one of the following:

Computational melody analysis

- Licks: *lick* (unspecified), *lick_bebop* (bebop lick), *lick_blues* (blues lick).
- Simple lines: *line_a* (ascending), *line_d* (descending), *line_cv* (concave), *line_cx* (convex).
- Tick lines (a = ascending, d = descending, s = short, l = long): *line_t_asdl*, *line_t_alds*, *line_t_dsal*, *line_t_dlas*.
- Interwoven lines (a = ascending, h = horizontal, d = descending, top line first) : *line_ah*, *line_ha*, *line_ad*, *line_hd*, *line_aa*, *line_ad*, *line_da*, *line_dd*.
- Wavy lines *line_w[_x]*, where x can be any specifier from simple and tick lines or missing, which is short for *line_w_h*, a wavy line that starts and ends roughly at the same pitch.
- Rhythms (s = single pitch, m = multiple pitches, r = regular rhythm, i = irregular rhythm): *rhythm_sr*, *rhythm_si*, *rhythm_mr*, *rhythm_mi*.
- Others: *melody, void, expressive, quote, theme*.

The specifier part is optional and can be any string, e. g., the name of the musical work a *quote* was taken from or the location in the theme of a *theme* reference. *Examples.* ~#2+*melody* is a glued melody that is an upwardly transposed variation of the MLU (not necessarily also a *melody*) two units before; *theme:t1* is a reference to measure 1 of the theme of the tune; *lick, #lick, #lick* is a chain *aa'a"* of successively varied licks. If more than one back reference is possible, as probably here for the last one, the shortest back reference should be taken.

Feature extraction

Feature extraction is one of the central tasks in computational musicology and a prerequisite to many analytical investigations. In a general sense, features can be conceived as characteristics, traits, or properties that describe specific entities, e. g., musical objects. They range from very simple features, which require only a trivial measurement or are part of the definition of an object, to very complex ones ('deep stucture'), which require elaborate measurement procedures or cognitive models. Moreover, features can be ascribed to the whole entity of interest or only to parts of it. They can be single values (e. g., the number of notes in a melody) or vectors of symbols (e. g., the title of a piece.)

Features often serve as dependent variables in models to predict target variables, e. g., music perceptions or style classification. For example, certain musical properties, such as tempo, articulation, or tonality, are known to contribute to the emotional expression or impact a piece of music can have. For classification, objects are grouped into classes, categories, or types according to certain properties, i. e., feature values, using suitable similarity measures. Features are essentially human constructions and seldom merit ontological status. They coordinate the relationship between the objects and operational models for the prediction and description of these objects, but are principally arbitrary and contingent on the purpose of the scientific model. In analogy to coordinate systems that describe physical objects in space, one can also speak of 'feature spaces' for the description of an object. Like coordinate systems in the physical world, certain features are more apt or easier to handle than others, depending on the tasks and objects at hand. Finding the most suitable features for a problem is often a central task, called 'feature selection'.

There are always possibilities for constructing new features from old ones using algorithmic or mathematical operations. This is basically the approach we followed in designing our feature extraction software (`melfeatures`). It has a flexible module ('feature machine') at its core that allows the definition of a large class of features based on certain predefined properties of the musical object (i. e., its basic representation) and a set of mathematical and statistical operations.

General concepts

It is useful to first define some general properties of features. Let $\mathcal{O} = \{o_i\}$ be a set of objects and $\mathscr{F} = F_1 \times F_2 \times \cdots \times F_N$ an arbitrary feature space. The number N is called the dimension of the feature space, where we assume that the components F_i are mostly elementary (one-dimensional). In most cases, the components are either real or integer numbers ($\mathscr{F}_i = \mathbb{R}, \mathbb{N}$) or a set of labels, i. e., an arbitrary set with no further internal structure.

A feature is then a map from the objects into the feature space. The primary or defining features are those which are used to define the objects. Please note that the abstract representation of objects here is not identical to the objects themselves, i. e., the objects of interest here are the digital representations of musical objects as defined in section p. 41. Hence, in our representation, the primary feature of a melody is the representation itself, i. e., tuples of onsets, durations, and pitches etc. In this approach, each object has to have its own feature space, since the dimension of the basic representation is dependent on the length of the melody. The representation space for a melody of length N is then effectively $3N$ dimensional with components $F_i = \mathbb{R} \times \mathbb{R}^+ \times [0:127]$. Feature maps where the feature spaces vary with the object are called sequential features or, alternatively and probably less confusingly, transformations. Such transformations can themselves, of course, become the starting point of another feature map and in this way transformation chains can be built. This is also the basic logic behind the 'feature machine' of the `melfeature` module of MeloSpyGUI software, where transformation chains are defined with the aid of a simple syntax.

An important special case of feature maps are global features, which map an object to one and the same feature space. If the feature space is one-dimensional, these are called scalar features, even if the feature space is not numerical. Metadata are an important case of global and scalar feature. For example, the solos in the Weimar Jazz Database have an annotated rhythm feel which is represented by the set of labels

$$\mathscr{R} = \{\text{SWING}, \text{LATIN}, \text{FUNK}, \text{TWOBEAT}, \text{MIX}\}.$$

Then, the 'rhythm feel feature' is a map from the solos $\mathscr{S} \to \mathscr{R}$ onto the set of rhythm feel labels. Similar constructions hold for all metadata, even though the feature space is not always a fixed set of labels, but often strings (character sequences), e.g., the title of a piece.

Phrase IDs are an example of a non-primary sequential feature. Since each solo has a different number of phrases, a global finite-dimensional feature space is not sufficient to represent all possibilities. We can formally solve this with the aid of sequence spaces, e.g., spaces of sequences of arbitrary length into a fixed target space. Let T be such a target space (in the case of phrase IDs, these are the integers, $T = \mathbb{N}$). A sequence of length N over T, denoted $\mathscr{S}_N(T)$, is a map $[0:N-1] \to T$. The space of all sequences over T is defined as the union of all sequences of positive length:

$$\mathscr{S}(T) = \bigcup_{N=1}^{\infty} \mathscr{S}_N(T) = \{\mathscr{S}_1(T), \mathscr{S}_2(T), \ldots\}.$$

Note that sequences of length 1 are identical to the target space itself, $\mathscr{S}_1(T) = T$. A sequential feature (also sometimes, a bit misleadingly, called vector feature) is a feature map with feature space $\mathscr{S}(T)$. The list of phrase IDs of a solo is then a sequence of integers from 1 to M, where M is the number of phrases in a solo. Of course, such a list of integers is not very informative, so it can be combined, for example, with the indices of start and end tones to unequivocally identify phrases within a certain solo.

Our basic representation of melodies can then be viewed as a sequential feature with feature space $\mathscr{S}(\mathbb{R} \times \mathbb{R}^+ \times [0:127])$. In the case of sequential musical objects, a sequential feature is called point-wise or local if the length of the sequence space is (a simple function of) the length of the melody. In other words, a transformation that results in a sequence of the same length as the original melody is 'local' in this sense.

Finally, a matrix feature is a feature map into the space of matrices (mostly over $\mathbb{R}$), where the dimension of the matrices can be dependent on the object itself. A prominent example, available in the MeloSpyGUI, is the self-similarity matrix of phrases (see p. 63).

An important class of—mostly global—features are statistical features. These are constructed by using descriptive statistics (e. g., mean, median, standard deviation etc.) of a sample distribution which in this case are the elements of a transformation chain. For example, the mean pitch of a melody is constructed by the projection on the pitch component and subsequent averaging all (MIDI) pitches p_i of a melody of length N, i. e.,

$$\overline{p} = \frac{1}{N} \sum_{i=0}^{N-1} p_i.$$

A more complicated example is the relative frequencies of a chordal pitch class. Chordal pitch classes are defined for a pitch p and an annotated chord C_p with root pitch class $r(C_p) \in [0:11]$. The chordal pitch class of p is then defined as the interval of p to the root modulo 12. The modulo 12 operation returns the remainder after an integer division by 12, e. g., 23 mod 12 = 11. This operation effectively disregards the octave. The full formula is then:

$$\gamma(p, C_p) = (p - r(C_p)) \mod 12.$$

Applying this transformation to a melody of length N results in a sequence of chord pitch classes $\gamma_i = \gamma(p_i, C_{p_i})$, also of length N, which can then be treated as a random sample over the numbers from 0 to 11. The frequency of chordal pitch class $\Gamma_j, j \in [0:11]$, $f(\Gamma_j)$ is the number of times it occurs in the sample $f(\Gamma_j) = \left| \{\gamma_i = \Gamma_j, i \in [0:N-1]\} \right|$. Clearly, the sum of all frequencies over all possible pitch classes equals the size of the sample, i. e., $\sum_{j=0}^{11} f(\Gamma_j) = N$. The relative frequency of a chordal pitch class $d(\Gamma_j)$ is then the absolute frequency divided by the size of the sample, which is a number between 0 and 1. This relative frequency can be regarded as an estimation of the probability that a certain chordal pitch class will occur. The twelve relative frequencies of single chordal pitch classes can also serve as global, scalar features for a solo.

Selected features

A classification of melodic features can be performed according to many different criteria. A first classification is with respect to the musical dimension they pertain to, e. g., pitch/intervals or rhythm/meter. But since there are also features that relate to several different musical dimensions at once, this schema is not without problems. Another approach is more technical, like the one presented in the preceding section, e. g., global, sequential, scalar, vector, matrix features etc., which gives some information about the structure but not about the meaning. In the feature definition files of the MeloSpySuite/GUI, a rough classification, mainly based on musical dimension, is already in use, so it seems natural to follow this approach. The reader can thus easily make a connection to the software. We will discuss global characteristics of each feature class and the most important features, but we have to leave many details to our online documentation[10] due to limitations on space.

Accents

Accent features (or better, accent transformations, also called 'structural markers') are exclusively sequential, local transformations. They result in a sequence of numerical values of the same length as the melody. Nearly all accent features provide boolean values (binary markers), i. e., TRUE (1) or FALSE (0), indicating, whether or not a certain condition is fulfilled for an event in a melody. They originated in a paper (Müllensiefen, Frieler, & Pfleiderer, 2009), in which perception of perceived accents (in pop music) was modeled with the help of a long list of so-called 'accent rules' taken from the literature. The MeloSpySuite/GUI currently includes all accent rules used in the paper and several others. A slight generalization leads to the concept of structural markers, which provide point-wise boolean values with respect to some structural conditions, e. g., phrase and bar beginnings and endings. These are particular useful for more complex analyses in conjunction with other features. For example, if one wants to find out the distribution of metrical positions of phrase endings in a solo, one could extract metrical positions and phrase ending markers, and examine the distribution of metrical position with respect to phrase endings.

Auxiliary

Auxiliary features (transformations) either export the basic representation of the melody (which also permits the export of raw melodic data, though we recommend using the melconv module of the MeloSpySuite/GUI for

---

[10] http://jazzomat.hfm-weimar.de/documentation.html

this purpose), or annotated values, such as phrase IDs, form labels, metrical position, and chords.

Contour

Pitch contour is an important concept in music psychology since melody perception and melodic memory seem to work mostly with the rough contour of pitch sequences (Dowling & Fujitani, 1971), i. e., the ups and downs, and its global shape.

Huron and Abeßer contour map a pitch sequence to a fixed contour shape class. The Huron contour was proposed by Huron (1996) in a study about the melodic arch in Western folk song. For a sequence of N pitch values (p_i) the algorithm proceeds as follows: Take the first and last pitch p_0 and p_{N-1} and the mean value of all pitches in between $\overline{p} = \frac{1}{N-2}\sum_{i=1}^{N-2} p_i$. Between the first and the mean pitch and the mean and the last pitch, three size relationships are possible: equal (=), less (<), or greater (>). This yields nine possible combinations, which represent certain global contour shapes, e. g., == is a horizontal, <> a convex, and << an ascending contour. A reduced version with only five classes is obtained by mapping mixed horizontal-ascending/descending contours to the ascending/descending parts. This procedure is more suited for shorter melodies, e. g., folk song phrases of about 7–10 pitches, and not meaningful for very long melodies such as entire jazz solos or even a long bebop line. For this, an extension of Huron's method proposed by Abeßer et al. (2015) is better suited. It was developed for frequency contours (cf. p. 113), but carries over to pitch sequences without modification. Generally, contour shapes are best calculated for phrases or other shorter melody sections in order to obtain meaningful results.

Interval

Intervals are another very important musical dimension. They are derived from the pitch dimension, but are generally invariant under pitch transposition which reflects the psychological phenomenon that most people have only relative and not absolute pitch. All interval features provided in the MeloSpySuite/GUI use the semitone interval transformation as a starting point, i. e.,

$$\Delta p_i = p_{i+1} - p_i.$$

This transformation has one fewer element than the original melody. It can be made a point-wise transformation by adding an empty element at the beginning or the end. Intervals have a sign indicating the direction of the pitch change, but sometimes only the magnitude is of interest, which can be

Computational melody analysis

retrieved by taking the absolute value, $|\Delta p_i|$. The interval features provided are mostly statistical descriptors (maximum/minimum, range, mode, mean, median, variance, standard deviation, entropy, and Zipf's coefficient).

Infobox 6: Information entropy and Zipf's coefficient

Information entropy is a useful concept in computational musicology. It was developed by Claude Shannon (Shannon, 1948) to measure the information content of messages. The definition is generally applicable to the distribution of random events. The information of an event is defined as being inversely proportional to its probability, since very common events are expectable and thus less informative, whereas rare events provide a lot of information. If we have a set of possible events e_i with probabilities p_i, the information content of e_i is defined as the logarithm of the inverse probability:

$$h_i = \log \frac{1}{p_i} = -\log_2 p_i.$$

The information content of an event can be interpreted as the number of average Yes/No-question (called *bits*) one has to ask to guess the outcome of an experiment. That is also why the logarithm appears in the above, because with every Yes/No-question one halves the space of possibilities. For example, to obtain the result of a fair coin toss, one has to ask one question on average. (For an unfair coin, which always lands heads up, no question has to be asked, because the result is always the same).

The information entropy is then the expected information gain over all possible events:

$$H = E[h] = \sum_i p_i h_i = -\sum_i p_i \log_2 p_i.$$

Entropy will have low values if few very likely events dominate the process and will have very high values if all outcomes are roughly equally likely. Indeed, for uniform distributions, i.e., $p_i = \frac{1}{N}$ if there are N possible events, the entropy is maximal:

$$H_{\max} = -\sum_{i=1}^{N} \frac{1}{N} \log_2 \frac{1}{N} = -\log_2 \frac{1}{N} = \log_2 N.$$

This can be used to define normalized entropy for a random process with N outcomes:

$$H_0 = \frac{H}{H_{\max}} = \frac{H}{\log_2 N}.$$

The Zipf coefficient can be regarded as a measure for the non-uniformity of a probability distribution: the higher the value, the more the distribution is dominated by the most frequent elements. Power laws are a very common

> phenomenon in a wide area of applications from income distribution to city sizes. Zipf observed his law for word frequencies in English texts, where he found that the frequency of words fell as $\propto 1/r$ with the frequency rank ($\alpha = 1$). Zipf's coefficient is generally defined as the slope of the logarithm of class frequencies vs. the frequency ranks, i.e., the coefficient α of a (supposed) power law $f(r) \propto r^{-\alpha}$, where r is the frequency rank (see Zanette, 2006, for discussion of Zipf's law in the context of music). Very often, however, the Zipf coefficient is strongly correlated with the information entropy of a distribution. In practice, information entropy is mostly preferred as a measure for non-uniformity of a sample distribution. since it is more well-known and more easily and robustly calculated.

For semitone intervals, two classifications are available: fuzzy intervals and Parsons's code. The latter is sometimes called 'contour', which is not to be confused with the contour measures in the sense defined above. Parsons (1975) devised his code in the context of cataloging musical themes, where he considered only the basic interval directions, i.e., U(p) (+1), D(own) (-1), or S(ame)/R(epeat) (0), to achieve a very rough but compact code for melodies. Formally, this is just the mapping of semitone intervals to their sign, i.e., $\Delta p_i \mapsto \text{sgn}(\Delta p_i)$, where positive numbers are mapped to +1, negative numbers to -1 and zero onto itself.

A more detailed classification is given by the fuzzy interval transformation, which is sometimes called 'refined contour' in the literature. There are, of course, many different possible classifications of intervals. We used one with nine symmetric classes which seemed to be a good compromise between compactness and specificity (cf. Table 3).

Metadata

This category consists of all available metadata (in the Weimar Jazz Database, or other corpora such as the EsAC folk song database). These are all global, scalar features. For a list of the most important metadata in the Weimar Jazz Database, see Table 1.

Meter

This category collects global and local features and transformations connected to the metrical annotation. Besides raw exports of metrical annotations such as bar, beat, and tatum positions, the Metrical Circle Map transformation (MCM) and derived statistical features are also provided. The Metrical Circle

Table 3: Fuzzy interval classes.

Name	Interval range	Numerical value
large jump down	< -7	-4
jump down	$[-7 : -5]$	-3
leap down	$[-4 : -3]$	-2
step down	$[-2 : -1]$	-1
repetition	0	0
step up	$[1 : 2]$	1
leap up	$[3 : 4]$	2
jump up	$[5 : 7]$	3
large jump up	> 7	4

Map (Frieler, 2007, 2008) was introduced to enable a comparison of melodies with all types of meters and highly diverse rhythms. Metrical measures are binned into N equally long segments and metrical positions are mapped to the closest bin. This ensures comparability, admittedly rather brute-force, of metrical positions in any metrical frame, as well as for music with changing meters. However, for actual comparisons using the MCM, care should be taken in regard to the different metrical frames in a set of melodies in order to achieve interpretable results. In the MeloSpySuite/GUI a MCM with $N = 48$ is implemented, i. e., each tone event is mapped to a number $m \in [0 : 47]$. This is a local transformation (provided a metrical annotation is available). For this mapping, several circular statistical descriptors are available (see Appendix *Brief introduction to circular statistics* for a short introduction to circular statistics).

There are two metrical complexity measures available, *compression complexity* and *division complexity* as well as the arithmetic mean of both. The first is based on the idea that metrical local sub-beat grids are more complex if fewer positions are occupied. The beat-local grid is defined by the local division of the beat. For example, a group of four sixteenths is 'simpler' than a group of one eighth and two sixteenths, since the third sixteenth position in the sixteenth sub-beat grid is unoccupied in the latter. The second complexity measure is inspired by the idea that frequently changing beat divisions are more complex, particularly if these are not related by doubling or quadrupling. Let us take again 'The Lick' as an example (Figure 1, p. 46), see Table 4. Compression complexity values are calculated as follows. For each beat i in a set of N beats with local divisions d_i, the number $1 \leq n_i \leq d_i$ of occupied tatum positions is counted. Then, the total compression complexity is given by the mean over all beats:

$$\frac{1}{N}\sum_{i=1}^{N}\frac{d_i - n_i}{d_i - 1}.$$

A rhythm where all tatum positions are occupied will receive the minimal value of zero and a rhythm with only syncopated events the maximal value of one. (Note that the division is ensured to be optimal due to the FlexQ algorithm in our metrical representation).

The division complexity is similarly calculated for all beats with at least one event, where a change in division will be penalized by 1 if the ratio of divisions is not a power of two, in which case the penalty is set to 1/2.

$$\frac{1}{N-1}\sum_{i=1}^{N-1}\theta(d_i, d_{i+1}),$$

where

$$\theta(x,y) = \begin{cases} 0 & x = y, \\ 0.5 & |\log_2(x/y)| \in \mathbb{N}, \\ 1 & \text{else.} \end{cases}$$

A rhythm with a constant beat division will be awarded the minimal division complexity of 0; a rhythm with constantly changing divisions, not related by a power of 2, will receive the maximal value. (Note that this construction also relies on the fact that the divisions are guaranteed to be local and optimal as provided by the FlexQ algorithm.)

MLA

From midlevel annotations as described above (p. 54), a set of sequential features can be derived, e. g., lists of raw MLUs, main types, duration, and back references.

Pitch

The base for all pitch features is the pitch dimension of the basic representation from which several representations are derived. The most important transformation of pitch is pitch classes (pc), which reflect the octave equivalence. In the common 12-tone equal tempered tone system, this is easily done by taking the MIDI pitch values modulo 12. Since, by convention, $C4 = 60$, all Cs are mapped to $\hat{0}$, where the hat over the zero conventionally indicates

Table 4: Compression and division complexity for 'The Lick'.

Measure	Beat	Division	Occupation	CC	DC
1	1	2	.X	0.5	0.0
1	2	2	.X	0.5	0.0
1	3	2	XX	0.0	0.0
1	4	2	XX	0.0	0.0
2	1	1	X	0.0	0.5
2	2	4	.X.X	0.5	0.5
			Sum	1.5	1.0

Note: ./X = unoccupied/occupied tatum position, CC = compression complexity value, DC = division complexity value.

pitch classes (Forte, 1973). The other tones are enumerated accordingly, i.e., C♯/D♭→$\hat{1}$, D→$\hat{2}$, D♯/E♭→$\hat{3}$ etc. Formally, given a fixed anchor pitch P, the pitch class transformation (PC) for pitches p_i with respect to P is given by:

$$p_i \mapsto (p_i - P) \mod 12.$$

It is an established tradition to use $P = 0$ for (absolute) pitch classes (Forte, 1973), but the anchor is basically arbitrary.

The idea is to use different anchors with respect to context. One option for this is the tonic of the key of the melody (if available). For example, for a melody in A♭ major, one sets the anchor to $P = 8$, and all A♭s are then mapped to $\hat{0}$, with the other pitches mapped accordingly. This transformation is called tonal pitch class (TPC) and is available in the MeloSpySuite/GUI.

Another option, which is especially important in chord-based jazz improvisation, is to use the root of the underlying chord as the anchor. For example, a C will be mapped to $\hat{0}$ if played in a Cmaj⁷ context, but to $\hat{11}$ in a D♭min⁷ context, and to $\hat{4}$ in a A♭°⁷ context. This is called chordal pitch class (CPC).

Another modification of the approach is to reflect the diatonic major/minor system, since under TPC and CPC minor thirds are mapped to $\hat{3}$ whereas major thirds are mapped to $\hat{4}$, even though both serve the function of a diatonic third scale degree in minor or major, resp. Diatonic scale degrees are mapped to the values 1 to 7 and special symbols are used for the remaining 'chromatic' tones. This leads to tonal and chordal diatonic pitch classes (TDCP, CDPC).

An extension of CDPC, called extended chordal pitch class (CDPCX), proved to be more important in practice and is often used in this book. For chords with a major third, the major scale is used as the underlying diatonic scale; for chords with a minor third (including diminished and half-diminished chords), the dorian scale is used[11] as the underlying diatonic scale. Exceptions are dominant seventh chords, where the minor seventh is mapped to the seventh scale degree (mixolydian). See Table 5 for a mapping of chord types to base scales. The remaining non-diatonic pitches are thus also dependent on the chord, or—to be more precise—from the diatonic context derived from the chord and are thus mapped to different symbols (Table 6). The resulting alphabet as implemented in the MeloSpySuite/GUI contains 13 symbols plus the symbol X for pitches without chord context (NC). Note that flat ninth, sharp fourth/flat fifth, and flat sixth are always considered to be non-diatonic, even when the chord prescribes these as a tension. The major/minor third is considered non-diatonic over chords with a minor/major third. The same rule also holds for major and minor sevenths.

Table 5: Mapping of chord types to diatonic scales for CDPCX.

Chord type	Diatonic scale
$maj^{(6,7)}$, aug	ionian
$dom^{7,\,alt}$, aug^7	mixolydian
$min^{(7)}$, $dim^{(7)}$, $min^{7\flat5}$, $sus^{(7)}$	dorian

Generally, all higher chord tensions are ignored for reasons of simplicity in conjunction with the fact that the chord annotations in the Weimar Jazz Database are taken from lead sheets. One should bear this in mind when interpreting CDPCX values. Some chords, such as the diminished seventh chords, do not fit to a classical diatonic scale over any of its chord tones or are, at least, ambiguous. These are in someway intrinsically non-diatonic chords (even though, e.g., a fully diminished seventh chord can be interpreted as a dominant seventh chord with an added minor ninth and without a root in a minor scale.) Moreover, linear movements should be considered too, since many of the non-diatonic pitch classes are produced not as 'free chromatics' but using passing and neighboring tones. Features derived from these pitch

---

[11]The choice to use the dorian scale and not the minor (aeolian) scale was based on the rationale that (1) a minor sixth (or ♭13) is generally considered a dissonant extension over a minor chord, (2) dorian minor chords are somehow more common in jazz due to the frequent use of ii7 chords, and (3) the transformation becomes simpler this way.

Table 6: Mapping of CPC to CDPCX.

CPC	Diatonic context			Name
	Ionian	Dorian	Mixolydian	
$\hat{0}$	1	1	1	
$\hat{1}$	-	-	-	♭9
$\hat{2}$	2	2	2	
$\hat{3}$	B	3	B	♯9
$\hat{4}$	3	>	3	♯10
$\hat{5}$	4	4	4	
$\hat{6}$	T	T	T	♯11
$\hat{7}$	5	5	5	
$\hat{8}$	%	%	%	♭13
$\hat{9}$	6	6	6	
$\hat{10}$	<	7	7	♭7
$\hat{11}$	7	L	L	♯7
NC	X	X	X	

transformations are mostly statistical descriptors, either continuous (PITCH), circular (PC and CPC), or nominal (CDPC, CDPCX), TDCPC).

Example. In Table 7 the most important pitch transformations are listed for 'The Lick' (cf. Figure 1, p. 46.)

Rhythm

For rhythms, the most important distinction is the one between durations and inter-onset intervals (IOI). Generally, IOIs are more relevant for rhythm perception whereas durations are mainly a matter of articulation and tone formation. Durations are already part of the basic representation of a tone event and IOIs can be easily calculated given the list of onsets. However, due to micro-timings and transcription imprecisions, the bare numerical values of either durations and IOIs are of little analytical help and require some binning processes. In the MeloSpySuite/GUI a classifications for time spans (durations and IOIs) are predefined in two different variants, absolute and relative. This classification has five classes, VERY SHORT, SHORT, MEDIUM, LONG, and VERY LONG. To calculate the classes, one first has to relate the time spans to a reference value. Absolute time span classes are constructed using a fixed reference value of 500 ms corresponding to the beat duration in

Table 7: Pitch representations of 'The Lick'.

Note	Chord	Name	PITCH	PC	TPC	TDPC	CPC	CDPCX
1	C^{maj7}	B4	71	11	11	7	11	7
2	C^{maj7}	B4	71	11	11	7	11	7
3	C^{maj7}	A4	69	9	9	6	9	6
4	C^{maj7}	B4	71	11	11	7	11	7
5	C^{maj7}	C5	72	0	0	1	0	1
6	C^{maj7}	D5	74	2	2	2	2	2
7	$F\sharp^{m7\flat5}$	B4	71	11	11	7	5	4
8	$F\sharp^{m7\flat5}$	G4	67	7	7	5	1	–
9	$F\sharp^{m7\flat5}$	A4	69	9	9	6	3	3

Note. PITCH = MIDI pitch, PC = Pitch class, TPC/TDPC = Tonal (diatonic) pitch class (based on C major), CPC/CDPCX Chordal (diatonic, extended) pitch class.

120 bpm. This value is a good approximation to preferred and spontaneous tempos reported in the rhythm research literature. In a way, it represents a 'natural' time unit for humans (e. g., Fraisse, 1982). Relative time span classes are constructed using the duration of the momentary beat as the reference value.

Formally, let T_i denote time-spans, i. e., durations d_i or IOIs Δt_i, and fix a reference duration $T_{0,i}$, possibly a function of the time-span itself, e. g., the local beat duration for relative time-span classes, or a fixed value (e. g., $T_0 = 0.5$ for absolute time-span classes). Furthermore, let $\epsilon < 1$ be a small numerical offset. Then the time-span classification $\hat{\Theta}$ is defined for normalized time-spans

$$\hat{\Theta}(T_i) = K\left(\frac{T_i}{T_{0,i}}\right)$$

with the time-span classification function $K(t)$:

$$K_\epsilon(t) = \begin{cases} -2 & t < 2^{-2+\epsilon} \\ -1 & 2^{-2+\epsilon} < t \leq 2^{-\frac{1}{2}-\epsilon} \\ +0 & 2^{-\frac{1}{2}-\epsilon} < t \leq 2^{\frac{1}{2}+\epsilon} \\ +1 & 2^{\frac{1}{2}+\epsilon} < t \leq 2^{2-\epsilon} \\ +2 & > 2^{2-\epsilon}. \end{cases}$$

In the time-span classifications in the MeloSpySuite/GUI $\epsilon = 0.1$ was used.

This gives a classification function, using verbal class labels, of

$$K(t) = \begin{cases} \text{VERY SHORT} & t < 0.268, \\ \text{SHORT} & 0.268 < t \leq 0.660, \\ \text{MEDIUM} & 0.660 < t \leq 1.560, \\ \text{LONG} & 1.560 < t \leq 3.732, \\ \text{VERY LONG} & t > 3.732. \end{cases}$$

The rationale behind these numerical class boundaries is based on a few ideas. First, a five-fold classification seems a good choice between specificity and compactness. Secondly, sixteenth notes should be mapped to VERY SHORT, eighth notes to SHORT, quarter notes to MEDIUM, half notes to LONG, and whole notes to VERY LONG. These correspond to normalized time-spans of $\frac{1}{4}, \frac{1}{2}, 1, 2, 4$, which are mapped to the desired classes. But besides these binary metrical time-spans, there are also triplets, quintuplets etc., as well as dotted and double dotted durations which have to be accommodated. Furthermore, in performance-based data such as Weimar Jazz Database, the time-spans are actually real-valued numbers. The choice of class boundaries was further motivated by the conditions that triplets should be mapped to the class short and dotted quarters to medium. Finally, the boundaries were determined by programming parsimony by tweaking powers of two, since—accidentally—$2^{\frac{1}{2}} = \sqrt{2} = 1.4142\ldots$ is less then 1.5, which is the normalized length of a dotted quarter note.

In the MeloSpySuite/GUI four different time-span classifications are available: relative and absolute duration and IOI classes. For these, standard statistical descriptors such as class frequencies and entropies are implemented as scalar global features.

Example. Let's calculate the relative IOI classes of 'The Lick' (Figure 1, p. 46). The first quarter note is of medium class (numerical 0), the eighth notes are of class short (-1), the prolonged quarter note in measure 2 still falls in the medium class, and for the last tone, no IOI class can be given, but let us assume that it ends a phrase, so it might be assigned to the class very long (2). As a result, we have a sequence of relative IOI classes

$$(0, -1, -1, -1, -1, -1, 0, -1, 2).$$

Another important set of features comes from the field of micro-timing (micro-rhythm). Micro-timing can be generally defined as the deviations of performed timing from a nominal timing as for instance prescribed in a score. However, in the case of jazz improvisation, where there is no score which could define nominal values, the definition of micro-timing is not as straightforward and is intrinsically intertwined with the metrical annotation process (see Frieler & Pfleiderer, 2017 for a more in-depth discussion of this topic). Nevertheless, if a metrical framework is given, the deviation from nominal onset can be measured. The MeloSpySuite/GUI contains some local features in this respect. For jazz solos, the swing ratio is a very important special case of systematic micro-timing. It is defined as the ratio of the first to the second eighth note in a binarily divided beat. The MeloSpySuite/GUI contains some local transformations and global scalar values for measuring swing ratios.

Sequence/Interval, Sequence/Pitch, Sequence/Rhythm

These classes of features deal all with direct sequential aspects of melodies, based on different abstractions (transformations) of the three main types: interval, pitch, and rhythm. Moreover, there are two main types of construction: N-gram based and run-length based sequential features.

N-gram-based features are closely related to the concept of patterns (see p. 78). N-grams are defined as subsequences $e_{j:k}$ of length $N = k-j+1$ of a sequence $\{e_i\}_{1 \leq i \leq L}$. The sequences of interest mostly originate from simple point-wise one-dimensional transformations such as semitone intervals, pitch classes, or duration classes. A sequence of length L has $L-N+1$ subsequences of length N, since at each position of a sequence except the last $N-1$ a subsequence can be found. Of interest then are distributions of subsequences, e.g., frequencies of N-grams and other statistical properties, particularly information entropies. This is also connected to Markov chains, since the frequencies of bigrams are an estimator for the transition probabilities between elements. Generally, N-grams are connected to Markov chains of order $N-1$.

Example. Consider all unigrams (1-grams), bigrams (2-grams), and trigrams (3-grams) for the relative IOI classes of 'The Lick' (numerical representation) listed above. For this sequence of nine elements, nine unigrams, eight bigrams, and seven trigrams can be extracted; see Table 8, where the N-grams are shown along with their frequencies. In the predefined features of the MeloSpySuite/-GUI only bi- and trigrams are available. This has mostly practical reasons, but is also motivated by the fact that N-gram spaces for finite sequences quickly become rather sparse with increasing N, e.g., the set of observed N-grams is much smaller than the space of all possible N-grams, which has size M^N, exponential in the size M of the alphabet (i. e., the set of all possible outcomes). This means that each N-gram is mostly observed only once, and certain features, such as the entropy, cannot be meaningfully estimated.

Table 8: Uni-, bi-, trigrams and runs of relative IOI classes for 'The Lick'.

Position	Unigram			Bigram		Trigram	
	Value	Count	Run length	Value	Count	Value	Count
0	M	2	1	MS	2	MSS	1
1	S	6	5	SS	4	SSS	3
2	S	6		SS	4	SSS	3
3	S	6		SS	4	SSS	3
4	S	6		SS	4	SSM	1
5	S	6		SM	1	SMS	1
6	M	2	1	MS	2	MSL	1
7	S	6	1	SL	1	—	—
8	L	1	1	—	—	—	—

Note. M = MEDIUM (0), S = SHORT (-1), L = VERY LONG (2).

If the alphabet is finite, the normalized (sample) entropy of an N-gram distribution of a sequence can be estimated to (cf. Infobox 6)

$$H_N^0 = -\frac{\sum_{n \in \text{all N-grams}} f_n \log f_n}{N \log M},$$

where the relative frequencies $f_n = F_n/(L-N+1)$ are based on the count F_n of N-grams n and the number $(L-N+1)$ of all subsequences of length N in a sequence of length L. The denominator is the maximal N-gram entropy for N-grams over an alphabet of M elements, i.e.,

$$H_N^{\max} = \log \frac{1}{M^N} = -N \log M.$$

Example. To calculate the normalized relative IOI class bigram entropy (ioiclass_bigram_entropy_norm) of 'The Lick' we need the relative frequencies $f_{\text{MS}} = \frac{2}{8} = \frac{1}{4}$, $f_{\text{SS}} = \frac{4}{8} = \frac{1}{2}$, and $f_{\text{SM}} = f_{\text{SL}} = \frac{1}{8}$, which can easily be read off from Table 8. The denominator is $2\log(5) = -3.22$, since the time-span classes have five possible outcomes. We have

$$\begin{aligned} H_2^0(\text{The Lick}) &= \frac{\frac{1}{2}\log\frac{1}{2} + \frac{1}{4}\log\frac{1}{4} + 2\frac{1}{8}\log\frac{1}{8}}{2\log(5)} \\ &= \frac{-1.23}{-3.22} \\ &= 0.377. \end{aligned}$$

Another important type of sequence features is based on run lengths. A 'run' in any sequence is a subsequence with only identical elements. Run lengths are a natural way of looking at sequences and have several applications, e. g., for statistical tests or for data compression. For example, in the relative IOI class abstraction of 'The Lick' there are four runs of length 1 and one run of length 5 (a sequence of eighth notes); see Table 8, Columns 2 and 4. Run lengths can be used to construct features either as mean lengths of specific elements, e. g., descending or ascending semitone intervals, or—more generally—as mean run lengths of all runs of all elements of a certain alphabet as well as derived constructions, e. g., ratio_chromatic_sequences, which is the percentage of chromatic (semitone) passages with respect to all passages, where a passage is defined as a run of at least three elements.

Structure

Structural features relate to musical form, which is viewed here as the self-similarity of a melody with respect to a given segmentation, e. g., phrases. To quantize self-similarity for melodies, one needs a melodic similarity measure (Müllensiefen & Frieler, 2004; Frieler, 2009), which is normally conceptualized as a (symmetric) map

$$\sigma(m_1, m_2) \to [0, 1],$$

for two melodies m_1 and m_2 with values in the unit interval, where the value 1 is interpreted as 'identity' and 0 as maximal dissimilarity. If a segmentation of a melody m into M segments $(m_i)_{1 \leq i \leq M}$ is given, then the self-similarity matrix is given by the values

$$\sigma_{ij} = \sigma(m_i, m_j).$$

Currently, in the MeloSpySuite/GUI only interval-based self-similarity matrices for bar and phrase segmentations are available and the similarity measure is defined via the edit distance (Müllensiefen & Frieler, 2004). From a self-similarity matrix, scalar features can be derived via statistical descriptors of distributions of similarity values, e. g., for adjacent segments or non-adjacent segments. Using a clustering algorithm to find clusters of segments with high inter-group similarity, the SSM can also be expressed as a form string, e. g., where similar segments are labeled with letters and primes, e. g., aaba'. (This is also available for duration classes.)

Tone formation

Tone formation means the actual process of performing a note (the map of abstract notes to performed tones). Currently, this falls into three main categories: articulation, f_0-modulation, and loudness. Micro-timing as an important fourth dimension is sorted under rhythm features.

Articulation is traditionally addressed with musical labels such as staccato, legato, portamento etc., which often also have special symbols in common Western musical notation, e. g., dots for staccato and horizontal lines for legato. There are also instrument specific articulations, such as spizzicato for bowed instruments. For our purposes, we approximately define the articulation of a tone event simply as the ratio of duration to inter-onset interval. Higher ratios indicate more legato and smaller ones more staccato articulation. This is only a first approximation, e. g., there is an absolute, tempo-dependent aspect to articulation which is ignored when using time-spans ratios—which are tempo invariant by definition. With this definition, the articulation values with a range of 0 to 1 for monophonic melodies can be easily calculated from the basic representation and scalar global features can be derived using statistical descriptors such as mean, median, and standard deviation.

f_0-modulation means the changing of the fundamental frequency (f_0) of a tone. The abstraction that a tone event has one single pitch is very often not justified in practice, particularly not for wind instruments and singing. Frequently, bends, slides, and vibratos can be observed. Measuring f_0-modulations is not an easy task. The techniques used for the solos in the Weimar Jazz Database are explained in detail in Chapter *Score-informed audio analysis of jazz improvisation*. In the MeloSpySuite/GUI only a basic set of features is available, which includes the deviation of the f_0 from the nominal 12-tone equal tempered pitch, the vibrato (modulation) frequency and the modulation range (in cents). Moreover, for the solos in the Weimar Jazz Database manual tone-wise annotations of f_0-modulation types are available, which can take on the values BEND, SLIDE, FALL-OFF, STRAIGHT (no modulation), and the empty value (no annotation).

Loudness and intensity are the third aspect of tone formation. Intensity values are not easily measured and the corresponding loudness (a psycho-physical concept) even less so. Nevertheless, for each tone event in the Weimar Jazz Database, intensity estimations were extracted using sophisticated audio algorithms, as described in detail in Chapter *Score-informed audio analysis of jazz improvisation*. This results in a frame-wise estimation of intensity values per tone, for which the maximum, median, and standard deviations are available. Furthermore, the relative position of the loudness maximum with respect to the duration of the tone and the temporal centroid of the frame-wise loudness distribution are provided. Finally, the ratio of the median loudness to the median value of the background track is included (signal-to-background ratio).

Patterns

In the context of jazz research, we are interested in the use of patterns during improvisation (e. g., Owens, 1974; Norgaard, 2014). To measure the pattern content in improvisations, we devised the melpat module of the MeloSpy-Suite/GUI, which helps with two basic tasks in this context: pattern search and pattern mining/extraction. In the first task, a certain pattern is given and instances of this pattern are to be found in a corpus of melodies. In the second task, all patterns, possibly subject to certain conditions, are to be extracted automatically from a corpus of melodies.

More specifically, patterns in the context of melodies are defined as subsequences, or N-grams, of a certain representation of the melody, e. g., interval or pitch sequences. Therefore, we recall and extend first the notations for sequences and N-grams as introduced earlier (p. 63).

Basic definitions

Our starting point is a corpus $\mathscr{C} = \{m_i\}$ of melodies and a local (point-wise) transformation F with target space T_F, so that the object of interest is the set of transformed sequences in the corpus $\mathscr{F} = \{s_i \equiv F(m_i), m_i \in \mathscr{C}\}$. For the sake of simplicity, we will write $\mathscr{C}$ for a transformed corpus as well.

The maximal length of the corpus is the length of the longest sequence in $\mathscr{C}$, notated as $l_{\max}(\mathscr{C}) = \max_{s \in \mathscr{C}} l(s)$, where $l(s)$ is the length of the sequence s. The size of the corpus is the number of sequences in $\mathscr{C}$, notated as $\sigma(\mathscr{C})$. The total length of the corpus is the sum of all lengths of all sequences

$$l_\infty(\mathscr{C}) = \sum_{s \in \mathscr{C}} l(s).$$

We denote subsequences of a sequence s with

$$s_{i:j} = (s_i, s_{i+1}, \ldots, s_j)$$

for $0 \leq i \leq j < l(s)$. The length of the subsequence is $l(s_{i:j}) = j - i + 1$. We denote the set of all subsequences of length n of s as $\mathbf{n}(s)$, e. g., $\mathbf{2}(s)$ is the set of all bigrams, $\mathbf{3}(s)$ the set of all trigrams of s.

Two sequences are said to be identical if they have the same length and the same sequence of elements. An N-gram is then the equivalence class of all identical sequences of length N (over the target space T_F). The standard representative of an N-gram is then the sequence $[0 : N-1] \to T_F$. The frequency of an N-gram n in a sequence s is the size of the set of occurrences of n in s:

$$\chi_s(n) = \{i \in [0: l(s)-1], \text{where } s_{i:i+N-1} = n\},$$

hence, $F_s(n) = |\chi_s(x)|$. $\chi_s(n)$ is the set of all indices for s where the N-gram n can be found. We say n is contained in s, $n \in s$, if the set of occurrences is not empty, i.e., $\chi_s(n) \neq \emptyset$.

The relative frequency of n in s is defined as the ratio of frequency to the maximal number of subsequences of length N in s, i.e.,

$$f_s(n) = \frac{F_s(n)}{l(s)-N+1},$$

see Table 8 for an example.

The frequency of an N-gram in a corpus $\mathscr{C}$ is the sum of all frequencies of the N-gram over all sequences in the corpus, i.e., the size of the set of occurrences of n in $\mathscr{C}$:

$$\chi_{\mathscr{C}}(n) = \bigcup_{s \in \mathscr{C}} \chi_s(n).$$

Hence,

$$F_{\mathscr{C}}(n) = |\chi_{\mathscr{C}}(n)| = \sum_{s \in \mathscr{C}} F_s(n).$$

The relative frequency of n in the corpus is then defined as

$$f_{\mathscr{C}}(n) = \frac{F_{\mathscr{C}}(n)}{\sum_{s \in \mathscr{C}} l(s) - N + 1}.$$

The number of occurrences of an N-gram n in the corpus is the number of sequences where n appears at least once, i.e., the size of the set of embedding sequences:

$$\omega_{\mathscr{C}}(n) = \{s \in \mathscr{C} \text{ where } n \in s\}.$$

Pattern search

Pattern search can be defined as searching for a given sequence in a corpus (after suitable transformation). For a given search pattern (N-gram) n in a corpus $\mathscr{C}$, the search result is just the set of subsequences and indices where the pattern can be found:

$$\rho_{\mathscr{C}}(n) = \{(j, i, l(n)) \mid i \in \chi_{s_j}(n) \neq \emptyset\}.$$

Example. Let us say we want to find all instances of 'The Lick' in the Weimar Jazz Database. To find a (possibly too large) set of candidates, it is recommended that we start with a plain interval search. The semitone interval sequence of the lick is $(0, -2, 2, 1, 2, -3, -4, 2)$ (cf. Table 1). Hence, we can first select the transformation intervals in the pattern search tab of the MeloSpyGUI and enter the string

```
0 -2 2 1 2 -3 -4 2
```

and start processing. This will result in a list of instances of this interval pattern (as a CSV file). Indeed, this search finds only one instance, in the Chet Baker solo.

This simple search process can be amended in two ways. Firstly, by secondary search, i.e., searching within the result set using secondary criteria, and secondly, by using regular expressions. Of course, both extensions can also be combined.

To define secondary search, we fix two transformations F_1 and F_2 over a given corpus and two search patterns with respect to the two transformations, say n_1 and n_2. The result of the secondary search is then simply the intersection of the single searches:

$$\rho_{\mathscr{C}_1 \times \mathscr{C}_2}(n_1, n_2) = \rho_{\mathscr{C}_1}(n_1) \cap \rho_{\mathscr{C}_2}(n_2).$$

It is desirable to have compatible results from both searches, in the sense that they should refer to exactly the same subsequences in the original untransformed melodies. This might be a problem where a local transformation is actually defined over subsequences, i.e., semitone or inter-onset intervals which need two consecutive elements for calculation. Retrieving the original subsequence in the melody is called back-lifting. We refrain from formalizing the process of back-lifting, but give an example for semitone interval transformations. An interval at position i in an interval sequence is back-lifted to the subsequence $m_{i:i+1}$ in the original sequence, if the indexing of the interval transformation was done in forward fashion, i.e., via $\Delta p_i = p_{i+1} - p_i$, or to the subsequence $m_{i-1:i}$ if the indexing is done in backward fashion $\Delta p_i = p_{i-1} - p_i$.

Regular expressions (regex for short) are a very powerful method for defining flexible search patterns for strings, i.e., sequences of characters. They have a longstanding tradition in computer science. They are defined using a rather cryptic syntax, which can be viewed as a very specialized computer language. Nearly all modern computer languages provide some native support for regular expressions and there are different flavors or variants of regular

Table 9: List of special characters for regular expression search.

Special character	Meaning
.	matches any element
^	matches beginning of sequence
$	matches end of sequence
*	zero or more repetitions
+	one or more repetitions
?	zero or one repetition
{m}	exactly m repetitions
{m,n}	between m and n repetitions
|	matches either regex before or after the symbol

expressions. The basic elements for regular expressions are character sets, quantifiers, and position indicators. For instance, the string [a-z] indicates the set of lower-case letters in most regex implementations. Wildcards, e. g., a single dot, which stand in for an arbitrary character are also very important. Examples for quantifiers are *, meaning 'zero or more instances', and + for 'one or more instances'. Examples for position parameters are ^ ('caret') for 'beginning of a string' and $ for 'end of a string' (cf. Table 9).

With only these few elements, rather complex search patterns can already be defined. For example, the regex ^A[a-z]+C will find all strings that start with an upper-case A, followed by at least one lower-case letter, and an upper-case letter C. For example. the strings ABC, AAbC, and AC would not match this pattern, but AbC and AabcC would.

Regular expressions are defined for finite alphabets, i. e., ASCII or unicode. To use the powerful regex machinery for melodic sequences, only transformations which have a finite alphabet can be used. For continuous transformations, i. e., inter-onset intervals, they are not applicable. On using regular expressions with the MeloSpyGUI, see Infobox 7.

Infobox 7: Using regular expressions for pattern search

The use of regular expressions (regex) for finite-sized transformations is done in the MeloSpySuite/GUI by mapping the target domain of the transformation to a consecutive segment in the unicode alphabet and using the regular expression library for Python. The basic syntax of regular expressions thus follows the Python rules (https://docs.python.org/2/library/re.html). However, this mapping to unicode characters cannot be used for actually inputting regular expressions, which makes a hybrid syntax necessary. Moreover, using fixed character classes such as \w, which means all alphanumeric characters (i.e., [a-zA-Z0-9_]) in standard Python regex syntax is of no use. Instead, the standard representations have to be used to define 'character sets' manually. For example, for semitone intervals, integer numbers are used, e.g., the sequence -1 0 1 -2 (without commas) means a sequence of a semitone down, a tone repetition, a semitone up, and a whole-tone down. All quantifiers and position parameters have to be (singly or doubly) quoted, e.g., '[' -1 0 ']+' means one or more occurrences of the elements -1 0 (semitone down and repetition). The most important special characters for the use of regexes in pattern search can be found in Table 9.

In case of the above example, the interval search for 'The Lick', one might think that the first tone repetition could be absent and the last tone could be varied. This can be expressed with the regex

```
0 "?" -2 2 1 2 -3 -4 "."
```

This will find variations of 'The Lick' with and without the first tone repetition, as expressed by the quantifier ? translating to 'zero or one tone repetition', and with all possible end tones, expressed by the dot . as a stand-in for all possible intervals. The actual search in the Weimar Jazz Database brings up six instances of four different patterns: the original instance with the tone repetition at the beginning, and five beginning with a descending whole tone (-2), two of which end in a descending fourth (-5) and two in a descending minor third (-3).

Pattern mining

The task of pattern mining or pattern extraction is to extract all patterns from a given corpus $\mathscr{C}$, which is subject to certain conditions for the patterns. A pattern database with minimal length K, maximal length M is the set of all N-grams with $k \leq N \leq M$. Often, we like to subject the pattern database to further conditions, e.g., minimal frequencies or occurrences. In fact, (sequential) patterns are often defined as N-grams that occur at least k times in at least l different entities in the corpus, with the minimal definition of $K = 2$ and $L = 1$. Obviously, $L \geq 1$ implies also $K > 1$.

Another useful restriction, available as a submodule to the melpat module in the MeloSpySuite/GUI, is called pattern partition. A pattern partition is defined for a single sequence s in the corpus with respect to the pattern database of the entire corpus (including the borderline case of a single-sequence corpus).

It is constructed by filtering sub-N-grams from a pattern database as defined above (possibly subject to length, frequency, and occurrence conditions). A sub-N-gram n is proper if there exists a super-K-gram k with $K > N$ and $n \in k$ such that all occurrences of n also imply the occurrence of k. If an N-gram n only occurs as a certain sub-N-gram, then it is not considered to be an independent entity but as completely derivative and hence as not interesting in itself. A pattern database can be substantially pruned by filtering out all derivative N-grams. The pattern partition of a sequence s is then the subset of N-grams of s in the so pruned pattern database.

Example. Consider the mini-corpus $\mathscr{C} = \{s_1, s_2\}$ of two sequences given in Parsons's code:

$$s_1 = \text{UUDUUD},$$
$$s_2 = \text{UUDUDD}.$$

Here, the pattern database of bi- and trigrams occurring at least twice is composed of the trigrams UUD (3) and UDU (2), and the bigrams UU (3), UD (4), and DU (2) (counts in parentheses). As one can readily see, the bigram UU only occurs as part of the trigram UUD. Hence, it would be filtered out for a pattern partition. On the other hand, the bigram UD, which is also a sub-bigram of UDD, would be kept, since it also occurs as a sub-bigram of DUD and UDD. (See also Figure 7 in Chapter *Trumpet giants: Freddie Hubbard and Woody Shaw* for a graphical representation of an interval pattern partition of at least length $N = 7$ in a solo by Woody Shaw.)

For pattern partitions and databases, certain global scalar features can be defined that try to capture how much the sequences in a corpus are determined by patterns, which are defined here as N-grams with the minimal condition of occurring at least twice in at least one sequence. For the following, we fix a corpus and drop the index $\mathscr{C}$ for simplicity. Likewise, we fix a pattern database

$$\mathscr{P} = \bigcup_{N \leq i \leq M} \mathscr{P}_i$$

as the union of (pruned) N- to M-grams. The pattern partition of a sequence s is then the intersection of $\mathscr{P}$ with all N-grams of s (of the same length range):

$$\mathscr{P}(s) = \mathscr{P} \cap \bigcup_{N \leq n \leq M} \mathbf{n}(s).$$

The coverage of a sequence s by patterns from $\mathscr{P}$ is the percentage of elements in s contained in at least one N-gram. If we define the set of index intervals in s where any n covered by any N-gram from $\mathscr{P}$ as

$$\Gamma(s) = \{\{i,\ldots,i+N-1\} \mid \exists_{n \in \mathscr{P}} : i \in \chi_s(n)\},$$

then the coverage is simply

$$\gamma(s) = \frac{|\Gamma(s)|}{l(s)}.$$

The over coverage is the average number of N-grams to which an element in s belongs. The average overlap is defined as the average number of elements two adjacent patterns $\mathscr{P}$ share, where the patterns are sorted with respect to start positions in s. The average N-gram length is defined as the mean length of N-grams contained in the pattern partition of s. Finally, the mean logarithm excess probability is defined using the ratio of the observed frequency of a pattern to the expected frequency derived from a Markov process of zeroth order. The latter is just a complicated term for the product of the probabilities of the elements that constitute an N-gram. For an illustration, consider the mini-corpus of Parsons's code sequences from above. The relative frequencies of the unigrams are $f_U = \frac{7}{12}$ and $F_D = \frac{5}{12}$. Using elementary probability theory, the *a priori* frequency is the probability under the assumption that all elements in the sequence are independently produced, i.e., the product of the single probabilities. The trigram UUD thus has an expected probability of

$$p_e(\text{UUD}) = p(\text{U})p(\text{U})p(\text{D}) = \frac{7}{12} \cdot \frac{7}{12} \cdot \frac{5}{12} = 0.142.$$

On the other hand, the observed frequency is three times out of a possible eight times, or $p_o = \frac{3}{8} = 0.375$. The ratio of observed to expected probabilities, the excess probability, is then

$$\frac{p_o}{p_e} = \frac{0.375}{0.142} = 2.64.$$

Hence the trigram UUD appears about 2.6 times more often than an independent (Markov) process would suggest. The logarithm of excess probability is then used to make the process of averaging excess probabilities over all patterns more meaningful.

Statistical feature selection: searching for musical style

Martin Pfleiderer and Jakob Abeßer

The Weimar Jazz Database offers myriads of possibilities to compare various subsets of data using musical features which are automatically extracted with MeloSpyGUI and statistical methods. In the following pilot study, one powerful statistical approach is chosen. It follows a simple idea: First, the database is divided into two subsets, e. g., the improvisations of a certain musician versus the improvisations of all other musicians, or all improvisations within one jazz style or played with a certain musical instrument versus all remaining improvisations. Next, the statistical values for a large number of musical features are automatically extracted for these two subsets. In the last step, those musical features that differ significantly between the two subsets are identified. In a statistical sense, these discriminative features can be interpreted as being particular or idiosyncratic for a musical characterization of the chosen subset, e. g., for the improvisations of a certain musician—at least in regard to those improvisations which are included in the Weimar Jazz Database. From these exploratory findings with regard to the particularities of certain musicians, jazz styles, or instruments, one can confirm or question existing claims about jazz styles as well as gain new insights into stylistic features within the history of jazz which, in turn, could be further examined with subsequent analytical case studies.

Within the 456 solos included in the Weimar Jazz Database, there are, however, only few musicians who are represented with more than five or six improvised solos. To expand the statistical base for the method, choruses instead of entire solos were chosen as basic investigation units, resulting in an extended corpus of 1416 (chorus) units. Thus, longer solos with many choruses receive more weight, while short solos with only a few choruses receive less weight. Likewise, however, improvisations with an open form, e. g., the solos of Ornette Coleman, also receive less weight.

For each of the 1416 choruses, 121 statistical values concerning various musical features were extracted. All statistical values discussed below were averaged over all investigation units of the subsets of interest. The features encompass several musical dimensions:

- Pitch: Extended chordal pitch classes are chosen, since this category is very relevant in a jazz improvisation context by relating pitch classes to each underlying chord. Additionally, there are several values concerning the overall range of pitch usage and the degree of chromaticity, as well as the entropy of the usage of pitches and pitch classes, e. g., how redundant (low entropy value) or unforeseeable (high entropy value), resp., the usage of pitch classes is within the improvisation.

- Interval: The usage of intervals is characterized by interval classes (fuzzy intervals) and several statistical values including interval entropy, range, and mean.

- Rhythm and meter: Rhythm is characterized by several measures of duration classes and classes of inter-onset intervals in regard to both tempo and absolute time (seconds). Moreover, there are general measures for event density and tempo. Meter is characterized by various measures, e. g., by syncopicity, metrical complexity, and entropy.

- Lines: The characteristics of longer lines are depicted, among others, by the mean lengths of ascending and descending passages, chromatic lines, and arpeggios. By measuring the run-lengths of identical duration classes or interval classes, one can characterize the uniformity of the improvised line, e. g., if a musician mainly plays eighth-chains of descending steps.

Sometimes, several statistical values indicate the same musical feature in a slightly different way, e. g., the event density in regard to the tempo or in regard to absolute time intervals in seconds. Some of those features are already explained in Chapter *Computational melody analysis*, others are introduced in this chapter during the interpretation of the results. The exact definitions of all features are documented with their corresponding feature definition files, which are listed in regard to musical parameters within the online documentation.[12]

---

[12] http://jazzomat.hfm-weimar.de/commandline_tools/melfeature/melfeature_features.html

In an exploratory study, the subsets of the data are built following the categories 'performer', 'style', 'tonality type', and 'instrument'. This results in several dozens of statistical investigations comparing each musician with all other musicians, each style (traditional, swing, bebop, cool/West Coast, hardbop, postbop, fusion, free) with all other styles, each tonality type ('functional', 'blues', 'modal', 'color' and 'free') with all other types and each musical instrument with all other instruments. However, to gain meaningful results, it is important that the size of a subset is not too small, since comparing just two choruses with the remaining 1414 choruses of the Weimar Jazz Database will evidently not lead to statistically robust and conclusive findings.

In order to identify those musical features that discriminate the two data subsets significantly, the statistical method of classification or decision trees was chosen (Breiman, 2001). Given a two-class partition of the dataset, a random forest classifier with 250 decision trees was trained using random subsets of both investigation units (choruses) and features, since this approach leads to more robust classification models.

As a next step, the 20 features with the highest differences between the two subsets were selected. For each of those features a two-sample t-test was performed in order to investigate whether the distribution means of both subsets for a particular feature differ significantly in a statistical sense. Furthermore, the Cohen's d effect size measure (Cohen, 1988) was computed in order to determine how big the difference between the subsets effectively is. Finally, all features with a significant difference of means ($p < 0.05$) and a rather strong effect size of $d > 0.5$ were selected. The ranking of the chosen musical features in the tables results from the absolute values of this effect size. However, due to space constraints, in the following only a small selection of the results are reported and interpreted in order to give just an impression of the potentials of the statistical procedure. The discussion is confined to some of the most striking examples in regard to the performers' personal style as well as to jazz style, harmonic style and instrument, respectively. The complete lists of features concerning all subsets are stored in an online repository[13] and are open for examination.

Characteristics of jazz style, tonality type and instrument

Could jazz styles be differentiated in regard to how jazz musicians improvise within these styles? Surprisingly, there are no statistical differences between

---

[13] https://github.com/jazzomat/python/tree/master/publications/book_2017/feature_selection

Table 1: Significant features of improvisations within swing style (106 choruses) compared to all other improvisations (1310 choruses).

Feature	Mean (class)	Mean (others)	Cohen's d	Sig.
ioiclass_abs_hist_01_very_short	0.306	0.452	−0.60	***
durclass_abs_hist_02_short	0.408	0.302	0.52	***
ioiclass_abs_hist_02_short	0.494	0.387	0.52	***

the subsets of all solos stylistically labeled as 'bebop', 'cool' or 'hardbop' and the respective remaining solo corpus. Apparently, the ways in which jazz musicians improvise within these modern jazz styles of the 1940s and 1950s are similar to a degree that makes it impossible to distinguish between them on a global statistical level. One could conclude that bebop, cool jazz and hardbop all lie at the core of jazz improvisation as represented within the Weimar Jazz Database.

Looking at the jazz styles beyond this modern 'common practice jazz', the statistically most significant differences lie within the domain of rhythm and duration rather than pitch and harmony. Looking, for example, at all 106 swing choruses in contrast to the remaining 1310 choruses improvised in other jazz styles (Table 1), there are only three distinguishing measures that are statistically significant and have a strong effect size: Swing solos have fewer 'very short' duration intervals (31 % vs. 45 %, durclass_abs_hist_01_very_short) and a much higher percentage of both 'short' durations (41 % vs. 30 %, durclass_abs_hist_02_short) and 'short' inter-onset intervals (49 % vs. 39 %, ioiclass_abs_hist_02_short), both in regard to absolute time, i. e., independent from tempo. Generally speaking, swing musicians play 'slower' lines (i. e., with more eighth notes and fewer sixteenth notes) than the players in the remaining corpus. The same holds true for musicians playing traditional jazz. In contrast, postbop musicians play a much higher percentage of 'very short' durations and inter-onset intervals, i. e., 'faster' lines.

Some jazz styles are tied to certain tonality types. Improvisations within functional tonality, blues tonality and 'color' tonality (defined as mainly non-functional chord changes employed in postbop or fusion jazz) display significant differences compared to the respective remaining improvisations only with regard to interval range (blues uses smaller intervals) and pitch range (higher within 'color' tonality). However, modal improvisations have many significant differences compared to all other, non-modal improvisations including those pieces classified as 'color' (Table 2). In the Weimar Jazz Database, there are 102 choruses of modal improvisation taken from 25 solos. Within those solos, there are fewer minor thirds ('blue notes') played

Table 2: Significant features of improvisations with modal tonality (102 choruses) compared to all other improvisations (1314 choruses).

Feature	Mean (class)	Mean (others)	Cohen's d	Sig.
int_range	29.500	21.068	0.93	***
abs_int_range	17.225	12.38	0.84	***
cdpcx_density_>	0.029	0.011	0.83	***
int_std	4.007	3.33	0.76	***
ioiclass_abs_hist_02_short	0.267	0.405	−0.67	***
cdpcx_density_B	0.008	0.036	−0.63	***
durclass_abs_hist_02_short	0.199	0.318	−0.59	***
abs_int_mean	3.017	2.661	0.58	***
ioiclass_abs_hist_01_very_short	0.570	0.431	0.57	***
pitch_std	5.946	5.038	0.56	***
durclass_abs_entropy	0.475	0.593	−0.54	***

over major scales or chords than within the remaining corpus (0.8 % vs. 3.6 %, cdpcx_density_B). Moreover, there are significantly fewer major thirds played over minor chords or scales (dorian, aeolian, phrygian, locrian) than within the remaining corpus (1.1 % vs. 2.9 %, cdpcx_density_>). While the percentage of these dissonant pitches is in general very low, those dissonances are clearly avoided within modal improvisation. Additionally, there is a higher range of intervals used within modal improvisation (see int_range and abs_int_range), and there are more 'very short' tone durations than 'short' tone durations (shown with significant differences with regard to ioiclass_abs_hist_02_short, durclass_abs_hist_02_short and ioiclass_abs_hist_01_very_short)—which is significant also for postbop in general.

With regard to musical instruments, improvisations played on the trombone display the most significant differences compared with improvisations played on all other instruments (Table 3). Included in the subset are 76 trombone choruses within 26 solos played by stylistically diverse jazz musicians, such as Kid Ory, Dickie Wells, J. J. Johnson, Curtis Fuller, or Steve Turre. These differences include a higher share of medium inter-onset intervals relative to tempo (31 % vs. 16 %, ioiclass_rel_hist_03_medium), a higher metrical complexity (0.22 vs. 0.17 for metric_complexity, and 0.17 vs. 0.10 for metric_complexity_compression) as well as a significantly higher percentage of tone repetitions (12 % vs. 5 % of all played intervals, fuzzyint_hist_05_repeat). Therefore, trombone players clearly play slower, but metrically more complex lines with much more tone repetitions than musicians improvising on other instruments.

Table 3: Significant features of improvisations played on the trombone (76 choruses) compared to all other improvisations (1340 choruses).

Feature	Mean (class)	Mean (others)	Cohen's d	Sig.
ioiclass_rel_hist_03_medium	0.305	0.163	1.11	***
art_median	0.776	0.849	−1.05	***
fuzzyint_hist_05_repeat	0.123	0.053	0.81	***
parsons_hist_constant	0.123	0.053	0.81	***
pitch_median	61.736	65.607	−0.78	***
metric_complexity	0.221	0.167	0.77	***
art_std	0.214	0.185	0.72	***
ric_mean_seg_len	1.811	2.320	−0.63	***
aic_mean_seg_len	1.698	2.314	−0.61	***
metric_complexity_compression	0.166	0.101	0.59	***
parsons_entropy	0.822	0.711	0.57	***
metric_complexity_division	0.276	0.232	0.56	***
pitch_range	18.934	23.461	−0.55	***
pitch_std	4.258	5.151	−0.54	***
parsons_bigram_entropy	2.485	2.168	0.53	***

By contrast, improvisations played on the alto saxophone seem to lie right in the center of our database (with no significant differences to the rest of the database), while tenor saxophone and trumpet solos mainly differ with regard to pitch range (tenor is lower, trumpet is higher) as well as in the case of trumpet solos with regard to the share of very long tones (2.9 % vs. 1.7 %, ioiclass_rel_hist_05_very_long).

Personal style of jazz musicians

Each jazz musician improvises on a variety of pieces exhibiting a variety of different chord changes, differing tempos and differing rhythmic feels. Despite these many different contexts and frameworks for improvisation, are there any musical peculiarities which, in general, differentiate the improvisations of one jazz musician from those of all other jazz musicians? Presumably, the issue of personal style is one of the most exciting topics with regard to jazz improvisation. Looking at the many results provided by our statistical approach, the answer seems to be ambivalent: On the one hand, there are significant differences between the solos of almost every jazz musician and the remaining corpus. But on the other hand, there are fewer differences than expected—and sometimes the significant differences are rather trivial, e. g., that a trumpet player's improvisations shows a higher and a baritone saxophonist show a lower mean pitch due to the tonal range of the instrument.

Table 4: Significant features of improvisations played by Benny Goodman (8 choruses) compared to all other improvisation (1408 choruses).

Feature	Mean (class)	Mean (others)	Cohen's d	Sig.
durclass_rel_hist_04_long	0.156	0.028	1.55	***
pitch_median	72.312	65.360	1.39	***
avgtempo	264.900	194.667	1.00	**
mean_length_chromatic_descending	4.562	2.896	0.98	**
mean_length_chromatic_mixed	4.657	3.542	0.89	*
syncopicity	0.191	0.314	0.87	*
int_min	−14.250	−10.020	−0.78	*
mean_length_arpeggio_ascending	3.713	2.598	0.76	*
mean_length_chromatic_sequences	4.171	3.177	0.74	*
mean_length_arpeggio_descending	3.558	2.541	0.72	*

In some cases, however, the statistical approach yields results which should be further examined. Here are five examples.

Swing clarinetist Benny Goodman is included in the Weimar Jazz Database with only seven solos and eight choruses. Goodman plays more long arpeggios, both ascending (3.7 tones vs. 2.6 tones on average, seemean_length_arpeggio_ascending) and descending (3.6 tones vs. 2.6 tones on average, mean_length_arpeggio_descending), more long chromatic sequences (4.2 vs. 3.2 tones on average, mean_length_chromatic_sequences) as well as more long tones relative to the beat (15.6 % vs. 2.8 %, durclass_rel_hist_04_long) (Table 4). Moreover, his improvisations display a smaller amount of syncopated tones (19 % vs. 31 % of all tones, syncopicity) than the improvisations of the other musicians. Unfortunately, all solos by Goodman in the Weimar Jazz Database are in a fast or very fast tempo (199 to 303 bpm). Therefore, it is disputable whether the significant features which distinguish Goodman's improvisations from all other improvisations are indeed peculiarities of his general personal style or are just due to the fast tempo. In particular, a high value for syncopicity could result from playing inaccuracies, e. g., tones played too early (or too late), which are detected as syncopations.

The next four examples are all related to postbop improvisation. Beside being played higher (as with all trumpet players) and faster (as with all postbop musicians), Woody Shaw's improvisations differ from all other improvisations by rather high percentages of fourths (11.2 % vs. 8.5 %, cdpcx_density_4) and minor seconds (5.5 % vs. 3.9 %, cdpcx_density_b2) in regard to the underlying harmony (see Table 5). By contrast, tenor saxophonist Wayne Shorter displays peculiarities in regard to choice of pitches (see Table 6): Compared with the improvisations of all the other musicians, he has a slightly but significantly

Table 5: Significant features of improvisations by Woody Shaw (23 choruses) compared to all other improvisations (1393 choruses).

Feature	Mean (class)	Mean (others)	Cohen's d	Sig.
pitch_median	71.326	65.301	1.21	***
ioiclass_rel_hist_01_very_short	0.607	0.438	0.68	**
cdpcx_density_4	0.112	0.085	0.59	**
cdpcx_density_b2	0.055	0.039	0.55	**

Table 6: Significant features of improvisations by Wayne Shorter (34 choruses) compared to all other improvisations (1382 choruses).

Feature	Mean (class)	Mean (others)	Cohen's d	Sig.
art_std	0.216	0.185	0.75	***
cdpcx_density_>	0.027	0.012	0.72	***
cdpcx_density_T	0.064	0.042	0.50	**

higher preference for playing tritones (6.4 % vs. 4.2 %, cdpcx_density_T) as well as major thirds over minor chords (2.7 % vs. 1.2 %, cdpcx_density_>).

David Liebman is a postbop saxophone player who reflected his individual approach to improvisation in several texts, including a comprehensive treatise called *A Chromatic Approach to Jazz Harmony and Melody* (Liebman 1991). Therefore, in regard to the improvisations included in the Weimar Jazz Database, one could ask to what degree he puts his chromatic approach into practice. In regard to the ten musical features which significantly differentiate Liebman's solos from all other solos, there are three features concerning chromaticity and another three features concerning the usage of non-diatonic intervals (Table 7). The mean length of both chromatic sequences and descending chromatic lines is higher within Liebman's solos than within other solos (3.9 vs. 3.2 tones, mean_length_chromatic_sequences, and 4.2 vs. 2.9 tones, mean_length_chromatic_descending) as well as the mean length of sequences with both ascending and descending semitones (which include trills, mean_length_chromatic_mixed). Liebman uses significantly more tritones (7.5 % vs. 4.2 %, cdpcx_density_T), minor seconds (6.1 % vs. 3.8 %, cdpcx_density_b2) and minor sevenths over major chords (0.8 % vs. 0.2 %, cdpcx_density_<) than the other musicians. Of course, chromaticity and dissonant pitches are interrelated. Additionally, both the pitch entropy (4.3 vs. 3.8, pitch_entropy) and standard deviation of pitch usage (6.3 vs. 5.1, pitch_std) are higher. It is remarkable that both pitch entropy and pitch stan-

Table 7: Significant features of improvisations by Dave Liebman (34 choruses) compared to all other improvisations (1382 choruses).

Feature	Mean (class)	Mean (others)	Cohen's d	Sig.
cdpcx_density_T	0.075	0.042	0.79	***
mean_length_chromatic_descending	4.193	2.874	0.78	***
cdpcx_density_b2	0.061	0.038	0.77	***
pitch_std	6.314	5.073	0.76	***
pitch_median	68.852	65.314	0.71	***
cdpcx_density_<	0.008	0.002	0.59	***
pitch_entropy	4.313	3.763	0.57	***
mean_length_chromatic_sequences	3.906	3.164	0.55	**
mean_length_chromatic_mixed	4.216	3.532	0.54	**

Table 8: Significant features of improvisations by Dave Liebman (34 choruses) compared to all improvisations labeled as "postbop" and played on the tenor saxophone (513 choruses).

Feature	Mean (class)	Mean (others)	Cohen's d	Sig.
pitch_median	68.852	63.633	1.31	***
pitch_std	6.314	5.383	0.55	**
ratio_chromatic_sequences	0.125	0.082	0.54	**
cpc_bigram_entropy	5.909	5.216	0.51	**
pitch_entropy	4.313	3.859	0.51	**

dard deviation are also higher in Liebman's improvisations than in the improvisations of all other postbop tenor saxophone solos (Table 8). Compared to that subset of the database, Liebman's improvisations show a higher percentage of chromatic sequences (12.5 % vs. 8.2 %, ratio_chromatic_sequences) and a higher entropy of chordal pitch classes (5.9 % vs. 5.2 %, cpc_bigram_entropy). However, the usage of dissonant non-diatonic pitches does not differ significantly for Liebman and other postbop tenor saxophone players.

According to the results of the statistical comparisons, trumpet player Freddie Hubbard is one of the jazz musicians whose improvisations differ over a rather broad variety of musical dimensions (Table 9). While playing more very long tones than the other musicians (in regard to absolute inter-onset intervals, 2.5 % vs. 0.6 %, ioiclass_abs_hist_05_very_long), sequences of very short tones played by Hubbard tend to be longer. The average length of lines with those 'very short' tones is 4.5 tones in Hubbard's improvisations, while only being 2.3 tones within the remaining corpus (mean_seg_len_01_very_short). In general, the event density is lower within Hubbard's improvisations (3.4

Table 9: Significant features of improvisations by Freddie Hubbard (19 choruses) compared to all other improvisations (1397 choruses).

Feature	Mean (class)	Mean (others)	Cohen's d	Sig.
ioiclass_abs_hist_05_very_long	0.025	0.006	1.18	***
avgtempo	114.257	196.163	−1.18	***
ric_mean_seg_len_01_very_short	3.191	1.622	1.11	***
syncopicity	0.449	0.311	0.97	***
event_density	3.429	4.81	−0.81	***
ioiclass_rel_hist_01_very_short	0.346	0.179	0.78	***
cdpcx_density_B	0.066	0.033	0.75	**
pitch_median	69.026	65.350	0.74	**
fuzzyint_hist_01_big_jump_up	0.040	0.022	0.72	**
parson_hist_ascending	0.344	0.433	−0.72	**
mean_seg_len_01_very_short	4.469	2.296	0.66	**
mean_length_step_descending	4.700	3.905	0.62	**
ratio_ascending_descending	0.755	0.928	−0.57	*

vs. 4.8 tones per second on average, event_density). However, the share of syncopated tones is higher, since 45 % of all tones played by Hubbard are syncopated in contrast to only 31 % in the solos of the remaining corpus (syncopicity). While playing fewer ascending lines than the other musicians, Hubbard contrasts this tendency with a relatively high proportion of big upward jumps (4 % of all intervals compared to only 2.2 % in the remaining solos, fuzzyint_hist_01_big_jump_up). Last but not least, in the solos of Hubbard the share of minor thirds played over major chords is twice as high as in solos of other musicians (6.6 % vs. 3.3 %, cdpcx_density_B).

Conclusion

Maybe the uniqueness of a personal sound cannot be found in the various musical features extracted in this study but rather in, e. g., more complex or higher-level melodic features such as a characteristic micro-rhythmic strategy or a personal signature lick, or in various features of an idiosyncratic instrumental sound, e. g., a characteristic timbre or attack (see Chapter *Score-informed audio analysis of jazz improvisation*). As exemplified in this chapter, however, the statistical approach both confirms findings about musical characteristics and, in many cases, can give further clues to significant features of improvisations and improvisers. Of course, these results of a comparative or 'distant reading' have to be further examined and differentiated with the 'close reading' of analytical case studies.

There are many more possibilities for creating data subsets and examining the distinguishing musical features of those subsets (cf. p. 175, where different subsets of cool jazz players are compared). One could create subgroups of jazz musicians according to various criteria, e. g., year of birth, origin, affiliation to a certain school or direction, or alleged influence, and then identify the most discriminative features of their improvisations. Or one could also compare improvisations within certain keys—say, all flat keys against all sharp keys—or tempo ranges in order to gain insights into learning and playing routines of jazz musicians. Moreover, there are statistical methods for identifying the differences between more than two classes. Additionally, one can choose less restrictive statistical criteria (higher significance threshold, lower effect size) for the selection of a larger set of relevant musical features, since these less robust features could also, nonetheless, both carry musical meaning and inspire further investigations and analytical case studies. However, if the reader gains some ideas of how to pursue this approach in regard to certain research issues, the aim of this chapter will be fulfilled—that is, to demonstrate some of the potentials of performing comparative music analysis with statistical methods.

Score-informed audio analysis of jazz improvisation

Jakob Abeßer and Klaus Frieler

One main challenge of analyzing recordings of ensemble music with computational tools is the inherent overlap of simultaneously sounding instruments. In particular, spectrograms of mixed audio tracks exhibit both horizontal structures (overtones) and vertical structures (tone attack transients), which often superimpose each other (M. Müller, 2015). Separating of a musician improvising within an ensemble is very complicated and in many cases impossible. Furthermore, the sound quality of many audio recordings, e. g., the early recordings of the transcriptions within the Weimar Jazz Database, is rather poor since they come from the early stage of audio recordings in the beginning of the 20th century.

We face these challenges using a score-informed analysis approach, i. e., we use the manually created transcriptions of the Weimar Jazz Database (cf. p. 19) of the soloists' melodies as additional cues during different steps of the audio analysis. p. 101 will detail how manual transcriptions of pitch, onset, and duration allow for an automatic separation of the ensemble recording into two audio streams: the isolated solo instrument and the accompanying instruments (rhythm section), respectively. This approach allows for an investigation of the audio recordings of jazz solos in regard to performance features such as dynamics (changes in intensity), intonation (pitch accuracy with respect to a given tone system), articulation (relation of tone duration to inter-onset interval), pitch modulation (temporal variation of the fundamental frequency over the tone duration) as well as timbre characteristics (sound).

The methods and results discussed in this chapter are complementary to the symbolic music analysis methods discussed in Chapter *Computational melody analysis*. Following this approach, we pursued several in-depth studies

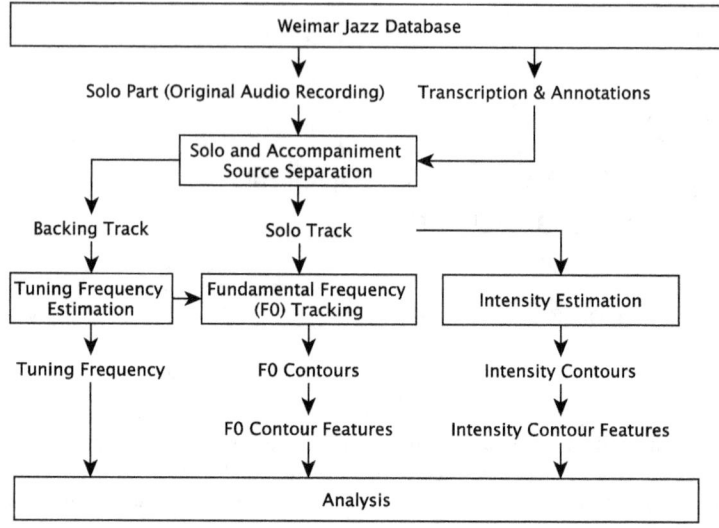

Figure 1: Score-informed audio analysis of jazz solos.

of the original audio recordings of the solos included in the Weimar Jazz Database which are motivated by jazz research questions and which we approach using several methods from audio signal processing and Music Information Retrieval (MIR).

Besides analyzing extracted solo parts, we also developed a new algorithm for the automatic transcription of the bass lines, based on a deep neural network. This representation measures the likelihood of different bass pitch values over time and can be used as a first step towards a transcription of walking bass lines as we show in p. 123.

The score-informed analysis procedure is summarized in Figure 1. At first, the transcribed part of the original audio recording is separated into a backing track, which includes the accompanying instruments, and a solo track, which includes the improvising soloist (cf. p. 101). Then, the underlying tuning frequency is estimated from the backing track (cf. p. 101). In the next step, we estimate tone-wise fundamental frequency contours and intensity contours from the isolated solo instrument track (cf. p. 104 and p. 109). Finally, we describe each contour using more abstract features such as the fundamental frequency modulation range or the median tone intensity (cf. p. 104).

Score-informed audio analysis

Table 1: Overview of performers, instrument(s), number of solos, and number of tones.

Performer	Instrument	# Solos	# Tones
Art Pepper	as, cl	6	3634
Ben Webster	ts	5	1826
Benny Carter	as	7	2650
Benny Goodman	cl	7	1144
Bix Beiderbecke	cor	5	680
Bob Berg	ts	7	4894
Branford Marsalis	ts	6	4691
Cannonball Adderley	as	5	2642
Charlie Parker	as	17	5672
Chet Baker	tp	8	1428
Chris Potter	ts	7	7156
Clifford Brown	tp	9	4232
Coleman Hawkins	ts	6	2609
David Liebman	ss, ts	11	7518
David Murray	ts	6	3005
Dexter Gordon	ts	6	4149
Dickie Wells	tb	6	870
Dizzy Gillespie	tp	6	1808
Don Byas	ts	8	2264
Don Ellis	tp	6	1458
Eric Dolphy	as, bcl	6	3330
Fats Navarro	tp	6	1968
Freddie Hubbard	tp	6	2222
Gerry Mulligan	bs	6	2621
Hank Mobley	ts	4	2118
Herbie Hancock	p	5	2769
J. J. Johnson	tb	8	3324
Joe Henderson	ts	8	4930
Joe Lovano	ss, ts, ts-c	8	6104
John Coltrane	ss, ts	20	19428
Johnny Dodds	cl	6	722

Performer	Instrument	# Solos	# Tones
Joshua Redman	ts	5	2422
Kenny Dorham	tp	7	2856
Kid Ory	tb	5	319
Lee Konitz	as	8	3519
Lee Morgan	tp	4	2243
Lester Young	ts	7	1787
Lionel Hampton	vib	6	1326
Louis Armstrong	cor, tp	8	1157
Michael Brecker	ts	10	7601
Miles Davis	tp	19	6734
Milt Jackson	vib	6	2302
Ornette Coleman	as	5	2857
Pat Metheny	g	4	2374
Paul Desmond	as	8	2169
Pepper Adams	bs	5	2343
Phil Woods	as	6	2802
Roy Eldridge	tp	6	1748
Sidney Bechet	ss	5	1078
Sonny Rollins	ts	13	5399
Sonny Stitt	as, ts	6	1759
Stan Getz	ts	6	3705
Steve Coleman	as, ss	10	5552
Steve Lacy	ss	6	2332
Wayne Shorter	ts	10	3815
Woody Shaw	cor, tp	8	3193
Wynton Marsalis	tp	7	3070
Zoot Sims	ts	6	1136
Total		423	191464

In each of the following sections, we describe for each processing step both the applied computational method and an exemplary corpus study to demonstrate the analytical potentials of our approach. Of course, there are many more research issues that could be approached within this analytical framework. Most of the data used in the case studies is included within the Weimar Jazz Database and is ready to be further explored.

In order to have a representative corpus in regard to personal styles, we focus on all soloists featured within the Weimar Jazz Database with at least four solos. This selection still covers around 95 % of all annotated tones within the Weimar Jazz Database. Table 1 gives an overview over the selected performers and their instruments as well as the total number of solos and tones for each performer.

Source separation

The main goal of the sound source separation step is to isolate the solo instrument from the accompanying instruments, i. e., the rhythm section. The algorithm applied for solo and accompaniment source separation was originally proposed in E. Cano, Schuller, & Dittmar, 2014. The high-quality solo transcriptions from the Weimar Jazz Database, which are perfectly aligned to the audio track, are used as prior information to the separation algorithm. The main approach is to iteratively model the tones of the solo instrument in the spectral domain. Typical characteristics such as inharmonicity (deviation of harmonic frequencies from integer multiples of the fundamental frequency), magnitude and frequency smoothness, as well as common amplitude modulation among partials are taken into account.

Tuning estimation

Tuning refers to the adjustment of the pitch frequencies of musical instruments to a given reference frequency. As will be shown in p. 102, jazz recordings exhibit a high variance with respect to the tuning frequency. While the first jazz recordings date back to the 1920s, a standardized reference frequency for the concert pitch A4 of 440 Hz was not defined until 1955 in the ISO 16 standard and later re-affirmed in ISO16:1975 (1975). Furthermore, pianos—the most important accompaniment instruments in jazz recordings—tend to detune over time (Fletcher & Rossing, 1998). A third reason for tuning frequency deviations in early jazz recordings lies in technical imperfections in the recording process, such as speed variations in gramophones or tape recorders (Ballou, 2008). As a consequence, the tuning frequency f_{ref} must be estimated before the intonation of jazz soloists in relation to the performing ensemble can be analyzed. Rhythm section instruments like the piano and double bass provide a suitable tuning reference for the soloist since they have mostly stable tone pitches. Therefore, we estimate f_{ref} exclusively from the backing track, which is automatically extracted using a source separation algorithm (cf. p. 101). Audible artifacts from the source separation process do not affect the tuning frequency estimation (Abeßer et al., 2015). An estimate of the tuning frequency from the rhythm section allows to investigate whether and to what extent a soloist tends to play "sharp" or "flat" by using slightly higher or lower pitch frequencies, respectively.

In a previous study (Abeßer, Frieler, Cano, Pfleiderer, & Zaddach, 2017), we compared two state-of-the-art methods for tuning frequency estimation proposed by Müller and Ewert (2011), as well as Mauch (2010) for tuning frequency estimation from jazz recordings. In the first approach, a multirate filter bank with semitone spacing is used. The center frequencies of the filters are systematically shifted in order to estimate the most likely tuning frequency from the averaged spectrogram. In the second approach, a note saliency representation is computed with a third-of-semitone spacing. This saliency is averaged over the full audio recording and analyzed using a Discrete Fourier Transformation (DFT). The most likely tuning deviation from 440 Hz is finally estimated from the phase of the DFT. Both methods showed a very high agreement over the solos in the Weimar Jazz Database with a sample correlation of $r = 0.96$ ($p < .001$). We finally decided to use the method proposed by Mauch since it is available as a time-efficient implementation as part of the NNLS Vamp Plugin[14].

Temporal development of tuning frequencies in jazz recordings

The Weimar Jazz Database includes recordings from almost every decade of the 20th century. In this study, we investigate the hypothesis that earlier recordings show a larger deviation from the later on standardized tuning frequency of 440 Hz than later recordings. Based on the estimated tuning frequency f_{ref} in Hz, we compute its deviation from the standardized tuning frequency as

$$\text{tuning\_dev} = 1200 \log_2 \frac{f_{ref}}{440}.$$

Figure 2 shows the absolute tuning deviation for all solos in the Weimar Jazz Database as a function of their recording years. We observe a negative correlation of $r = -0.286$ ($p < .001$). Similarly, Figure 3 illustrates the distribution of the tuning deviation over four different recording periods of

---

[14] http://isophonics.net/nnls-chroma (last accessed: 01.09.2017)

Score-informed audio analysis

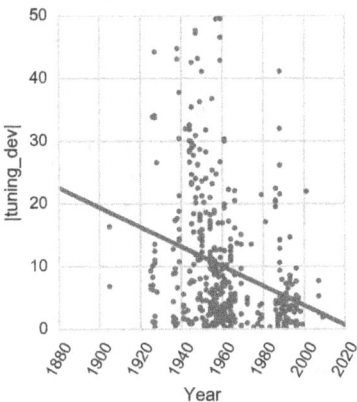

Figure 2: Absolute tuning deviation from 440 Hz over the recording year for all solos in the Weimar Jazz Database.

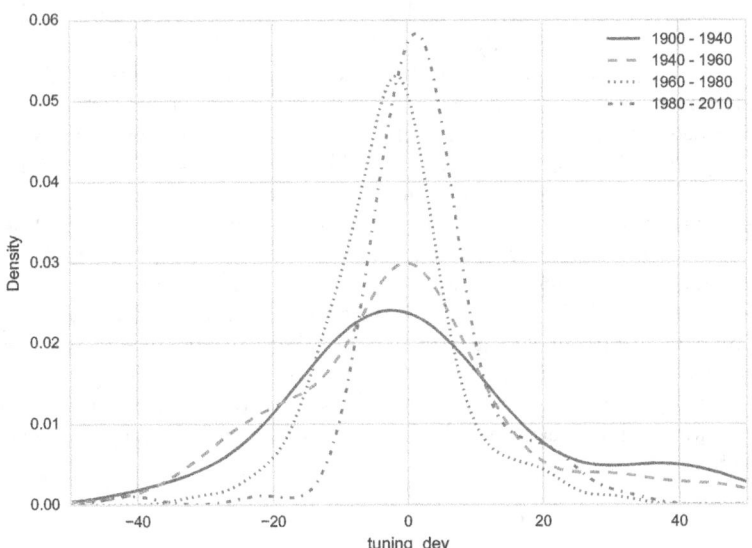

Figure 3: Tuning deviation from 440 Hz in cents over different recording periods of the 20th century.

the 20th century. Both figures confirm that the absolute tuning deviation of jazz recordings from the ideal concert pitch decreased over the 20th century.

Notably, before 1960, absolute tuning deviations larger than 30 cents can be observed, while afterwards, the highest tuning deviations drop to below 25 cents with the exception of three solos recorded around 1990. Probable reasons are the technical progress of audio recording technology as well as the delayed adoption of the standardized 440 Hz tuning frequency.

Analysis of fundamental frequency contours

Fundamental frequency contour tracking

An important means of expression for musicians is the ability to shape the fundamental frequency (f_0) contour of a tone. Abeßer, Frieler, et al. (2017) evaluated two algorithms which automatically extract tone-wise f_0 contours from jazz solos in ensemble recordings. With the first method proposed by Abeßer, Pfleiderer, Frieler, and Zaddach (2014), a spectrogram representation of the mixture track is analyzed in order to track neighboring spectral peaks over time and join them to contours. The algorithm is score-informed, i. e., the search region in the spectral domain is restricted by the annotated tone parameters pitch, onset time, and offset time. The second algorithm was the pYIN algorithm proposed by Mauch and Dixon (2014), which estimates the predominant fundamental frequency from monophonic signals based on an autocorrelation analysis in the time domain. Naturally, this approach allows one to achieve a better frequency resolution compared to spectrogram-based methods. At the same time, however, it is less robust if multiple harmonic signals overlap. We applied the pYIN algorithm to the solo track, which is extracted in the source separation step. Finally, we segmented the extracted f_0 track using the tone onset and offset times to extract tone-wise f_0 contours. In the experiments described in the following sections, we used the pYIN algorithm as it outperformed the first approach by showing a slightly higher pitch accuracy.

Fundamental frequency contour features

We extracted several features to characterize important aspects of the contour shape, such as periodic modulations, or general trends, such as vibrato or pitch bends. Table 2 summarizes all features used in this chapter. The tone-wise f_0 contours are denoted as $f_0(n)$, with n being the frame number.

Table 2: Fundamental frequency contour features.

Feature	Description
mod_range_cent	Modulation range in cents around the annotated pitch (taking into account the estimated tuning frequency); computed as the difference between the 95th and the 5th percentile over $f_0(n)$.
dev_median	Median tone-wise frequency deviation from the annotated pitch frequency $f_{0,A}$ (taking into account the estimated tuning frequency); computed as the median over $1200\log_2\left(\frac{f_0(n)}{f_{0,A}}\right)$ in cent.
mod_freq_hz	Modulation frequency in Hz; computed as the most prominent peak in the autocorrelation function over $f_0(n)$ within a lag range that corresponds to modulation frequencies between 2 and 15 Hz.

Sharp and flat intonation

In this study, we investigate whether and to what extent saxophone and trumpet players systematically show flat or sharp intonation in their solos. To this end, we group the solos by musicians and compute the dev_median feature for each tone. Figure 4, Figure 5, and Figure 6 show comparative box plots for all selected alto saxophone, tenor saxophone, and trumpet players.

As a general observation across all instruments, sharp intonation is more prevalent than flat intonation, while the median of absolute f_0 deviation rarely exceeds 20 cents. Of all the alto saxophone players listed in Figure 5, Steve Coleman, Ornette Coleman, and Benny Carter show a slight tendency to flat intonation while particularly Sonny Stitt, Lee Konitz, and Charlie Parker clearly intonate sharply with positive dev_median values around 20 cents and higher. A similar picture emerges with the tenor saxophone players in Figure 5. While only Ben Webster shows a clear tendency towards flat intonation, a number of players such as Don Byas, Branford Marsalis, Sonny Stitt, Coleman Hawkins, Dexter Gordon, and John Coltrane show positive dev_median values between 10 and 20 cents. Finally, Figure 6 shows that, for the most part, trumpet players Roy Eldridge, Clifford Brown, Dizzy Gillespie, Wynton Marsalis, and Kenny Dorham use sharp tone intonation of around 10 to 20 cents. In general, there are no intonation commonalities

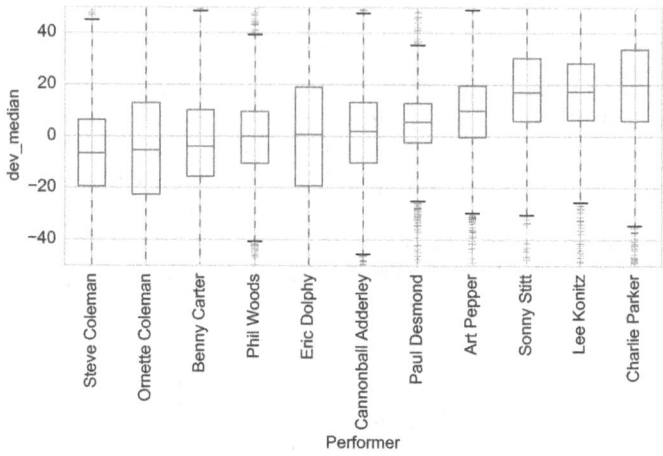

Figure 4: Boxplot over median tone-wise f_0 deviations in cents for alto saxophone players.

in regard to different recording periods or different jazz styles. Furthermore, the findings are only tendencies in regard to personal idiosyncrasies since the range of deviations is rather large across all musicians.

Context-dependency of fundamental frequency contour features

Is there any correlation between f_0 contour features of tones (see Table 2) and parameters that characterize their musical context? These parameters are median tone intensity (intensity_solo_median, see p. 109), note number (noteid), tatum value (tatum, cf. p. 51), relative tone position within the corresponding musical phrase (normalized to [0, 1], rel_pos_in_phrase), as well as the tone parameters pitch, onset, and duration. An initial test (D'Agostino, 1971) showed that none of the contour features nor the contextual parameters showed a normal distribution. Therefore, throughout the analyses discussed in this section, we used Kendall's τ as a rank correlation coefficient. The correlation results between pairs of features and contextual parameters are shown in Table 3.

In general, we only observed only very small correlations with small effect sizes. However, at least in the case of a tone's duration, its intensity and its position within a phrase, these correlations indicate some overall trends. The

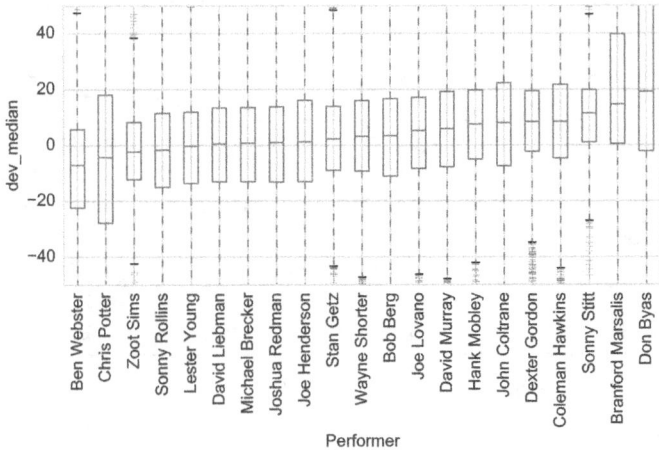

Figure 5: Boxplot over median tone-wise f_0 deviations in cents for tenor saxophone players.

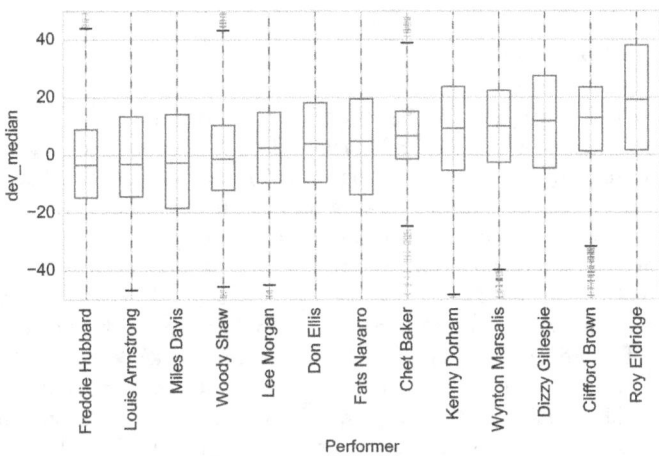

Figure 6: Boxplot over median tone-wise f_0 deviations in cents for trumpet players.

Table 3: Kendall's τ correlation coefficient. Only significant correlations ($p < .05$) are shown.

	mod_range_cent	dev_median	mod_freq_hz
intensity_solo_median	−0.11***	+0.04***	−0.11***
noteid	−0.02*	+0.02***	−0.06***
tatum	−0.03***	+0.02*	−0.05***
rel_pos_in_phrase	+0.07***	−0.11***	+0.18***
pitch	−0.08***		−0.04***
onset	−0.02*		−0.04***
duration	+0.16***	−0.22***	+0.32***

*$p < .05$, **$p < .01$, ***$p < 0.001$

f_0 modulation range is generally larger for longer tones but smaller for louder tones. Longer tones as well as tones in a later position within phrases tends to show a better intonation (i.e., lower values for dev_median).

Vibrato modulation frequency

Within the Weimar Jazz Database there are 4,163 tones that have been manually annotated as "vibrato tones". Each vibrato is characterized by a certain 'vibrato frequency', i.e., the frequency of the f_0-modulation. To what extent does vibrato frequencies differ between certain musicians? Figures 7 to 9 show boxplots over all trumpet, alto saxophone, and tenor saxophone players. For the trumpet players, there are median mod_freq_hz values between 6.5 Hz and 9.5 Hz, whereas alto players show higher values of 7.5 Hz to 10 Hz. The largest variance can be observed for tenor saxophone players with median values of 6 Hz and 10.5 Hz. In general, modern tenorists like Bob Berg, Michael Brecker, and Chris Potter tend to play a faster vibrato compared to older players like Chu Berry, Ben Webster, or Lester Young. In contrast, trumpet and alto saxophone players' vibrato frequencies vary within style, e.g., the frequencies of well-known swing trumpet players Harry Edison and Roy Eldridge differ significantly. However, there is a high overall variance of vibrato frequencies within the tones played by certain musicians. Therefore, all observations should only be interpreted as general trends.

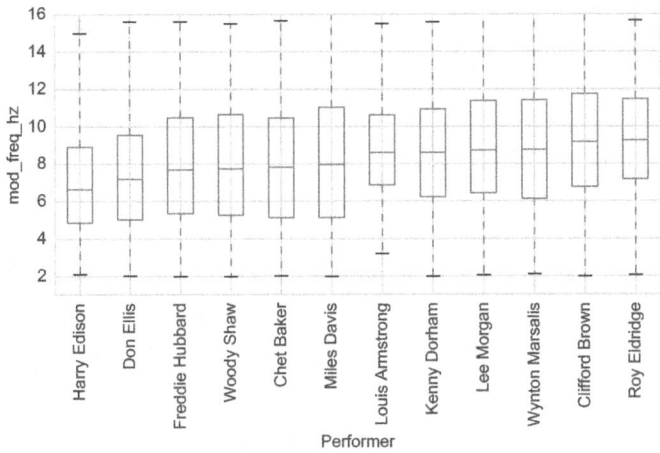

Figure 7: Boxplot over vibrato modulation frequency for trumpet players.

Tempo dependency of vibrato modulation frequency

Another interesting question is whether the modulation frequency of vibrato tones depends on the tempo of a song. In order to answer this, we detected the most prominent modulation frequency f_{mod} between 2 Hz and 15 Hz, as explained in p. 104. We computed the ratio $r = T_{\mathrm{mod}}/T_{\mathrm{solo}}$ between the 'modulation tempo', which follows from $T_{\mathrm{mod}} = 60 \cdot f_{\mathrm{mod}}$, and the average tempo over the solo T_{solo} in beats per minute. Figure 10 shows the relationship between r and T_{solo}.

As can be observed in Figure 10, there is no evidence in the Weimar Jazz Database that performers adapt the speed of their vibrato to integer multiples of the current tempo. For tempos above 150 bpm (medium and fast solos), the modulation frequency varies between the beat level (quarter note) and the 16th note level. For slower tempos, the vibrato can be up to 10 times faster than the beat tempo.

Intensity estimation

Dynamics are essential to any music performance (Fraisse, 1982; Langner & Goebel, 2003). Supposedly, implicit syntactical rules as well as expressive intentions influence how musicians apply dynamics. Musicians can accentuate certain parts of musical phrases by playing tones with different intensities,

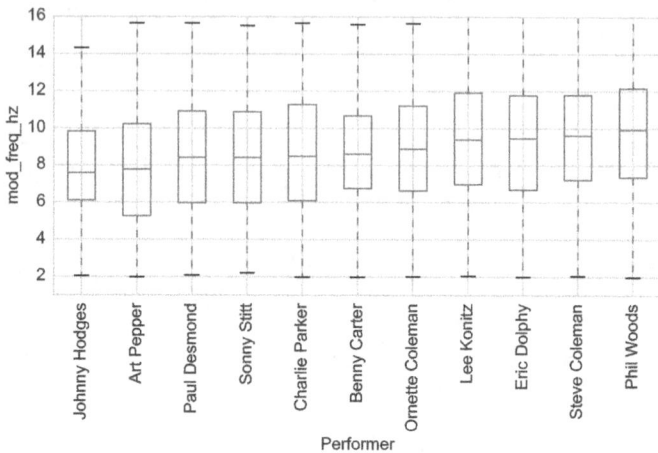

Figure 8: Boxplot over vibrato modulation frequency for alto saxophone players.

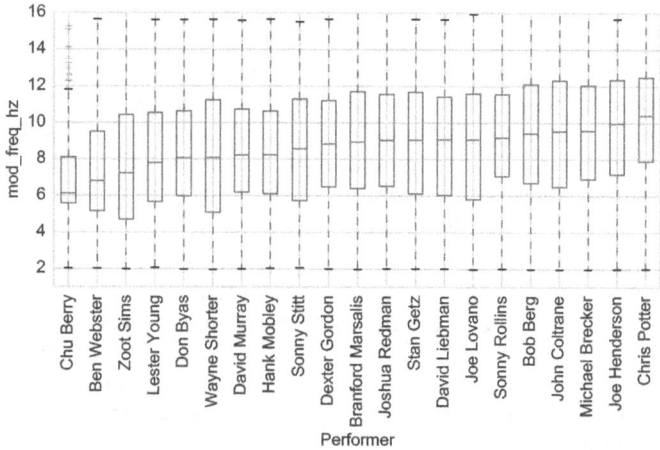

Figure 9: Boxplot over vibrato modulation frequency for tenor saxophone players.

i. e., "local stresses" (Lerdahl & Jackendoff, 1983). In regard to meter, the emphasis of certain tones via intensity changes allows musicians both to underline the given metrical structure and to imply additional rhythms, e. g., by using syncopation (Pfleiderer, 2006). Two prominent examples are clarinet

Score-informed audio analysis 111

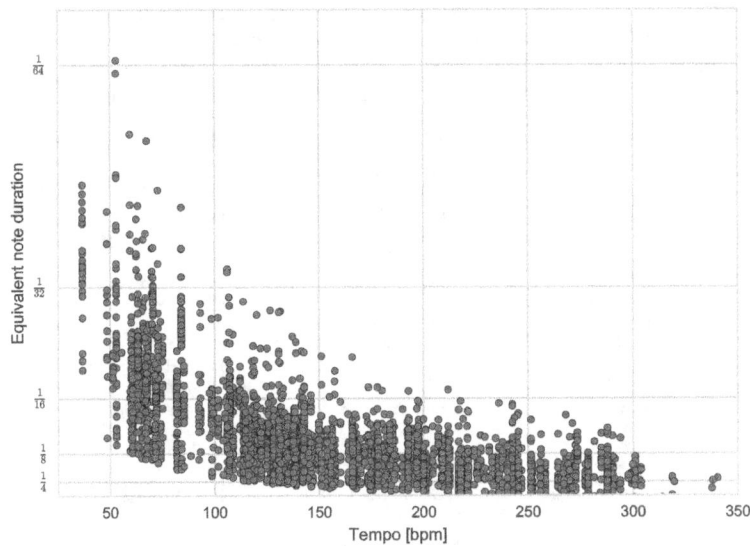

Figure 10: Modulation frequency of vibrato tones as equivalent to the note duration according to the average solo tempo in beats per minute; the note lengths according to the tempo are indicated on the left side.

and soprano saxophone player Sidney Bechet and saxophonist Charlie Parker, who are said to use accentuation either of off-beat or of cross-rhythmic superposition in their improvisations (Owens, 1995).

As measuring the dynamics of a solo instrument within an ensemble recording is complicated, the use of dynamics has hitherto been mostly neglected in jazz research so far. As detailed in Abeßer, Cano, Frieler, and Pfleiderer (2014), we measure the dynamics of the separated solo instrument (solo track) by computing intensity values on a short time scale of around 10 ms. Essentially, we compute and aggregate intensity values for the 24 critical bands of the human auditory system using a method that originates from psychoacoustics (Painter & Spanias, 2000). Using tone onset and offset times from the solo transcriptions, we obtain intensity contours by aggregating frame-wise intensity values. Finally, we compute five features from the intensity contour of each tone—maximum, median, standard deviation, temporal centroid, and relative peak position within the tone's duration. The Weimar Jazz Database contains intensity features, which were computed from the tones in the solo track both as absolute and relative values (normalized to the backing track).

Table 4: Highest-ranked and lowest-ranked performers sorted in descending order according to Pearson correlation coefficient values between median tone intensity and pitch, note duration, or relative note position within a phrase (averaged over all solos by a performer); both mean and standard deviation values are given.

#	pitch	duration	rel_pos_in_phrase
1	Don Ellis (tp) (0.55 ± 0.06)	Lionel Hampton (vib) (0.29 ± 0.09)	Branford Marsalis (ts) (-0.09 ± 0.02)
2	Sonny Stitt (as, ts) (0.53 ± 0.18)	Fats Navarro (tp) (0.26 ± 0.04)	John Coltrane (ss, ts) (-0.09 ± 0.02)
3	Chet Baker (tp) (0.52 ± 0.18)	Phil Woods (as) (0.18 ± 0.05)	Stan Getz (ts) (-0.12 ± 0.01)
4	Bix Beiderbecke (cor) (0.50 ± 0.10)	Dizzy Gillespie (tp) (0.15 ± 0.01)	Sonny Stitt (as, ts) (-0.14 ± 0.03)
5	Fats Navarro (tp) (0.48 ± 0.11)	Michael Brecker (ts) (0.12 ± 0.04)	Ben Webster (ts) (-0.15 ± 0.01)
6	Lee Konitz (as) (0.46 ± 0.15)	Cannonball Adderley (as) (0.11 ± 0.01)	Ornette Coleman (as) (-0.16 ± 0.02)
7	Kenny Dorham (tp) (0.45 ± 0.16)	John Coltrane (ss, ts) (0.10 ± 0.12)	Clifford Brown (tp) (-0.16 ± 0.06)
52	Michael Brecker (ts) (0.14 ± 0.02)	David Murray (ts) (-0.23 ± 0.08)	Paul Desmond (as) (-0.28 ± 0.14)
53	Hank Mobley (ts) (0.14 ± 0.01)	Gerry Mulligan (bs) (-0.27 ± 0.11)	David Murray (ts) (-0.29 ± 0.09)
54	Wynton Marsalis (tp) (0.09 ± 0.24)	Paul Desmond (as) (-0.29 ± 0.11)	Lester Young (ts) (-0.29 ± 0.04)
55	Bob Berg (ts) (0.07 ± 0.14)	Don Byas (ts) (-0.30 ± 0.12)	Coleman Hawkins (ts) (-0.30 ± 0.03)
56	Johnny Dodds (cl) (-0.02 ± 0.27)	Louis Armstrong (cor, tp) (-0.34 ± 0.02)	Louis Armstrong (cor, tp) (-0.32 ± 0.10)
57	Joshua Redman (ts) (-0.22 ± 0.02)	Steve Lacy (ss) (-0.34 ± 0.21)	Don Byas (ts) (-0.36 ± 0.04)
58	Chris Potter (ts) (-0.24 ± 0.04)	Bix Beiderbecke (cor) (-0.51 ± 0.17)	Bix Beiderbecke (cor) (-0.41 ± 0.08)

Context-dependency of tone intensities

Are there any correlations between a tone's intensity and its pitch height, its duration, or its position within a phrase? In order to find an answer to these issues, we computed the Pearson correlation coefficient between tone-wise median intensity values and the context parameters pitch, duration, and rel_pos_in_phrase as explained in p. 106. In Table 4, the artists in the Weimar Jazz Database with the highest and lowest average correlation coefficients averaged over the corresponding solos are listed; both the mean and standard deviation are shown, and only musicians with significant correlations are displayed. It is not surprising that most of the solos show a positive correlation between intensity and pitch since, in general, higher notes are played more loudly. Notable exceptions are the two modern tenor saxophone players Joshua Redman and Chris Potter with negative correlation values of around

−0.2, presumably due to several loud tones which are 'honked' at the very bottom of the tenor saxophone range.

The correlation between tone intensity and duration seems well balanced among artists and no instrument-specific tendencies towards positive or negative correlation values could be observed. As it becomes obvious from the third column, tones at the beginning of musical phrases are generally played more loudly than tones at the end. This seems to be true in particular for earlier trumpet and cornet players such as Bix Beiderbecke and Louis Armstrong and tenor saxophone players like Don Byas, Coleman Hawkins, Lester Young, and David Murray. However, saxophone players such as Branford Marsalis, John Coltrane, and Stan Getz manage very well to play at the same dynamic level throughout an entire phrase.

Phrase-wise intensity and pitch contours

The movement of pitch and intensity within melodic phrases has a strong influence on the overall perception of a melody (Müllensiefen, Wiggins, & Lewis, 2008). In this study, we compare pitch contours and intensity contours of phrases taken from the solos in the Weimar Jazz Database. We modified Huron's classification of melodic contours of folk songs (Huron, 1996) in order to make it suitable for the very long phrases which are often encountered in jazz (Abeßer, Frieler, et al., 2017). For both parameters, pitch and intensity, five contour types, 'horizontal', 'ascending', 'descending', 'convex', and 'concave', are distinguished. We first compute the median intensity values v_1, v_2, and v_3 within the first 25%, the central 50%, and the final 25% of the phrase duration over tone-wise pitch and intensity values. Based on both the median intensity and pitch values of all tones in a given phrase, the first 25%, the central 50%, and the final 25% of tones are grouped into three segments. Furthermore, based on the median values v_i within the i-th group, the differences between adjacent groups are computed using a tolerance value $\Delta v_{\min}$.

Then, we compare the segment intensity difference Δv_i via

$$\Delta v_i = \begin{cases} \text{sign}(v_{i+1} - v_i), & \text{if } |v_{i+1} - v_i| \geq \Delta v_{\min}, \\ 0, & \text{otherwise.} \end{cases}$$

using the threshold $\Delta v_{\min} = 0.1\,(\max_i v_i - \min_i v_i)$. Finally, the contour type is determined using the heuristic given in Table 5, based on the pairs of segment intensity differences $(\Delta v_1, \Delta v_2)$. Phrases with a length of fewer than 4 tones are grouped into an additional category.

Table 5: Heuristic for the classification of phrase contours. Each phrase contour type is based on differences Δv_1 and Δv_2 between adjacent segment pairs according to either pitch or intensity.

Contour Type	$(\Delta v_1, \Delta v_2)$
Horizontal	(0, 0)
Ascending	(0, 1), (1, 0), (1, 1)
Descending	(0, −1), (−1, 0), (−1, −1)
Concave	(−1, 1)
Convex	(1, −1)

Table 6: Percentage of intensity and pitch contour types in jazz solo phrases.

Contour Type	Intensity	Pitch
< 4 notes	10.1	10.1
Horizontal	12.9	3.5
Convex	13.4	17.4
Concave	9.7	10.9
Ascending	13.6	20.0
Descending	40.3	38.1

Intensity and pitch contour types in musical phrases

How often do the the pitch and intensity contour types detailed in the previous section occur within the solos in the Weimar Jazz Database? Are there any correlations between pitch contours and intensity contours?

As shown in Table 6, descending contours appear most often for both intensity and pitch. Ascending and convex pitch contours also appear quite often, while for intensity, almost non-descending contour types appear comparably often, except for horizontal contour, i. e., playing at one and the same dynamic level throughout a phrase.

Table 7 illustrates how often different intensity and pitch contours co-occur. All pitch contour types most often coincide with the corresponding intensity contour (32.9 % on average) or with a descending intensity contour (41.4 % on average). This finding is confirmed by the positive correlation between intensity and pitch shown in p. 112.

Table 7: Percentage of co-occurrence of intensity and pitch contour in jazz solo phrases (minimum length is 4 tones).

Pitch Contour Type	Intensity Contour Type				
	Horiz.	Conv.	Conc.	Ascend.	Descend.
Horizontal	24.5	7.2	7.8	19.1	41.3
Convex	10.6	30.1	7.9	13.7	37.7
Concave	16.9	7.4	23.6	11.0	41.2
Ascending	14.7	16.3	11.7	28.5	28.8
Descending	14.1	10.1	8.3	9.5	57.9

Alternating eighth-note accentuations

It is claimed that many jazz musicians contribute to the swing feeling of their playing by accentuating every second eight-note within eight-note chains. The tone-wise intensity values extracted by our score-informed audio analysis methodology allow for an inspection of this hypothesis. For each solo, we performed a paired t-test between the median tone intensity values of the second and first eighths in eight-note sequences. We selected all solos with at least 10 eight-note pairs, which led to a subset of 77 solos from the Weimar Jazz Database.

After selecting solos with significant differences between both eighths ($p < 0.05$) according to the t-test, we computed Cohen's d to measure the effect size (Cohen, 1988). In total, we found 67 solos with positive values for d and only 10 solos with negative values for d. Therefore, most jazz musicians tend to play the first or on-beat eighth note louder than the second or off-beat eighth. In contrast to the hypothesis cited above, there is a clear trend towards on-beat accentuation, at least within the Weimar Jazz Database solos. The ten solos with the highest and lowest effect size values are shown in Table 8. In general, there is a higher effect size for solos with positive d, i.e., with emphasis on the first eighths.

Since the five solos with the highest effect size are played by traditional and swing musicians, there seems to be a tendency to accent the on-beat eighths by playing them more loudly in older styles. However, modern saxophone players such as David Liebman, Zoot Sims or Joe Henderson follow this tendency, too. It has to be further explored whether intensity differences of eighth pairs are stylistic traits of individual musicians or depend on other aspects such as the overall tempo.

Table 8: Ten solos with the highest effect size for both positive intensity differences (first eighths louder than second eighths) and negative intensity differences.

Performer	Title	Cohen's d
Bix Beiderbecke (cor)	Margie	1.23*
Sidney Bechet (ss)	Limehouse Blues	1.04***
Lionel Hampton (vib)	High Society	0.90***
Benny Goodman (cl)	Tiger Rag	0.89***
Johnny Dodds (cl)	Heebie Jeebies	0.87*
David Liebman (ss, ts)	Nica's Dream	0.85**
Zoot Sims (ts)	Night and Day	0.83***
Joe Henderson (ts)	Totem Pole	0.83*
J.C. Higginbotham (tb)	Baby Won't You Please Come Home	0.80**
Coleman Hawkins (ts)	It's Only a Papermoon	0.77**
Stan Getz (ts)	Blues in the Closet	−0.19**
Herbie Hancock (p)	Hand Jive	−0.23*
Clifford Brown (tp)	I'll Remember April	−0.28*
Chet Baker (tp)	You'd Be So Nice to Come Home to	−0.33*
Phil Woods (as)	Strollin' with Pam	−0.34**
Kai Winding (tb)	Tiny's Blues	−0.36*
Milt Jackson (vib)	Don't Get Around Much Anymore	−0.40*
Hank Mobley (ts)	Soul Station	−0.40*
Fats Navarro (tp)	Good Bait	−0.52*
Steve Turre (tb)	Steve's Blues	−0.58***

*$p < .05$, **$p < .01$, ***$p < 0.001$

Timbre analysis

Jazz musicians are said to create and develop an individual personal 'sound' in order to be acknowledged as unique and creative artists (Berliner, 1994; Jackson, 2012) While young musicians learn and grow by imitating older musicians, they are generally not appreciated as 'real' jazz musicians by their peers or by critics and the audience until the have found their own instrumental 'voice' with a distinctive 'sound'. However, what actually contributes to a personal style or 'sound' is not easy to grasp. One might define the 'sound' of a jazz musician as a combination of a characteristic instrumental timbre and preferred sound effects (such as growls or slides), dynamics and articulation, as well as structural idiosyncrasies such as the usage of certain rhythmic or melodic patterns or catch-phrases, or an individual approach to harmony or to solo dramaturgy. While in this usage the term 'sound' tends to become synonymous with 'style', we prefer to focus on aspects of timbre as detectable from single tones within a musician's instrumental improvisations. Could timbral characteristics of single tones or a certain amount of tones played by a jazz musician be used to distinguish his 'sound' from that of other musicians? And if so: Which sonic features are the decisive factors?

In this section, we aim to distinguish between the 'sound' of different jazz musicians by examining timbral characteristics of their improvisations. In particular, we focus on trumpet (tp), alto saxophone (as), and tenor saxophone (ts) musicians with at least four solos included in the Weimar Jazz Database.

Method

We approach the task by first separating the solo instrument from the ensemble recording using automatic source separation as explained above (p. 101). Then we extract several acoustic features from the solo instrument track by analyzing the corresponding magnitude spectrograms of each tone. These features quantify spectral and temporal properties such as the tone's envelope contour shape and the energy distribution across the tone's partials. Finally, we apply machine learning algorithms to learn artist-specific timbre patterns from a large set of representative solo excerpts taken from the Weimar Jazz Database.

Based on the STFT magnitude spectrogram M of a tone in the separated solo track, we use Non-Negative Matrix Factorization (NMF, D. D. Lee & Seung, 2001) with one component to represent each tone as a product of a spectral envelope S and a temporal envelope A. An example of such a simple decomposition is shown in Figure 11. In the temporal envelope A, the short attack part as well as the decay and release parts of the tone's envelope are visible. The peaks in the spectral envelope S indicate the partials (overtones) of the tone. Also, it becomes apparent that higher partials show higher energy than lower partials.

Since the temporal envelope, in particular the attack part with its rising amplitude shape, is important for the human recognition of instrument timbres, we compute two additional representations. We calculated the first derivative ΔA of the temporal envelope A as a second representation and the histogram values $N_{\Delta A}$ over ΔA with 10 equally spaced histogram bins as a third representation.

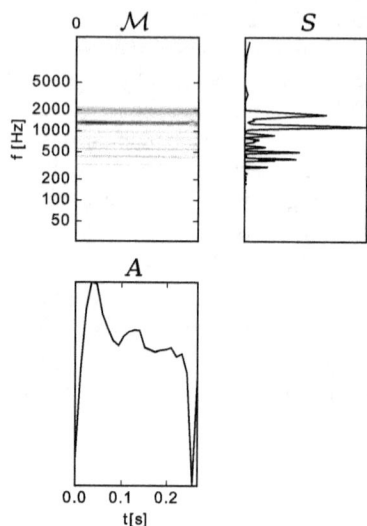

Figure 11: Decomposition of a tone's magnitude spectrogram M into a spectral envelope S and a temporal envelope A.

Based on these two representations S and A, we extracted 127 audio features which combine state-of-the-art features from the field of MIR with several novel contributions. The main categories of these features are listed in Table 9. The first group of features based on the spectral envelope S includes standard low-level features such as the statistical measures spectral centroid, spread, skewness, and kurtosis as well as spectral shape characteristics such as spectral decrease, slope, flatness, and roll-off frequency. Most of these features implement summative statistical measures while some of them capture higher-level properties such as the energy distribution over partials (relative harmonic magnitudes, odd-to-even ratio, tristimulus 1-3) or the tone envelope shape (log attack time, log decay time, multi-resolution gamma filter bank) (Peeters, 2004).

Mel-Frequency Cepstral Coefficient (MFCC) features originate from speech processing and give a compact description of the spectral envelope shape. We use the MFCC coefficients 2 to 13. The Octave-Based Spectral Contrast (OSC) features characterize spectral peaks and valleys in different octave-related frequency bands, which can indicate the presence of harmonic peaks (overtones) and noise-like components in an audio signal (C.-H. Lee, Shih, Yu, & Lin, 2009).

Table 9: Spectral and temporal features to characterize the timbre of tones in a jazz solo.

Category	Feature
Spectral features	Statistics (centroid, spread, skewness, kurtosis), shape (decrease, slope, flatness, roll-off), Mel-Frequency Cepstral Coefficients (MFCC), spectral contrast (octave-based, shape-based), inharmonicity coefficient, relative partial magnitudes, odd-to-even ratio, tristimulus 1-3
Temporal features	Statistics (centroid, spread, skewness, kurtosis), shape (decrease, slope, flatness, roll-off), relative attack part length, log attack time, log decay time, Multi-Resolution Gamma Filter Bank (MRGF)

Furthermore, features to quantify the relationships between partial frequencies and between partial magnitudes are computed. Therefore, we first estimate the fundamental frequency of a given tone as the frequency position that corresponds to the highest cross-correlation between the spectral envelope S and an idealized harmonic spectrogram with unit peaks at the harmonic frequency positions (Abeßer & Schuller, 2017). The 'inharmonicity coefficient' measures how strong the partial frequencies deviate from integer multiples of the fundamental frequency. We estimate the coefficient from the spectral envelope S as proposed in (Abeßer & Schuller, 2017). By normalizing the partial magnitudes in S to the magnitude of the fundamental frequency, we compute the 'relative partial magnitudes'. As proposed by Peeters (Peeters, 2004), we additionally compute the 'odd-to-even ratio' and the three 'tristimulus' features, which provide alternative relationship measures between the partial magnitudes to describe the timbre of a given tone.

The second set of features includes temporal features. Similarly to the spectral audio features, we compute the aforementioned low-level statistic descriptors on the three temporal representations A, ΔA, and $N_{\Delta A}$ to characterize their general distribution. Based on the position of the global peak in A, we segment the temporal envelope into an attack part and a decay part. From the durations of the two parts, we compute the 'relative attack part length' (by normalizing to the overall tone duration) and the log attack and decay time. In addition, we compute the 'Multiresolution Gamma Filterbank Response' (MGFR) features (Tjao & Liu, 2010). The applied filter bank consists of 32 gamma filter kernels that resemble different temporal envelope shapes with varying attack times and overall durations. The proposed set of 127 features is computed for all tones in a given solo.

Table 10: Data set for automatic performer identification for trumpet (tp), alto saxophone (as), and tenor saxophone (ts) players.

Instrument	Performer
tp (13)	Chet Baker, Clifford Brown, Dizzy Gillespie, Don Ellis, Fats Navarro, Freddie Hubbard, Kenny Dorham, Lee Morgan, Louis Armstrong, Miles Davis, Roy Eldridge, Woody Shaw, Wynton Marsalis
as (11)	Art Pepper, Benny Carter, Cannonball Adderley, Charlie Parker, Eric Dolphy, Lee Konitz, Ornette Coleman, Paul Desmond, Phil Woods, Sonny Stitt, Steve Coleman
ts (21)	Ben Webster, Bob Berg, Branford Marsalis, Chris Potter, Coleman Hawkins, David Liebman, David Murray, Dexter Gordon, Don Byas, Hank Mobley, Joe Henderson, Joe Lovano, John Coltrane, Joshua Redman, Lester Young, Michael Brecker, Sonny Rollins, Sonny Stitt, Stan Getz, Wayne Shorter, Zoot Sims

Timbre-based performer classification

To what extent can a soloist be identified among his instrument peers based on the tone-wise features specified above (cf. p. 116)? In the following, we focus on all trumpet, alto saxophone, and tenor saxophone players included in the Weimar Jazz Database with at least four solos as listed in Table 10. For each solo, we extracted features from the first 100 tones with a duration of more than 100 ms.

The classification was performed using leave-one-label-out cross-validation. Here, the total data set of tones is repeatedly split into a training set, which is used to train the classification model, and a test set, which is used to evaluate the model's performance. The leave-one-label-out strategy implies that in each cross-validation fold, tones from all solos of a given artist except one solo are used to train the classification algorithm while the tones from the remaining solo are used as a test set. This strategy reflects the use case, in which a trained system is used to classify an artist with tones taken from a previously unseen solo. The final model performance is computed by averaging the performance measures in each cross-validation fold.

In each fold, we first standardize the features to zero mean and unit variance and then apply Linear Discriminant Analysis (LDA) to transform the initial feature space. LDA maximizes the variance between tones of different performers and minimizes the variance between tones of the same performer in

Table 11: Performer identification results (accuracy values).

Instrument	tp	as	ts
Number of performers	13	11	21
Baseline accuracy	0.08	0.09	0.05
Tone-wise classification	0.29	0.36	0.25
Solo-wise aggregation	0.57	0.69	0.57

the feature space. The goal is to achieve a good separability among different performers. Our main assumption here is that at least some of the proposed timbre features are more or less consistent over tones played by an individual musician and therefore allow us to characterize his or her sound. Finally, we train a Random Forest classifier (Breiman, 2001) with 200 trees.

Table 11 shows the mean class accuracy values for the trumpet (tp), alto saxophone (as), and tenor saxophone (ts) groups. Based on the number of performers, we provide the random choice accuracy as a baseline for the classifiers. The accuracy values for tone-wise classification between 0.25 and 0.36 are low even considering the high number of classes of 11 (as), 13 (tp) and 21 (ts). We can significantly improve upon these results by applying majority voting over all tone-wise classification results in order to obtain one classification result for each solo. Here we make use of the trivial assumption that all tones in a solo are played by the same performer.

As an example, Figure 12 illustrates the confusion matrices for the automatic performer classification among all 11 alto saxophone players. The tone-wise classification results shown at the top indicate that in particular tones by Art Pepper, Charlie Parker, Lee Konitz, and Paul Desmond can be well discriminated from those of their instrument peers. The lower plot shows that by applying majority voting in regard to all tones used within a certain solo, the number of misclassifications drastically decreases, especially for Benny Carter and Steve Coleman. Interestingly, the majority voting worsens the results for Ornette Coleman, which show many confusions with Benny Carter and Steve Coleman.

In future work, listening tests could be used to compare tone pairs of these performers in order to investigate, whether these confusions can be interpreted as timbral similarities between musicians that are associated with their individual 'sound' or whether they have to be traced back to rather superficial similarities in regard to more general characteristics of musical instruments or to the recording quality.

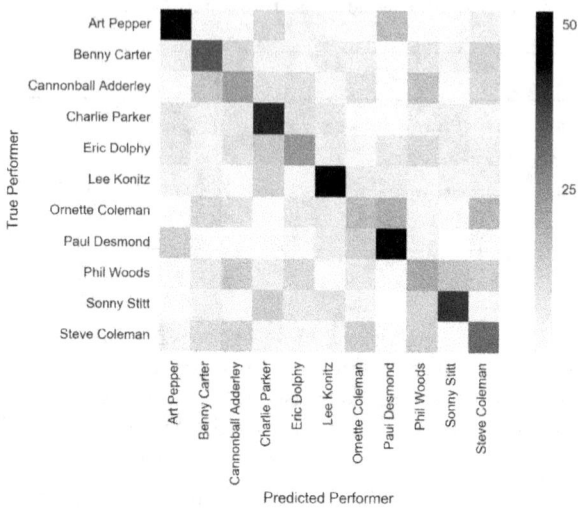

(a) Tone-wise classification.

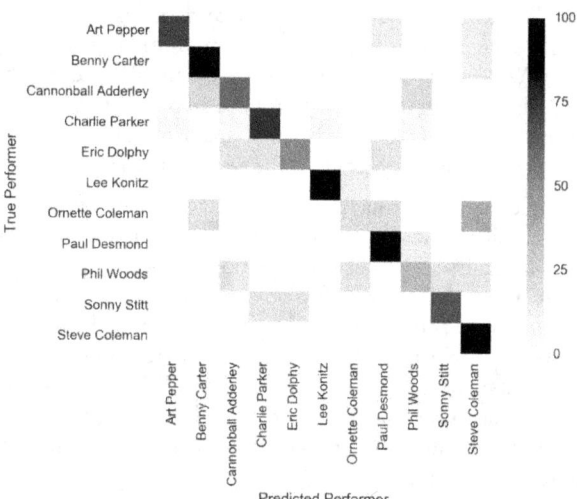

(b) Solo-wise classification using majority voting.

Figure 12: Confusion matrices for performer identification (alto saxophone players).

With our approach, known sonic similarities between jazz musicians can be systematically verified and formerly unknown sonic similarities between musicians might be uncovered. Moreover, an automatic analysis of large archives of jazz recordings would permit an investigation of how the timbral characteristics of the most common jazz instruments have changed over the course of jazz history. Using an algorithmic procedure of timbre characterization could also help to clean up metadata annotations in jazz archives and to enrich algorithms for automatic performer identification in jazz ensemble recordings.

Walking bass transcription

Method

Walking bass lines are a significant and even defining feature of many jazz styles. They mostly consist of quarter-note chains to support the main metrical structure and to provide harmonic orientation by emphasizing chord tones such as roots, thirds, and fifths. In a recent study (Abeßer, Balke, Frieler, Pfleiderer, & Müller, 2017), we proposed a novel method to automatically transcribe the walking bass line from jazz recordings. The central idea is to train a deep neural network to learn a mapping from a mixture (constant Q) spectrogram to a bass saliency representation. This representation measures the likelihood of the bass line playing certain pitches at a certain time. The mapping is learned automatically based on labeled training data, i. e., 31 jazz recordings selected from the Weimar Jazz Database with manually created bass line transcriptions.

Based on the bass saliency representation, we avoid the error-prone step of automatic tone formation, i. e., grouping salient pitches to tone events, but instead use manual beat annotations from the Weimar Jazz Database and estimate the most salient bass pitches for each beat. Based on a separated test set of ten bass lines, the proposed approach achieved a beat-wise pitch accuracy of 83 % and outperformed three state-of-the-art bass transcription algorithms for the given task.

Walking bass analysis

To demonstrate the analytical potential of our method for walking bass transcription, we will present some first exploratory studies of walking bass pitches, mostly with respect to the underlying harmony. It is the usual task of the bass player to convey the chords of a tune while also creating smooth and interesting lines. The golden rule (in common practice jazz, at least) is to play the root of the chord on the first beat of a bar. Doing so clearly presents harmonic guidance for the other players and leaves also the piano (or other chord) player the freedom to omit the root and to play more modern sounding voicings, often using harmonic extensions (e. g., ♭9, ♯11, ♭13). Besides the root, the fifth, the third and, to some extent, the seventh are the next most important tones for conveying a chord. However, focusing exclusively on chord tones would create arpeggios with rather large intervals in between, which neither form smooth lines nor are they generally easy to play on a double bass. Hence, besides the 'root-on-the-first-beat rule', bass players have some freedom (or are even supposed) to create well-sounding lines. Quite probably, they rely here on a large repertoire of patterns, particularly for frequently occurring accord transitions, e. g., II-V combinations in the more common keys such as F, B♭, and C. An in-depth analysis of walking bass patterns cannot be carried out here, but by using simple distributions of pitch classes some insights into the principles of creating walking bass lines can already be gained. We used 422 walking bass lines with annotated rhythm feel 'swing' extracted from the solos of the Weimar Jazz Database using the method described above. This resulted in 110,703 bass tones for which context information was also gathered, most importantly the annotated chords.

First, it might be interesting to look at the distribution of pitch classes[15]). In Table 12, the distribution of pitch classes across all solos is shown. Interestingly, this distribution does not so much reflect the most common keys, as it does the specifics of the double bass. The pitch classes which are available as open strings, i. e., E, A, D, and G, are the most frequent, with G being the most frequent of all, which might be explained by the fact that the pitch G is a more frequent chord root in the most common keys than the other three pitches E, A, and D. Besides these four most frequent ones, the other pitch classes are basically uniformly distributed.

Secondly, we take a look at the distribution of chordal pitch classes, i. e., the pitch class of each bass tone in relation to the root of the chord. Since major and minor chords have different thirds, we also annotated each chord with its basic triad type (major or minor) to see whether the thirds are used differently. In Figure 13, boxplots for chordal pitch classes differentiated with respect to basic triad types are shown. One clearly sees that the root of the chord (cpc = 0) is by far the most frequent chord pitch class (about 30 % on average for both minor and major), followed by the fifth (cpc = 7), with about 10 %. In both major and minor contexts, the next most common chordal pitch class

---

[15] We restrict ourselves to pitch classes here to circumvent problems with octave errors introduced by the extraction algorithm.

Score-informed audio analysis

Table 12: Percentage of walking bass pitch classes.

Rank	Pitch Class	Percentage
1	G	14.3
2	A	10.7
3	D	10.2
4	E	8.3
5	C#/Db	8.0
6	C	7.4
7	F#/Gb	7.4
8	F	7.0
9	B	6.9
10	Bb	6.8
11	D#/Eb	6.7
12	G#/Ab	6.2

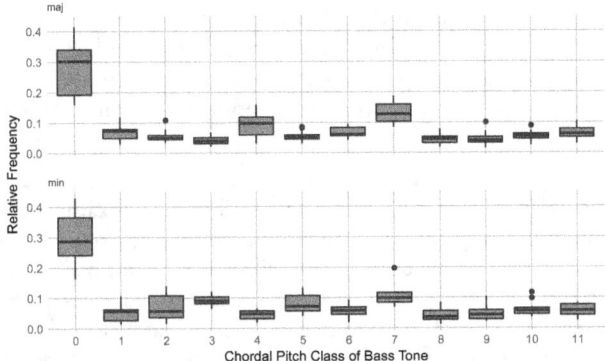

Figure 13: Relative frequencies of chordal pitch classes with respect to basic triad type of the underlying chord. Top: major, bottom: minor.

is indeed the major (cpc = 4) or the minor third (cpc = 3), respectively. The most significant differences appear for the relatively high frequency of the supertonic (cpc = 3) and the subdominant (cpc = 5) for minor-based chords. Besides this, the distribution of the other scale degrees is more or less the same for both chord types.

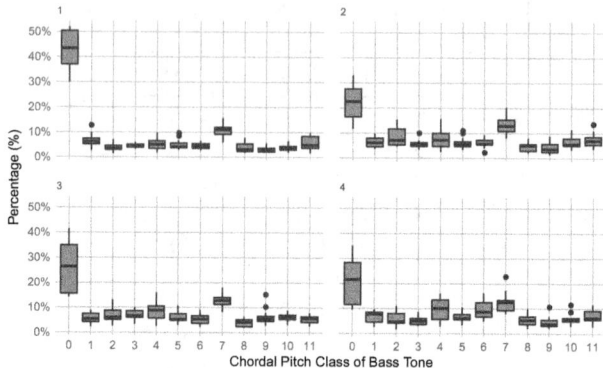

Figure 14: Relative frequencies of chordal pitch classes with respect to beat position.

Since all selected solos are in common $\frac{4}{4}$ time, we can easily differentiate the distribution of chordal pitch classes with respect to beat positions as seen in Figure 14. The root is still the most common chordal pitch class for all four positions, but, as expected, even more so for the first beat with more than 40%, which is, however, at the same time rather unexpectedly low. Interestingly, no clear pattern for the other chordal pitch classes can be identified, which hints at a rather large variation and fluidity of walking bass lines.

Thirdly, one could conjecture that differences in chordal pitch class usage might exist with respect to commonness of chords. To examine this point, we calculated chordal pitch class frequencies with respect to the frequency of the root of the underlying chord, again differentiated for major and minor basic triad types (Figures 15 and 16, for the relative frequencies of chord root pitch classes see Table 13). Pearson's correlations can be found in Table 14. Clear trends can be seen for both triad types. For instance, the chord root pitch class occurs less often for more common chord roots in both cases, very strongly so for major chords ($r_{maj} = -.92$), slightly less so for minor chords ($r_{min} = -.64$). The second scale degree (cpc = 2) increases in frequency for more common chords, particularly for minor chords ($r_{maj} = .63, r_{min} = .85$). Interestingly, the frequency of major thirds (cpc = 4) increases for more common chord roots as well as for minor chords ($r_{maj} = .86, r_{min} = .8$), but the frequency of minor thirds (cpc = 3) *decreases* for minor chords. The increase in major thirds could be partly explained by their use as chromatic passing tones to the root of a following dominant seventh chord, since minor chords very often occur in ii7-V combinations. An examination of beat

Table 13: Relative frequencies of chord root pitch classes for major and minor triad type chords.

Rank	Major			Minor		
	Root PC	Rel. Frequency		Root PC	Rel. Frequency	
		Major	All		Minor	All
1	F	0.18	0.12	C	0.20	0.06
2	Bb	0.17	0.12	G	0.17	0.05
3	Eb	0.15	0.10	F	0.15	0.05
4	C	0.12	0.08	D	0.14	0.04
5	G	0.10	0.07	A	0.07	0.02
6	Ab	0.08	0.06	Bb	0.07	0.02
7	D	0.07	0.05	Eb	0.06	0.02
8	Db	0.05	0.03	E	0.04	0.01
9	A	0.02	0.02	Gb	0.04	0.01
10	B	0.02	0.01	B	0.02	0.01
11	Gb	0.02	0.01	Db	0.02	0.01
12	E	0.02	0.01	Ab	0.02	0.01

Note. Chord root frequencies are counted beat-wise.

positions of major thirds over minor seventh chords shows that they occur more often on weak beats 2 and 4 (54 % vs. 46 % for beat 1 and 3). The frequency of fifths (cpc = 7) decreases for less common chord roots in the case of major chords ($r_{maj} = -.41$), but not significantly so, and increases for minor chords ($r_{min} = .68$). Finally, the frequency of major sixths (cpc = 10) and minor sevenths (cpc = 11) are higher for major chords with increasing commonness of the chord roots ($r_{maj} = .81$ and $r_{min} = .66$).

How to interpret these interesting trends? The increased use of roots with less common chords might indicate a "safe playing" strategy, since there might be fewer preconceived patterns at hand, so bass players tend to rely on the easiest and safest solution, the root. On the other hand, the more common a chord (root), the more freedom and the more patterns the bass player might have at their disposal due to their playing and practice routines. Complementarily, one might conjecture that the more common chords tend to occur in longer stretches, i. e., as a tonic or subdominant chord in a standard 12-bar blues (e. g., F or Bb blues) where chords can last up to four bars and more in a row. This leaves room for the bass player to create longer, more diverse, and interesting lines, possibly also including spontaneous, temporary, and

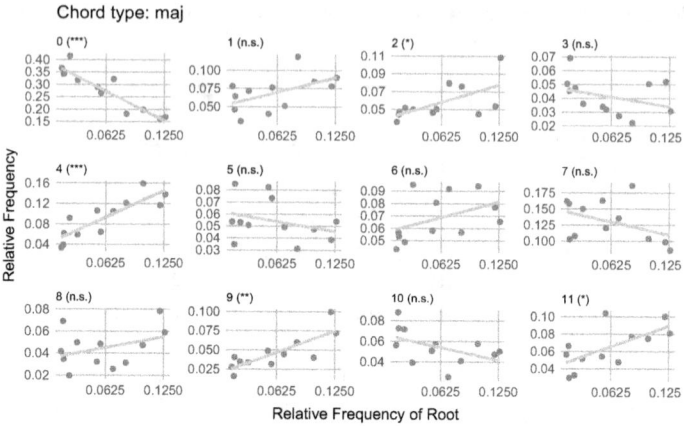

Figure 15: Relative frequencies of chordal pitch classes plotted against relative frequencies of chord roots for major-based chords. Each panel shows the relative frequency of the corresponding chordal pitch class on the y-axis for all 12 chord root pitch classes with the relative frequency on the x-axis. Asterisks in parentheses indicate the significance of the trend (n.s. = not significant, * = $p < .05$, ** = $p < .01$, *** = $p < .001$).

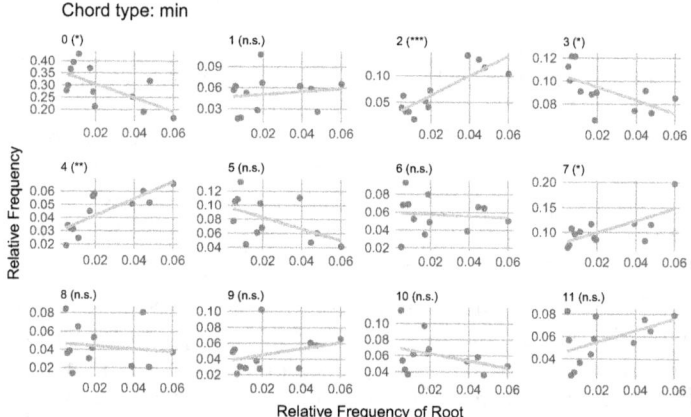

Figure 16: Relative frequencies of chordal pitch classes plotted against relative frequencies of chord roots for minor-based chords. Each panel shows the relative frequency of the corresponding chordal pitch class on the y-axis for all 12 chord root pitch classes with the relative frequency on the x-axis. Asterisks in parentheses indicate the significance of the trend (n.s. = not significant, * = $p < .05$, ** = $p < .01$, *** = $p < .001$).

Table 14: Pearson's correlations of chordal pitch classes with respect to frequency of chord root pitch classes.

cpc	Type	r	p	Sig.	cpc	Type	r	p	Sig.
0	maj	−0.92	0.00	***	6	maj	0.44	0.15	n.s.
	min	−0.64	0.02	*		min	−0.08	0.81	n.s.
1	maj	0.54	0.07	n.s.	7	maj	−0.41	0.18	n.s.
	min	0.15	0.64	n.s.		min	0.68	0.01	*
2	maj	0.63	0.03	*	8	maj	0.37	0.23	n.s.
	min	0.85	0.00	***		min	−0.13	0.68	n.s.
3	maj	−0.34	0.28	n.s.	9	maj	0.81	0.00	**
	min	−0.60	0.04	*		min	0.34	0.28	n.s.
4	maj	0.86	0.00	***	10	maj	−0.48	0.11	n.s.
	min	0.80	0.00	**		min	−0.35	0.26	n.s.
5	maj	−0.31	0.33	n.s.	11	maj	0.66	0.02	*
	min	−0.50	0.10	n.s.		min	0.49	0.10	n.s.

Note. cpc = chordal pitch class, type = triad type of chord, n.s. = not significant, * $p < .05$, ** $p < .01$, *** $p < .001$, all df = 10.

implicit chord substitutions. Moreover, modal pieces, such as "So What" or "Impressions", which have very slow-varying chords sequences (or modes, for that matter) are typically written using common chords (e. g., Dmin^7 / D dorian, cf. Pfleiderer, Frieler, & Zaddach, 2016).

These interesting first observations merit further examination in more detailed studies. Clearly, these results already demonstrate the power of having high-quality automated transcription algorithms at hand.

Solos: Case studies

Don Byas's "Body and Soul"

Martin Pfleiderer

Coleman Hawkins's solo on "Body and Soul" is generally viewed as a milestone in the history of jazz improvisation (see, e. g., Schuller, 1989, pp. 441-445; Porter et al., 1993, pp. 173-175; DeVeaux, 1997, pp. 98-110). Coleman Hawkins recorded "Body and Soul" in October 1939 and the recording unexpectedly sold over 100 000 copies in the first six months after its release (DeVeaux, 1997, p. 99). In these times, this was a remarkable success for a jazz recording with no singer and no big band—all the more so as Hawkins does not play the melody but just improvises two choruses, accompanied by a rhythm section and, during the second chorus, by some horn chords. With "Body and Soul", Hawkins proved that improvisation is the central artistic achievement of jazz—given that sound recordings could transform elusive improvisations into a lasting art form (cf. DeVeaux, 1997, p. 11). With this recording, the "father of the jazz tenor saxophone" (Porter et al., 1993, p. 62) influenced subsequent musicians in their focus on improvisation and, in particular, tenor saxophonists in their improvisations over "Body and Soul" (cf. Bowen, 2011, pp. 23ff.; Pfleiderer, 2011). This chapter is dedicated to one of those follow-up improvisations over "Body and Soul" recorded in January 1947 by the tenor saxophonist Don Byas and to a comparison with Hawkins's seminal improvisation.

Don Byas—a side figure in jazz history

Today, Don Byas is far less well-known than Hawkins, but nevertheless a widely acknowledged master of the jazz tenor saxophone. He was born in 1912 as Carlos Wesley in Muskogee, a little town in Oklahoma, and started playing in local swing bands at the age of 17. During his college years (1931-32, at Langston College, Oklahoma), he led a band called Don Carlos and

His Collegiate Ramblers. After a four-year stay in Los Angeles, Byas moved to New York in 1937 where he started to work with several swing bands, e. g., those of Don Redman, Lucky Millinder, Andy Kirk, Edgar Hayes, and Benny Carter, and recorded with Billie Holiday. In early 1941, Byas was chosen by Count Basie to be Lester Young's successor in his big band; he recorded with Basie's big band and small groups, and started to play at clubs on 52nd Street. Moreover, Byas recorded with Coleman Hawkins, Charlie Parker, and Dizzy Gillespie as well as for several Hollywood films. Like Coleman Hawkins, Don Byas participated in bebop jam sessions right from its beginnings in the early 1940s. In 1941, a jam session at Minton's Playhouse was recorded by Jerry Newman, featuring Byas with the Minton's 'house band', including Joe Guy on trumpet, Thelonious Monk on piano, and Kenny Clarke on drums. They played, among other songs, "Body and Soul"; later, parts of the session were issued on a vinyl album called *Midnight at Minton's* under the name of Don Byas. In February 1944, Don Byas participated in one of the first bebop studio recordings which was made with a twelve-man group led by Coleman Hawkins including, among others, bebop pioneers Dizzy Gillespie, Oscar Pettiford, and Max Roach.

In September 1946, Don Byas went to Europe—following the example of Hawkins, who lived in Europe from 1934 until 1939. At first, Byas toured with Don Redman's big band in Denmark, Belgium, Switzerland, and Germany. Then, he settled in France and in the early 1950s moved to the Netherlands where he lived until his death in 1972. During his residence in Europe, Byas had only loose connections to the US jazz scene. Although he played and sometimes recorded with US jazz musicians such as Dizzy Gillespie, Mary Lou Williams, Bud Powell, or Ben Webster, Byas mostly worked and recorded with European musicians.

Presumably, his absence from the United States is the main reason why Byas is a rather underrated figure in jazz history. Nevertheless, he has been highly praised by musicians and connoisseurs. As an example, saxophonist and composer Leo T. Sullivan writes on an internet website dedicated to Don Byas:

> Byas was a masterful swing player with his own style, an advanced sense of harmony, and a confidence that was unmistakably his own, immediately recognizable. His sense of drama coupled with a brilliant use of dynamics and timbre, a deeply-felt romanticism—accomplished both the tenderest warmth and the most strident sting. He never picked up the rhythmic phrases, the lightning triplets, that are indigenous to bop. Yet Charlie

> Parker said of him that Byas was playing everything there was to play.
>
> One of the greatest of all tenor players, Don Byas' decision to move permanently to Europe in 1946 resulted in him being vastly underrated in jazz history books. His knowledge of chords rivaled Coleman Hawkins, and, due to their similarity in tones, Byas can be considered an extension of the elder tenor. (Sullivan, n.d.)

Despite such enthusiastic assessments, there is almost no analytical research on Byas's style of improvisation. For example, Thomas Owens's stylistic account of countless modern jazz musicians dedicates only one paragraph to Byas, focusing on his relation to bebop playing (Owens, 1995, p. 72).

In January 1947, one year after his arrival in France, Byas recorded "Body and Soul" with Billy Taylor, piano, Jean Bouchety, double bass, and Buford Oliver, drums. The following analytical case study is an attempt to appreciate several characteristics of this improvisation. First, several techniques of improvisation will be exemplified by analyzing parts of the solo. Then, a comparison between the solos of Byas and Hawkins will investigate commonalities and differences between their styles of improvisation.

Don Byas's "Body and Soul" (1947)

The formal structure of Byas's "Body and Soul" is clearly modeled after Hawkins's 1939 version. The recording starts with a four-measure introduction, passes through two improvised choruses, and ends with a rubato cadenza. In contrast to Hawkins, however, Byas returns to paraphrasing the melody in the last A section of the second chorus. When listening to Don Byas improvising two choruses on "Body and Soul", I am in particular impressed by both his warm and intimate tenor sound and his elegant and highly ornamented melodic lines. His articulation of each tone of these lines is pin-sharp, like a pearl on a string, and he plays with an amazing rhythmic variability, including several moments of brief hesitation and laid back phrases. After paraphrasing and commenting on the original melody in the first A section, he departs from the melodic template with sophisticated lines, which flow up and down the whole range of the tenor saxophone. Additionally, there are clear melodic statements that are accentuated both by sequencing certain motifs as well as by retarding certain tones and playing them louder at the same time. One climax of the solo, at least in regard to instrumental virtuosity, consists of several lines shortly after the beginning of the second chorus (mm. 38–40), which flow up and down with both astonishing velocity and precise articulation. Another climax is in the last B section (mm. 52 and 53), where Byas jumps two times to the top of the saxophone range, first to D5 and then to G5.

In the following, I will give examples for several creative strategies employed in Byas's solo. The music examples are based on the transcription included in the Weimar Jazz Database. The score has been re-worked in several respects in order to make it easier to read. In regard to rhythm, the original transcription strictly follows the position of the tones in relation to a constantly tapped metric framework. Since Byas tends to play some tones or whole phrases deliberately behind the beat, however, there are many odd note values and note shifts with many slurs over metric positions. In most of the music examples below I prefer a simplified and more readable notation where these rhythmic shifts are marked by 'laid back' above certain notes and phrases. Moreover, several rests which were omitted by the conversion algorithm are added as well as a few tones which seemingly went unnoticed by the human transcriber. Some accidentals are adjusted to the harmonic framework. The rubato cadenza at the end is ignored both for transcription and analysis. Since it is not known which chords Byas actually had in mind while improvising his version of "Body and Soul", the annotated chords follow a more sophisticated jazz re-harmonization of "Body and Soul" in the key of D♭ major, which is included in the Weimar Jazz Database transcription too, rather than the simple chord progressions in C as originally composed by Johnny Green (Krieger, 1995, pp. 20f.).

Melodic strategies for improvisation

Following proposals by André Hodeir and Gunther Schuller, jazz scholar Barry Kernfeld categorizes three types of jazz improvisation which may occur within a certain solo (Kernfeld, 1995, pp. 119-158). While in paraphrase improvisation there is a close reference to the original melody of a piece, in so-called chorus phrase or formulaic improvisation musicians invent new lines that fit to the harmonies of the original composition. Often, this strategy relies on a vocabulary of melodic building blocks, patterns or formulas. In motivic improvisation, the musicians vary one or several motifs, sometimes taken from the theme of a piece but more often drawn from the ongoing stream of improvisational ideas. All three strategies for improvisation can be found in Byas's solo on "Body and Soul".

Byas starts and ends his solo with a paraphrasing of the original melody (first A section and last A section). An immediate comparison with the original

Don Byas's "Body and Soul" 137

Figure 1: Original melody of "Body and Soul" (in Db major) and Byas's improvisation in the first and last A section.

melody (see Figure 1) reveals many of Byas's techniques of paraphrasing, ornamenting and varying the melody as well as some general features of his style of improvising. In a few cases, he keeps playing the longer and metrically important tones of the original melody, e. g., the F at beat one of m. 6 (both sections), but more often he does not place the melody tone but a tone from the underlying chord on beat one, e. g., at mm. 3 and 5 (both sections), and then plays the melody a bit later and in a varied and rhythmically condensed manner, such as in mm. 1, 3, 4, and 5. In between the individual parts of this melodic skeleton, he often adds ornamenting phrases within the second half of a measure, such as in mm. 2, 6, and 8 of the first section or mm. 2, 3, 5, and 6 of the last section. As another strategy of ornamentation he plays short

Figure 2: Don Byas "Body and Soul", second A section.

figurations before a goal tone, e. g., E and F (end of m. 4) before E♭ (m. 5) or D♭ and E♭ (end of m. 5) before F (m. 6) in the first section. Several times Byas emphasizes certain tones by retarding them. Interestingly, all the clearly laid back tones in the first section A (see mm. 3, 4 and 7) also stand out as the highest tones within the melodic contour. In m. 7, he repeats a four-tone motif one semitone lower. This technique of sequencing is employed by Byas regularly throughout the solo and contributes to the motivic coherence of his improvisation.

In the second A section (see Figure 2), Byas departs from paraphrasing the original melody by playing the ascending E♭ minor scale. Now, a chorus phrase improvisation in the sense of Kernfeld starts. Byas switches from the pulse in the first eight measures, which is mainly based on eighth triplets, to a sixteenth note pulse. However, he continues to employ strategies of figuration (see, e. g., B and A at the end of m. 9 leading to B♭ in m. 10) and of sequencing by repeating motivic cells a semitone lower, e. g., in m. 12, where a line upwards is twice followed by a jump down (the third time in m. 13 by a line down). In m. 15, he repeats a four-tone figure, with a jump up a sixth, a semitone lower. Therefore, chorus phrase improvisation is closely intertwined with motivic improvisation.

Another strategy of Byas to generate melodic coherence seems to be the usage of an open system of melodic patterns. His pattern vocabulary encompasses both melodic lines which have a certain salience and recognition value and more amorphous melodic building blocks that mostly pass unnoticed for the listener. MeloSpyGUI offers a comfortable functionality to search for various kinds of these building blocks or patterns. In general, patterns are defined as certain sequences of elements (pitches, intervals, etc.) which are repeated at least a second time within one solo or within a set of several solos. Although these patterns are often part of longer lines, their double or multiple occurrences indicate that they are characteristic for a solo—or, if occurring in other solos too, for Byas's overall personal melodic vocabulary.

Within his improvisation on "Body and Soul", Byas repeats several long pitch patterns (see Figure 3). The longest pattern is part of the paraphrasing in the first A section, containing twelve tones played in m. 6 and then repeated in the last section over the same chord in mm. 61 and 62 (Figure 3a). Both melodies start on beat one with an ascending E♭ minor seventh arpeggio and sound similar despite their slightly different rhythms. The second long pattern, consisting of ten tones, is played in m. 26 and repeated closely in m. 29 (Figure 3b). Both patterns start on different metric points and are part of longer lines, which continue differently.

Furthermore, there are three pitch patterns containing seven tones (e. g., in mm. 30 and 62, see Figure 3c), five patterns with six tones, and twelve patterns with five tones. While most of the patterns occur only two times, two of the five-tone patterns appear three times at different positions within the solo. The coverage with patterns of five or more tones within the whole solo is almost 27.6 % (disregarding overlapping patterns). If one looks at patterns of four or more pitches, the percentage rises to more than 50 % and to about 80 % if one disregards absolute pitch and instead allows for patterns of three identical intervals. Of course, these patterns encompass chord arpeggios and simple scale sections, too. Nevertheless, the repeated use of such building blocks may contribute to an overall impression of melodic coherence.

Comparison: Coleman Hawkins and Don Byas

In his performance history of "Body and Soul", José Antonio Bowen states that jazz musicians in general learn tunes as performed by other musicians—and not by studying the original score (Bowen, 2011, p. 25). Most likely, Byas was familiar with the famous recording by Hawkins from 1939. At least in regard to form, Byas widely modeled his recording after Hawkins's.

Figure 3: Several melodic patterns (marked by brackets), which are played at different positions of "Body and Soul" by Don Byas.

Beside other examples, Bowen points at two motivic allusions several jazz musicians have made to the Hawkins recording of "Body and Soul": the upbeat three-tone repetition of the first melody tone (E♭) and the alternation of the second E♭ by a G♭ (Bowen, 2011). While Byas chooses other tones at the beginning of his solo, he plays an upbeat too, and emphasizes the G♭by playing it, not as Hawkins does on an offbeat, but prominently on beat four (see Figure 1).

There are several further parallels between the two solos. First of all, the climax of Byas's solo in mm. 53–54 recalls the climax at the end of Hawkins's solo (mm. 58–59, see Figure 4). There, Hawkins plays a sequence of three motifs, each consisting of three upwards interval jumps to a high tone which result in an ascending guide tone line E♭5–E5–F5 at the top of the tenor range. The climax of Byas's solo encompasses only two salient tones at the top, D5 and G5, which are embedded in flowing lines. However, those two tones are approached by big upward jumps of an octave and a seventh respectively. While differing in detail, the climaxes of both solos follow the same strategy of accentuating high tones, which are highlighted by exceptionally large interval jumps.

Figure 4: Top: Don Byas "Body and Soul", mm. 53–54; bottom: Coleman Hawkins "Body and Soul", mm. 58–59.

Additionally, there are some striking examples concerning the usage of identical patterns. There are 34 identical interval patterns consisting of five tones and another twelve patterns consisting of six to eight tones which are played at least once by both players in their improvisations on "Body and Soul". While some of these patterns, including chord arpeggios and scale extracts which are part of a common vocabulary of jazz patterns of these times, others are more specific to the styles of both Hawkins and Byas. Figure 5 shows two examples of such specific patterns, which Byas and Hawkins both played in the course of their solos on "Body and Soul". While the first pattern (a), an ascending diminished chord followed by a descending augmented triad, is played by both musicians over the same chords and at the same metrical position, the second pattern (b) is played with a different rhythm and a whole tone apart. Notably, these patterns only appear in these two solos and are not picked up within other solos transcribed in the Weimar Jazz Database. Therefore, it seems to be probable that Byas deliberately or unconsciously borrowed these patterns from Hawkins's "Body and Soul" recording.

Parallels in regard to the usage of particular motifs and patterns aside, it is not an easy task to compare two improvisations. In the following, I shall choose a comparative perspective of a 'distant listening' of the two solos, mainly with statistical values and distributions. Although in a slightly faster tempo (99 bpm versus 95 bpm), Byas plays more tones than Hawkins, resulting in a higher event density. Even if one disregards the final cadenza of Byas as well as a few short tones (which were both omitted in the transcription), his solo includes 723 tones while Hawkins's solo includes only 635 tones. The resulting event density of Hawkins's solo is lower (3.79 tones per second or

Figure 5: Two examples of patterns used by both Byas (1st and 3rd line) and Hawkins (2nd and 4th line) in their solos on "Body and Soul".

9.57 tones per measure) in comparison to Byas (4.65 and 11.2 tones, resp.). However, the rate of syncopicity (40 and 39, resp., of all tones) the overall ambitus (two and a half octave) are rather similar for both solos. Rather subtle differences between the two solos are revealed if one examines the choices of pitches and intervals as well as of melodic contour and metric placement. In regard to harmony, both Hawkins and Byas clearly prefer the constituting intervals of a chord, i. e., the fifth, the root and the third, followed by the seventh (see Figure 6). This mirrors the orientation of both musicians towards chords and vertical playing.

However, more than 20 % of all tones fall outside the scales prescribed by the chords. This indicates both a high degree of harmonic flexibility with regard to the chord changes, including different kinds of chord substitutions, and a high degree of chromatic figuration and ornamentation employed by the two musicians. They both play many non-diatonic tones, however these dissonances quickly find their resolution, as Scott DeVeaux put it in regard to Hawkins (DeVeaux, 1997, p. 97) and as can be seen in Byas's solo, too.

Apparently, both musicians employ the technique of tritone substitution for the Ab^7 chord in the second measure of the A section as well as a substitution by one of the whole-tone scales (cf. DeVeaux, 1997, pp. 104-107). In three cases, m. 2 of the first and second A sections and m. 6 of the first A section,

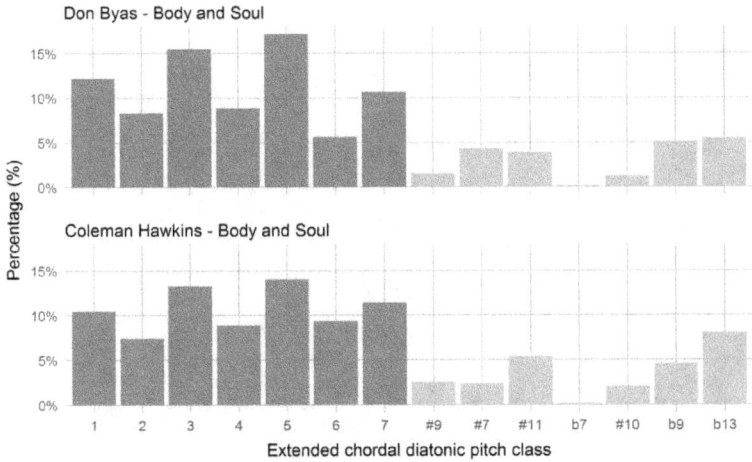

Figure 6: Percentage of both diatonic pitch classes (1 to 7) and non-diatonic pitch classes in relation to the underlying chord root within the solos of Hawkins and Byas.

Byas plays phrases based on a whole-tone scale—which, of course, fits both to the $A\flat^7$ and D^7 chord. Coleman Hawkins has employed this strategy widely, although this device has already been used before, e. g., by Benny Goodman (DeVeaux, 1997, p. 107ff.).

There are many commonalities but also some striking differences between the two musicians concerning the usage of intervals (Figure 7). Hawkins plays more tone repetitions than Byas and almost twice as many falling minor thirds. In contrast, Byas prefers descending minor and major seconds, which is much more typical for musicians of modern jazz. By contrast, the distribution of contours of melodic phrases are similar in both solos and dominated by descending contours, followed by convex, concave and ascending contours (Figure 8).

In regard to the metric positions where Byas and Hawkins place their tones, there is a broad variation in general. Judging from the metrical map (Figure 9), tones on the eighth offbeat level occur almost as frequently as tones on beats. Therefore, an overall eighth pulse dominates the solo while a sixteenth pulse is clearly discernible, too. However, this sixteenth pulse is blurred by additional eighth triplets and sixteenth triplets that lie near the second and fourth sixteenth of each beat. However, there are slight differences betweenn Byas's and Hawkins's solo, too. For example, while Hawkins plays tones on all beat positions more often than on eighth or sixteenth positions, Byas plays on the

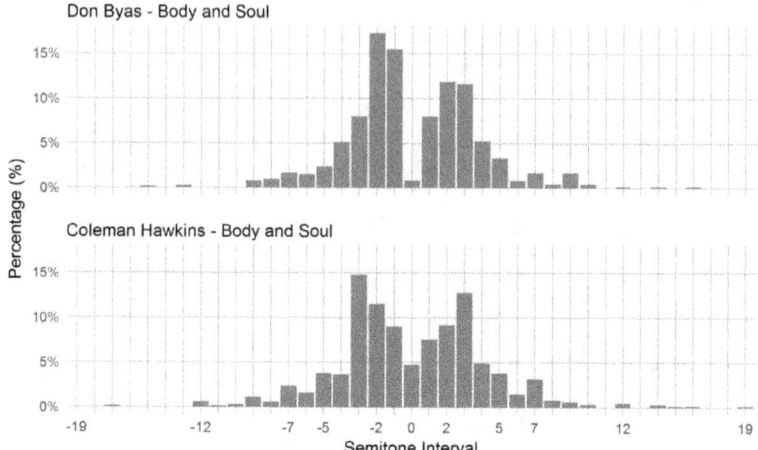

Figure 7: Percentage of intervals within the two solos.

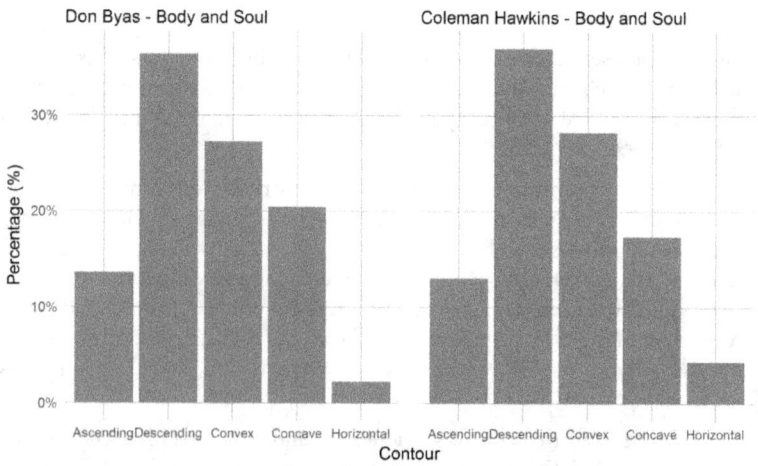

Figure 8: Percentage of five melodic contour types in regard to all phrases within the two solos.

eighths between the beats more often than on beats 2 and 3. Nevertheless, syncopations, i. e., tones played on a metric subdivision without a tone on the following beat, occur rather frequently in the improvisations of both

Don Byas's "Body and Soul"

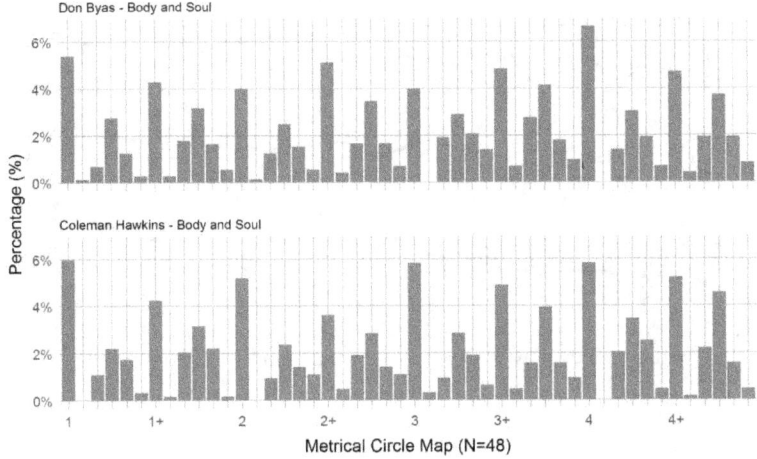

Figure 9: Metrical Circle Map of Don Byas's solo on "Body and Soul" (top) and Hawkins's solo on "Body and Soul" (bottom). Each tone is assigned to the closest of 48 equidistant time points within a bar.

musicians: 39 % of all tones are syncopations, however, including those tones within passages that are generally played behind the beat or 'laid back'.

Comparison of overall dramaturgy

In his analysis on Hawkins's solo on "Body and Soul" Schuller writes of a "seamless inner unity" and that Hawkins "steadily builds up his solo to an anguished climax fifty-seven measures later, using the various compositional and articulative elements at his command to shape and guide the line of progression" (Schuller, 1989, p. 441). As Schuller puts it, this progression encompasses the expansion of pitch range, the rhythmic intensification from eighth triplets to sixteenth triplets as well as the usage of dynamics and sonority, developing from a "warm friendly sound" at the beginning to "an ever keener edge" and "almost strident bursts of sound" at the climax (Schuller, 1989, p. 444). He illustrates this progress of intensification in regard to pitch range, rhythm and dynamics with graphic representations (Figure 10). However, it is neither clear what exactly Schuller depicts in these graphs nor how he arrived at his slightly ascending wavy lines. In the following, I shall attempt to reconstruct the three graphs by statistical means in order to compare the overall dramaturgy of the solos by Byas and Hawkins.

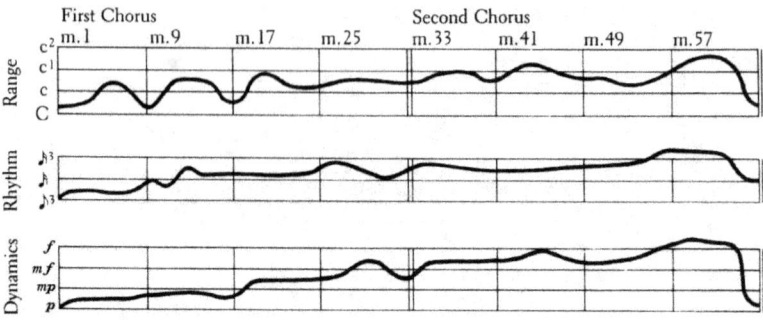

Figure 10: Progression of Coleman Hawkins's "Body and Soul" in regard to pitch range, rhythm and dynamics. Graphic representation by Gunther Schuller (1989, p. 444).

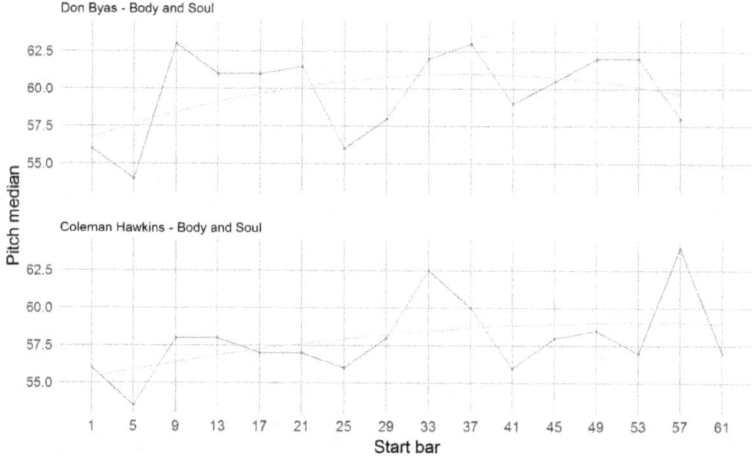

Figure 11: Median pitches over successive four-measure groups over the course of both solos.

Obviously, the first of Schuller's graphs describes not the course of all pitches but an overall tendency of pitch range in the course of the solo. Since the median is a statistical measure for the central tendency of a distribution, the median pitches in regard to successive four-measure units of both solos are depicted in Figure 11, ranging from F2 (MIDI pitch 53) to E3 (MIDI pitch 64). There are striking differences to the graph "range" of Schuller. For Hawkins's

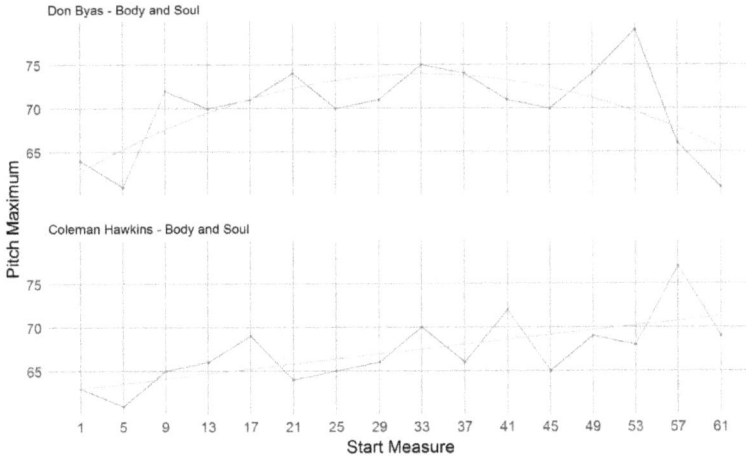

Figure 12: Highest pitches over successive four-measure groups over the course of both solos.

solo, the curve shows two peaks (mm. 33–36 and mm. 57–60). Byas in general plays tones with higher pitches, despite a low beginning and a trough at the third A section (mm. 25ff.).

Following the intuitive assumption that the highest pitches may have the strongest impact on the overall impression of pitch height or range, the highest pitches in successive four-measure groups are depicted for both solos in Figure 12. Now the continuously ascending tendency within both solos becomes apparent by the zigzagged upward lines, notwithstanding the fact that Byas moves down during his reprise of the theme in the last eight measures of his improvisation.

It is not easy to reconstruct what exactly Schuller depicts in his graph titled "rhythm". Both solos show a rather large variety of rhythmic values with a clear dominance, however, of an eighth and sixteenth note pulse during most passages of the solo. This finding is affirmed by the metrical maps of the two solos (Figure 9) that depicts the occurrence of tone onsets in regard to a fine metric grid. Unfortunately, examining the metrical maps for successive groups of four and eight measures did not result in a more detailed graph concerning a tendency towards a shift of metric pulse. However, looking at the overall event density in regard to successive four-measure groups (Figure 13) brings to light that the total amount of tones played by Hawkins remains the same overall: On average, Hawkins plays four tones per second. Therefore, Schuller's

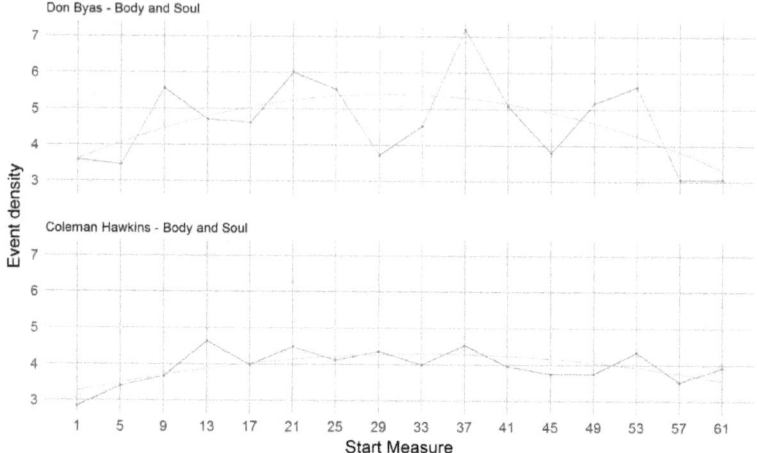

Figure 13: Amount of tones per second averaged in regard to successive four-tone groups for both solos.

impression of an increasing tendency in regard to rhythm or metric pulse could not be confirmed. However, the graph for Byas's improvisation clearly shows both a much higher variety of event densities and, at certain passages during his solo, a much higher density, extending up even to seven tones per beat averaged over four measures.

Last but not least, the median dynamics of all the tones played by Byas and Hawkins varies in the course of both the solos (see Figure 14). Both solos start on a relatively high level and, towards the end of the bridge or the start of the third A section (around m. 21 or 25), go down in regard to loudness. While in the case of Byas the dynamics vary around roughly the same level for the rest of the solo, Hawkins's solo shows a clear tendency towards rising dynamics until the start of the first half of the A section, which at the same time is the climax of his solo (cf. Figure 4).

Summary and outlook

In his solo on "Body and Soul" (1944), Byas combines several strategies of improvisation. He uses the strategies of ornamenting and sequencing within passages dedicated to both paraphrasing the theme and improvising over the harmonies. Moreover, both strategies are intertwined with passages of

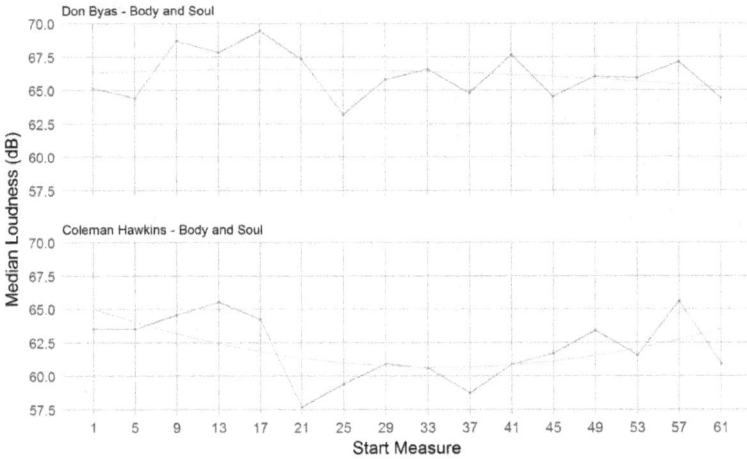

Figure 14: Median loudness of tones in regard to successive four-tone groups for both solos. The loudness of each tone is extracted automatically by a method described in section p. 109.

motivic variation. In the case of Byas, therefore, Kernfeld's categorization of three distinct types of improvisation (paraphrase, chorus phrase and motivic improvisation) would appear to be a rather simplifying analytical heuristics. Besides an evident motivic approach to improvisation there is an astonishing variety of pitch and interval patterns, which Byas plays two or more times within the course of two choruses. Moreover, many of these patterns are shared by Byas and Hawkins in their versions of "Body and Soul". Further studies will be required to reveal commonalities and differences between their usage of musical building blocks and patterns—in regard to the improvisations over certain chord changes as well as in regard to personal style.

Don Byas modeled his recording of "Body and Soul" in 1944 after Hawkins's seminal recording made five years earlier. He was familiar with Hawkins's improvisation on "Body and Soul" as well as Hawkins's style of improvisation. Since jazz improvisation is an open-ended process of giving and taking playing ideas and musical patterns, it is not surprising that there are several parallels between the two improvisations. However, there are differences, too, e. g., in regard to overall event density or preference for intervals. Byas seems to play even more virtuosic and with a higher variety concerning several musical dimensions. In regard to solo dramaturgy, Hawkins seems to focus more on an intensifying process while Byas follows a more arch-like process with much more variety in between. However, the impression of an overall intensification during the course of Hawkins's solo, which has been formulated and visualized by Gunther Schuller, arises not so much from a continuing overall tendency concerning metric subdivision, pitch range or an averaged mean pitch, but seemingly from a tendency concerning the highest pitches in the course of the solo as well as dynamics within the second half of the solo only. This demonstrates that the task of unambiguously relating overall listening impressions to certain musical dimensions is not as easy as it seems at first glance. A statistical exploration of musical features can contribute to this analytical task.

Mellow Miles?
On the dramaturgy of Miles Davis's "Airegin"

Benjamin Burkhart

Miles Davis is generally acknowledged to be one of the most flamboyant figures in the history of jazz. Davis is one of the canonical artists of jazz—besides Louis Armstrong, Charlie Parker, Dizzy Gillespie, or John Coltrane—whose influence is believed to be essential for following generations of musicians. Hence, it is hardly surprising that a number of researchers have already investigated multiple aspects of the musical work of Miles Davis. For instance, various authors have concentrated on the recordings of the late 1950s (Barrett, 2006)—quite often with a focus on modal compositions and improvisations—, the ensemble recordings of the 1960s (Meyers, 2015; Waters, 2011), or on fusions with musical styles other than jazz during the late 1960s (Grella, 2015; Svorinich, 2015), to collaborations with pop or rap music artists in the 1970s and 1980s (Cole, 2006; Tingen, 2001). On the other hand, relatively little attention has been paid to Miles Davis's early recordings and early improvisational style (Kerschbaumer, 1978; Owens, 1995, pp. 113ff.; Sagee, 2003). Using the solo on "Airegin" (1954) as an example, this chapter's objective is to analyze aspects of Davis's personal style in the first half of the 1950s—that is to say, in a relatively early stage of his career. Since Miles Davis is well known for his highly thought-out improvisational style, the solo's general dramaturgy as well as the motivic development will be central focal points of the analysis.

The (early) improvisational style of Miles Davis

Compared with the virtuoso playing of his contemporaries and mentors Charlie Parker or Dizzy Gillespie, Miles Davis's early improvisational style in the late 1940s and early 1950s has often been described as 'reductive' or 'calm' (Kerschbaumer, 1971, p. 226; Wilson, 2001, p. 39). Nevertheless, there were elements of bebop-like lines and a focus on vertical—that is, chordal rather than melodic (horizontal)—playing in his recordings even in the mid-1950s (Sagee, 2003, p. 27). But as prior analytical work has also shown, certain solos in the late 1940s demonstrate that Davis's personal style in this early stage of his career deviated clearly from the fast and virtuoso playing of other bebop trumpeters such as Dizzy Gillespie, Fats Navarro, or the early Kenny Dorham. In his analysis of the solo on "Israel" (*Birth of the Cool*) from April 1949, Peter Niklas Wilson characterizes Davis's style as rhythmically simple, dynamically regular, and reductive—according to Wilson, there are no extravagant or dramatic effects with regard to musical features such as rhythmic diversity or pitch range (Wilson, 2001, pp. 61ff.). In a further examination of the characteristics of Miles Davis's personal style, especially in the 1950s, Wilson speaks of an "aesthetics of reduction" ("Ästhetik der Reduktion", Wilson, 2001, p. 43) or of a "combination of simplicity and sophistication" ("Verbindung von Simplizität und Raffinesse", Wilson, 2001, p. 226). This deliberate kind of melodic and thought-out improvisation, rather than virtuoso playing, was further developed during the 1950s. According to John Szwed, the "effect is one of hearing him think, with the audible thought process itself becoming part of the music" (cited from Sagee, 2003, p. 27). Meanwhile, Davis's style of improvisation has even been described with the aid of quantitative methods: a comparison between solos by Miles Davis, John Coltrane, and Cannonball Adderley on "So What" (1959) has shown that both saxophonists roughly play twice as many tones as Davis does (Frieler et al., 2016a, p. 5).

This leads to another central stylistic component of Miles Davis's recordings during the (late) 1950s—the modal compositions and improvisations. In modal compositions, scales or modes but not chords form the basis for improvisation. This new approach to jazz improvisation was established by the Miles Davis Sextet with the seminal recording *Kind of Blue* (1959), which contains the modal compositions "So What" and "Flamenco Sketches". But it is generally acknowledged that Davis had already experimented with modal compositions at least one year earlier—the piece "Milestones" (1958) is assumed to be the first modal tune in jazz history (Kerschbaumer, 1978, p. 90; Sagee, 2003, p. 30). What makes Davis's modal approach interesting in the context of this chapter is the way he himself describes the prospects and benefits of improvising modally. In his autobiography, Miles Davis states:

> The challenge here, when you work in the modal way, is to see how inventive you can become melodically. It's not like when you base stuff on chords, and you know at the end of the thirty-

two bars that the chords have run out and there's nothing to do but repeat what you've done with variations. I was moving away from that and into more melodic ways of doing things. And in the modal way I saw all kinds of possibilities (cited from Sagee, 2003, p. 30).

That is to say, for Davis himself, the focus on melodic (horizontal)—and explicitly not chordal (vertical)—improvisation and on melodic inventiveness was one key argument in favor of modal playing. As mentioned before, the melodic style is already apparent in certain recordings of the late 1940s. Moreover, prior research has highlighted Miles Davis's ability to develop motivic ideas over the entire duration of a single solo. Davis often introduced melodic ideas which he further developed and varied in different stages of the improvisational process—a technique he especially differentiated during the 1950s (Kerschbaumer, 1978, p. 80).

To sum up: The focus on melodic improvisation can be described as one key feature of many solos recorded by Miles Davis. Additionally, expanding the possibilities for melodic inventiveness during the improvisational process was described as one central motivation for the development of modal playing by Davis himself. Still, his focus on motivic, thought-out improvisation was already apparent several years before *Kind of Blue* (Wilson, 2001, pp. 61ff.). In the following, several features and elements within Davis's improvisation on "Airegin" will be systematically described and compared with improvisations by other bebop trumpeters.

Listening and describing

Composed by saxophonist Sonny Rollins, "Airegin" was recorded on June 29th 1954 and first released on the LP *Miles Davis with Sonny Rollins* (1954). The line-up consisted of Miles Davis (tp), Sonny Rollins (ts), Horace Silver (p), Percy Heath (b), and Kenny Clarke (dr). The key is A♭-maj and the average tempo is 241 bpm. Miles Davis plays three choruses and the solo has a duration of approximately 1:50 min. The analysis starts with a description of my own impressions when listening to Miles Davis's solo on "Airegin". The tempo is quite high, but this is, of course, not unusual in the context of jazz. In fact, there are several lines of fast eighth notes in the solo that could also be described as typical for the style of other bebop trumpeters, too, but they certainly do not dominate the structure of the solo. On the contrary, these lines are mixed with passages that sound more melodic or even cantabile, or with rather rhythmic passages. In general, there seems to be no real climax in the solo: The improvisation sounds calm and there are

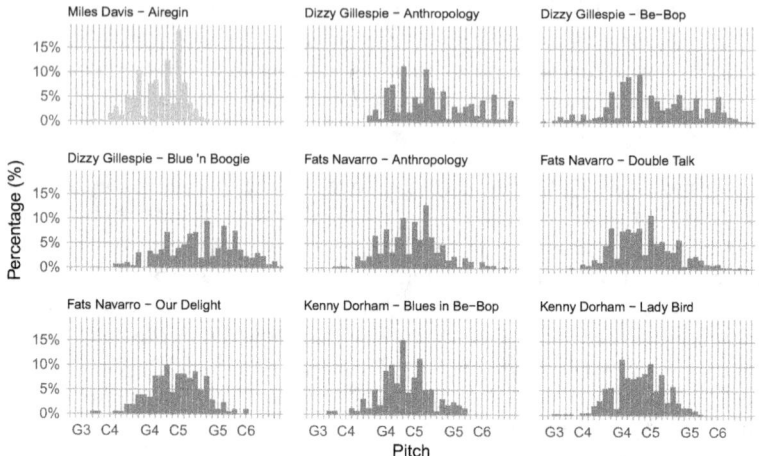

Figure 1: Pitch distributions in "Airegin" and selected bebop trumpet solos.

few elements that imply an increase in musical expressiveness. By contrast, the improvisation is structured quite homogeneously and there are no expressive 'outliers'. This rather rough description confirms the findings of the authors cited: rather than playing several fast and virtuoso lines, Davis seems to concentrate instead on the homogeneity of the improvisation and on melodic inventiveness.

Basic computational analysis

In a second step, one has to transfer these rather vague overall impressions into definite musical features that can be verified by examining the solo. For example, as the degree of expressiveness appears to be relatively low, the pitch range of the solo might also be rather low. While examining the regularity of the improvisation, the interval structure might also be of interest. Additionally, as the solo, from time to time, sounds quite cantabile, it can be assumed that Davis improvises fairly harmonically and without many dissonances; this could be explored by using the features for chordal pitch class analysis. Furthermore, the rhythm might be quite regular as well, which can be analyzed by using the features for rhythmic analysis or by examining the durations of tone events. First of all, in Figure 1 the pitch distribution of Davis's solo on "Airegin" can be seen.

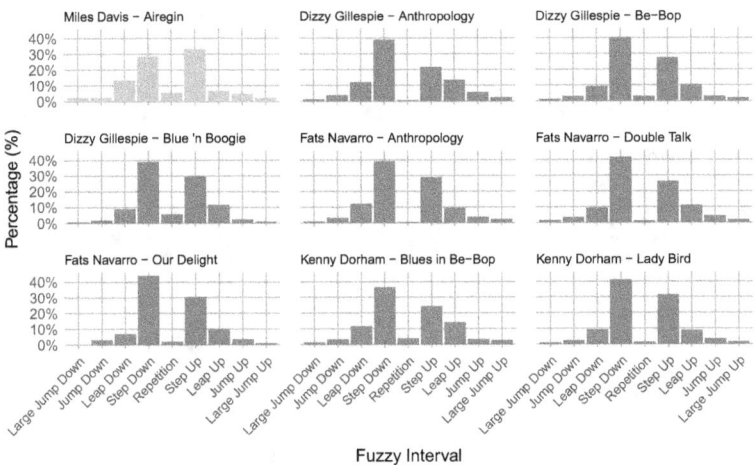

Figure 2: Fuzzy interval distributions in "Airegin" and selected bebop trumpet solos.

The histogram shows that the pitch range is nearly two octaves, from A3 to A♭5—that is to say, it is comparatively small and Davis avoids extremely high or low tones. Moreover, he obviously concentrates on the pitches between, approximately, E♭4 and D5, which means that the greater part of the tones played is within roughly one octave. Regarding the pitch range and pitch distribution, the solo seems to be quite restrained. This is strengthened when we compare "Airegin" with solos by other bebop trumpeters played in similar tempi: In this case, solos by Dizzy Gillespie ("Anthropology", 1946; "Be-Bop", 1945; "Blue 'n Boogie", 1945), Fats Navarro ("Anthropology", 1948; "Double Talk", 1948; "Our Delight" (1948), and Kenny Dorham ("Blues in Be-Bop", 1946; "Lady Bird", 1955) were chosen.

Concerning the pitch range, the solos by Dizzy Gillespie in particular differ clearly from Miles Davis's improvisation on "Airegin". In "Be-Bop", the ambitus is over three octaves and Gillespie frequently plays high notes up to D♭6, besides several outliers ranging as high as G♭6. In the solos by Fats Navarro and particularly in those by Kenny Dorham, the differences are not comparably distinctive—nevertheless, they are obvious, since the pitch ranges are always larger than in the case of "Airegin". The homogeneity of Davis's improvisation can be explored further by analyzing the interval structure of the solo: Figure 2 shows rough categorizations of intervals, from 'large jump up/down' (seven semitones or more) to 'step up/down' (two or one semitones), and tone repetitions. Miles Davis focuses distinctly on interval

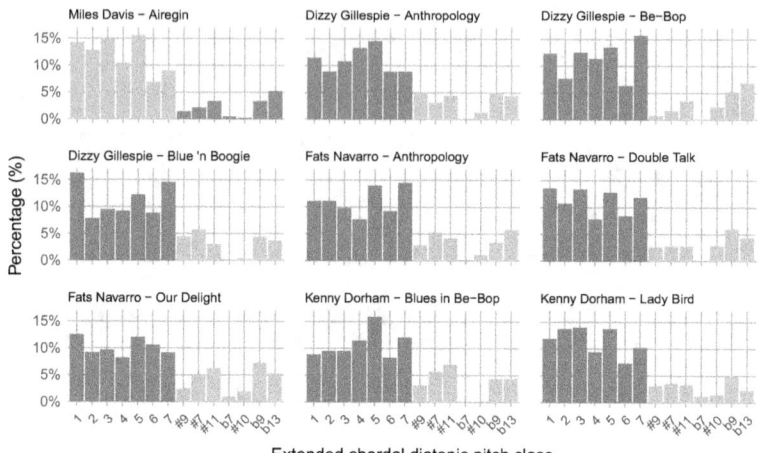

Figure 3: Extended chordal diatonic pitch class distribution in "Airegin" and selected bebop trumpet solos.

steps, mostly upwards but also often downwards, while almost completely avoiding (large) jumps. These results suggest an interval structure without any expressive outliers. The interval structures of the aforementioned solos played by Dizzy Gillespie, Fats Navarro, and Kenny Dorham are quite similar. One key difference concerns the direction of the interval steps: All the other trumpeters prefer steps downwards, while Davis focuses on steps upwards.

Figure 3 lists the pitch classes in relation to the underlying chord roots and chord types ('cdpcx' = chordal diatonic pitch class extended, see Chapter *Computational melody analysis*). The fifth is the pitch class played most often by Davis, followed by the third and the root. Pitch classes outside of the range of tones from root to seventh are played quite seldom, the highest value being approximately five percent (♭13). In comparison with the other solos, there are several small differences. A special emphasis on the third—as in "Airegin"—is only apparent in Fats Navarro's "Double Talk" and Kenny Dorham's "Lady Bird", whereas the other trumpeters show a slight tendency to play more chromatically than Miles Davis does. Furthermore, Dizzy Gillespie ("Be-Bop", "Blue 'n Boogie") and Fats Navarro ("Anthropology") clearly emphasize the seventh (Figure 3).

When listening to Davis's improvisation, it seems obvious that he combines several motivic and rhythmic features; relatively fast lines as well as short, rather melodic passages. Hence, it might be interesting to find out whether

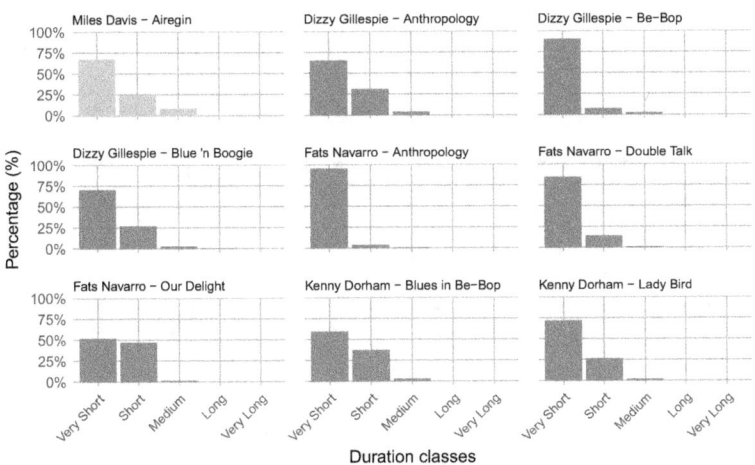

Figure 4: Duration classes in "Airegin" and selected bebop trumpet solos.

such combinations lead to high rhythmic flexibility. One option for exploring rhythmic tension is to analyze whether a soloist plays rather long or short tones, or a mixture of different elements. Figure 4 illustrates that Davis, for the most part, plays short tones relative to the tempo and very short tones in relation to 0.5 seconds (abs). The solo is clearly dominated by short tone events, which could be interpreted as another constitutive feature for the perceived homogeneity. In this respect, the other improvisations do not clearly differ from "Airegin".

In summary, these rather basic descriptions of the solo, based on the author's listening experience and the use of just a small sample of musical features, which were described statistically by using MeloSpyGUI, already provide an overview of the central structural details of Miles Davis's improvisation on "Airegin". It becomes obvious that the improvisation's overall structure lacks highly expressive tonal or rhythmic moments. These findings confirm the descriptions by the authors mentioned above.

One central point of interest for this chapter is the overall dramaturgy of the solo as well as its motivic development. Since the solo is for the most part played without highly expressive moments, it could be even more interesting to see how Davis organizes the improvisation on a higher structural level, or how he further develops and varies melodic ideas. For these reasons, the focus will now be on the analytical tools used to describe the temporal dramaturgy of Davis's improvisation on "Airegin".

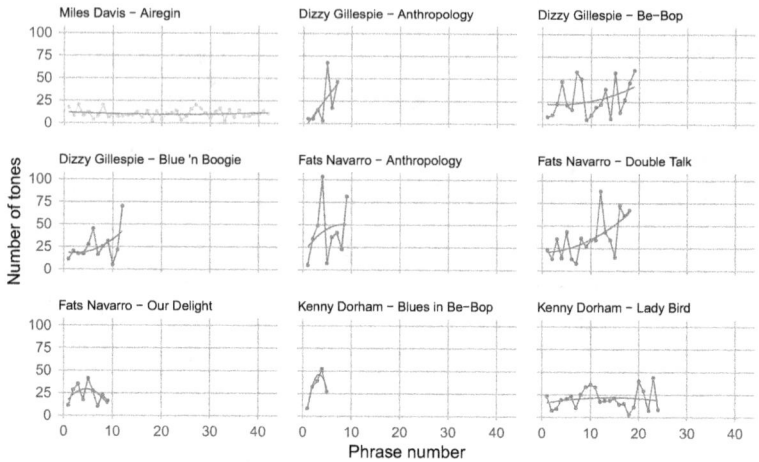

Figure 5: Number of tones over phrases in "Airegin" and selected bebop trumpet solos.

Interpreting the dramaturgy of "Airegin"

In the following, several aspects of the musical dramaturgy of Miles Davis's improvisation on "Airegin" will be analyzed. According to Frieler, Pfleiderer, Abeßer, & Zaddach, 2016b, p. 70, "[j]azz solos possess distinct curves of musical parameters that are commonly associated with arousal, tension and intensity and might follow certain trends of dramatic development as, for example, arched or concave curves". To analyze the dramaturgy of jazz improvisations, as the authors further argue, is to investigate the "internal logic" (Frieler et al., 2016b, p. 69) of a solo. Miles Davis is especially well known for his calm and thought-out improvisations that often lack a real climax in a dynamic or virtuoso sense—as is the case in the solo on "Airegin". For this reason, it seems particularly necessary to explore the overall dramaturgy of the solo. Other key questions are how the impression of calmness might be confirmed analytically and how the inner logic of the improvisation might be characterized. Frieler et al. (2016b, pp. 74f.) suggest twelve features for describing the musical dramaturgy of a jazz improvisation, which will, in part, also be considered in this chapter. For instance, the number of tones played, the pitch range, or the variance of intervals or tone durations (Frieler et al., 2016b) might be of interest.

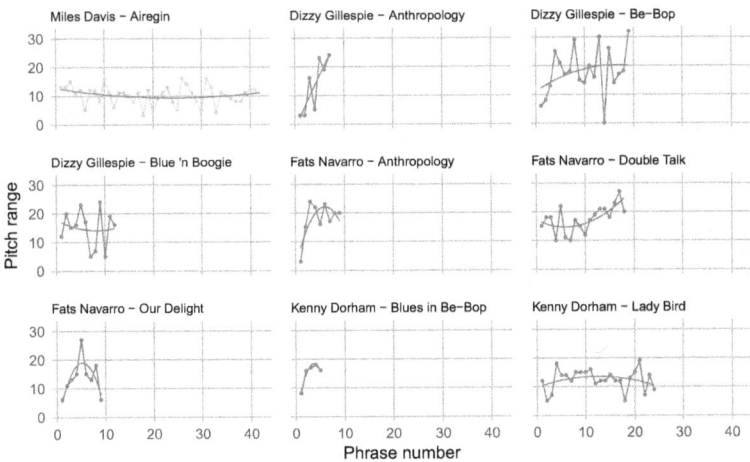

Figure 6: Pitch range over phrases in "Airegin" and selected bebop trumpet solos.

Phrases can be understood as rather short and meaningful units with a musical sense of their own. For each solo in the Weimar Jazz Database, such units were annotated manually during the transcription process. When exploring the musical dramaturgy and the inner logic of a solo, analyzing the succession of musical phrases might be quite helpful, since various musical characteristics may differ meaningfully from phrase to phrase. In the solo on "Airegin", 42 phrases in total are annotated. The number of tones contained in each single phrase ranges from three to twenty, the median number is ten. Figure 5 illustrates the development over the solo: the number of tones (y-axis) and the number of phrases (x-axis). The variability is fairly low and, like the mean length of phrases, does not clearly de- or increase over the course of the solo. When comparing Davis's variability on "Airegin" with that of the selected solos by other bebop trumpeters, one can clearly see the differences (Figure 5). Especially in the rather short solos by Dizzy Gillespie ("Anthropology"), Fats Navarro ("Our Delight"), and Kenny Dorham ("Blues in Bebop"), but also in Navarro's longer solo on "Double Talk", the number of tones over phrases is more variable.

The following analytical features will refer to the musical parameters discussed in the previous section—pitch, interval, and rhythm—in order to contextualize the prior findings regarding homogeneity and calmness. Figure 6 provides an overview of the development of pitch range over the 42 phrases of the solo. The figure illustrates the development over the solo: the number of

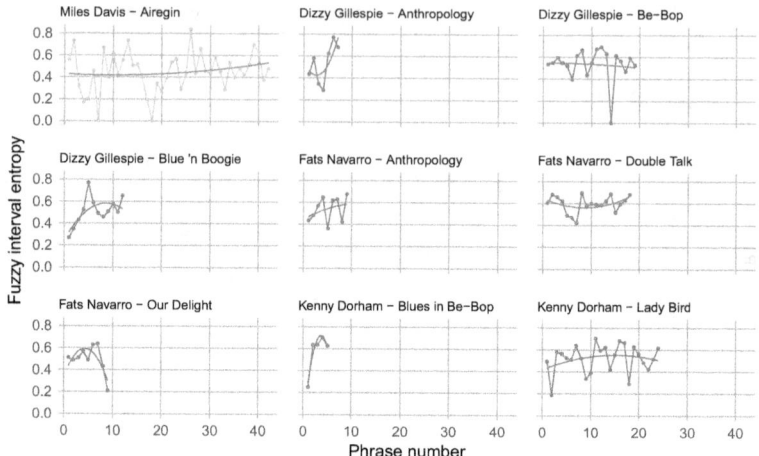

Figure 7: Entropy of fuzzy intervals over phrases in "Airegin" and selected bebop trumpet solos.

tones (y-axis) and the phrase number (x-axis). The minimum pitch range over the phrases is three semitones, the maximum sixteen, and the median range is thirteen. The variability is again quite low, but the pitch range over the phrases clearly decreases in the middle of the solo. Additionally, when reaching the 16 semitone peaks, Davis immediately and clearly reduces the pitch range over the following phrases. As an analysis of improvisations by Gillespie, Navarro, and Dorham shows, the differences between the pitch ranges over phrases are very apparent. Again, especially in the short solos (e. g., Gillespie's "Anthropology"), the variability is clearly higher than in "Airegin" (Figure 6). The variability of fuzzy intervals (as explained above) can be analyzed in a similar fashion by calculating the entropy (cf. Chapter *Computational melody analysis*). Figure 7 was generated by measuring the variability of interval classes, whereby smaller values indicate lower variability (Frieler et al., 2016b, p. 75). Therefore, the variability increases slightly in the second half of the solo. With regard to the other solos, the variability is more comparable here than in the foregoing examples. However, Davis's tendency towards smaller values is also apparent.

The variability of the chosen pitches in reference to the underlying chords might also be of interest when analyzing the musical dramaturgy. Figure 8 illustrates an overview which was created by calculating the entropy (cf. Chapter *Computational melody analysis*) of the distribution of extended chordal

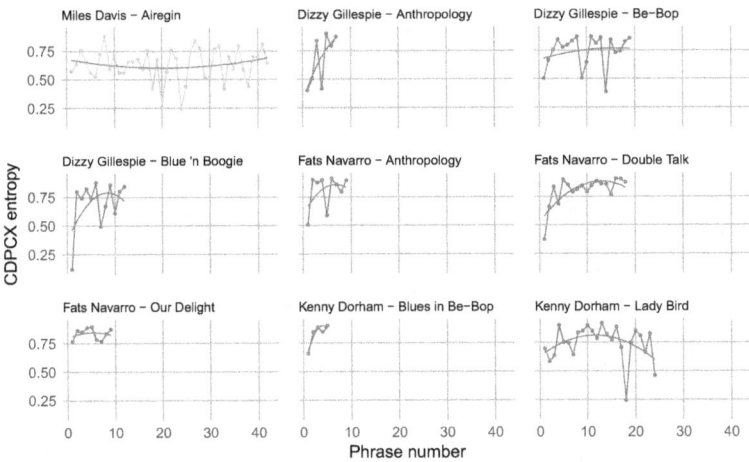

Figure 8: Entropy of chordal diatonic pitch classes over phrases in "Airegin" and selected bebop trumpet solos.

diatonic pitch classes: In this case, smaller values signify a higher variability (Frieler et al., 2016b, p. 75). As the figure illustrates, there are four obvious outliers, while the general variability remains quite constant over the course of the solo. Gillespie's "Blue 'n Boogie" and Navarro's "Double Talk" in particular are clearly different, since both trumpeters start their improvisations with high values which decrease radically over the following phrases (Figure 8). Furthermore, the development of the duration classes per phrase must also be mentioned. Similar to the previous figures, smaller values indicate a lower variability, since the entropy (cf. Chapter *Computational melody analysis*) of duration classes was calculated (Figure 9; Frieler et al., 2016b, p. 75). There are three clear outliers in the middle of the solo—but as in all other figures, the variation increases at the end of the improvisation. Hence, Davis does not clearly change the phrase durations over the course of the improvisation. In particular the solos by Gillespie ("Be-Bop") and Navarro ("Anthropology") are of higher variability (Figure 9).

In summary: All of the figures concerning "Airegin" depict fairly similar concave curves. The intensity and variability always decreases slightly until the middle of the improvisation, and then increases slightly again until the end of the solo. But in general, the solo appears to be very homogeneous—especially in comparison with more expressive solos in the context of modern jazz and compared to several solos by other bebop trumpeters. All in all,

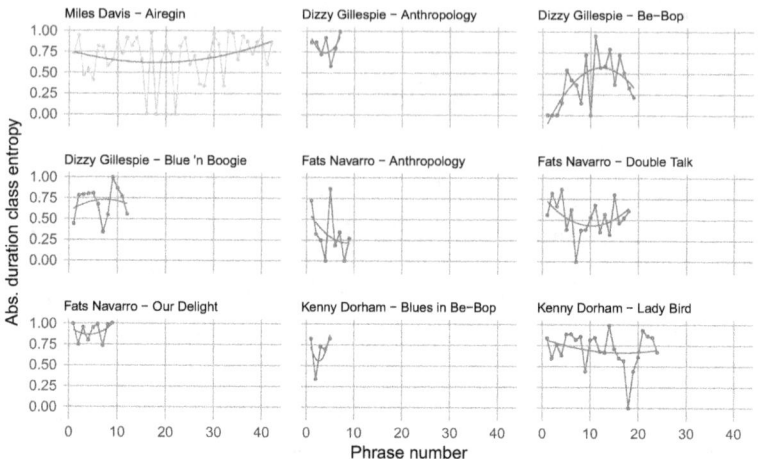

Figure 9: Entropy of duration classes over phrases in "Airegin" and selected bebop trumpet solos.

the tools for a dramaturgical analysis confirm the results of the previous sections. That is, the calmness of Miles Davis's improvisational style can also be described in terms of statistics. However, one further and important feature that cannot be explained by drawing on the statistical tasks outlined here is the motivic and melodic development of the improvisation. But this appears to be a central component, since the solo is played very regularly in various regards, and too much regularity might even bore listeners.

Midlevel analysis part 1: analyzing the motivic development

The overall structure of an improvisation probably cannot adequately be understood if one concentrates solely on certain excerpts of jazz solos—for this reason, the foregoing section focused on the structural variability of musical phrases over time. The recently developed method of "midlevel analysis" (MLA, Frieler et al., 2016a; Frieler & Lothwesen, 2012; Schütz, 2015) provides an opportunity to explore the motivic structure of an improvisation. In general, the MLA system encompasses nine main categories, 18 subcategories, and 41 sub-subcategories that are annotated manually to midlevel units. Additionally, the so-called *back reference* is part of the system. This term describes the relationship between two or more successive or non-successive midlevel units within a solo (cf. Chapter *Computational melody analysis*). Whether two units can be described as related to each other is, as is midlevel annotation in general, based on the perception of the annotators. Since relations sometimes pass unnoticed, there may be even more references than those actually annotated. There are various kinds of relationships or references: For instance, musical ideas such as *lick* can simply be repeated or further developed while rhythmically or melodically varying just a small excerpt of the foregoing unit. Furthermore, midlevel units can be transposed or varied tonally by changing the accompanying chords. Additionally, elements of a certain type of a midlevel unit can be reused in order to create a midlevel unit of another type—for example, melodic fragments can form the basis for *line* MLUs. Miles Davis's ability to develop and recombine motivic ideas over the entire duration of a single solo has already been highlighted by other researchers (Kerschbaumer, 1978, p. 90). Hence, *back references* may help to describe these central creative strategies of Davis's personal style in a quantitative manner. That is to say, this new approach to studying improvisation might be a suitable toolkit for analyzing one of the central components of Davis's personal style. For instance, midlevel analysis has already shown remarkable differences between Davis and his contemporary John Coltrane (Frieler et al., 2016a, pp. 158f.). In general, this method appears to be highly suitable for an exploration of Davis's so-called thoughtful improvisational style.

In "Airegin", 48 midlevel units in total were annotated by the author of this chapter; 29 musical ideas were labeled as *lick*, 16 as *line*, and three as *melody* (for definitions, see p. 54 and Frieler et al., 2016a, pp. 146f.). Their minimum duration is 0.48 seconds, the maximum 3.59, and the median is 1.45. The units contain two to twenty tones, the median number is eight. As for the musical phrases in the previous section, the following figures shall provide an overview of the variability of lengths—referring to the number of tones—and durations of the midlevel units (in seconds) during the improvisation (Figure 10, Figure 11).

Once more, the variations are structured quite homogeneously and they form concave curves. If peaks in duration or length are reached, Davis always immediately goes back to shorter midlevel units. In general, there are no conspicuous differences between the trends of musical phrases and midlevel units. In Figure 10, the variations are compared with those of solos played by other bebop trumpeters. Regarding the length (number of tones) of midlevel units, the graphs do not at first sight show any clear differences in comparison with "Airegin". The variability is predominantly low, as is the case in Fats Navarro's solo on "Double Talk", and even decreases over the course of the improvisation. Differences become apparent when one compares the length of individual units. Whereas the longest unit in "Airegin" encompasses 20 tones, all the other trumpeters play distinctively longer units up to 77

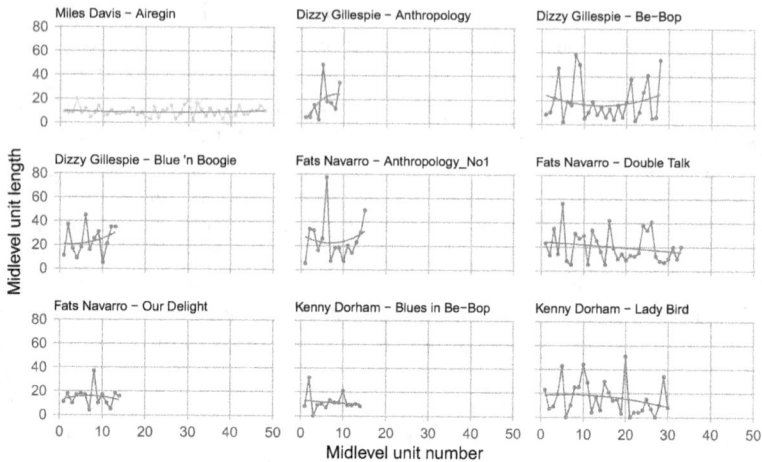

Figure 10: Length of midlevel units in "Airegin" and selected bebop trumpet solos.

tones (Fats Navarro, "Anthropology"). A comparison between durations (in seconds) of midlevel units yields comparable results (Figure 11). Davis's longest midlevel unit is 3.6 seconds, while Gillespie, Navarro, and Dorham play longer units up to 7.5 seconds—only Kenny Dorham's improvisation on "Blues in Be-Bop" seems to be directly comparable to "Airegin".

In the following, the motivic relations are analyzed. The transcription of the solo, including midlevel units and back references, is used to reconstruct the process of improvisation with a special focus on the back references. In total, there are nine back references in the solo (Figure 14, see end of the chapter). However, it must be mentioned that in certain cases the categorization of midlevel units is ambiguous. Therefore, the results should always be interpreted within the specific context of a single solo. For instance, what might sound expressive in solos by cool jazz musicians could instead be perceived as melodic in the context of postbop jazz improvisations. Furthermore, while in highly virtuoso solos the differentiation between the characteristics of *lick* (rhythmic conciseness) and *line* (uniformity of eighth-note chains) is generally obvious, in the case of Miles Davis's improvisations, the annotation is, from time to time, rather ambiguous. In particular, certain midlevel units have the characteristics both of a *lick* and of a *line*. Decisions must be made after carefully listening to the improvisation several times. In some cases, both types of midlevel annotation are possible.

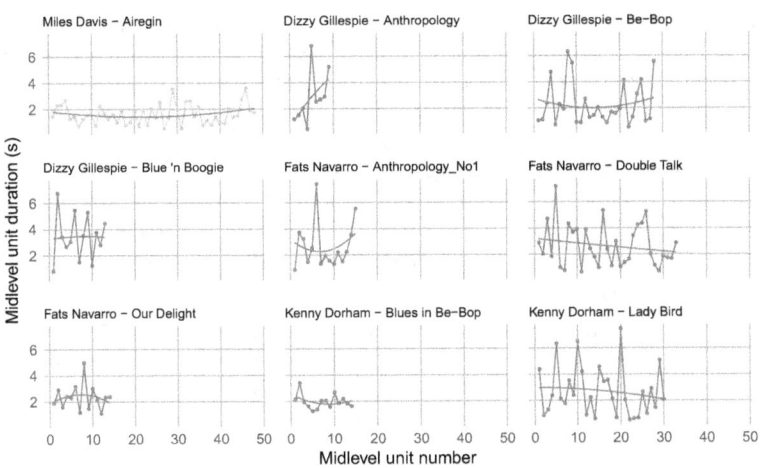

Figure 11: Duration of midlevel units in "Airegin" and selected bebop trumpet solos.

Miles Davis starts with three *licks* of similar length and continues with three *lines* of different subtypes. What follows is an oscillation between one *lick*, two *lines*, and again one *lick*. The following *lick*, midlevel unit 11 in mm. 23 to 24, is the first *back reference*. The group of six tones is not simply copied from the convex *line* in mm. 19 and 20, but played at a different metrical position, and the underlying chords are also different. As a result, the *line* in bar 20 is reinterpreted as an *lick* in mm. 23 and 24. In the following, Davis again plays a mixture of *licks* and *lines*. In mm. 46 to 48, he improvises a convex *line* which occurs in a similar fashion two units later, in mm. 50 to 52, at different metrical positions. After a subsequent concave *line*, Davis virtually repeats the first *lick* of the solo, which functions as an introduction, and ends up in the first bar of the first chorus; the new *lick*, played in mm. 55 to 57, introduces the last A section of the second chorus. That is to say, Miles Davis reuses an idea developed 17 midlevel units before, in the same harmonic and metrical context. Additionally, the following *lick* in m. 58 refers to the same idea, as the characteristic interval jump over a fifth is extended to a sixth. After several more *licks* and *lines*, Davis introduces the first more melodic or cantabile midlevel unit (labeled as *melody*) in mm. 72 to 74 and further develops this idea in the following two bars. The label #+ indicates that the idea was partially transposed upwards. The next *back reference* (mm. 88 to 89) is the reinterpretation of the third *lick* in the solo, which means that Davis reuses an idea he introduced 38 midlevel units before. In detail, the *back reference* concerns only the last three tones of the original *lick*, the accompanying chord in both bars is $B\flat^7$. After the following wavy *line*, the next two *licks* are nearly an exact repetition. In this late part of the solo, there are only four midlevel units left: *lick*, *melody*, *convex line*, and one more *lick*. The last *lick*—mm. 107 to 109—is a variation of the *lick* played in mm. 55 to 57. Hence, it is also highly similar, in a metric and harmonic sense, to the first midlevel unit of the solo. Miles Davis uses this idea three times: when starting the improvisation, approximately in the middle, and at end of the solo. Davis reuses improvisational ideas he introduced or already reused 17 and 22 midlevel units earlier.

It is important to mention that Miles Davis's solo on "Airegin" lacks any midlevel units, such as *expressive* or *rhythm*, that might rather create musical tension, since timbral effects or rhythmicity are foregrounded, while melodic qualities are more in the background (Frieler et al., 2016b, p. 78). In addition, these types of musical ideas are generally more likely to occur in the later parts of jazz improvisations (Frieler et al., 2016b, p. 79), when reaching the dramaturgical climax. The overall structure of midlevel units in "Airegin"—that is to say, the sequences and combinations of *licks*, *lines*, and melodic elements—does not indicate any clear dramaturgic preferences. This aspect can also be interpreted as an integral component of the perceived homogeneity of the improvisation.

Midlevel analysis part 2: some comparisons

In the following, the results of the foregoing midlevel analysis will be further contextualized. In doing so, all other transcriptions of solos by Miles Davis contained in the Weimar Jazz Database will be explored with a focus on midlevel units and *back references*. All in all, the Weimar Jazz Database contains 19 solos by Miles Davis, from 1951 ("K.C. Blues") to 1969 ("Bitches Brew" and "Miles Runs the Voodoo Down"). In both tunes from 1969 as well as on "Oleo" (1956), Davis plays two solos and in each case both solos were transcribed. Ten of the solos were recorded in the 1950s, nine in the 1960s. It is therefore possible to analyze the historic development of Davis's improvisational strategies by comparing older recordings, before the modal improvisations on *Kind of Blue*, with solos from the 1960s. At this stage of his career, Davis even played rather virtuoso and started to experiment with rock music.

Drawing on the foregoing analytical steps, several graphs illustrate the development of midlevel units over the entire duration of individual solos. As in the previous section, there will be two analytical features: the length (the

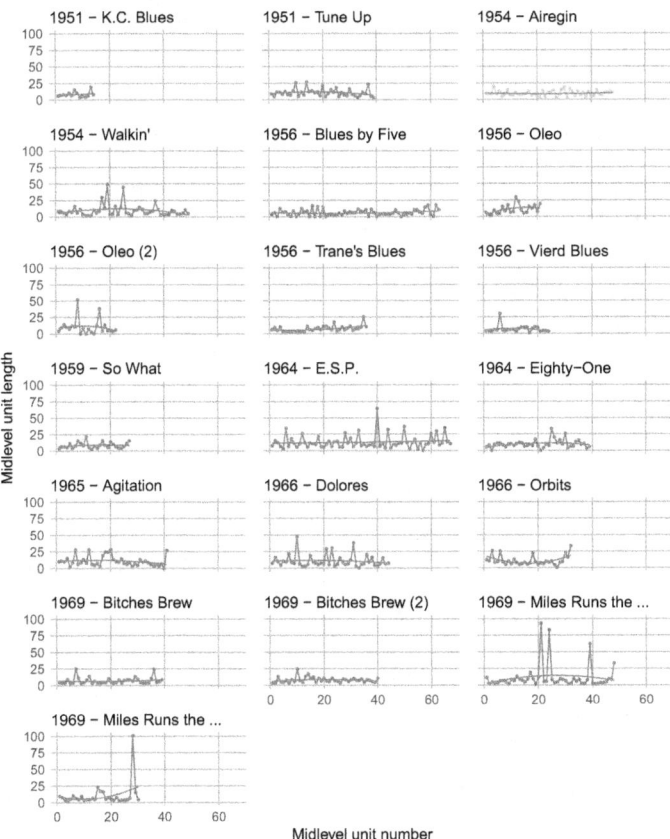

Figure 12: Length of midlevel units in all solos by Miles Davis contained in the Weimar Jazz Database.

number of tones per unit) (Figure 12) and the duration of midlevel units (in seconds) (Figure 13). The durations are generally comparable with those of the solo on "Airegin". Davis tends to avoid expressive dramaturgical climaxes. The graphs further confirm the impression that the uniformity of musical ideas over the course of a solo can be considered a central aspect of Miles Davis's personal style. One particularly striking example is the solo on "E.S.P.". In this rather virtuoso improvisation, the durations of midlevel units hardly de- or increase at all. The analysis of lengths leads to similar results.

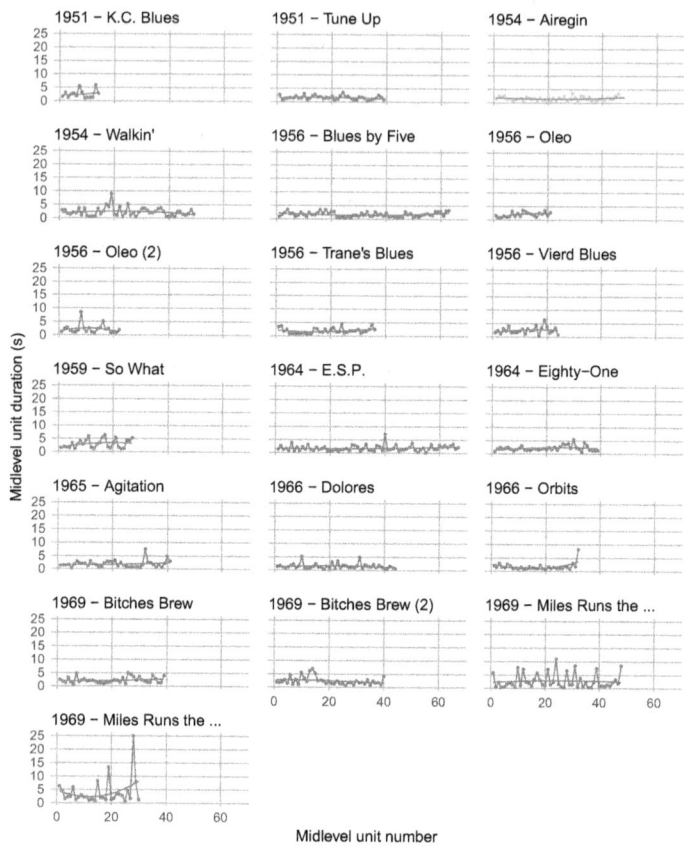

Figure 13: Duration of midlevel units in all solos by Miles Davis contained in the Weimar Jazz Database.

One recurring feature that was already shown in the analysis of "Airegin" is Davis's tendency to ultimately reduce the duration or length of musical ideas after reaching conspicuous peaks. On the one hand, this leads to zigzag structures. On the other hand, as in the case of the second solo on "Miles Runs the Voodoo Down", there can sometimes be only one clear outlier, whereas all other midlevel units are of comparable, rather short duration. "Miles Runs the Voodoo Down" further illustrates that Davis significantly lengthened some of his ideas in recordings during the late 1960s—the longest midlevel units contain up to 100 tones in both solos due to fast rhythmic oscillations.

Table 1: Midlevel back references in solos by Miles Davis in the Weimar Jazz Database.

Solo	Year	MLU	BR	BR (%)	MD
K.C. Blues	1951	14	1	7.1	1
Tune Up	1951	39	4	10.3	13
Airegin	1954	48	9	18.8	38
Walkin'	1954	49	6	12.2	1
Blues by Five	1956	63	1	20.6	2
Oleo (1)	1956	21	5	23.8	2
Oleo (2)	1956	22	4	18.2	2
Trane's Blues	1956	36	10	27.8	16
Vierd Blues	1956	24	3	12.5	1
So What	1959	27	8	29.6	1
E.S.P.	1964	67	11	16.4	60
Eighty One	1964	39	6	15.4	5
Agitation	1965	41	14	34.2	19
Dolores	1966	44	3	6.8	1
Orbits	1966	32	1	3.1	1
Bitches Brew (1)	1969	39	3	7.7	2
Bitches Brew (2)	1969	40	21	52.5	24
Miles Runs the Voodoo Down (1)	1969	48	12	25.0	10
Miles Runs the Voodoo Down (2)	1969	30	7	23.3	10

Note. MLU = count of midlevel units, BR = count of back references, MD = maximum distance.

As demonstrated in the analysis of "Airegin", it seems worthwhile to explore Davis's usage of back references, too. Table 1 provides an overview of *back references* in all 19 solos by Davis contained in the Weimar Jazz Database. Back references do occur in every solo, but to a varying degree. In the solo on "Orbits", the percentage of back referenes in relation to all midlevel units is only 3.1, whereas in the second solo on "Bitches Brew" it is 52.5. Furthermore, in several solos Davis simply develops ideas introduced one unit before, but in "E.S.P." he refers back to an idea he played as many as 60 units earlier. All in all, 19.2 % of all midlevel units in the solos analyzed are based on ideas already introduced beforehand. The extensive usage of *back references* can be described, not as a feature necessarily occurring in every analyzed solo, but as a regularly recurring and sometimes essential feature. These findings should be verified by analyzing more solos. Nevertheless, *back references*

Table 2: Midlevel back references in selected bebop trumpet solos.

Performer	Title	MLU	BR	BR (%)	MD
Dizzy Gillespie	Anthropology	9	1	11.1	1
Dizzy Gillespie	Be-Bop	28	4	14.3	4
Dizzy Gillespie	Blue 'n Boogie	13	0	0.0	0
Fats Navarro	Anthropology	15	1	6.7	1
Fats Navarro	Double Talk	33	0	0.0	0
Fats Navarro	Our Delight	14	0	0.0	0
Kenny Dorham	Blues in Bebop	14	3	21.4	3
Kenny Dorham	Lady Bird	30	3	10.0	3

Note. MLU = Count of midlevel units, BR = count of back references, MD = maximum distance.

can certainly be described as an important feature of Davis's personal style. Furthermore, the reinterpretation of musical ideas can be found not only in recordings released in the late 1950s—that is, in the context of modal, rather melodic improvisation—, but even in the early 1950s and the late 1960s.

Interestingly, the average percentage of *back references* in all other solos contained in the Weimar Jazz Database is 24.5. Hence, this feature might also be of interest when analyzing improvisations by other soloists. But when we compare "Airegin" with the aforementioned solos by other bebop trumpeters, the differences are obvious (Table 2). On average, *back references* appear to be of no importance in the bebop solos analyzed here, even though they occur in more than half of the improvisations. In particular, high values in the category "maximum distance" are lacking. Hence, when compared with other bebop trumpeters, the usage and development of musical ideas can be assumed to be a distinctive feature of Miles Davis.

Conclusion

The analysis of several musical features as well as of the overall dramaturgy of Miles Davis's solo on "Airegin" clarifies why the improvisation sounds so calm and homogeneous—in particular when contrasting his solo with those by other bebop trumpeters. Interestingly, jazz historian Alyn Shipton describes "Airegin", and additionally "Oleo" and "Doxy" from the same recording (*Miles Davis with Sonny Rollins*), as being characteristic for Davis's "future direction" (Shipton, 2007, p. 667). While Davis was generally seen as a bebop trumpeter in the mid-1950s, pieces such as "Airegin" can retrospectively be interpreted as early hardbop tunes. Furthermore, the analysis of the motivic relations created by Miles Davis illustrates his 'thoughtful' style of improvising. In this specific example, variability seems to be created not by virtuoso lines or expressiveness, but by melodic and motivic references. Therefore, a statistical approach can help to systematically describe and further understand characteristics of Davis's (early) personal style that have frequently been discussed in jazz studies over the last decades. Midlevel annotations, in particular, provide deep insights into Miles Davis's improvisational strategies.

Figure 14: Transcription with midlevel annotations of Miles Davis's solo on "Airegin".

Figure 14: (Continued).

West Coast lyricists: Paul Desmond and Chet Baker

Benjamin Burkhart

The term "West Coast jazz" itself often occurs in jazz historiography, even though there is no general agreement as to what it exactly refers to. The question of whether it can be characterized as a distinctive musical style or, as jazz critic and researcher Ted Gioia puts it, merely "a somewhat unified phenomenon" (Gioia, 1992, p. 363) often arises. This chapter explicitly does not aim at answering this question, but instead focuses analytically on musicians such as Chet Baker and Paul Desmond who are generally acknowledged to be among the most prominent protagonists of West Coast jazz—either because of their origins or because of their long-term activities in the western part of the US, principally Los Angeles and San Francisco. The focus will be on a comparison between their personal improvisational styles, with reference to analytical writings published on West Coast jazz up till now. One main goal is to explore characteristics often associated with West Coast jazz musicians and to provide a foundation for further analytical research.

In terms of public attention and commercial success, West Coast jazz was the most popular jazz style since the swing era. In the first half of the 1950s, musicians such as Gerry Mulligan and Dave Brubeck formed ensembles which soon attracted national attention. Hence, it is hardly surprising that the West Coast stars were criticized by journalists and jazz musicians alike for their alleged commercialism or musical primitivism. One key aspect in discussions of West Coast jazz is the assumption that it somehow deviated from the cool jazz of the East Coast, mainly New York City. Generally described as a 'Euro-American' equivalent to 'African-American' cool jazz in the tradition of Miles Davis, several sociocultural influences are believed to be essential for the development of West Coast jazz. Being based in California, mainly in Los Angeles, many jazz musicians profited from an artistic and economic infrastructure that was distinctly different from that of the East Coast. Thanks to the recording studios of Hollywood and a number of big bands and orchestras, musicians often had the opportunity to be paid relatively well for their work—as a result, working as a jazz musician on the West Coast was described as a regular employment rather than an artistic, creative activity (Hellhund, 1985, p. 240; Jost, 2003, pp. 160–171).

According to Ekkehard Jost, the employment of jazz musicians in big bands and orchestras further led to an unusual degree of musical standardization. To be a member of these big ensembles, one had to fulfill certain criteria relating to instrumental sound, since the music was an integral part of California's cultural industry—people wanted to hear the sound they already knew and appreciated. Furthermore, pianist Stan Kenton's big band was of great significance for West Coast jazz. Kenton in particular tried to create a 'European' sounding version of contemporary jazz, one influenced by symphonic compositions by, for instance, Richard Strauss, Nikolai Rimsky-Korsakov, or Sergei Prokofiev (Jost, 2003, pp. 158–162). However, West Coast jazz became famous not for its big bands and orchestras but for the small ensembles of Gerry Mulligan and Dave Brubeck, and for instrumentalists such as Chet Baker, even though most of the musicians were former members of the large Hollywood ensembles. According to Herbert Hellhund, the music of the small ensembles can be characterized by distinctly non-virtuoso and rather cantabile improvisations and by technical sophistication in arrangements and ensemble playing. Furthermore, Hellhund believes that the various syntheses of musical styles of African-American and European descent are significant for West Coast jazz (Hellhund, 1985, pp. 236–241). Ted Gioia further notes that the sound of West Coast jazz "was cleanly articulated, the execution fluid and polished" (Gioia, 1992, p. 362). Among the most prominent instrumentalists who became well-known especially for their melodic, lyrical improvisations are the alto-saxophonist Paul Desmond and the trumpeter Chet Baker. The analysis of these two musicians forms the basis of this chapter, since they appear to be directly comparable. Additional comparisons with other musicians generally associated with West Coast jazz, Gerry Mulligan, Stan Getz, and Zoot Sims, are also undertaken in order to contextualize the findings. In a last step, solos by East Coast cool jazz instrumentalists (Lee Konitz, Warne Marsh) are analyzed in order to compare aspects of West and East Coast jazz.

"The world's slowest alto player"—Paul Desmond

A description like "the world's slowest alto player" might seem quite unflattering—however, it is a description formulated not, as one might think, by journalists or resentful musicians, but by Paul Desmond himself. And indeed, Desmond, who became especially well-known for his collaboration with pianist Dave Brubeck and for his composition "Take Five" (1959), does not seem directly comparable with the virtuoso alto style of the 1940s and 1950s popularized by Charlie Parker and his fellows. Nevertheless, he is assumed to be one of the most well-known alto players of the 1950s and 1960s, referring directly to the style of saxophonists such as Lester Young or Benny Carter in the two foregoing decades (Harrison & Kernfeld, 2001, p. 605).

Desmond began his career as a professional musician when studying the clarinet at San Francisco Polytechnic; in 1943, he switched to the alto saxophone. After being drafted into the army, he worked as a military musician and was part of the 253rd AGF (Army Ground Forces) Band. In the following years, he was first hired to play in Alvino Rey's and Jack Fina's ensembles before working with Dave Brubeck. He was a member of Brubeck's famous quartet from 1951 to 1967. Besides his collaboration with Dave Brubeck, Desmond released several recordings with musicians such as Gerry Mulligan, Jim Hall, Chet Baker, and the Modern Jazz Quartet (Gioia, 1992, p. 77).

Even though Desmond's work has largely been ignored by academia up until now, some of his contemporaries describe him as one of the most central figures in jazz during the 1950s and 1960s. Dave Brubeck states:

> Of all the alto saxophonists of his day, so under the influence of Charlie Parker, Paul was the one who struck his own path and found his own sound, integrating in his improvisations a great sense of melody, harmonic and rhythmic invention—and wit (cited from Ramsey et al., 2005, p. 11).

Musicologist Thomas Owens further describes Desmond as being one of the "three most prominent non-members of the Parker school", besides Art Pepper and Lee Konitz (Owens, 1995, p. 2). Not being part of the so-called 'Parker school' means that the alto saxophonist was among those jazz musicians who created musical styles that deviated from the bebop idiom of the late 1940s and early 1950s. Ted Gioia even assumes that Desmond had "perfected a 'cool' alternative to the bebop style" (Gioia, 1992, p. 122). But at the same time, he describes Desmond as "a saxophonist who seemed completely out of touch with musical modernism" (Gioia, 1992, p. 69) and who had polished "a retrograde, almost anti-modern saxophone style" (Gioia, 1992, p. 75).

What Gioia both praises and criticizes is the probably most prominent feature of Desmond's personal style: the melodic, rather simple improvisations that clearly distinguish him from the virtuosity of jazz musicians associated with the aforementioned 'Parker school'. Most of the authors who have published biographical or analytical works on Paul Desmond highlight the alto player's melodic inventiveness (Harrison & Kernfeld, 2001, p. 605; Kunzler, 2002, p. 292), or again in Gioia's words: his "talent for melodic construction" (Gioia, 1992, p. 90). According to Günter Gliesche, Desmond played jazz like a thinking person with lyrical intelligence, and improvised clear and melodic lines (Gliesche, 2006, p. 9). In his analytical study on cool and West Coast jazz, musicologist Herbert Hellhund further highlights Desmond's simple, motivic style which, according to the author, led to highly structured and continuous improvisations (Hellhund, 1985, pp. 259f.). One other striking and frequently mentioned feature is Desmond's personal sound. When attempting to describe Desmond's sound, adjectives such as "lyrical", "tender", "airy", "romantic" (Kunzler, 2002, p. 292), "lucid", or "bright" (Gioia, 1992, p. 90) are used. In summing up, biographer Dough Ramsey states that Paul Desmond was "famous for the warmth, inventiveness and lyricism of his playing" (Ramsey et al., 2005, p. 13).

The writings mentioned above demonstrate that Paul Desmond's melodically inventive and motivic improvisations are among the most distinctive features of his personal style. Even though this talent is frequently highlighted by a number of authors, Desmond's technical abilities are generally described as being quite limited. The parallels to writings on Chet Baker are obvious, since Baker is acknowledged to be another great melodic improviser of so-called West Coast jazz.

"There's a little white cat out on the West Coast who's gonna eat you up"—Chet Baker

This section heading refers to a quote attributed to Charlie Parker. According to Chet Baker himself, Parker had warned Miles Davis and Dizzy Gillespie after having played a short tour on the West Coast with Baker—a tour that is generally acknowledged as being a breakthrough in Baker's career (Gioia, 1992, p. 172). As a child, Baker started playing music on the trombone before switching to the trumpet at the age of thirteen. Like Paul Desmond, Baker became a military musician in the 1940s. In 1946, he first joined the 298th Army Band in Berlin, and then the Presidio Army Band in San Francisco in 1948. After being discharged in 1952, Baker intermittently played local jobs until he first met Charlie Parker at an audition hosted by Parker in

Los Angeles (Gordon, 1986, p. 72). At that time, Baker was already highly interested in the music of trumpeters such as Miles Davis, Fats Navarro, and Red Rodney (Gioia, 1992, p. 170). Miles Davis in particular is believed to have had a huge influence on Chet Baker. But, as Alain Tercinet assumes, Baker had already developed some highly characteristic elements of his own personal style before becoming more and more inspired by Davis (Tercinet, 1986, p. 95). That is to say, it might be difficult to decide which trumpeter influenced the other to what degree at any given time. In 1952, Baker and baritone saxophonist Gerry Mulligan formed their famous quartet and Baker became well-known as a solo artist with his later groups, too (Gordon, 1986, p. 82).

Like Paul Desmond, Baker deviated from the virtuoso solo style of the bebop era. According to Robert Gordon, his style as a trumpeter was dominated by "a tendency towards introspection, a limited emotional range"—something Gordon further characterizes as the "very worst faults of Baker's trumpet style" (Gordon, 1986, p. 83). Gordon was not the only writer to criticize Baker's technical abilities. Jeroen de Valk assumes the expressivity of Baker's playing to be his key talent, whereas in a technical sense, he calls him an "[a]nalphabet" (Valk, 1991, p. 15). But Ted Gioia also highlights Chet Baker's ability to deal with his technical limitations and to thereby create a distinctive style of playing:

> [H]e did so much with his limited musical tools that one scarcely kept track of what he couldn't or didn't do. In an age of incessant virtuosity, Baker's work was a telling and much-needed reminder that technical mastery was not the only path to musical expression, and indeed could often be a beguiling dead-end street (Gioia, 1992, p. 169).

As in the case of Paul Desmond, Baker's playing has been described as "uncommonly lyrical" (Gioia, 1992, p. 181). Alain Tercinet further states that Chet Baker's improvisations were characterized by a "disenchanted lyricism" ("lyrisme désenchanté") (Tercinet, 1986, p. 95) and had an "intimate and romantic character" ("charactère intimiste et romantique") (Tercinet, 1986, p. 234). Furthermore, his contemporaries highlight his ability to react intuitively to new or unfamiliar musical situations, as stated by Gerry Mulligan (Valk, 1991, p. 35). According to Mulligan, Baker could not even read sheet music and played everything by ear (Gioia, 1992, p. 174). Herbert Hellhund further praises Baker's talent for melodic inventiveness and states that this ability led to an "atmospheric intensity" ("atmosphärische[n] Intensität") (Hellhund, 1985, p. 264).

What therefore seems interesting about the improvisational styles of Paul Desmond and Chet Baker is their melodic and technically limited but nonetheless—according to the authors quoted above—lyrical playing. The following sections aim particularly at exploring and comparing these characteristics in improvisations by both musicians. Furthermore, the results are contextualized by analyses of selected solos by other jazz musicians commonly associated with West and East Coast cool jazz.

Analyzing pitch classes

The Weimar Jazz Database contains eight solos each by Desmond and Baker. Six of Desmond's tunes were released on his album *Bossa Antigua* (1964); he played two solos on "Alianca" and "Samba Cantina" and in each case, both solos were transcribed. Two more solos are from "Blue Rondo a la Turk" and "The Girl from East 9th Street", which appeared on the album *Time Out* (1959) by the Dave Brubeck Quartet. Six of Baker's solos were recorded in the mid-1950s (1954/1955), whereas his improvisations on "Two's Blues" and "You'd Be So Nice to Come Home to" are from 1975. Most of Desmond's solos are played on bossa nova pieces. The available recordings of Chet Baker are more heterogeneous, ranging from the slow ballad "I Fall in Love Too Easily" (1954) to the up-tempo tune "You'd Be So Nice to Come Home to".

In order to gain an impression of the degree of harmony or consonance, the distribution of pitch classes—diatonic or consonant vs. chromatic or dissonant pitches—will be analyzed. The following histograms provide an overview of the (extended) chordal diatonic pitch class distribution—that is, the diatonic and non-diatonic pitches according to the root of the underlying chord—in all solos by the two musicians, in total (Figure 1) and per tune (Figure 2). In the case of Paul Desmond, the fifth is the pitch class played most often, followed by the third and the root note. Chet Baker, on the other hand, emphasizes the root note, the fifth, and the fourth. But the pitch distribution per solo also illustrates that there are only a few obvious preferences for certain pitch classes in both musicians' improvisations. Interestingly enough, Desmond and Baker often focus on the third (Desmond: "Alianca (1)", "Alone Together", "Samba Cantina (1)", "Samba Cantina (2)"; Baker: "Long Ago and Far Away", "Two's Blues", "You'd Be So Nice to Come Home to"), which indicates a highly consonant melodic structure that emphasizes the underlying chords. On the other hand, Desmond sometimes emphasizes the second and fourth ("Bossa Antigua"), and Baker even the sixth and seventh ("Just Friends") or fourth ("Let's Get Lost", "There Will Never Be Another You (1)"). Hence, there are no overall preferences in either musicians' solos.

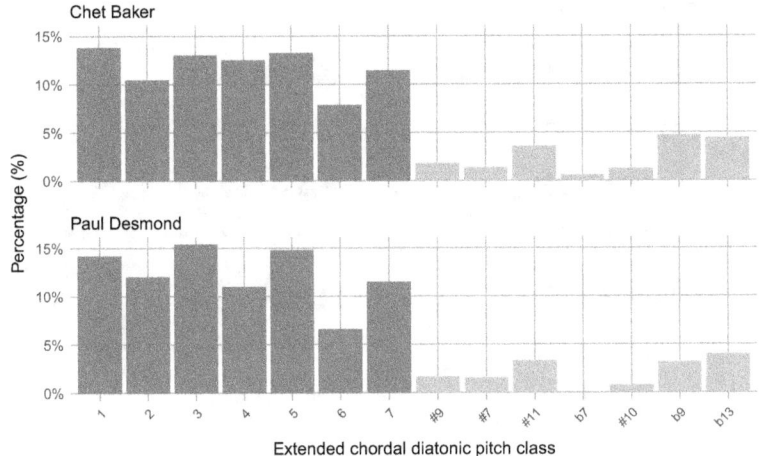

Figure 1: Extended chordal diatonic pitch class distribution in solos by Chet Baker and Paul Desmond (in total).

If the 'lyrical' melodic features of Desmond's and Baker's improvisations are to be explored, non-diatonic pitch classes would seem to be relevant as well, since these pitch classes might intensify or, vice versa, counteract the consonant 'lyricism'. Clearly, Desmond only rarely plays non-diatonic pitch classes; the highest percentage per pitch class is 4.4 for the minor sixth (b13)—which will only sound (mildly) dissonant in the context of major chords or a major context—, whereas he never plays dissonant minor sevenths over major chords in the solos analyzed here. In the case of Baker, the percentage of single non-diatonic pitch classes per solo is always less than 5 %—the highest value is 4.8 % for the minor ninth (b9). All in all, 14.1 % of Desmond's and 18.2 % of Baker's tones are non-diatonic pitch classes.[16]

The next question is how both musicians use non-diatonic tones or dissonances dramaturgically—especially since they obviously do not have any preferences for certain pitch classes. In order to understand the improvisational dramaturgy, it seems reasonable to analyze the musical phrases, which

---

[16]This difference is statistically highly significant; a χ^2-test revealed a p-value of $p = .01$ ($\chi^2(1) = 6.54$) with Cramer's $V = .043$, which means that Desmond plays slightly but consistently more diatonically than Baker. A comparison of the full distribution of chordal diatonic pitch classes showed even greater differences ($\chi^2(13) = 30.68$, $p = .002$, Cramer's $V = .093$) which, besides the non-diatonic tones, is mostly due to Desmond's preference for thirds and fifths and Baker's preference for fourths and sixths.

Figure 2: Extended chordal diatonic pitch class distribution in solos by Chet Baker and Paul Desmond (per tune).

were annotated manually for each solo contained in the Weimar Jazz Database. Phrases, which can be understood as fairly short and meaningful units with a musical sense of their own, can help to understand the "internal logic" (Frieler et al., 2016b, p. 69) of jazz improvisations by allowing one to examine the variation of musical features over phrases. The following graphs illustrate the development of playing non-diatonic tones over phrases in the solos of Paul Desmond and Chet Baker (Figure 3). There, the phrase-wise percentage of non-diatonic tones is depicted along with quadratic polynomial trend lines.

In the case of Desmond, there are various strategies for playing dissonances over phrases. Ongoing variations lead to zigzag curves ("Alianca (1)", "Alone Together", "Blue Rondo A La Turk"), convex curves ("Alianca (2)", "Bossa Antigua", "Samba Cantina (2)"), and low variability with few outliers ("Samba Cantina (1)", "The Girl From East 9th Street"). In Baker's solos, there are convex curves ("I Fall in Love Too Easily", "There Will Never Be Another You (1)"), strongly increasing trend lines ("Let's Get Lost", "Long Ago And Far Away"), and examples with low variability ("Just Friends", "There Will Never Be Another You (2)", "You'd Be So Nice to Come Home to").

In the following, both musicians' strategies for playing non-diatonics are compared. In doing so, it is fairly essential to choose comparable examples. First of all, solos played on comparatively slow and balladic tunes, which at the same time display certain distinctive features regarding outliers or trend lines, are selected. Desmond's first improvisation on "Samba Cantina" is one of the slower solos contained in the Weimar Jazz Database; the average tempo is 150.8 bpm. The structure of non-diatonic playing is quite conspicuous, since there are several phrases without any chromatic pitch classes at all, as well as obvious outliers (up to 70 %). Chet Baker's "I Fall in Love Too Easily" is by far the slowest tune among the selected recordings (65.2 bpm) and, as in "Samba Cantina", there is a pendulum structure of non-diatonic and diatonic phrases—whereas the convex trend lines clearly differ from those in the figure referring to Desmond's solo. The strategies of playing diatonically or non-diatonically over phrases can be explored by analyzing both the percentage of non-diatonic pitch classes and the number of tones per phrase. In doing so, the focus is on whether the soloists choose non-diatonic pitch classes in short phrases, thereby creating attention for brief moments only, or if the non-diatonics are played over longer passages. In this case, it could be argued that non-diatonic tones are highlighted as more integral elements of the overall dramaturgy.

Figure 4 illustrates the percentage of non-diatonic pitch classes and the number of tones for each phrase in Paul Desmond's first solo on "Samba Cantina". First of all, the trend lines are clearly reversals of one another—convex for non-

Figure 3: Non-diatonic tones over phrases in solos by Chet Baker and Paul Desmond.

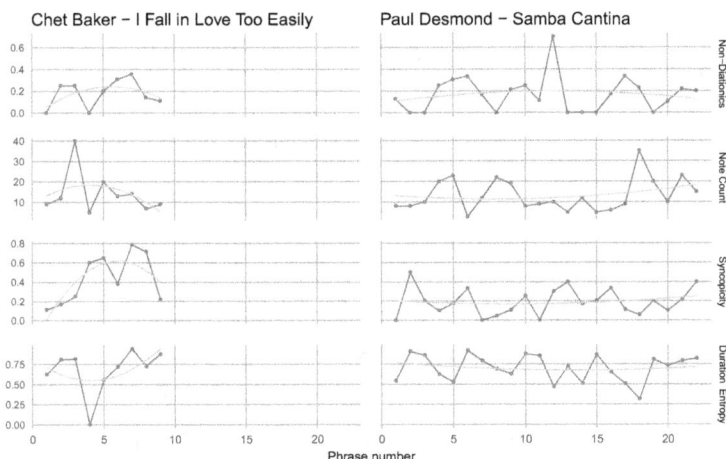

Figure 4: Non-diatonic tones, number of tones, syncopicity, and duration entropy over phrases in Chet Baker's solo on "I Fall in Love Too Easily", and Paul Desmond's first solo on "Samba Cantina".

diatonic tones and concave for the number of tones per phrase. Desmond's first three phrases are relatively short, and as the percentage of non-diatonic tones is zero twice, it could be argued that he improvises very consonantly. In phrases four and five, both trend lines display the same direction, whereas in the following phrases up until number eleven, the directions are sometimes opposed. Additionally, the next dissonance peak in phrase 17 is not accompanied by a strong increase in the number of tones. In contrast, the directions of both trend lines over the last three phrases are quite similar. But as in the case of phrase 8 or 19, Desmond sometimes plays comparatively long phrases of 20 tones or more without any non-diatonic pitch classes. That is to say, he uses rather long phrases to play fairly consonantly rather than create tonal tension or smooth out his lines with chromatic passing tones. Figure 5 illustrates an example of a long diatonic phrase. The melodic quality might be attributed to the four-eighth-note pattern which Desmond repeats three times in bars 21 and 22. Desmond repeats a pendulum between the minor seventh, minor third, minor seventh, and fifth in bar 21, and between the fourth, minor seventh, fourth, and second in bar 22.

Figure 4 also illustrates the development over phrases in Chet Baker's solo on "I Fall in Love Too Easily". In this case, the trend lines look fairly similar. Baker starts with a phrase without any non-diatonic pitch classes, whereas in

Figure 5: Diatonic phrase in Paul Desmond's first solo on "Samba Cantina".

Figure 6: Dissonant accents in Chet Baker's solo on "I Fall in Love Too Easily".

the second phrase, the percentage clearly increases up to 25. Furthermore, the number of tones increases as well. When the peak of played tones is reached in the following third phrase, the percentage of non-diatonic pitch classes nearly remains the same, while both values clearly decrease in the fourth phrase. With the exception of the sixth phrase, the directions of both lines are similar until the end of the solo. Figure 6 illustrates phrases one and two—that is, the transition from a short phrase without any non-diatonic tones at all to a slightly longer phrase with a higher number of played tones as well as a higher percentage of non-diatonic pitch classes. The figure shows the first four bars of Baker's solo; the second phrase starts at the end of bar two. The dissonant impression results mainly from playing E♭ as a short figuration and then a long dissonant major seven C♯ over $D^{m7♭5}$, a half-diminished chord, which is already a rather dissonant chord in its own right. The C♯ can also be interpreted as an anticipated augmented fourth of the ensuing $G^{7♭9}$ chord, with a distinct blue note character. Hence, in this case Chet Baker's usage of dissonant and consonant pitch classes differs from Paul Desmond's strategy. In "I Fall In Love Too Easily", Baker uses the comparatively longer phrases for playing more non-diatonic pitch classes and thereby, it could be argued, creating more tension.

In summary: Both soloists are well known for their melodic and harmonic improvisations, and the analysis of chordal diatonic pitch classes over phrases shows that they often improvise in a rather diatonic fashion. As shown above, Paul Desmond's and Chet Baker's strategies for implementing dissonances in the overall dramaturgy of the improvisations sometimes differ, although a comprehensive comparison would necessitate the analysis of more solos.

For further contextualization, certain results of the foregoing analysis will now be compared with improvisations by other musicians commonly associ-

Table 1: Phrase lengths (number of tones) in solos by West and East Coast jazz musicians.

Soloist	Median	Range
Paul Desmond	12	2–63
Chet Baker	14.5	1–63
Gerry Mulligan	18	2–65
Stan Getz	14	2–71
Zoot Sims	13	3–48
Lee Konitz	24	3–79
Warne Marsh	24	2–66

ated with West Coast jazz. For the comparisons, solos by Gerry Mulligan, Stan Getz, and Zoot Sims are taken into consideration. Furthermore, solos by Lee Konitz and Warne Marsh—East Coast cool jazz musicians in the tradition of Lennie Tristano—are analyzed as well, in order to explore possible differences between West and East Coast jazz soloists. According to Herbert Hellhund, short phrases are especially typical for Paul Desmond's personal style (Hellhund, 1985, p. 258).[17] These characteristics were also evident in the foregoing analysis. For this reason, the number of tones per phrase was chosen as one analytical feature for the comparison with other jazz musicians. The following table lists the median phrase lengths and their range over all the solos by each musician (Table 1).

As a matter of fact, the median phrase length of Desmond's solos is the lowest, followed by Sims and Getz. The median length of Baker's phrases is slightly higher than Getz's, whereas Mulligan plays the most tones per phrase compared with the other West Coast players. The median values of Konitz's and Marsh's solos are both, at 24 tones per phrase, generally higher, even twice as high as Desmond's median value, which can be regarded as a considerable difference. However, the differences with respect to the minimum and maximum values are rather small.[18]

Furthermore, we will also compare the distribution of chordal diatonic pitch classes (extended)—summarized for all solos (Figure 7). The root note, the

---

[17] This can in fact be corroborated with a t-test ($t(105.14) = 2.769$, $p = .007^{**}$), with a mean phrase length of 13.6 tones for Desmond and 18.3 for Baker. Baker also displays a higher variability of phrase lengths ($SD = 14.0$) than Desmond ($SD = 8.43$).

[18] A one-way variance analysis (ANOVA) of phrase lengths by performer revealed highly significant differences ($F(6,778) = 13.84$, $p = .000^{***}$, adj. $R^2 = .09$), with Konitz and Marsh playing much longer and Desmond playing much shorter phrases. Baker is in the middle field.

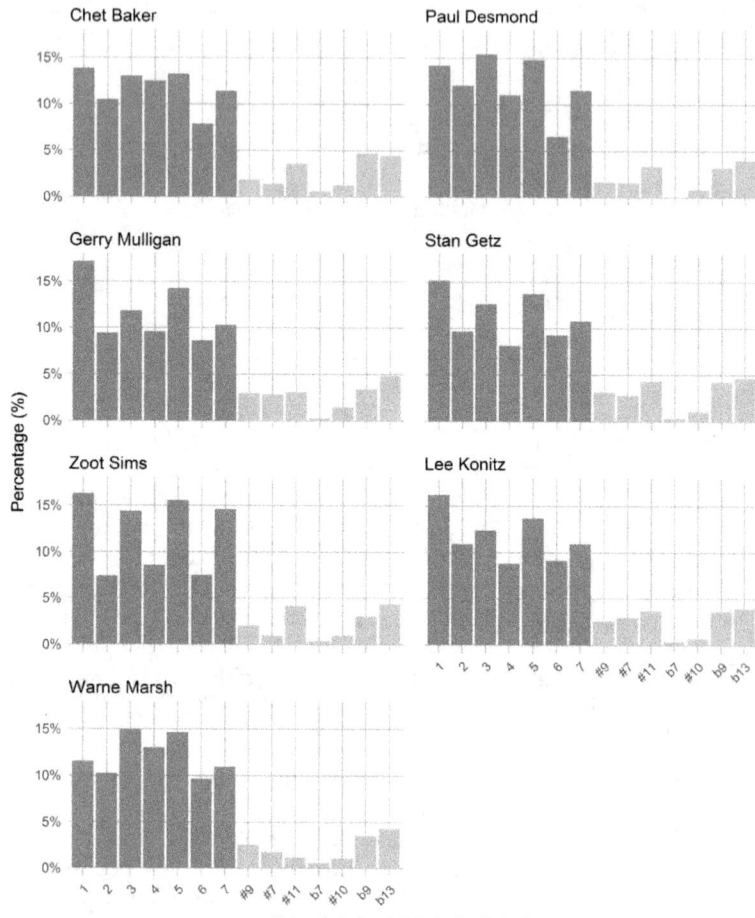

Figure 7: Distribution of extended chordal diatonic pitch classes in solos by West and East Coast jazz musicians.

third, fifth, and the seventh are the pitch classes most often played by West Coast jazz musicians, while the emphasis on the third is also apparent in their improvisations. The percentages of non-diatonic pitch classes are slightly higher compared to Desmond and Baker: 18.1 % (Gerry Mulligan), 19.6 % (Stan Getz), and 15.4 % (Zoot Sims). Regarding the chordal diatonic pitch class distribution, the results for Konitz's and Marsh's solos do not differ significantly. The percentages of non-diatonic pitch classes are comparable, too: 17.6 % (Lee Konitz), 14.3 % (Warne Marsh).[19]

Analyzing rhythm

When analyzing musicians who are acknowledged to be melodic 'lyricists', it seems appropriate to concentrate on stylistic features that might reflect rhythmic tension. One can explore how musicians use or don't use such features, especially as part of the overall dramaturgy of an improvisation. Syncopicity, i.e., tones on offbeats with no event on the following on-beat, was chosen as a first basic feature that is assumed to create rhythmic tension.[20] The following figure provides an overview of the percentage of syncopicity in all solos by Paul Desmond and Chet Baker contained in the Weimar Jazz Database, and by the other West and East Coast jazz musicians (Figure 8). The figure clearly illustrates that, on average, less than half of all tone events are syncopated events. These results seem obvious in view of the two musicians' calm, lyrical style of improvising. One might assume that they do not try to create rhythmic tension by an extensive use of syncopated events.

As in the previous section, the relevance of the analyzed features for the overall dramaturgy of improvisations is to be explored here, too. Again, the examples chosen are Desmond's first solo on "Samba Cantina" and Baker's "I Fall in Love Too Easily"—the percentage for Baker's solo is the highest, the values for two solos on "Samba Cantina" are the lowest. Figure 4 illustrates the development of syncopated tone events over phrases. In Desmond's solo, the peak is already reached in the second phrase (50 %). In the following bars, the percentages of syncopated events oscillate regularly between values of up to 40 %, which leads to a slightly concave trend line. Chet Baker, on the

---

[19] A one-way ANOVA of the number of non-diatonic pitch classes per phrase by performer revealed a significant effect ($F(6,766) = 3.49$, $p = .002$, adj. $R^2 = .019$), with Gerry Mulligan, Stan Getz and Zoot Sims playing slightly more non-diatonic tones than average, and Paul Desmond and Warne Marsh playing fewer. However, the effect is rather small.

[20] Note that metrical positions in the Weimar Jazz Database are provided by a metrical annotation algorithm, which means that not only proper syncopations contribute to the *syncopicity* value, as used here, but also micro-timing aspects, such as laid-back or loose (or sloppy) playing, which might result in higher values.

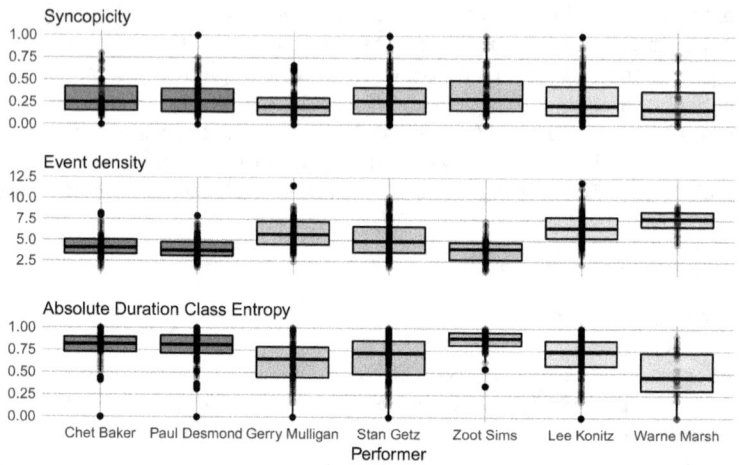

Figure 8: Syncopicity, event density, and absolute duration class entropy in solos by West and East Coast jazz musicians.

other hand, seems to purposefully make use of syncopicity, since the highest value is 80% and the trend line increases strongly over the course of the improvisation. While the structure of Paul Desmond's solo can be described as relaxed and calm, Baker appears to improvise more 'expressively'.

The next feature is event density, measured as the number of tones per second. Figure 8 summarizes the event densities of all solos by both musicians, and by the other West and East Coast musicians. In this case, the differences between Desmond and Baker are rather small—the event densities are comparatively low. What event density cannot explain is rhythmic flexibility. But this might be a relevant analytical feature if improvisational calmness is to be explored, especially in a dramaturgical sense. For this reason, the entropy of absolute duration classes, which measures the variability of duration classes which are defined in relation to a tempo-independent reference value of 500 ms, was calculated. Here, smaller values indicate lower variability (Frieler et al., 2016b, p. 75). Figure 8 provides an overview of entropies for all solos, Figure 4 illustrates the entropy of duration classes over phrases in Desmond's "Samba Cantina" and Baker's "I Fall in Love Too Easily". In Desmond's solo, the values oscillate regularly between approximately 0.5 and 0.9, leading to a trend line that decreases slightly in the middle and increases again slightly at the end of the solo—the variability is quite low. Chet Baker's solo appears to be more varied, especially due to phrase four, where the entropy is clearly decreasing. But in general, the values are rather similar (Figure 4).

In summary: Concerning mean values of syncopicity, event density, and duration classes, the improvisations by Paul Desmond and Chet Baker are highly similar. The differences become obvious when one explores the dramaturgy and the concordances of different analytical features. Baker appears to be the more 'expressive lyricist'. Whether the analytical findings described here are special in the context of West Coast jazz (and in part that of East Coast jazz as well) will be explored by a comparison with the aforementioned jazz musicians (Figure 8).

First of all, the percentage of syncopicity was calculated for each solo. West Coast jazz instrumentalists Stan Getz and Zoot Sims play distinctly more syncopations, whereas Lee Konitz and Warne Marsh clearly play fewer syncopated tone events—probably due to the higher amount of fast eighth-note chains. Baker, Desmond and Mulligan are located in between the extremes. In comparison with the other West Coast jazz musicians, Desmond and Baker seem to create less rhythmic tension in terms of syncopicity, but more than their East Coat fellows. Furthermore, Figure 8 illustrates the event density (tones per second) per soloist. Evidently, Gerry Mulligan's event density is noticeably higher than that of Desmond and Baker, whereas Zoot Sims's improvisations do not clearly differ—in this case, Stan Getz is located in between the extremes. In contrast, the values of Konitz's and Marsh's solos are generally much higher, indicating that these players appear to be more clearly rooted in the bebop tradition of playing fast lines.[21] Finally, the values for the entropy of duration classes are compared in regard to all instrumentalists. Gerry Mulligan's and Stan Getz's values are lower in comparison to Desmond and Baker, whereas those of Zoot Sims are clearly higher. The values of the East Coast jazz musicians are comparable with Desmond's and Baker's solos in the case of Lee Konitz, but clearly lower in Warne Marsh's improvisations. The variability of duration classes in Paul Desmond's and Chet Baker's improvisations is apparently higher than in the solos by most of the other musicians.[22] It can be assumed that this higher flexibility of rhythmic structures is due to a lesser importance of fast note chains, indicating a more 'melodic' playing.

---

[21] A one-way ANOVA of event density by performer revealed that this is indeed a very strong difference ($F(6, 38) = 9.917$, $p = .000^{***}$, adj. $R^2 = .549$)

[22] A one-way ANOVA of the entropy of absolute duration classes by performer yielded moderate differences ($F(6, 48) = 3.327$, $p = .01^{**}$, adj. $R^2 = .249$).

Table 2: Most discriminating features between Paul Desmond and Stan Getz / Gerry Mulligan / Zoot Sims.

Feature	PD	GMS	Cohen's d	Sig.
Rel. freq. dur. class short (abs)	0.47	0.24	1.41	***
Event density	3.71	4.71	−1.29	***
Rel. freq. dur. class very short (abs)	0.37	0.67	−1.24	***
Rel. freq. CDPCX (3)	0.16	0.11	0.96	***
Dur. class bigram entropy	2.61	1.90	0.95	***
Dur. class entropy (abs)	0.75	0.57	0.92	**
Mean length chromatic ascending	3.86	2.77	0.70	*
Mean length of eighth-note chains	3.03	3.94	−0.58	*

Note. Significance is coded as * = $p < .05$, ** = $p < .01$, *** = $p < .001$; PD = Paul Desmond, GMS = Stan Getz, Gerry Mulligan, and Zoot Sims; duration class bigram entropy is a measure for rhythmic variability; duration class short is the relative frequency of short durations (approx. eighth notes); duration class very short is the relative frequency of sixteenth and shorter notes; event density is the number of tone events per second; CDPCX density (3) is the relative frequency of the thirds of the contextual chord; duration class entropy is also a measure of rhythmic variability. Finally, mean sequence lengths are calculated by identifying chains of identical elements and averaging the number of elements of these sequences across a solo. Cohen's d is a measure of effect size, defined as the mean difference divided by the (pooled) standard deviation, i. e., it is the difference in units of standard deviations. (Absolute) values between .2 and .5 are commonly considered to be small, values between .5 and .8 to be medium, and values beyond .8 to be strong effects. The sign indicates the direction of the effect. Hence, a positive value of d means that Paul Desmond has a higher mean value than all the other soloists.

Concluding statistical comparisons

In the following, the foregoing analysis will be complemented by further statistical analyses. The Weimar Jazz Database provides the opportunity to statistically cross-check multiple musical features in order to compare the personal styles of individual musicians with a number of other soloists, or even with all the other musicians and solos contained in the database. The following tables list only those differences that are statistically significant. Paul Desmond and Chet Baker will be compared with West Coast jazz musicians on the one hand and East Coast cool jazz instrumentalists on the other. Interestingly enough, when comparing Paul Desmond's and Chet Baker's solos, the only statistically significant differences concern the mean length of

Table 3: Most discriminating features between Paul Desmond and Lee Konitz / Warne Marsh.

Feature	PD	KM	Cohen's d	Sig.
Event density	3.17	5.79	−2.43	***
IOI class entropy (rel)	0.72	0.39	2.08	***
Dur. class bigram entropy	2.61	1.53	1.61	***
Rel. freq. IOI class short (rel)	0.51	0.78	−1.29	***
Mean length of homogeneous rhythms	2.06	3.10	−1.09	***
Mean length of eighth note chains	3.03	5.26	−1.03	**
Mean length sequences descending	4.06	4.84	−0.95	**
Mean length step descending	3.38	4.47	−0.78	*
Mean lengths of chains of very short tones	1.38	2.63	−0.76	*
Mean number of unique pitch classes per phrase	6.04	7.75	−0.74	*

Note. Significance is coded as * = $p < .05$, ** = $p < .01$, *** = $p < .001$; PD = Paul Desmond, KM = Lee Konitz and Warne Marsh.

chromatic ascending tone-chains (Desmond: 3.9; Baker: 2.0) and the standard deviation of the intervals played (Desmond: 3.6; Baker: 2.7). The first table illustrates a comparison (mean values) between Paul Desmond and other West Coast jazz musicians—Gerry Mulligan, Stan Getz, and Zoot Sims (Table 2). In this case, there are various significant differences. Results that especially confirm the findings presented in the foregoing sections concern Desmond's higher variability regarding duration classes and his special emphasis on the third, and furthermore, the clearly lower value for event density. The results of a comparison with the East Coast cool jazz musicians mentioned above—Lee Konitz and Warne Marsh—appear to be confirmed (Table 3). For instance, the differences concern the inter-onset intervals—Konitz and Marsh play faster tone chains, whereas the variability of IOIs is clearly higher in the case of Desmond (IOI class entropy), as is the variability of duration classes. Table 4 shows significant differences between Chet Baker and other West Coast jazz musicians. There are less significant deviations from other West Coast jazz instrumentalists, as in the case of Paul Desmond, while some results appear fairly similar. This concerns differences regarding short and very short duration classes, and furthermore, the rhythmic variability (duration class entropy). One last table illustrates a comparison between Chet Baker and Lee Konitz / Warne Marsh (Table 5). As in the case of Paul

Table 4: Most discriminating features between Chet Baker and Stan Getz / Gerry Mulligan / Zoot Sims.

Feature	CB	GMS	Cohen's d	Sig.
Rel. freq. duration class short (abs)	0.42	0.26	1.05	***
Duration class very short (abs)	0.45	0.67	−0.87	**
Duration class bigram entropy	2.50	1.90	0.78	**
Mean length of quarter note chains	1.90	1.49	0.75	*
Duration class entropy (abs)	0.69	0.57	0.60	*

Note. Significance is coded as * = $p < .05$, ** = $p < .01$, *** = $p < .001$; CB = Chet Baker; GMS = Stan Getz, Gerry Mulligan, and Zoot Sims.

Table 5: Most discriminating features between Chet Baker and Lee Konitz / Warne Marsh.

Feature	CB	KM	Cohen's d	Sig.
Mean length of quarter note chains	1.89	1.20	1.74	***
IOI class entropy (rel)	0.66	0.39	1.66	***
Dur. class bigram entropy	2.50	1.53	1.39	***
Rel. freq. of IOI class short (rel)	0.55	0.78	−1.29	***
CDPCX density (4)	0.13	0.08	1.06	**
Mean length descending sequences	4.15	4.84	−0.77	*
Mean length of very short tone chains	1.33	2.63	0.75	*
Mean length of eighth-note chains	3.54	5.26	−0.73	*
Mean length of rhythmically uniform chains	2.35	3.10	−0.71	*

Note. Significance is coded as * = $p < .05$, ** = $p < .01$, *** = $p < .001$; CB = Chet Baker; KM = Lee Konitz and Warne Marsh.

Desmond, the deviations repeatedly concern the variability of IOI classes and duration classes. Additionally, Baker tends to avoid chains of fast tones (see 'Rel. freq. of relative IOI class short'), and he especially emphasizes the fourth.

Conclusion and outlook

The results of the foregoing section reveal that several differences regarding improvisational styles of the 'lyricists' Paul Desmond and Chet Baker and other musicians of West Coast or East Coast cool jazz can be described in terms of statistics of musical features. Furthermore, in terms of statistics, Chet Baker's improvisations appear to be more similar to solos by other musicians mentioned in this chapter. What could not be taken into consideration in this analysis is the personal sound of Paul Desmond and Chet Baker, which has been described as "lyrical", "airy", "romantic", "tender" (Kunzler, 2002, p. 292), "bright", or "lucid" (Gioia, 1992, p. 90). As shown above, musical features regarding pitch choices and rhythm can be adequately explored in order to describe aspects of personal style. However, it must be assumed that the phenomena of personal sound are of at least similar relevance. Future studies would be well advised to consider these distinctive traits of Desmond's and Baker's styles.

Trumpet giants:
Freddie Hubbard and Woody Shaw

Benjamin Burkhart

In the liner notes of the album *The Eternal Triangle* (1988), producer Michael Cuscuna describes Freddie Hubbard and Woody Shaw as "the two most volatile and most creative living jazz trumpeters" (cited from Richardson, 2006, p. 3). Obviously, Cuscuna was highly impressed by the collaboration of the two 'trumpet giants'. Both Hubbard and Shaw stand for the transgression of the technical limitations of their instrument, for an unusually virtuoso approach to trumpet playing. This chapter aims at systematically describing two characteristics of the virtuoso improvisational styles of both musicians: the internal structure of tone chains and the use of wide intervals.

Frederick Dewayne "Freddie" Hubbard was born in Indianapolis in 1938 and played the trumpet, mellophone, tuba, and french horn during his high school years. He started his career as a professional musician in the mid-1950s when he had lessons with the first trumpeter of the Indianapolis Symphony Orchestra, and performed live and on recordings with various jazz ensembles. After moving to New York in 1958, he frequently played with renowned jazz musicians such as Sonny Rollins and J. J. Johnson, before replacing Lee Morgan in Art Blakey's Jazz Messengers in 1961. During the 1960s, he formed his own ensembles and continuously performed as a sideman for, e. g., John Coltrane, Eric Dolphy, and Herbie Hancock. With the latter, he participated in the recording of the seminal LP *Maiden Voyage* (1965). Besides his experiments with various styles of jazz and popular music during the 1970s and 1980s, he occasionally gave lessons at colleges (cf. Barnhart, 2005, pp. 117f.; Kernfeld, 2002a, pp. 288f.; Kerschbaumer, 2003, pp. 435ff.).

According to Randy Sandke, Hubbard can be regarded as "one of the major voices in jazz of the sixties and seventies" (Sandke, 2000, p. 623). He is further praised as being one of the best and most important hard bop trumpeters, and especially his improvisational diversity is highlighted by several authors (Kernfeld, 2002a, p. 289; Kerschbaumer, 2003, p. 436). Musicologist Thomas Owens even speaks of Hubbard as "one of the most powerful and distinctive trumpeters and flugelhorn players in jazz" (Owens, 1995, p. 134). Among the musical features mentioned most often in writings on Freddie Hubbard are motivic development, melodic sophistication, and especially fast tone chains (cf. Kernfeld, 1995, p. 150; Owens, 1995, p. 134). Furthermore, his personal style was not only praised by jazz critics and musicologists, but by jazz musicians as well. For instance, Wynton Marsalis states: "He brought the big sound, he had great phrasing, and he had a sense of being extremely modern" (cited from Goldsher, 2002, p. 22). The trumpeter and flugelhorn player Valery Ponomarev especially emphasizes Hubbard's rhythmic precision: "His rhythmic approach was so accurate, so precise. His precision was incredible—ridiculous, really" (cited from Goldsher, 2002, p. 23). According to Thomas Owens, Hubbard's very precise and fast tone chains often consist of repetitions of several smaller units (Owens, 1995, p. 135). Additionally, as Harold Ousley states, Hubbard often made "scales out of certain intervals, like alternating seconds and minor thirds" (cited from Berliner, 1994, p. 224) and from these created various patterns that he combined while improvising. Another often proposed characteristic of Hubbard's style as a trumpet player is that he was influenced by saxophone players, especially John Coltrane and Sonny Rollins (Kunzler, 2004a, p. 582; Richardson, 2006, p. 4). According to trumpeter Chuck Mangione, he even sounded as if "Sonny Rollins [was] playing the trumpet" (cited from Goldsher, 2002, p. 25).

Woody (Herman II) Shaw was born 1944 in Laurinburg, North Carolina as the son of a gospel singer. He began to play the trumpet at the age of 11 and became a member of a YMCA (Young Men's Christian Association) big band when he was 14. As a professional musician in the 1960s, Shaw performed with Eric Dolphy, Max Roach, and Herbie Hancock and was a member of Art Blakey's Jazz Messengers from 1971–1972. Like Freddie Hubbard, he further worked as a jazz educator in schools and colleges during the 1970s (Kernfeld, 2002c, pp. 557f.; Kerschbaumer, 2006, p. 685). The trumpeter Brian Lynch characterized Woody Shaw as "the last innovator in the trumpet lineage" (cited from Goldsher, 2002, p. 31) and he was further called a "trumpet machine" or even "monster" (Sandke, 2000, p. 541). As in the case of Freddie Hubbard, Shaw's ability to improvise unusually fast tone chains with high precision is described as one of the key characteristics of his personal style (Kernfeld, 2002c, p. 557). And, like Freddie Hubbard, Woody Shaw is also believed to be strongly influenced by jazz saxophonists, mainly John Coltrane and Eric Dolphy (Kunzler, 2004b, p. 1205; Richardson, 2006, p. 4). According to Randy Sandke, Coltrane was the main influence, since Shaw had systematically developed Coltrane's melodic and harmonic ideas (Sandke, 2000, p. 624). What fascinated Shaw's contemporaries even more was his characteristic manner of intervallic playing. None other than Freddie Hubbard once stated: "He played intervals that made him sound different from *anybody*. He called his style 'intervallic playing'. He was one of the most modern trumpeters of his era" (cited from Goldsher, 2002, p. 30, italics in original). Fourths in particular are described as essential for Woody Shaw's personal style and sound, even in fast tone chains, requiring a high level of technical mastery (Berliner, 1994, p. 165; Goldsher, 2002, p. 30; Kerschbaumer, 2006, p. 685).

To sum up, important components of the personal styles of Freddie Hubbard and Woody Shaw appear to be a 'saxophone-like' approach to the trumpet and their fast and virtuoso playing, including a characteristic use of (wide) intervals. According to Edward Rex Richardson, the intervallic playing in particular can be regarded as an important influence of reed-instrumentalists or even pianists. He assumes that Hubbard's and Shaw's personal styles are "typified by the unusually wide intervals [...], intervals that defy 'natural' idiomatic trumpet playing and that seem derived more from the instrumental language of reed-players and keyboardists than from brass players" (Richardson, 2006, p. 4). Indeed, Hubbard and Shaw have frequently been compared; Hubbard is often believed to be a great influence on Shaw (Kunzler, 2004b, p. 1205; Owens, 1995, p. 136)—which Hubbard himself emphasized, too (Goldsher, 2002, p. 31). Shaw, on the other hand, rejected any comparisons with Hubbard and stated that he had never been directly influenced by him.

Usage of intervals within lines

The following analysis does not aim at describing and comparing the personal styles of Freddie Hubbard and Woody Shaw in total, but instead focuses on fast virtuoso lines and the approach to intervallic playing. It will examine whether there are concordances regarding the use of wide intervals in virtuoso parts of the improvisations. Furthermore, structural details of tone chains will be explored, especially the use of patterns. Thereby, the usage of characteristic intervallic patterns will be analyzed in order to estimate to what degree both musicians make use of memorized and pre-practiced musical formulas. Therefore, in this section only musical units that can be characterized as lines or fast tone chains will be analyzed in detail, while other aspects of their personal styles, e. g., motivic improvising or the general dramaturgy of solos, are treated as side issues.

Table 1: Percentage of midlevel units in solos by Freddie Hubbard and Woody Shaw.

MLU main type	Hubbard	Shaw
lick	58.9	48.9
line	21.9	22.2
melody	10.9	14.7
rhythm	6.8	4.9
void	0.0	1.1
fragment	0.0	1.5
expressive	1.0	4.9
quote	0.5	0.0
theme	0.0	1.9

The Weimar Jazz Database contains six solos by Freddie Hubbard, recorded during a period from 1960–1966. In the case of Woody Shaw, the database encompasses eight solos, recorded in 1977, 1978, and 1987. The improvisational units that shall be explored were chosen with the aid of the midlevel analysis approach (cf. Chapter *Computational melody analysis*). In doing so, jazz improvisations are interpreted based on successions of musical units based on various ideas. There are nine main categories for labeling those units: line, lick, melody, theme, rhythm, expressive, quote, fragment, and void. Table 1 provides an overview of the percentages of midlevel units in the solos by Freddie Hubbard and Woody Shaw. In total, 192 midlevel units were annotated in the solos by Hubbard, and 266 in the solos by Shaw. The percentages of midlevel units labeled as lines are similar for both musicians. Still, there are clear differences regarding the overall percentage of midlevel categories. Hubbard plays more licks, and he also improvises more rhythmically. Shaw, on the other hand, clearly plays more melodies, fragments, and expressive passages, or leaves voids. In general, Woody Shaw's solos are more variably structured, since the entropy of midlevel units is 1.45, whereas in Hubbard's solos it is 1.23 (cf. Chapter *Computational melody analysis*). A first step for a comparison of the structural details can be undertaken by statistically analyzing the durations, numbers of played tones, and event densities of all the lines by Freddie Hubbard and Woody Shaw (Table 2). The obvious differences concern the median number of tones per line and the median event density, for which Shaw's values are clearly higher. Overall, the values for both musicians appear to be comparable. Especially the large range for duration, number of tones, and event density can be regarded as one obvious concordance in the personal styles of Hubbard and Shaw.

Table 2: Duration, number of tones, and event density (tones per second) in lines by Freddie Hubbard and Woody Shaw.

	Hubbard	Shaw
Median duration (sec)	2.16	2.58
Range of durations	0.84–9.23	0.70–9.08
Standard deviation of durations	1.82	1.63
Median number of tones per line	16	21
Range of number of tones per line	6-65	6-58
Standard deviation of number of tones	3.63	2.33
Median event density (tones/sec)	7.21	8.90
Range of event density (tones/sec)	3.11–16.36	3.89–13.67
Standard deviation of event density	10.37	11.35

In order to compare the intervallic structures of tone chains played by Hubbard and Shaw, which are believed to be unusual in general but characteristic for both musicians, one can refer to an analysis of 'fuzzy intervals'. Table 3 provides an overview: 'Large jump up' stands for interval steps bigger than a fifth (seven semitones), 'jump up' for five to seven semitones, 'leap up' for three or four semitones, and so forth—the values signify the percentage for all lines and for all solos, respectively. Additionally, the entropy of fuzzy intervals was calculated, whereby higher values signify higher variability (cf. Chapter *Computational melody analysis*; Table 3). While in general there are many large jumps in the solos, both musicians tend to avoid large interval jumps and tone repetitions in their lines. Furthermore, the values for interval jumps and leaps are clearly higher in the case of Shaw, whereas one concordance is the tendency to play more decreasing intervals than increasing ones. Since the variation of intervals is obviously higher in Shaw's lines, it is hardly surprising that the entropy of fuzzy intervals is also significantly higher (Wilcoxon test $W(99) = 622$, $p = 0.000$). Regarding intervallic variability, the lines of Woody Shaw appear to be more complexly structured—especially since the event density is also higher. Clearly, Woody Shaw plays interval jumps or leaps even in very fast lines with a high level of technical difficulty. The virtuoso lines played by Freddie Hubbard appear to consist primarily of comparatively small interval steps. Furthermore, the percentage of fourths in the lines illustrates obvious differences: Shaw's percentage for ascending (3.6) fourths is more than three times as high as Hubbard's (1.2). Regarding ascending fourths, the difference is even bigger: 6.0 % in Shaw's improvisations, and 1.5 % in Hubbard's. Figure 1 provides an overview of semitone

Table 3: Distribution and entropy of fuzzy intervals in solos by Freddie Hubbard and Woody Shaw.

	Freddie Hubbard		Woody Shaw	
	lines (%)	solos (%)	lines (%)	solos (%)
Large jump up	1.0	3.5	0.3	1.6
Jump up	2.5	3.7	7.8	8.3
Leap up	7.2	8.8	9.0	9.3
Step up	27.9	24.6	24.6	23.4
Repetition	1.5	7.1	1.2	5.6
Step down	46.5	34.6	38.4	31.6
Leap down	11.2	12.6	13.7	13.7
Jump down	1.8	3.9	4.9	6.2
Large jump down	0.4	1.1	0.1	0.3
Entropy (median)	0.42	0.76	0.59	0.72

interval distribution in all lines by Freddie Hubbard and Woody Shaw. Since Woody Shaw obviously plays wide intervals even in high-speed tone chains, one may ask if he makes use of pre-conceived patterns to meet the technical challenge of playing wide intervals in fast lines.

Usage of long patterns

According to musicologist Thomas Owens, patterns play a distinctive role for the improvisational language of jazz musicians: "Every mature jazz musician develops a repertory of motives and phrases which he uses in the course of his improvisations. His 'spontaneous' performances are actually pre-composed to some extent" (Owens, 1974, p. 17). The improvisations of Freddie Hubbard and Woody Shaw are assumed to be influenced by modal scales, e. g., "a pentatonic sort of scale" (cited from Berliner, 1994, p. 228). Such assumptions imply clear concordances of their improvisational styles, especially regarding the usage of certain interval patterns.

When searching for recurring formulas in Hubbard's and Shaw's solos, there were various exclusion criteria for the selection of passages that can be defined as patterns. On the one hand, repetitions of single tones, which appear several times in solos by both musicians, were not considered. The same applies to oscillations of two or more tones. Additionally, since only tone chains were analyzed and as the aim was to exclude short patterns that might only

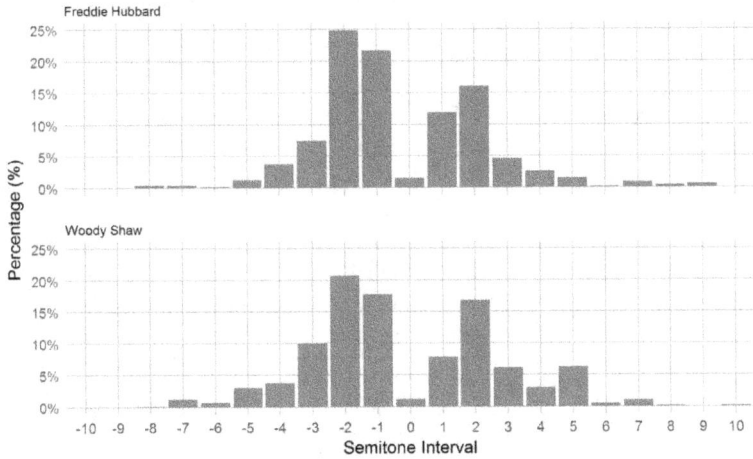

Figure 1: Interval histogram over lines in solos by Freddie Hubbard and Woody Shaw.

be repeated by accident, comparatively long patterns of at least eight tones occurring at least twice in at least two different solos were searched for. It can be assumed that patterns of at least eight tones that occur in different improvisations and in different metrical or harmonic contexts are unlikely to have been created 'on the fly' but are instead practiced and learned in advance. Since one focus of this chapter is on interval structures, interval patterns were taken into consideration—that is, patterns of the same intervals, independent from actual pitches. Searching for patterns meeting the above mentioned criteria results in 77 patterns in Hubbard's improvisations, and 125 in Shaw's. Most of those patterns are played within different solos, while patterns played twice (or more) in only one solo are rather seldom (Table 4).[23]

In the solos contained in the Weimar Jazz Database, Freddie Hubbard seldom plays patterns longer than eight, and never longer than nine tones occurring in two or more improvisations. Woody Shaw makes use of interval patterns more extensively than Freddie Hubbard, even though the numbers of patterns occurring in more than one solo are comparable. However, there are two striking exceptions: Freddie Hubbard's solo on "Maiden Voyage" and Woody Shaw's solo on "In a Capricornian Way". All patterns that are alike with respect to the intervallic structure, independent of duration or rhythm, are listed. Hence, the results must be cross-checked (by ear) in order to check if

---

[23] Since mistakes in the transcriptions must be expected, it is just possible that there are even more patterns in the solos that cannot be analyzed in this chapter.

Table 4: Interval patterns in solos by Freddie Hubbard and Woody Shaw.

Performer	Solo	Interval patterns
Freddie Hubbard	245	0
	Dolphin Dance	2
	Down Under	0
	Maiden Voyage	30
	Society Red	9
	Speak No Evil	0
	All eight solos	77
	At least two solos	59
Woody Shaw	Dat Dere	7
	If I Were a Bell	9
	Imagination	8
	In a Capricornian Way	26
	Rahsaan's Run	8
	Rosewood	6
	Stepping Stone	4
	Steve's Blues	6
	All eight solos	125
	At least two solos	72

Note. Only interval patterns counted with at least eight elements occurring at least twice.

they sound similar, too. This is of particular relevance in this chapter, since the aim is to explore characteristics in fast tone chains. In a first step, one can refer to the durations of patterns—only comparatively short durations can refer to lines. Secondly, if durations of two or more listed patterns are similar, musical similarities should be checked by ear. When checking the 59 interval patterns that can be found in at least two of Hubbard's solos, it must be stated that there are only two results: an ascending line of eight tones he plays both on "Dolphin Dance" (2:21 min, original recording) and "Maiden Voyage" (3:15 min, original recording). That is, Hubbard largely avoids long interval patterns occurring in two or more solos that sound similar with respect to duration and rhythm. Additionally, patterns that appear to be highly similar are almost not part of the fast tone chains that are in the focus of this chapter.

Figure 2: Interval patterns (13 intervals) in solos by Woody Shaw: "In a Capricornian Way" (top) and "Rahsaan's Run" (bottom). The beams above the staves mark the patterns, the numbers signify the interval steps in semitones.

Woody Shaw, on the other hand, plays several patterns that are similar in a musical sense within different solos and parts of high tempo tone chains. One striking example is a pattern of 13 intervals occurring in the solos on "In a Capricornian Way" and "Rahsaan's Run" (Figure 2). Rhythmically, the two examples are slightly different, but the patterns are obviously parts of comparatively fast tone chains. The durations are 1.15 s ("In a Capricornian Way"), and 1.36 s ("Rahsaan's Run"). Whereas the patterns mainly consist of small interval steps up to three semitones, Shaw also plays a major third (4) and a fourth (5). Tellingly, not only the intervals but also the pitches are identical. Another example that illustrates Woody Shaw's usage of wide intervals in virtuoso lines even better is a twelve-interval-pattern occurring in "In a Capricornian Way" and "Rosewood" (Figure 3). In this case, the durations are again very similar: 1.21 seconds ("In a Capricornian Way"), and 1.14 s ("Rosewood"). Woody Shaw plays fifths (7), fourths (5), and major thirds (4), which is rather challenging due to the very high tempo. Interestingly enough, the absolute pitches are transposed by one semi-tone here. Tonally, the first instance is clearly outside, utilizing A major tones over an Eb^{7sus4} chord, whereas in the second instance the pattern neatly aligns with the underlying Gm^9 chord. One further long pattern can be found in the same two solos (Figure 4). Shaw avoids wide intervals until the end of the pattern, where he plays two fourths. Again, the absolute pitches are identical here, but the metrical location is shifted by half a beat. Tonally, the first instance uses tones from the Eb minor scale over an F^{7sus4} chord, which is slightly off, whereas the second instance fully fits the Ab^{7sus4} chord, with a rather outside Eb minor pickup on beat four of the preceding measure.

As a matter of fact, fourth-steps indeed appear to be an essential characteristic of Shaw's improvisations, even at very high tempi. The interval patterns oc-

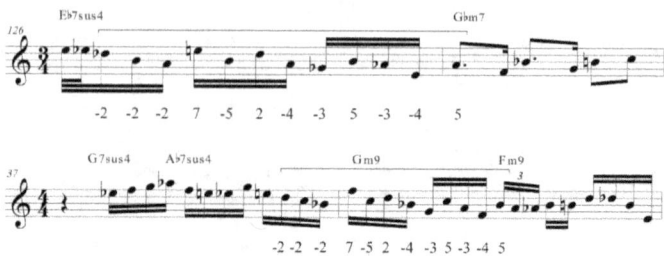

Figure 3: Interval patterns (twelve intervals) in solos by Woody Shaw: "In a Capricornian Way" (top) and "Rosewood" (bottom).

Figure 4: Interval patterns (eleven intervals) in solos by Woody Shaw: "In a Capricornian Way" (top) and "Rosewood" (bottom).

curring in two or more solos by Freddie Hubbard encompass no fourths at all. Hubbard clearly focuses on seconds and, to a lesser extent, on thirds—which matches the aforementioned assumption of playing "scales out of certain intervals, like alternating seconds and minor thirds" (cited from Berliner, 1994, p. 224). In the following, two solos by Hubbard and Shaw ("Maiden Voyage" and "In a Capricornian Way"), in which the numbers of patterns are clearly higher than in all others, will be analyzed in order to contextualize the previous findings.

A Comparison: "Maiden Voyage" vs. "In a Capricornian Way"

The modal tune "Maiden Voyage", composed by Herbie Hancock, was recorded in March 1965 and released on Hancock's LP of the same title. The lineup consisted of Hancock on piano, Freddie Hubbard on trumpet, George Cole-

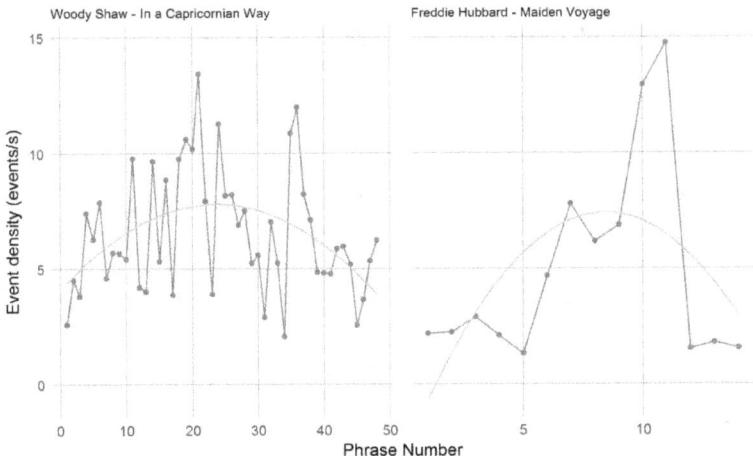

Figure 5: Event density (tones per second) over phrases in Freddie Hubbard's solo on "Maiden Voyage" and Woody Shaw's solo on "In a Capricornian Way".

man on tenor saxophone, Ron Carter on bass, and Tony Williams on drums. Hubbard's solo has been described as "a magnificently creative improvisation", due to the combination of melodic, rhythmic, and rapid scalar passages (Kernfeld, 1995, p. 150). When listening to the improvisation, the impression of a clearly thought-out dramaturgy and an increasing intensity arises—ranging from fairly cantabile passages at the beginning to virtuoso scalar lines at the end. To illustrate the course of intensity, Figure 5 demonstrates the development of event density (number of tones per second) per phrase. The event density clearly increases over the course of the solo, while decreasing at the end; the values range from 1.31 (phrase 5) to 14.76 (phrase 11).

The high event density results from the fast tone chains that start at 3:48 min in the original recording. The high number of patterns in Hubbard's improvisation is due to these lines: Hubbard constantly repeats and further develops scalar passages. The longest interval pattern encompasses 20 tones, and also consists of shorter, but still comparatively long patterns of 14 and 12 tones occurring in other stages of the improvisation. These rapid tone chains, as notated by Barry Kernfeld in his easy-to-read transcription of the solo (Kernfeld, 1995, pp. 147ff.), only consist of interval steps up to minor thirds. Hubbard seems to play these lines in a very high tempo in order to increase the improvisation's intensity at the end of the solo. He does not re-use ideas introduced in other stages of the improvisation or even in other

Figure 6: Interval patterns (twelve intervals) in Woody Shaw's solo on "In a Capricornian Way".

solos contained in the Weimar Jazz Database. Additionally, he clearly focuses on small interval steps—pentatonic scales described as characteristic for Hubbard's pattern vocabulary (Berliner, 1994, p. 228) cannot be found in the improvisation on "Maiden Voyage".

"In a Capricornian Way", a composition by Woody Shaw, was recorded in 1978 and released on the album *Stepping Stones. Live At The Village Vanguard* in the same year. The following musicians participated in the recording session: Woody Shaw (cornet), Carter Jefferson (tenor saxophone), Onaje Allan Gumbs (piano), Clint Houston (bass), and Victor Lewis (drums). Figure 5 illustrates the event density over phrases in Shaw's solo. The values range from 2.05 to 13.42 tones per second, which is comparable to Hubbard's improvisation on "Maiden Voyage". The dramaturgical increase of intensity is not as clear as in "Maiden Voyage", since there are several peaks and a general zigzag structure.

Besides the patterns occurring in "In a Capricornian Way" as well as in other solos by Shaw, there are further examples he plays twice in this improvisation, too. One striking example is a twelve-interval-pattern occurring two times (Figure 6). Obviously, Woody Shaw re-uses a pattern he introduced 39 bars earlier. The harmonic and metrical contexts are rather similar, since Shaw simply shifts the starting position of the pattern from the first to the second beat of a bar. Additionally, the absolute pitches are the same. Shaw frequently re-uses long interval patterns over the course of the solo, which is illustrated in Figure 7.

Pitch patterns as shown above are no exception in Shaw's improvisations: Altogether, he plays 56 pitch patterns of at least eight tones occurring in two or more solos. Freddie Hubbard, on the other hand, only plays 19 comparable patterns. Clearly, Shaw is more apt to long patterns than Hubbard, interval

Trumpet giants

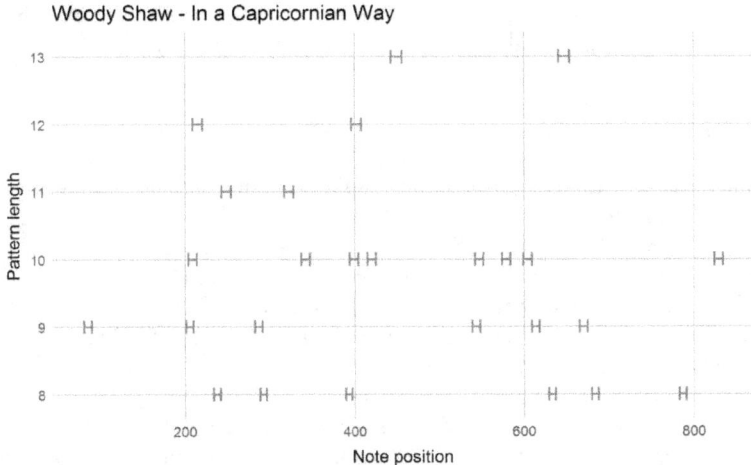

Figure 7: Distribution of interval patterns (eight to thirteen intervals) in Woody Shaw's solo on "In a Capricornian Way".

Table 5: Pitch patterns in the solos by Freddie Hubbard and Woody Shaw.

Performer	Solo	Pitch patterns
Freddie Hubbard	245	0
	Dolphin Dance	0
	Down Under	0
	Maiden Voyage	12
	Society Red	7
	Speak No Evil	0
Woody Shaw	Dat Dere	4
	If I Were a Bell	4
	Imagination	6
	In a Capricornian Way	22
	Rahsaan's Run	8
	Rosewood	4
	Stepping Stone	4
	Steve's Blues	0

Note. Only pitch patterns counted with at least eight elements occurring at least twice.

or pitch patterns alike. This impression can be confirmed when summarizing the pitch patterns over all solos by both musicians (Table 5).

Summary

When listening to the improvisations by Freddie Hubbard and Woody Shaw contained in the Weimar Jazz Database, some parallels can be found. As shown above, Hubbard's and Shaw's tone chains are comparable to a certain degree—especially regarding the percentages of lines in relation to other midlevel units, or concerning the durations and the numbers of tones per line. But when examining structural details, the differences become obvious. The intervallic structures of Shaw's tone chains clearly differ from Hubbard's, since Hubbard rather tends to make use of wide intervals when playing musical ideas other than lines. On the other hand, Shaw's focus on fourths, even in high tempos, could clearly be confirmed. Furthermore, and possibly as a result of the high technical difficulty resulting from his intervallic playing, Woody Shaw seems to refer to a repertory of memorized patterns that is much easier to retrace than in the case of Freddie Hubbard.

Michael Brecker's "I Mean You"

Wolf-Georg Zaddach

Due to his outstanding instrumental skills and enormous workload as a recording and performing artist, Michael Brecker is "widely regarded as the most influential tenor saxophonist since John Coltrane" (Gans, 2017). In fact, his personal style includes bebop and postbop improvisation as well as soul and pop music. Therefore, analyzing his solos can be a fruitful approach to help understanding the widely shared opinion about Brecker. Brecker (1949–2007), born and raised in the metropolitan area of Philadelphia, already worked with renowned jazz and fusion musicians like Billy Cobham and Horace Silver in his early 20s, and gained wider recognition with the Brecker Brothers, with his brother Randy on the trumpet. After 1980, Brecker made more than 15 recordings as a leader. Besides these, he went on appearing as a sideman on recordings by Chick Corea, Herbie Hancock, John Abercrombie as well as Art Garfunkel or Billy Joel, among others. When Brecker died due to complications of leukemia in 2007, he had participated on more than 700 recordings and won 15 Grammy Awards.

In 1995, Brecker was featured on *Infinity* with the McCoy Tyner Trio. Here, Brecker once again demonstrates his energetic and creative improvisation abilities. Besides a version of John Coltrane's "Impressions"—for which Brecker won a Grammy as "Best Jazz Instrumental Solo"—, the album also contains the jazz standard "I Mean You". Originally written and first recorded by swing saxophonist Coleman Hawkins in 1946, the tune was rearranged by pianist Thelonious Monk in 1948 to become the ultimate version with an additional intro that is repeated after the regular form of 32 measures. It is this historic background of the song which challenges the improviser on a different level than, e.g., a modal tune.

When McCoy Tyner starts playing the first A section without bass and drums, he recalls the tune's origin and connection to the swing and early modern jazz era by using techniques of stride piano comping as well as walking bass lines in the left hand and unison lines in both hands. The band enters for the second A section and completes the head, including an odd last measure of $\frac{2}{4}$ instead of $\frac{4}{4}$ that functions as an upbeat to the repetition of the intro section. The tempo is a relaxed medium-up swing with about 180 bpm. Brecker starts his solo right after the head and the repeated intro section. During his rather short solo, he makes use of several modern jazz improvisation techniques, such as bebop scales, superimposition of chord progressions, symmetric scales such as the augmented and the half-step/whole-step scale, and constant structures. Yet these contemporary approaches are contrasted as well as interlinked with a rather traditional, early modern jazz style. How he manages to balance out the jazz tradition with advanced postbop techniques of improvisation during that short solo is remarkable, demonstrating Brecker's class. In the following, I will provide several analytical observations to corroborate this thesis.

The solo

The recording of "I Mean You" on *Infinity* follows the standard AABA form of 32 measures as can be found in the *557 Standards* compilation (p. 159). The solo form reads as follows:

A1	F^6	F^6	$D\flat^7$	D^7	Gm^7	C^7	F^6	$Gm^7\ C^7$
A2	F^6	F^6	$D\flat^7$	D^7	Gm^7	C^7	F^6	F^6
B1	$E\flat^7$	$E\flat^7$	F^6	F^6	$D\flat^7$	$D\flat^7$	$G\flat^7$	$Gm^7\ C^7$
A3	F^6	F^6	$D\flat^7$	D^7	Gm^7	C^7	F^6	F^6

Brecker plays two solo choruses. His solo sounds relaxed and bluesy, and yet modern and contrasting at certain points. When the solo starts, the listener detects the restraint of the rhythm section: After the head is played by the complete band, McCoy Tyner stops playing. He accompanies Brecker during the first chorus only within the B section. Due to this, the A sections of Brecker's first chorus are played as a saxophone trio without any chords, whereas the second chorus is fully accompanied by piano, bass, and drums. However, during the first chorus the bass plays out the harmonic progression rather clearly, as does McCoy Tyner, who renders the underlying chords with optional tones, fourth chords and bluesy minor third suspensions on major chords.

Brecker starts his solo in a somehow relaxed feeling with laid-back eighth notes. Additionally, possibly in reaction to McCoy Tyner's absence during the first two A sections, he plays phrases that span over four measures each (cf.

Michael Brecker's "I Mean You"

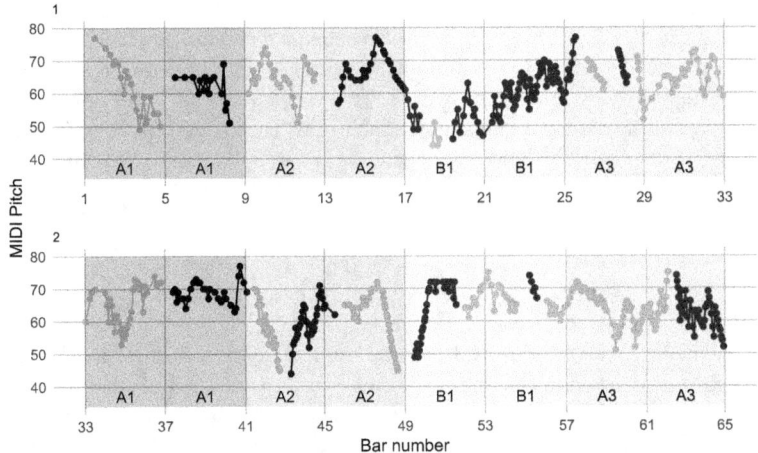

Figure 1: Piano roll of Brecker's solo. Phrases are alternatingly colored, form parts shaded gray. Pitch is displayed in MIDI pitch (C4 = 60). Top: first chorus, bottom: second chorus.

Figure 1). The beginning of all four phrases is a little delayed and set towards the middle of each measure, with the exception of the third phrase (m. 9, see Figure 3 at the end of this chapter). In doing so, Brecker emphasizes the regular structure of the sections and offers the opportunity to hear the roots of the underlying chords played by the bass at the beginning of each measure. At the same time, that strategy may give Brecker the chance to develop and react to the playing of the accompanying band. The tonal material outlines the somewhat uncommon chord progression of the tune, especially with the $D\flat^7$ and the following D^7 in the A section. The overall contour of the phrases is mostly descending. In combination with the laid-back phrasing, he recalls the motion of the theme of the A section and demonstrates a relaxed attitude. As I will show later on in detail, this is also supported by certain tonal choices.

During the second half of the B section, Brecker begins to play lines consisting of sixteenth notes. During the third A section, he seems to start mixing the relaxed feeling of the first half of the chorus and the intensity of the B section in terms of speed. The second chorus becomes more intense in terms of dramaturgy and speed, while the peak is reached in the last A section, right at the end of the solo. Overall, Brecker emphasizes a heavy swing feeling with a swing ratio of 1.77:1 on average, and occasionally almost triplet eighths with a ratio of 2:1. Other solos by Brecker in the Weimar Jazz Database demonstrate similar ratios in tunes with a similar, slightly slower mid-tempo ("Midnight Voyage", 126 bpm, with 1.7:1 and "Naked Soul", 92.4 bpm, with 1.8:1) as well as rather straight eighths such as in "Peep" (320 bpm) and "Cabin Fever" (300 bpm). This seems to depend on the overall tempo of the tune, see Figure 2.

Harmonic treatment, phrase structure and motifs

Over the first two A sections, Brecker plays phrases of four measures length which start delayed in the middle of each measure (see the full transcription based on the Weimar Jazz Database at the end of this chapter). The solo begins with an accent on beat three of the first measure that repeats the underlying root and tonic, as if he were shouting out "You", possibly derived from the three-tone motif of the theme whose rhythm fits the phrase "I Mean You". What follows is a descending line using the F major scale referring to the descending motif of the theme. Since the line expands onto four measures, Brecker needs to adjust and transform the line harmonically to the $D\flat^7$ chord in m. 3, while he is still on a descending move. Here, Brecker plays a descending $G^{7\sharp 5}$ arpeggio as the tritone substitution to the underlying $D\flat^7$.

During that first phrase, Brecker offers an interesting strategy to connect the somewhat unusual progression of F^6 | F^6 | $D\flat^7$ | D^7. While the first measures are purely inside F major, the following $D\flat^7$ and D^7 create an interesting tension due to their chromatic connection as well as an implied conversion of a dominant cycle or cycle of fifth to a cycle of fourths, if the $D\flat^7$ is interpreted as the tritone substitution of G^7. How does Brecker handle this progression exactly? Due to a slight and chromatic adjustment of the F on the last beat of m. 3 to an E on the first beat of m. 4, he displays the harmonic shift moving from the major third of the $D\flat^7$ to the ninth of the D^7. At the same time, he repeats the B natural from m. 3, the minor seventh of $D\flat^7$, again over the D^7. If one interprets the D^7 in F and therefore as the secondary dominant (V7/II) to the following Gm^7, the B♭ as a flatted 13th would be the required pitch for the D^7. But on the contrary, in m. 4 Brecker uses a D major pentatonic with the B natural on a strong beat. Nonetheless, in playing the natural B over the D^7, Brecker creates a specific connection between both measures in stressing the meaning and relevance of this prominent chromatic progression that is typical for the music of Thelonious Monk, for example in tunes like "Well You Needn't" or "Epistrophy". Brecker keeps using the B natural instead of the B♭ over the D^7 for the rest of solo, but contextualizes

Michael Brecker's "I Mean You"

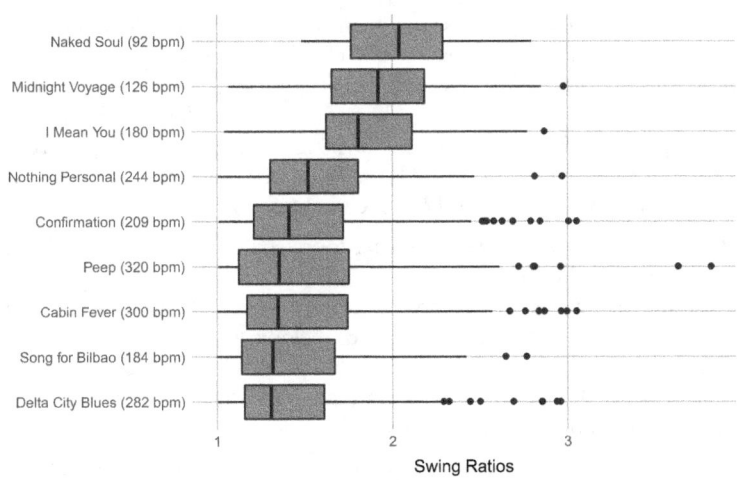

Figure 2: Box plot of swing ratios of Michael Brecker solos in the Weimar Jazz Database. Only swing ratios between 1:1 and 4:1 are kept. "I Mean You" has a median swing ratio of 1.92:1 and forms together with "Naked Soul" and "Midnight Voyage" a group of 'heavy swinging' solos.

it differently, e.g., as part of a A minor pentatonic implication in m. 28 or an augmented E^7 in m. 44. Additionally, this approach in the first four measures allows Brecker to divide the A sections into two harmonically consistent and coherent phrases of four measures with a harmonically rather interesting first part and a traditional II–V–I-cadence in the second part.

In the first B section, Brecker already deviates from a regular four-measure phrasing. He enters and leaves the B section by connecting with the A sections through expansions of the ongoing phrases so that they each end in the next section (cf. Figure 1). Even though he kind of jumps into it, this first B section follows the overall phrase division of four measures. Nevertheless, he marks the beginning of the B section with a new motif: From the descending F bebop scale in m. 16, he develops a motif that is striking due to its distinctive rhythm and tonal material of B♭ minor pentatonic over the E♭^{7}. The B♭ minor pentatonic creates a sus4 sound over the underlying E♭^{7}, but is also a coherent consequence of the descending F bebop dominant scale that Brecker plays in the preceding measure. Brecker transforms this idea into a leap sequence of ascending fourths in mm. 19 and 20, suggesting an F^{7sus4} that is resolved into a F^7. At this point, the first four measures of the B section are completed following the previous structure and yet varying it with distinctive motifs and breaks in between. The second half of the B section offers the first fast played line of mostly sixteenth notes. This phrase, which peaks in the first measure of the following A section with a high F, makes use of superimposed scales. The last A section is less clearly structured, though Brecker outlines the II–V–I progression and an additional turn-around with a superimposed chord progression that will be discussed later. The function of that superimposition is to clearly mark the end of the first chorus with a first climax.

The second chorus follows the rather loose structuring introduced in the second half of the first chorus. This allows Brecker to develop complex phrases with features of postbop improvisation such as four-tone patterns in combination with advanced harmonic or melodic ideas. Nevertheless, during the first two A sections of the second chorus, Brecker still seems to rely on the middle of the section as a focal point, releasing the tension mainly in terms of speed, but also harmonically.

In the B section, Brecker does not follow the regular phrase division anymore, but instead indicates the section again through motivic development. In m. 54, he plays in a descending motion the flatted fifth, the fourth and the major third of the underlying $D\flat^7$, which he repeats transposed and adjusted to the underlying C^7 in m. 56. Both are connected and seem to be a spontaneous invention. In doing so, he creates a guide tone line that descends chromatically in m. 54 from a B♭ to an E (though the A♭ is missing in m. 54) and is then interrupted by a measure and yet connected throughout the repetition of the $G\flat^7$ and the chromatic descending contour. The interrupting m. 55 stands out due to its harmonic content as well: Over the underlying $G\flat^7$, one can hear a clear Gm^7 arpeggio, with the minor third and root at the end of the phrase. One could interpret this in two different ways: a) Brecker makes use of side-stepping as a typical technique for playing outside (see below); b) Brecker approaches these last two measures with a horizontal displacement in which he anticipates the Gm^7 chord of the first half of the last measure having a full measure to fill with the C^7. At the same time, easily perceivable for the listener, the descending motif sounds bluesy and sly, which is an important general feature of Brecker's solo. The last A section is the highlight of the solo and contains mainly lines of sixteenth notes. Concerning the structuring of the phrases, it is the most outstanding section of the whole solo, making use of advanced techniques.

The usage of blues and bebop scales

During his relatively short solo, Brecker clearly makes references to the stylistic context of the piece, the late swing era as well as the bebop era as personified by the composers of the piece, Hawkins and Monk. Brecker uses several distinct techniques that echo this origin of modern jazz in particular: He re-harmonizes the tonic into a dominant seventh chord, uses blues and bebop scales, and quotes Charlie Parker. Brecker already uses the re-harmonization of the tonic F^6 in the first measure of the A2 of the first chorus (mm. 9 and 10). Here, he clearly plays the E♭ as the dominant seventh over two measures, the first on the strong beat three of m. 9. He does the same over the last two measures of the same section and the two measures of F in the first B section (mm. 19 and 20). For rest of the solo, Brecker avoids playing any sevenths over the F tonic with two exceptions in mm. 25 and 26 right after the first B section and in m. 52 in the second B section. Even though he does not repeat the minor seventh, the strong implication of the bluesy tonic has already been established by Brecker and picked up by the band. Interestingly, bassist Avery Sharps reacts already immediately to the first E♭ in m. 9 on beat three played by Brecker and plays an E♭ on beat four, leading into an F on the next beat followed by a descending chromatic line towards D, which can be understood as a typical F bebop dominant scale. At the end of the section, when Brecker again plays a F^7, Sharps incorporates the E♭ again in a bass line rising from the root to the fifth with the minor and major third and adding the E♭ and F on top. In the B section, both Sharps and McCoy Tyner emphasize the F^7 as well. McCoy Tyner has obviously been listening during the previous A sections and plays the F^7, with the additional blues influenced grace note of the minor third, simultaneously with Brecker's E♭ on beat three. In m. 25 in the A3 section, when Brecker switches back to the original F major seventh, Sharps outlines tones of the F major pentatonic while avoiding any sevenths. During m. 31 at the end of the section, he plays F–E♭–D–A♭, which amounts to an F^7 and D^7, respectively, the substitution $A♭^7$, which easily leads to the following Gm^7 and C^7 to complete the turn-around. During the following F^6 chords, when Brecker tends to avoid the seventh, the band seems to be still aware that he could repeat the blues influenced re-harmonization: In m. 33, right at the beginning of the second chorus, Sharps uses the E♭ again as a passing tone; in m. 47 before the second B section, he clearly plays an F^7 in the first measure with repeated insistence (F–F–E♭–E♭) while Brecker plays a fast descending line that implies A^7 with the additional blues interval of the flatted fifth—a possible indication of the coming $E♭^7$ as a tritone substitution. McCoy Tyner keeps the re-harmonization in mind as well, indicated by a bluesy F in m. 45 with the grace note of a minor third.

Blues and bebop scales are another feature that Brecker uses during his solo. According to Levine, a blues influenced scale is one of the "oldest, most basic melodic material" that has been played on the blues (Levine, 1995, p. 202ff.).

The motivic improvisation of the blues-influenced ascending guide tone line in mm. 54 and 56 is a reference to blue notes played earlier on. The first appearance of blue notes is again in the second A section of chorus one. In m. 11 he plays a descending line F–E–E♭ which creates a bluesy line with the major and minor third in regard to the underlying D♭^{7}. The descending line in m. 48, interpreted earlier as an anticipated tritone substitution to the E♭^{7} in the following measure due to its strong implications of A major on beat one, contains the flatted fifth as a chromatic passing tone in the sequence E–E♭–D–C♯. How might we interpret this phrase? Levine suggests as a practical approach to play the blues scale over major seventh chords a major third above the root. The underlying chord here is the F^6, the A blues scale would be a major third above the root F. That would contradict the previous interpretation as tritone substitution of an anticipated E♭^{7}. And yet, Brecker doesn't play a pure A blues scale, since he plays the major sixth and the major third while avoiding the minor third. It seems rather that he merges the A major pentatonic with the A blues scale and additional chromatic passing tones as a not-unusual addition for blues scales in modern jazz (Terefenko, 2014, p. 195-200). Again, the high tempo of this phrase creates an interesting major and somehow bluesy yet modern sound.

Levine also points out that Louis Armstrong already used chromatic passing tones in his solo on "Hotter Than That" from 1927, which later became known as the bebop scale (see Baker, 1985, p. 1; Levine, 1995, p. 158). According to Levine and Baker, certain bebop scales can be used for certain chord qualities: the bebop dominant scale for dominant seventh chords, the bebop major scale for major chords, and two different bebop minor scales for dorian and melodic minor. What they all have in common is that they use additional chromatic passing tones at certain positions, such as the major seventh in the bebop dominant scale or the raised fifth in the bebop major scale. Which bebop scales does Brecker use? In his solo on "I Mean You", Brecker uses the most well-known bebop scale, the bebop dominant scale, several times, while avoiding the other bebop scale options. The first dominant bebop scale appears at the end of the A2 section of the first chorus. After introducing a possible replacement of the F^6 with a F^7 at the beginning of the section, he plays a descending line ranging over more than one octave and leading into the previously discussed rhythmic figure at the beginning of the B-section. Interestingly, Brecker does not play a traditional bebop dominant scale: Starting at the F, he plays the E and E♭ as typical for that scale, but instead of the major 6th as the expected following tone, he plays the minor 6th (D♭). On one hand, Brecker plays a minor cadence with the following B♭m pentatonic in m. 17 for which the minor 6th, or respectively the flatted 13th, would be the most inside interval. On the other hand, this adjusted bebop scale is discussed in jazz theory as one of the 'altered bebop scales', in this case the F bebop dominant ♭13 scale (Terefenko, 2014, p. 205). Brecker even mixes both dominant scales, with the F bebop dominant scale and the major sixth during the second half of m. 16, leading into a B♭ minor triad. The next bebop dominant scale appears during the A3 section of the first chorus over the D♭^{7} in m. 27. Here, Brecker plays the characteristic major and minor seventh and the major sixth. What is new at this point is that he alters the meaning of the scale by altering the positions of the intervals. While the appearance of the bebop scale is often explained by ensuring that the important chord intervals (root, third, fifth and seventh) fall on the strong beats by adding chromatic passing tones, Brecker reverses that logic at this point. Starting with the root D♭ on an offbeat, he places the major seventh as one of the chromatic passing tones on a strong beat. With that phrase, which spans roughly two beats, he augments the D♭^{7} over the bar line into the following D^7, which therefore sounds like a moment of outside playing, describable as side-slipping (Liebman, 2006, p. 55–58). The last appearance of the bebop dominant scale is rather hidden and embedded in a phrase that spans two and a half measures right at the end of the solo (mm. 62–64). Embedded in a superimposed chord progression, Brecker plays the E♭ bebop dominant scale in m. 63 on beat three and the C bebop dominant scale on beat four, merging a modern superimposition with a rather traditional bebop phrasing.

Another connection to the bebop era can be found in a perhaps rather unconscious quote from well-established Parker formulas (Owens, 1974). Again, it is the A2 section of the first chorus that offers such a lick. In m. 13, Brecker starts a convincingly bebop-ish phrase which ends with the usage of the F bebop dominant scale discussed above. After a rather long break of two-and-a-half beats, he plays an ascending B♭ major triad initiated by a chromatic approach from the leading tone below. Thomas Owens identifies this phrase—in the exact rhythm with a triplet—as a typical formula often played by Charlie Parker over a B♭^{maj} chord (Owens, 1974, p.87-93). It is very likely that Brecker plays that formula here rather unconsciously since he probably practiced Parker solos a lot. Also, even if the pause before that formula gives Brecker some time to consider such a quote, he may have had something more "traditional" or "bebop-ish" in mind, rather than planning to play that exact formula.

Superimposed scales and virtual chord progressions

The superimposition of an improvised chord progression over the composed chord progression has, ever since its popularization by John Coltrane, been a typical feature of postbop improvisation (see Porter, 1998, p. 145–170; Liebman, 2006, p. 13). Since the 1960s, improvisers have developed a variety of superimpositions, often combined with further techniques of outside playing such as constant structures or tonal sequences of the same interval structure, side-slipping/-stepping, and symmetric scales (see Levine, 1995, p. 169-176; Liebman, 2006, p. 21–33; Kissenbeck, 2007, p. 95–112). In general, playing outside can be understood as an approach to creating a certain tension in contrast to the underlying chord progression provided by the rhythm section. As Kissenbeck puts it (2007, p. 95), it is important to organize outside playing with a certain musical logic to create coherence on its own. What can be heard then are two parallel musical systems—the chord progression of the rhythm section and the outside playing of the soloist—each of which makes sense on its own, musically. Superimposition aims for such a logic and means the "placement of one musical element over another to be sounded simultaneously", which is not the same as a replacement (Liebman, 2006, p. 16). It is the potential tension of that simultaneity that creates a certain modern sound. Brecker uses this approach often in his solos (see Poutiainen, 1999, p. 32–37; Rawlings, 2003, p. 68f.). On "I Mean You", Brecker uses that specific tension with a dramaturgic sense. As will be shown in the following, he uses tonal material which tends to be more outside, especially at the end of sections, while using superimpositions that sound rather "inside" with little or almost no tension here and there. Let's first have a look at the latter.

During the solo, Brecker regularly superimposes scale material over dominant seventh chords. The motif at the beginning of the first B section has already been discussed as a structuring element. The first two measures of that section, which offer the E♭^{7} chord for the first time in the solo, display certain common practice techniques: Above the E♭^{7}, Brecker uses the B♭ minor pentatonic, which is a fifth above the root of the chord. With that technique, he creates a certain sound which can be interpreted as an E♭$^{7\text{sus}4}$, without resolving the suspension. Right after that, he uses a stack of fourths in mm. 19 and 20, which starts at the C. Again, this creates an F$^{7\text{sus}4}$ character, a sound that became an independent chord category especially in modal jazz during the 1960s (Terefenko, 2014, p. 55f.). Following this, he seems to make use of another typical modern jazz approach: superimposing the A♭ melodic minor scale, which at the same time provides the underlying D♭^{7} as well as its tritone substitution G^7 with fitting scale material. In m. 22, he even supports the A♭ melodic minor with an E♭ major triad on beat two, followed by an ascending A♭ minor scale on beat three and partly four. He uses the same approach again during the second chorus in mm. 35 and 43. The usage of melodic minor as the superimposed scale material instead of outlining the underlying chord itself became a common feature in postbop improvisation.

He continues with superimpositions till the end of the first B section. In m. 23, he superimposes four independent four-tone patterns over the $G\flat^7$ which imply a chord sequence that could be interpreted as the following: Gm^7, C^7, $B\flat$, D^7. The Gm^7 and C^7 can be understood as a II–V tritone substitution to the underlying $G\flat^7$, while the $B\flat$ is a major third above the $G\flat$. The D^7 leads to the following Gm^7 in m. 24. Here, Brecker continues to color the C^7 with $D\flat$ melodic minor, which gives the C^7 an altered sound.

The next superimposition at the end of the first chorus offers the usage of another feature of outside playing. The lines in mm. 31 and 32 at the end of the chorus could imply a turnaround with an additional D^7, Gm^7 and C^7 as a common practice in jazz. During that turnaround, indicated by the bass, Brecker plays the following sequence: an F major triad in an ascending motion, an F♯ major triad in a descending motion, an E major triad in an ascending motion and again a descending F♯ major triad leading to the tonic F at the beginning of the second chorus. Each arpeggio consists of four notes and fills up the space of two beats—the same way a turnaround does. The triad structure and regular contour of the phrases creates its own logic and consistency. Yet Brecker does not play a complete turnaround of I–VI–II–V but rather expands resp. augments the dominant C^7 over mm. 31 and 32. In doing so, he is able to play a longer line that has a dominant function. Following this reading, the F♯ major triad can be understood as a tritone substitution to the C^7. The E major triad then could be a sideslipping from the tonic F. The F♯ again repeats the dominant function of that superimposition.

However, the usage of the E major triad could also be interpreted as a derivation of the augmented scale. The augmented scale can be understood as an interlocking combination of two augmented triads which are a minor third apart from each other (Weiskopf & Ricker, 1993). This creates a certain scale sequence of minor thirds and minor seconds. In C, the scale consists of an augmented C triad and an augmented E♭ triad and builds the following scale: C–E♭–E–G–G♯–B. It is likely that Brecker uses the C altered and C augmented scale in an interlocking fashion here to create this sequence of triads. While the tritone substitution of the C^7 can easily be derived from the C scale (or likewise be understood as alterations of the upper structure), the E major triad is provided in the C augmented scale. This specific usage of the augmented scale on dominant chords—a triad (with or without the raised fifth and an additional major seventh) built a major third above the root—had often been identified in Brecker's playing (see Weiskopf & Ricker, 1993, p. 7; Rawlings, 2003, p. 121, 124, 127, 163). He seems to use that approach on the second chorus in m. 44 as well, superimposing an E augmented triad derived from the C augmented scale over the underlying D^7. Only the D during beat three seems to be an adjustment of the C augmented scale (which would require an E♭). The superimposition here functions as a dominant chord to a following sounding F^6. Interestingly, during that specific measure the original chord would be a Gm^7, which the band played during the other A sections. Nevertheless, the band reacts to that C dominant sound played by Brecker immediately, demonstrating a high level of interplay. Especially McCoy Tyner emphasizes the F tonic right at beat one of m. 45.

The last A section is the climax of the solo. Here, Brecker plays fast lines that are especially pacey. The section starts with a descending, almost chromatic guide tone line that lands on the E♭ over the $D♭^7$ chord in m. 59. From here, he creates a phrase that can be interpreted as outlining the following chord progression: $A♭m^{mmaj7}$ in m. 59, $A♭m^7$ on beat one of m. 60, then A^7, A^{maj7}, followed by A♭ on beat one of m. 61, G^7 on beat two and C^{7sus} leading into a $C^{7♯9}$ in m. 62. In doing so, he again uses melodic minor scales to alter the underlying chord progression of $D♭^7$ and D^7.

The final phrase, starting in m. 62, is the definite highlight of the solo. Here, after beginning the measure with the ♯9 of the C^7, he again plays inside the C mixolydian scale with an implication of the tonic F through an A minor pentatonic four-tone pattern on beat four. The following measures are salient. In mm. 63 and 64, Brecker outlines rhythmically straight four-tone patterns in contrast to the overall laid back or swing eighths feeling of his solo, which somehow epitomizes the whole solo: the contrast and yet deep connection between traditional and contemporary ways of improvising. Measure 63 can be understood as making use of the symmetrical octatonic half-step/whole-step scale.[24]

During m. 63, Brecker plays material from the C half-step/whole-step scale. And as if he were urging for a final demonstration of contemporary sound, he structures the tonal material of that scale in two pairs of sequences. These sequences can be understood as constant structures that are repeated on different positions of the underlying scale. The first constant structure can be interpreted as an A^7 arpeggio with the characteristic flatted 9 and natural 13 on beat one, and on beat two a minor third below as an $F♯^7$ with the same upper structure. The chord structure itself can be viewed as a typical chord voicing

---

[24] It most likely not the first appearance of such symmetrical scales, though. Brecker plays a sequence of four-tone patterns in mm. 41 and 42, which aren't a constant structure of the exact same interval structure, but give a similar impression. While the first and the last of these patterns outline the underlying F major, the second one creates a certain whole tone scale impression due to its interval structure of two pairs of major seconds a tritone apart. Nevertheless, it sounds outside and fulfills the logic of the symmetric whole-tone scale, a scale Thelonious Monk used frequently as well (Berliner, 1994, p. 162). Alternatively, the tonal material could be described analytically as derived from the F lydian scale as another possible major scale besides F ionanian.

for symmetric scales (Goodrick, 1987, p. 89). The constant structure used by Brecker reflects the symmetric structure of the half-step/whole-step scale (Levine, 1995, p. 73ff.). Though the scale can be thought of as two interlocking fully diminished chords (e.g., $C°$ and $D\flat°$), it may well be possible to derive chords from the half-step/whole-step scale that differ slightly from the fully diminished sound: in C, e.g., $C^{7\flat9}$-$D\flat°$-$E\flat^{7\flat9}$-$E°$-$F\sharp^{7\flat9}$-$G°$-$A^{7\flat9}$-$B\flat°$. The dominant seventh chords (as well as the diminished ones) are a minor third apart, their roots reflect the fully diminished frame. This also means that a half-step/whole-step scale built on the root of every dominant seventh chord (C-E$\flat$-F$\sharp$-A) share the same tonal material. Brecker uses the scale's logic that enables a certain use of constant structures: He first starts an arpeggio on A, which is a minor third below the C, and moves it a minor third down to the F$\sharp$ and repeats it—that's the distinct constant structure—as the exact same interval sequence. The second constant structure during the second half of the measure mixes the logic of the symmetric scale with the chromatic steps of the dominant bebop scale: Starting on E$\flat$, a minor third above C, and playing the major and minor seventh of the E$\flat^7$, he repeats that exact structure a minor third below on the C. After this heavily outside and yet coherent sounding measure, he continues playing the original II-V-I, outlining an F^{maj7} on beat one, a Gm^7 on beat two and a C^7 using the mixolydian scale with an additional flatted fifth to land on the root of the tonic. While the logic of the solo tends to follow the path from traditional to contemporary playing, he subverts this routine during the last measures to end his solo not too far 'outside', giving it some closure as a sort of reconciliation.

Summary

Even in a short solo of two choruses, Brecker demonstrates his ability to play in a unique and coherent way. Using various approaches of modern jazz improvisation, he creates a traditional as well as modern jazz sound. On the one hand, he develops little motifs that give the solo a certain structure. On the other hand, he balances and combines different techniques such as playing bebop scales as well as harmonic superimpositions and symmetric scales in a certain way. During the last measures, Brecker's personal way and class is highlighted when he combines those techniques in only one fast line spanning over two measures. In line with his relaxed time feeling and timbre on the instrument, it becomes clear once again why he has been considered "one of the most important saxophone player after Coltrane" (Gans, 2017).

Figure 3: Full transcription of Michael Brecker's solo, based on the digital transcription of the Weimar Jazz Database.

Figure 3: (Continued.)

Right into the heart. Branford Marsalis and the blues "Housed from Edward"

Wolf-Georg Zaddach

Branford Marsalis, saxophonist and member of the Marsalis family, the "First Family of Jazz" (Raz, 2012), was born in 1960 and raised in Louisiana. While his younger brother Wynton Marsalis developed a widely-known advocacy of jazz heritage during the 1980s, Branford followed his own path. Growing up playing in rhythm and blues bands and listening to contemporary funk and pop music, he started digging deeper into jazz rather late, while studying jazz saxophone at the Berklee College of Music in Boston from 1979 and 1981. Nonetheless, he quickly became one of the most renowned saxophonists of his generation. His employers during the 1980s, such as Art Blakey or Miles Davis, were important influences on his development as a jazz musician as well as on his career. In 1985, the Chicago Tribune called him "a jazz star of the brightest magnitude", referring to a quote by Miles Davis, who supposedly called him the "greatest saxophonist since Coltrane" (Brogan, 1985). During that year, Marsalis also started working for Sting, the former The Police member, and experienced the glamorous but also—in his own words—"gross" world of pop music business (Brogan 1985). While at that time Wynton criticized Branford for this step as selling out his jazz heritage (Polkow, 1989), Branford remembers it as an important learning progress:

> That was one of the things about playing with Sting that was very helpful for me. Because I used to play these long rambling solos with a lot of space in them and just really didn't know how to start and finish solos when I was playing in Wynton's band. And then suddenly I had 90-second solos for a year and a half. And when you have that kind of discipline, where you have to get to it and get out, when I came back to jazz, my solos had a lot more intensity and a lot less overthinking (Milkowski, 2012).

Just a few years after working for Sting, he summarizes that he especially learned "aggressive playing" and judged his own playing in the band of his brother Wynton during the first half of the 1980s as being "far too tentative". After his pop experience, when he started playing a lot more jazz again, it felt to him that he had "a lot of fervor and it was really fresh" (Polkow, 1989). Besides his encounters with pop music, he also recorded classical music by Debussy, Stravinsky and others for the album *Romances for Saxophone* (1986). Here, he gained a different sense for melody, and the "discipline to play with simplicity" (Milkowski, 2012). When Marsalis recorded *Trio Jeepy* in 1988, his sixth album as a leader, he surely could rely on those different experiences in modern jazz, pop, and classical music.

Trio Jeepy is a trio recording with bass and drums exclusively, and was recorded in New York City. Marsalis chose Milt Hinton (1910–2000) and Delbert Felix (*1958) for bass and Jeff Watts (*1960) for drums. The saxophone trio setting without a harmony instrument is a rather modern approach in jazz, called 'strolling'. After Sonny Rollins's *Way Out West* (1957), one of the first full-length recordings with that specific setup, it became a frequently used format, especially by the 1960s avant-garde (e. g., Ornette Coleman, Albert Ayler). Marsalis had adopted the strolling approach several times on recordings before, e. g., on the first track of his first solo release *Scenes in the City* (1984), but had not yet used it for a complete recording. The title list consists mainly of standards and compositions spanning from the Great American Songbook era to the 1960s, as well as three original compositions by the band. In one of his previous albums, *Renaissance* from 1987, he followed a similar mixed approach, yet the standards there are played rather in a contemporary postbop style, while *Trio Jeepy* has a somehow traditional sound. This is mostly due to Hinton's bass playing but also to certain improvising strategies of Marsalis, as will be shown later.

Apparently, *Trio Jeepy* partly gives the impression of a recorded live concert (though without an audience) or even a rehearsal recording. As Scott Yanow states, the performances seemed to happen "quite spontaneous[ly]"; it seems that the band "had a lot of fun" (Yanow, 2017). False starts and discussions were left, which was not completely unheard of before in Marsalis's releases. The short conversations give interesting insights into the band's social interactions, especially between the jazz veteran Hinton and the 27-year-old Marsalis. The false start of "Three Little Words" (track 3) is one such example. Here, Hinton throws a harsh and yet demanding "You gotta play it, man" at Marsalis (0:13-0:20 min), forcing him to concentrate and start over in a convincing fashion. This straight-up and demanding mode of communication wasn't new to Marsalis at all, it was part of his socio-cultural background: "I grew up in the South, in New Orleans, where guys torture you all the time

[…]. When you were lousy at something, they told you you were lousy, and they told you how to fix it," recalls Marsalis, talking about the similar way Art Blakey used to speak to him (Raz, 2012). Pianist and singer Harry Connick Jr. (*1967), a student of Branford's father Ellis Marsalis in New Orleans, remembers playing with the Marsalis brothers: "Those guys were harsh, man! They would verbally cut me down. […] They would beat you up emotionally. At the time it was tear-inducing" (Panken, 2016). In a recent interview, Marsalis admits that music students nowadays judge this demanding and hands-on mentality as a rather "hostile environment" (Milkowski, 2012).

Two of the originals on *Trio Jeepy* are blues tunes, which is remarkable insofar as Marsalis's originals on his previous albums were exclusively postbop compositions at its best. Turning to the blues might be related to an event in the mid 80s, when Marsalis was accused by Dizzy Gillespie, with whom he worked at that time, that "he didn't hear any blues" in his playing (Goodwin, 2015). Marsalis admits that his main goal during the first half of the '80s was to sound like Coltrane and somewhat modern. Until *Trio Jeepy*, he had recorded traditional and blues songs only with Wynton's band and occasionally as a leader. The blues tunes on *Trio Jeepy* sound especially old-fashioned in a way that Marsalis hadn't released on a solo recording before. Marsalis's first solo of the blues "Housed from Edward" will be in the focus of the analysis in the following.

"Housed from Edward"—in the safe house of blues?

"Housed from Edward", the first track of the album, is a blues in F and listed as an original composition by Marsalis. The almost nine-and-a-half-minute recording is in a relaxed time feel (approx. 127 bpm). Marsalis plays one longer and one short solo; in between are solo choruses by Milt Hinton. The song starts with Hinton and Marsalis as a duo. At first, Hinton accompanies in a half-time feel with half notes outlining the blues progression. Watts enters at the second chorus, and the band plays another two theme choruses in a typical swing $\frac{4}{4}$-feeling with walking bass, before Marsalis starts his first solo of 10 choruses. During those first three theme choruses, Marsalis plays a head-like melody which places dotted half notes on the second beat of every measure (Figure 1). The tones mainly emphasize the root, third or fifth of the underlying chord progression outlined by the bass. Most of the tones are the length of half notes—during the first twelve measures there are no faster tones. The rhythmic placement outlines the downbeats, with an emphasis on the second beat during the first chorus. The first and second repetitions vary

Figure 1: The theme of "Housed from Edward" as played for the first time, before the solo starts.

the placement with onsets on beat one. However, due to Marsalis's variations and embellishments it sounds improvised rather than composed.

Watts offers a consistent swing drumming that emphasizes beats two and four of every measure, while reacting to Marsalis's solo with fills. Hinton's lines clearly emphasize the jazz blues chord progression without employing advanced (postbop) strategies such as covering up the underlying chord or harmonic progression, e.g., playing the second of the underlying chord on beat one. Furthermore, he plays constant quarter notes with only few rhythmic embellishments, supplying a steady swing groove together with Watts. His time feeling is rather on the beat provided by Watts's ride cymbal instead of pushing forward or playing laid back. When Hinton recorded with Marsalis in 1988, he had more than five decades of experience since he started playing as a professional in the Cab Calloway Orchestra in the 1930s (Chilton & Kernfeld, 2002). According to Kipperman, Branford Marsalis became especially attracted to Hinton's voluminous as well as percussive bass sound (Kipperman, 2016, p. 23). That sound is strongly influenced by the jazz era Hinton grew up with. In those times, the upright bass was usually played without any amplification, which required a certain technique to allow the bass to be heard. Playing linear and harmonically clear lines with a certain drive which provides a specific acoustic foundation became a trademark of Hinton's playing. In line with his unique approach to the New Orleans slap-bass technique, which he demonstrates on *Trio Jeepy* as well, he became a "prototypical model for generations of jazz bassists" (Kipperman, 2016, pp. 1; 25–36). Tonally, he outlines the harmonic progression by playing the chord tones on strong beats with frequent chromatic connections. As Kipperman summarizes, there is only one measure during the whole recording where Hinton avoids playing the root F right at the beginning of a new chorus (Kipperman, 2016, p. 49). Moreover, Hinton uses different techniques that are typical for old-school playing, like the repetition of a single, riff-like motif for several measures in a row. For example, right at the beginning of the third chorus, he repeats a simple figure basically repeating the F in the lower octave. He plays that two more times, weakening the underlying chord change F^7 | $B\flat^7$ | F^7 and thereby creating a certain tension that is resolved by Hinton when he arrives at the $B\flat^7$ in the fifth measure (Kipperman, 2016, p. 55), while Marsalis continues with the tension by playing a faster line.

Marsalis's first solo

The first solo right after the repeated head is the main solo of the performance, spanning over 10 choruses. The strong emphasis of the blues progression by Hinton and the absence of a harmonic instrument both enable Marsalis to develop his solo in different facets, balancing out simplicity and complexity through rhythmic and melodic aspects. In fact, the improvisation can be understood as a reflection on blues improvisation, oscillating between melodic simplicity and postbop devices such as outside playing, by a saxophonist who grew up in a family of renowned jazz musicians in New Orleans.

Melody and simplicity

It is a distinct feature of that setup that the listener hears two simultaneous melodies provided by the bass and the saxophone rather than a melody embedded in chords. Thus, tones played by the saxophone are more difficult to contextualize since the bass produces a constant flow of quarter notes which are rather easy to hear. For example, tones that are rather outside the harmonic framework create less tension than they would if a harmonic instrument such as a piano were present. On the other hand, tones and melodies that strongly support the underlying chord progression can create a certain sound of cohesion. The timbre and Marsalis's approach to improvisation are important here, too. His overall tone is the opposite of aggressive, and he plays and flows with the band rather than just continuously blowing fast lines. For Marsalis, it is a conscious decision to put the focus on the band's overall sound. In a recent interview, he recalls that he got confused by different concepts of a good jazz performance when he moved to New York City in the early 80s. Here, other musicians started to ask him what he thought about their solos:

> And then I started to realize, as I got older [...]: There are guys who actually separate themselves from the larger context, and their idea of a good song or a good performance is completely

based on how they felt about their solo. That's deep, man. And it was foreign to me. That shit is anti-music (Milkowski, 2012).

On the other hand, Marsalis was already known for his fast and complex lines. He remarks that playing fast and complex was "what everybody was doing back then in the '80s. You become a product of your environment" (Milkowski, 2012). He describes his search for an adequate musical expression in jazz as a long-term endeavor that had a lot to do with exploring the music's past, a fact he states in an interview in 1988 (Reid, 2010). Hence, he judges his skills at the beginning of his career as a fresh graduate of the Berklee College as having "no fuckin' idea how to play jazz" (Milkowski, 2012). Working with older and experienced jazz musicians like Blakey and Gillespie enabled him to discover their musical socialization through constant conversation and playing experience. This urge and the resulting conscious attempts to understand why the older generation of jazz musicians sounded as they did influence his playing—besides the other aforementioned experiences he acquired during the 1980s—especially in terms of melody, simplicity and phrasing. Those musical facets attracted his attention because most of the older musicians told him that the most influential music when they grew up was "church music and rhythm and blues" (Milkowski, 2012). He learned that it requires "discipline to play with simplicity" (Milkowski, 2012). In fact, during the first solo on "Housed from Edward", Marsalis oscillates between rather simple melodic ideas and postbop devices of playing outside, such as side-stepping or superimposing different chord changes.

The theme may be improvised. However, its main feature of half notes seems to work as a template for the solo (Figure 1). During the first chorus, Marsalis picks up and turns the theme into a template based on quarter notes. He plays a variation of the theme by rhythmic displacement (mm. 3 and 4), diminution (mm. 5–9), and harmonic variation (minor third in m. 1 and 4, flatted fifth in m. 9). Further, The quarter-note template in mm. 8 and 9 is a motif that Marsalis picks up several times during the solo. The line in mm. 8 and 9 is rather quiet and softly played, with gentle onsets in a slightly laid-back feeling (Figure 2).

During the first seven measures, he continues the rhythmic placement of tones on beat two from the theme and alters it with shifts to beats one and four in mm. 3 and 4. In m. 8, Marsalis starts playing a rhythmic motif of exclusively quarter notes for four more measures, with a slight rhythmic variation and offbeat accents in m. 7. During the whole solo, Marsalis gets back to this simple quarter-note template, varying it in different ways, e. g., at the beginning of chorus three as well as during chorus eight and at the end of the solo during chorus ten (Figures 3 to 5) in chorus three, Marsalis plays

Figure 2: Branford Marsalis, "Housed from Edward", mm. 1–9.

a variation of the half-note center of the theme with embellishments and combination with previous rhythmic displacements of the longer notes. The shift of the rhythmic placement within these three measures is remarkable: At the beginning of m. 25, the embellishment of the half note A is emphasized by placing it on the second beat, while the half note itself falls on beat three. In the following measure, the embellishment starts on beat one, the half note G falls on the strong beat two, and the phrase ends in m. 27 on beat one. By applying this slight but effective variation of placements, Marsalis creates a certain tension with the swing accompaniment of the drums by alternating between contrasting and emphasizing the swing feel. In chorus eight, Marsalis plays again the theme's quarter-note template with rhythmic and tonal displacement and diminution. The variation in mm. 90 and 91 is realized through syncopation and the repetition of the same note over different chords, an approach Marsalis already used during the first chorus (mm. 8 to 12). This can be understood as a variation of the first two measures of the theme, where an F is played—albeit in octave displacement—over the changes of F^7 and Bb^7. By repeating the same tone over the chord changes, he creates a certain tension with the harmonic progression outlined by the bass. In chorus ten, at the end of the solo, Marsalis gets back to the quarter-note template outlining the harmonic progression with a slight extension (Am^{7b5}). Here, he plays a reference to the first chorus (mm. 8 and 9, see Figure 2), where he played a sequence of similar quarter notes for the first time at the exact same position of the blues chord progression.

These rather simple variations are an important feature of the solo's uniqueness. Slight harmonic variations of the blues progression such as the Gm^{7b5} or the C^{7b9} have a long tradition. But in combination with his timbre, dynamics and rhythmic variations as well as his postbop devices, he creates a certain personal note. This is supported by his rather unconventional approach to the dramaturgy of the solo.

Figure 3: Branford Marsalis, "Housed from Edward", mm. 25ff.

Figure 4: Branford Marsalis, "Housed from Edward", mm. 89ff.

Figure 5: Branford Marsalis, "Housed from Edward", mm. 116f.

Freedom in dramaturgy—free-floating spontaneity and interaction

Besides taking the time of improvising to almost four minutes, Marsalis develops an interesting dramaturgy during those ten choruses (Figure 6). Surprisingly, the high point in terms of event density is already reached in chorus four and five, when he plays a dense line of sixteenth and even faster notes for almost six measures. Until that point, the event density of the phrases builds up from the beginning. Chorus four prepares the high point with the highest mean pitch and second most dense section of the solo. On the contrary, Marsalis plays pretty low in chorus five, so that the mean pitch here is the lowest of the whole solo. Nevertheless, he also plays a wide range of pitches during this chorus, spanning over two octaves. During the first three choruses, the mean pitch increases slowly while the pitch range decreases slightly. While chorus one provides a rather low mean pitch, the overall range is significantly wider than in chorus two or three, but not yet as wide as in chorus four and five. While chorus two and three differ just slightly in terms of mean pitch and pitch range, the latter is significantly denser than the first two choruses.

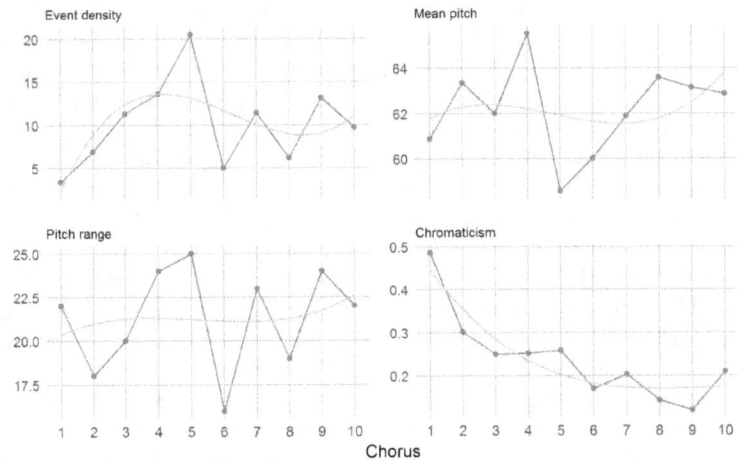

Figure 6: Event density (tones per second), mean pitch (averaged across all MIDI pitches), pitch range (difference between highest and lowest pitch), and chromaticism (percentage of non-diatonic tones) for each chorus.

The values for the degree of chromaticism differ and seem not to follow the overall dramaturgy. The proportion of chromatic or harmonically outside tones decreases constantly. While chorus one as the most chromatic or harmonically outside chorus with almost 50% outside tones, the other choruses consist of about 20 to 30% outside tones. Chorus one differs due to Marsalis's tonal choices their durations especially in mm. 8–12, when he uses altered tones.

In fact, it is Marsalis's choice of tonal material that follows a postbop logic of outside playing and his rather melodic and rhythmic flow of ideas. During the first chorus, most of the notes are a quarter note or longer. As mentioned above, the theme-melody is reflected and varied here. The first seven measures can be heard as harmonically rather inside (Figure 2), though he plays the blue note A♭ over the F^7 in mm. 1 and 4 which is outside in strict terms, but rather indicates the blues. In mm. 8 to 12, Marsalis makes extensive use of altered tones. On the one hand, he avoids outlining the chord progression Am^7 | D^7 in m. 8, and instead plays an F triad which he begins already in m. 6. Following this, he starts a rhythmic motif and seemingly picks up its repetitive character by repeating the same D♭ until m. 11. In doing so, he continues with altered tone over the chord progression of Gm^7 | C^7 | F^7. This tone repetition creates a certain tension of different altered tones ($Gm^{7♭5}$ | $C^{7♭9}$ | $F^{7♭13}$). The

D♭ implies a reference to F minor. Marsalis played the minor third over F just previously in mm. 1 and 4; now the D♭ appears as characteristic intervals of the F minor cadence, with the flatted fifth of the Gm⁷ and the flatted ninth of the C⁷. The following tones played over the turnaround in mm. 11 and 12 are derived from this D♭ sequence. Over the D⁷ he again plays a D♭ and E♭ which can be read as side-stepping to create a moment of outside, which is resolved to a C. Another interpretation may also be persuasive: Instead of outlining the chord progression as provided by the bass, the altered tones can be read as part of an extension of the dominant C⁷ that leads to the tonic F over the last three measures. Marsalis decides to develop this sequence of D♭—E♭—C further and repeats it in a chromatic motion downwards into m. 14, the second measure of chorus two (Figure 7). The interval structure remains the same (+2, -3) and follows the logic of the postbop technique of constant structures, the repetition of an identical interval structure on different starting pitches regardless the underlying chords. Yet the motif itself is rather short and singable, and even though it is shifted in chromatic steps, it lands on the root of the B♭⁷ (m. 14), and in the second half of the measure on the A as the major seventh of the B♭⁷. However, the line itself sounds due to its interval structure melodically and harmonically convincing. Following this, the first chorus already installs an intense dramaturgy due to its rhythmic motifs and variations as well as the use of altered tones.

Figure 7: Branford Marsalis, "Housed from Edward", mm. 11–14.

Yet the first chorus is far from being perceived as the most dramatic one. In fact, in combination with the increasing density of the phrases and occasional outside tones, the perceived dramaturgy increases until chorus five. In chorus four, for example, the percentage of outside tones is lower than in chorus one, yet Marsalis plays certain lines that extend the facets of the solo with postbop sounds. The first of these outstanding phrases already occur in m. 39, where he plays the minor and major third over the F⁷, and in mm. 41 and 42, when he plays the minor third over the B♭⁷ (Figure 8).

The second half of chorus 4 contains one long phrase and one short phrase during the last measure. While the longer phrase balances out inside and outside tones, the short phrase is completely outside, superimposing different chords. The first phrase starts in m. 43 and outlines the F major, avoiding

Figure 8: Branford Marsalis, "Housed from Edward", m. 39 and mm. 41f.

the bluesy dominant seventh. The first four-note group in m. 44 consists of F—C—C♯—G♯, and could be interpreted as first outlining the F major triad, followed by side-stepping chromatically upwards. Marsalis continues with chromatic passing tones and occasional implications of chord superimpositions, such as an F♯$^{7\flat9}$ with the last four-note group in m. 45. The second phrase superimposes an E^{add9} and E♭^{add9} over the turnaround at the end of the chorus. The placement of that short phrase between breaks at the end of the chorus over the turnaround emphasizes the outside tension and intensifies the dramaturgy. The chord progression can be interpreted either from a motivic perspective, as a melodic sequence, i. e., a transposition of the original motif onto another pitch; or it could be viewed from a harmonic perspective, either as chromatic side-stepping from F or as derivations of the dominant C (E major triad as part of the C augmented scale, E♭ major triad as part of C altered scale), though the added 9 does not fit into those superimposed scales in a strict sense.

The occasional outside implications in combination with the high density during the second half of the fourth and the first half of the fifth chorus create the high point of the solo. Chorus five splits into two parts as well. The first half keeps up the pace of the previous chorus and offers two fast lines, the fastest of the whole solo. During the second half, Marsalis surprisingly slows down and plays lines of quarter notes that are a reference to and, in part, a repetition of the motifs of the first chorus. He plays those fast lines during the first half of the chorus highly chromatically and outside the harmonic framework. At the same time, he employs melodic ideas implying guide-tone lines and side-stepping.

At the beginning of m. 50, he plays almost inside over an underlying B♭^{7} (Figure 9). Yet Marsalis adds the D♭ in the middle of the measure, which would be the bluesy minor third of the B♭^{7}. During the second half, he reaches the highest note of the whole line, the A. Though this note is only a short one within the fast-played line, he seems to spontaneously start an embellished melodic line moving downwards chromatically from A to A♭ (beat two in m. 51) to G on the fourth beat of m. 51. Marsalis fills the space in between with a wavy melodic contour, using partly chromatic material. The notes filled in between the A and A♭ are mostly inside, while the second half superimposes material which not only fills up the space between the melody tones but also implies arpeggios from chords other than the underlying F^7 (m. 51). The tones of beat one can be interpreted as an arpeggiated E$^{maj7\sharp11}$ and a G major triad or as an Em^{11}. Marsalis reaches that line centered on E easily by side-stepping a half-tone downwards from F. By rising up along an arpeggiated Em^{11}, he approaches the A♭/G♯. He plays pitches suggesting an E$^{7\sharp11}$ chord on beat two again. Both guide tones, the A and the A♭, are followed by a leap of a major third down, which suggests an F major triad and an E major triad, respectively. The guide tone G, placed on beat three, does not follow that logic and neither emphasizes the F^7 nor the side-stepping of E^7. In fact, the tonal material he plays may also belong to a B♭$^{7\sharp11}$ chord, which would be the tritone substitution for the previously introduced E$^{7\sharp11}$. However, the melodic aspect—implying a a descending guide-tone line—is outstanding, while the superimposition of additional chords adds a certain modern postbop sound. The second fast line of that chorus in m. 52, still over an F^7, is mainly played inside the blues changes and makes use of only the raised eleventh as a chromatic extension. Those two fast lines, creating the high point, are followed by a clear motivic reference to the beginning of the solo, using quarter notes and breaks. Additionally, he repeats the C♯/D♭ over the Gm^7 and C^7 (see mm. 9f. and 57f.). Once again, he creates a certain F minor sound with that distinct note, suggesting Gm$^{7\flat5}$ and C$^{7\flat9}$, yet softens that effect by alternating between the C♯ and D in a quarter-note rhythm during the Gm^7 and weakening the C$^{7\flat9}$ by avoiding the third.

While the first half of the solo appears to follow a logic of constantly intensifying dramaturgy, the second half of the solo differs. Chorus 5 seems to be the high point; the dramaturgy and intensity of Marsalis's playing is also supported by Watts's drumming, the latter keeping an intensity in his accompaniment with cymbal hits and ghost notes on the snare in triplet figures. During the second half of chorus five, he realizes that Marsalis has suddenly slows down and switches back to his swing accompaniment. Chorus six seems to be a relaxation of the previous dramaturgic peak. Density, pitch range, chromaticism as well as the mean pitch in Marsalis's playing are low. At this point, the solo could be over. The second half of the fifth chorus with the references to the first chorus might function as a reprise and

Figure 9: Branford Marsalis, "Housed from Edward", mm. 49–52.

signalize the end of the improvisation. Yet Marsalis decides to continue. He does so in the same way in which he connected chorus one and two: with a repetition of a sequence that connects both sections (Figure 10). It seems that he reacts to a spontaneous invention of his motif at the end of chorus 5 (m. 60). That motif is built around a $Gm^{7\flat5}$ triad. The first measure of chorus seven (m. 61) already introduces a variation of that motif: Handled as a sequence, it is repeated a half step below, adjusted to the F^7, and therefore played as an F major triad. The half note is converted into quarter notes and extended by a third one, recalling the quarter-note motif at the beginning of the solo and the second half of chorus five. What follows during the first half of chorus six is a call-and-response-inspired sequence of two motifs grouped around the C as one of the highest notes during that time. The motif in m. 61 becomes motif 1 of a sequence which alternates with motif 2 introduced in the following measure (m. 62). The sequence of both motifs is played two more times and characteristically starts with a D, leaping down a fourth or fifth to rise up to the C again. When it comes to the third repetition, Marsalis also varies the rhythmic placement of both motifs. While motif 1 started on beat one and motif 2 started on beat three the first two times, this time he shifts motif 1 forward to the fourth beat of m. 66 but keeps the break in between two motifs, so that motif 2 starts earlier on beat two as well (m. 68). That variation ends the sequence and Marsalis continues with offbeat accents

Figure 10: Branford Marsalis, "Housed from Edward", mm. 60–69.

and a strong laid-back phrasing (mm. 68ff.) which counteracts the regular flow of the previous motifs and sounds rather ragged.

During the last three measures of that chorus (mm. 70–73), Watts again starts playing a triplet-influenced groove that continues until the beginning of chorus eight. His triplets stabilize at the end of chorus six into a group of two triplets which he repeats several times. With this continued superimposition Watts creates a rhythmic displacement of the swing accents on two and four and thereby, in combination with Hinton's continued walking bass line in quarter notes, a certain tension and fragility. Marsalis picks up Watts's rhythmic intention immediately after his introduction in m. 72 (Figure 11). Instead of playing single quarter notes, he splits them up into two eighths, still interrupted and somehow ragged, while the tonal material is inside and outlines the underlying chord progression. At the end of m. 73, he slowly combines that rhythmic motif with Watts's triplet motif, a varying two-note motif, and lines in triplet feeling. He starts playing additional notes as well as outside notes, such as the minor third over a Bb^7 (mm. 74, 78), the sharp eleventh over an F^7 (m. 75), the flatted ninth over a D^7 and C^7 (mm. 80 and 82), as well as the flatted fifth over the Gm^7 again (m. 81). During the second half of this chorus, he even doubles the triplet feeling and plays sixteenth-note triplets. At that point, he creates another high point by repeating an ascending motif with the target tone C, starting from a C below and varying the tonal material in between just slightly by repeating the motion three times. As stated previously, Watts stops playing his superimposition right at beat one of chorus eight, and Marsalis ends his intense phrase in chorus seven on the same accent.

During chorus eight and nine, Marsalis works with the previously mentioned tone repetition (mm. 90 and 91) and varies it into fast and repeated trills built around the same notes of C and D with a rhythmic placement on beat three for each trill (mm. 106–108). Additionally, he once more emphasizes the

Figure 11: Branford Marsalis, "Housed from Edward", mm. 72–76.

blues by oscillating between the minor and the major third over the F^7 right at the beginning of chorus nine (m. 97). In the last chorus, Marsalis refers again to the theme with half notes on F placed on beat two, embellished, and approached from faster notes from below (mm. 109 and 111). The references back to the theme and its variation in the first chorus are obvious and give the solo some kind of closure. Yet, due to the continuation of the solo after the high point in chorus five, the end isn't necessarily predictable.

The solo is followed by a bass solo, which mainly outlines the chord progression in walking bass lines. Marsalis's second solo spans over two choruses. Here, he emphasizes the bluesy minor third of F^7 as a kind of anchor tone, frequently repeated and approached throughout the chord changes as the highest pitch. He repeats the A♭ and F in a trill in mm. 14 and 15, in some sense recalling blues and boogie piano trills. The band slows down a bit from 127 bpm to 122 bpm and the share of syncopated tones played by Marsalis is slightly higher than during the first solo (35.6 % compared to 31.5 %). The song ends with a repetition as well as a variation of the theme, with the drums strolling out.

Conclusion

Marsalis's first entire recording in a trio setup without a harmony instrument has a remarkable inclusion of traditional jazz sounds. Especially the blues "Housed from Edward" supports that impression. The traditional bass playing by Hinton and the setup both enable Marsalis balance out traditional improvisation techniques with postbop devices. A focus lies on the creation and variation of simple melodies that effectively fit the blues. Here, Marsalis applies call-and-response-inspired motivic work as a typical feature of traditional blues. These ideas are contrasted with fast lines that utilize postbop devices such as side-stepping and the superimposition of chord progressions.

Yet Marsalis embeds those modern sounds in larger melodic ideas such as implied guide-tone lines that are built around the major and minor third of F^7, again emphasizing the blues. The dramaturgy of the solo is the most outstanding overall characteristic. After reaching a peak in terms of event density and usage of postbop devices in chorus five, he continues for another five choruses, following a stream of motivic inventions and an interplay with Watts on the drums.

The solo as well as Marsalis's approach to play the blues in a trio setup with Milt Hinton on bass could be understood as a meditation or aesthetic reflection on his own processes of accumulating and internalizing jazz history and tradition—from the perspective of a postbop player who had already gathered diverse musical experiences at the time. The recording of "Housed from Edward" is an outstanding testimonial of a saxophonist who grew up in New Orleans and became involved in contemporary jazz in Boston and New York City in the search to flourish and to establish his own voice of many facets.

Bob Berg's solo on "Angles"

Klaus Frieler

Introduction

The present study attempts to reconstruct the creative processes underlying a specific jazz solo improvisation—Bob Berg's solo on "Angles"—using all available data from the musical surface as provided in the Weimar Jazz Database. To this end, we also try to integrate classical and computational analysis methods to gain a more complete picture than might be possible with either method alone. This includes general statistical descriptions, a look at tonal and intervallic choices as well as the metrical and rhythmical design. Central to our analysis will be an attempt to re-tell the 'story' of the solo with a special focus on playing ideas (midlevel units) and dramaturgic curves. We also take a closer look at the construction principles for lines, including a classification of line types, and in conclusion investigate the usage of interval and pitch patterns in order to arrive at a maximally complete picture of the creative devices and processes involved.

The object under study is a solo by Bob Berg (1951–2002), who was an eminent postbop tenor sax player of Miles Davis fame. He was born in Brooklyn, New York, and of Italian-Jewish origin. Unfortunately, only very little information is available about his life and personality. What is known is that he started playing saxophone at age 13 and studied at the Juilliard School, but never graduated. He became a professional musician already at the age of 18 and immersed himself in the New York loft jazz scene. He also dipped briefly into free jazz at the end of the 1960s. He was strongly influenced by John Coltrane and, in the 1970s, he initially shunned the then very popular fusion jazz, preferring more classical settings. From 1973 to 1976, he worked with Horace Silver, and was part of Cedar Walton's band from 1977 to 1981. His first record as a leader was *New Birth* from 1978, which featured Cedar Walton on keyboards and piano. In the 1980s, Bob Berg came to the attention of Miles Davis, who included him in his famous electric band from 1984 to 1987, where he became known as an eminent fusion saxophonist. After he left Davis's Band, Bob Berg diversified his interests and played postbop, fusion, and other styles in various settings and groups. In an interview from 1996, he stated: "I feel pretty comfortable moving between different areas of music." Amongst others, he was a frequent collaborator with his band mate from the Miles Davis band, guitarist Mike Stern, and with another Davis alumnus, Chick Corea, on whose Stretch label he also released several albums. After his untimely death in a tragic car accident in 2002, Berg left a musical legacy of 12 records as a leader and 33 records as a sideman.

The piece "Angles" is a Bob Berg original from his 1993 record *Enter the Spirit*. The composition can be described as a typical postbop tune, with a chord progression that is halfway between tonality and modality, very much in the spirit of Wayne Shorter's compositions from the 1960s. The theme melody is angular, which might have been an inspiration for the title of the song. The form and chords of the theme are not maintained during the solos; instead, a simplified 48-bar scheme AAB of 16 bars each is used, with four chords lasting over four bars each (cf. Table 1). The tonality is not fully clear, but a tendency to A♭ major can be stated, since the A sections start with A♭^{maj7} and end with E♭^{7} and most of the chords more or less fit into A♭ major. Deviations can be found in the D♭$^{7(\sharp11)}$ in the A and B sections, which belong to G♭ major/minor, as well as in the altered G$^{7\sharp9}$ and D^{7alt} chords at the ends of the B sections, which do not fit into A♭ major and have a rather unusual falling fourth relationship. The D^{7alt} leads back to the A♭^{maj7} with a tritone step, and hence these two chords might be interpreted as a semitone downward shifted variant of a A♭^{7}–E♭^{7} connection, which would fit better tonally. Due to the unusual chord connections, the overall loose tonality and rather long chord lengths, the solo form is located somewhere between tonal and modal conceptions.

The tempo is rather high with 270 bpm and the rhythmic feel oscillates constantly between latin in the A sections and swing in the B sections. The accompaniment is very dense. In particular, pianist David Kikoski playing is rhythmically very accentuated, relentlessly pushing the energy, while often filling the phrase gaps in Berg's solo with rhythmical impulses. Drummer Dennis Chambers employs a modern, complex and busy drum style, while frequently reacting to Berg as well as driving him forward.

The solo comprises 799 tones in 38 phrases and 144 bars over three choruses. Most of the tones (85.4 %) are very short on an absolute scale (i. e., absolute duration class) which in this high tempo equals mostly the level of eighth notes (cf. Table 2). The syncopicity, i. e., the percentage of syncopated tones,

Table 1: General characteristics of Bob Berg's solo on "Angles".

Composer	Bob Berg
Record	*Enter the Spirit* (1993)
Personnel	Bob Berg (ts), David Kiskoski (p), James Genus (b), Dennis Chambers (dr)
Tempo	270 bpm
Signature	$\frac{4}{4}$
Key	Mostly A♭ major
Form	A(16) A'(16) B(16)
	4-bar chord changes throughout
Chord Changes	A: A♭^{maj7} | Cm^7 | D♭^{7} | E♭^{7} |
	B: Fm^7 | D♭$^{7\sharp11}$ | G$^{7\sharp9}$ | D^{7alt} |
Rhythm feels (theme)	A: Latin, B: Swing
Rhythm feels (solos)	A: Latin, B: Latin
Lengths	799 tones
	144 bars
	3 choruses
	8 phrases
Duration	127 s
Densities	6.3 tones/sec
	5.6 tones/bar
	21 tones/phrase
Metrical centroid	3+
Start of phrases	42 % (beat 3)
	13 % on 3+
	10 % on 1
	10 % on 2+
Syncopicity	9.2 %
Tessitura	A♭3 — A♭5
	(36 semitones / 3 octaves)

is rather low (9.4 %) compared to the average value of about 30 % in the Weimar Jazz Database. This seems to be mostly due to Berg's highly precise timing, since, due to the metrical annotation with the FlexQ algorithm (cf. Chapter *Computational melody analysis*), syncopicity values in the Weimar Jazz Database are partly driven by laid-back playing and rhythmical freedom. The listening experience corroborates this conjecture, as Berg's solo shows a very tight rhythmical performance.

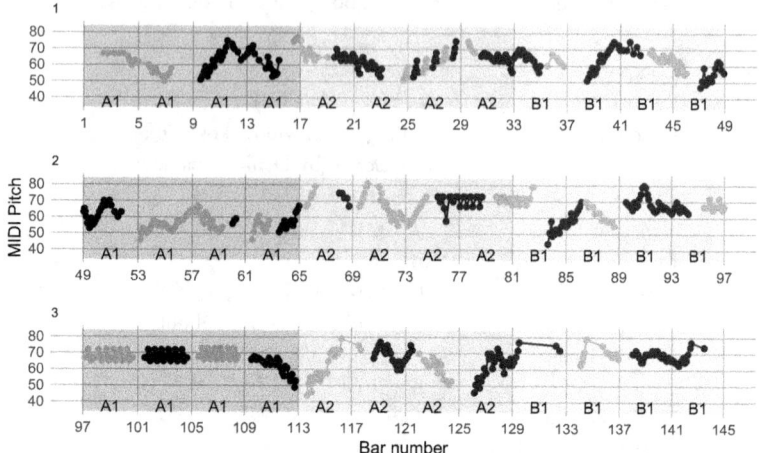

Figure 1: Piano roll representation of Bob Berg's solo. The single panels correspond to choruses. Phrases are colored alternatively; form parts are shaded with different gray tones.

The metrical placing of tones is uniformly distributed over all eighth note positions in the $\frac{4}{4}$ bar (Figure 2, middle panel). Interestingly, Berg has a strong preference for starting his phrases on and around the third beat of a bar (Figure 2, top panel; Table 1). As can be seen in Table 3, 22 of all 38 phrases start on beat 3, very often (ten times) also right after a chord change (see also Figure 1 for a visual overview of the interplay of phrase lengths, form sections, and four bar units). Another interesting fact is that Berg nearly always continues his phrases over the changes of contrasting form sections, i.e., A2 →B1 and B1 →A1, but not on the transition A1 →A2. The change of rhythm between the A and B sections under an ongoing phrase has a certain surprise effect and also contributes to the flow of the solo. The phrase endings are more diversely distributed but tend to fall on on-beats and also on the metrically strong first and third beats of a bar (Figure 2, lower panel).

With respect to accentuation in loudness, Berg shows a certain tendency to play (mostly in his fast lines) four eighth groups with descending loudness, starting from the strong first and third beat (Figure 3).

Table 2: Distribution of absolute and relative duration classes.

Duration Class	Absolute (%)	Relative (%)
very short	85.4	9.9
short	12.0	78.3
medium	1.9	9.4
long	0.6	1.6
very long	0.1	0.8

Table 3: Distribution of metrical and hypermetrical positions of phrase beginnings.

Bar phase	Beat position				Sum
	1	2	3	4	
0	1	1	10	0	12
1	4	2	4	1	11
2	1	2	6	1	10
3	2	1	2	0	5
Sum	8	6	22	2	38

Note. Bar phase = distance in bars from a chord change / four-bar block. Beat position = beat in the bar disregarding tatum position.

Tonal and interval choices

The overall pitch range is three octaves from A♭2 to A♭5, with a strong focus on the middle octave; 83 % of all tones are between A♭3 and E♭5 (Figure 4, top). Tonally, the pitch classes fit very well into A♭ major, even though G is the most common pitch class (accordingly, G4 is the most common tone), but this is due to some repeating patterns ('oscillations') in the third chorus, where G4 is the central tone. Looking at the pitch class distribution (Figure 4, bottom) the A♭ major seems to be rather dominant, with about 84 % of all tones coming from A♭ major. However, the solo makes a much more chromatic impression during listening. This can be explained by looking at the chordal diatonic pitch class distribution (Figure 5) and the chord-wise distribution of non-diatonic tones (Figure 6). There is a clear contrast between very inside, sometimes pentatonic playing on the one hand, and highly chromatic and even outside playing on the other hand. The latter mostly takes place in the second half of the B sections over the altered dominant seventh chords $G^{7\sharp 9}$

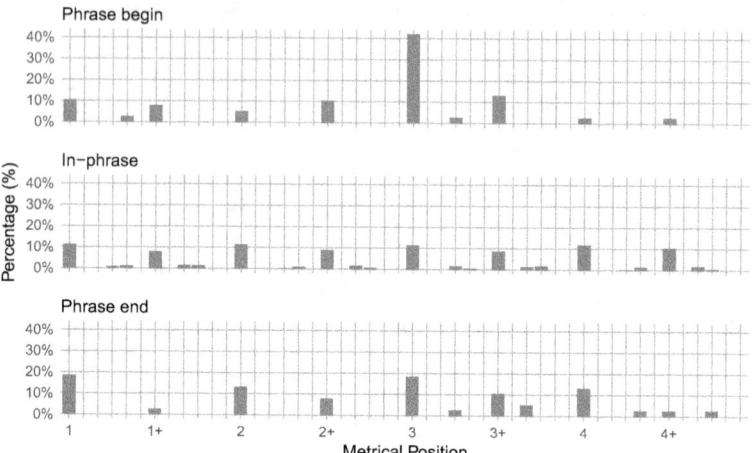

Figure 2: Metrical distribution in Bob Berg's solo differentiated for phrase position. Top: phrase beginnings ($N = 38$), middle: in-phrase tones ($N = 723$), bottom: phrase endings ($N = 38$).

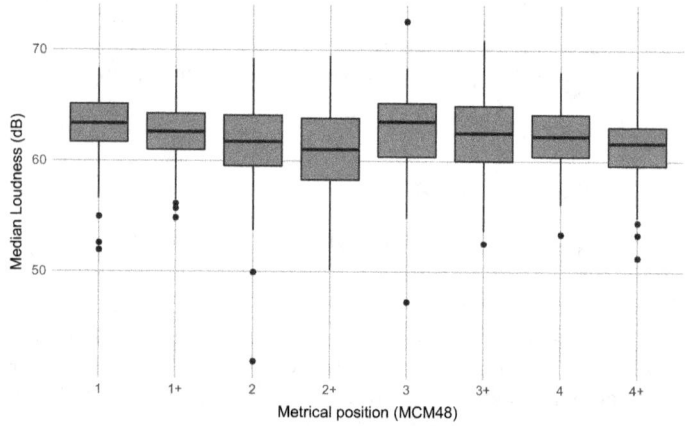

Figure 3: Loudness vs. metrical positions in Bob Berg's solo.

and D^{7alt}, but also once on the Cm^7 of the first A section in the second chorus and on the second $E\flat^7$ in the second A section of the first chorus, as well as the first A section of the last chorus. Interestingly, and this explains why the pitch class distribution fits so well in A♭ major: He often plays A♭ ionian on the $G^{7\sharp 9}$

Bob Berg's solo on "Angles"

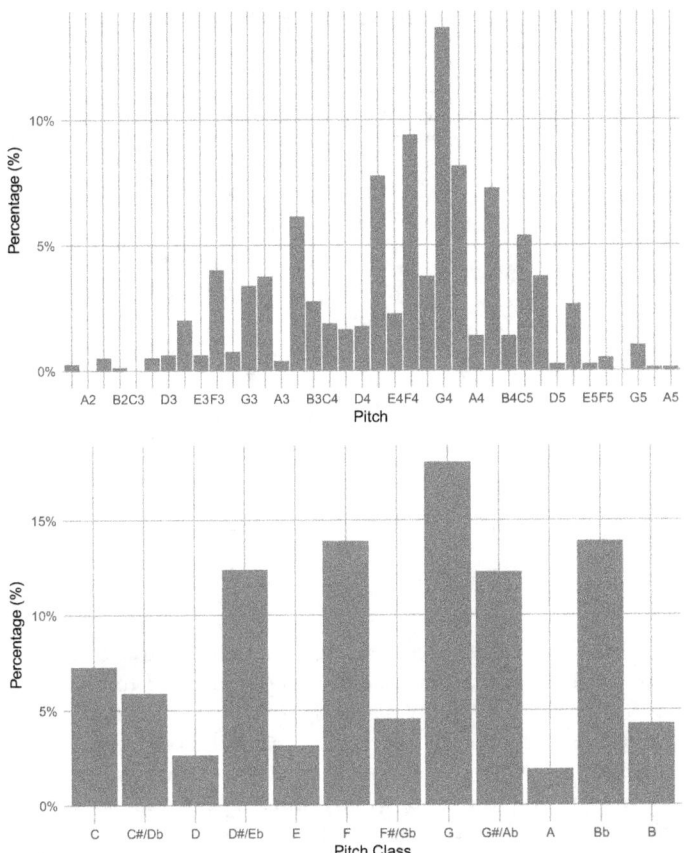

Figure 4: Pitch distribution (top) and pitch class distribution (bottom) in Bob Berg's solo.

and D^{7alt} at the end of the B section (e. g., in mm. 89–91 with a long $A\flat^{maj7}$ arpeggio). This is an interesting technique, since $A\flat$ ionian fits well with the altered chords but also with the overall tonality. These are also the points of highest harmonic tension, so in some way this outside playing results mostly from ignoring these odd chords in the overall harmonic progression.

Another reason for the modern sound of the solo is Bob Berg's preference for upper structures. For example, he plays Cm over $A\flat^{maj7}$ (mm. 2–4, mm. 65–67), Gm^7 over Cm (mm. 4–7), and $Fm^{7\flat5}$ over $D\flat^7$ (mm. 8–19, mm.25–28).

Table 4: Mean and median of chordal diatonic pitch classes mapped to third layers. See text for details.

Form section	Chord	Median	Mean
A1	A♭^{maj7}	7.0	6.6
	Cm^7	5.0	6.9
	D♭^{7}	5.0	6.7
	E♭^{7}	7.0	6.2
A2	A♭^{maj7}	7.0	7.1
	Cm^7	7.0	6.3
	D♭^{7}	7.0	6.9
	E♭^{7}	7.0	6.3
B1	Fm^7	5.0	6.3
	D♭$^{7\sharp 11}$	9.0	8.5
	G$^{7\sharp 9}$	9.0	7.8
	D^{7alt}	9.0	8.9
All		7.0	7.02

This observation can be corroborated by mapping chordal diatonic pitch classes to third layers. This is done by mapping 1 and 3 to itself, and the mappings (7, ♯7, ♭7) → 7, (2, ♭9, ♯9) → 9, (4, ♯11) → 11, and (6, ♭13) → 13. Afterwards, mean and median values of the mapped chordal pitch class distribution are a measure for the amount of upper structures used. The results can be seen in Table 4, broken down by chords. The overall median is 7, i. e., the seventh, which is right in the center of a chord's expansion into thirds. The interval distribution is somewhat unusual, as can be seen in Figure 7. Compared to the overall interval distribution (lower panel), there are many more tone repetitions but also a flat plateau for small descending intervals. This however can be explained by the long oscillating figures in mm. 75–81 and mm. 95–108, in which similar figures are repeated very often. These oscillations are responsible for the unusual interval distribution, but are nevertheless very important for the solo as a whole.

Re-telling the story

The storytelling metaphor is an important aspect in jazz parlance and jazz research (Frieler et al., 2016b) and might also be an active guiding principle for improvising jazz solos. Of course, there are no 'real' stories to be told

Bob Berg's solo on "Angles"

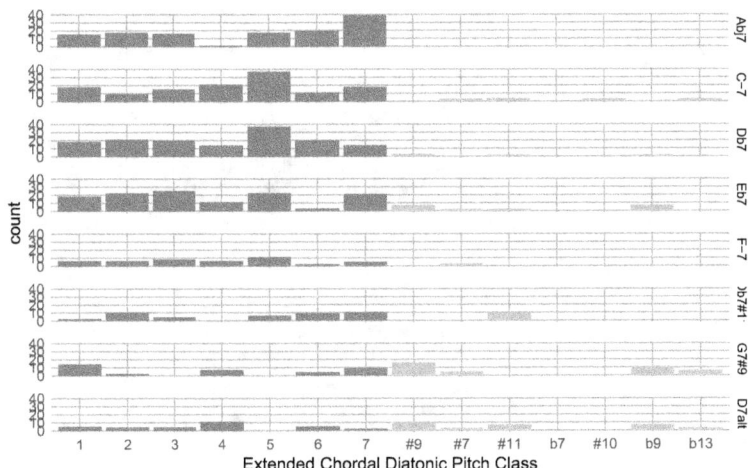

Figure 5: Tonal choices in Bob Berg's solo broken down for individual four-bar chords. Dark blue: diatonic pitch classes; light blue: non-diatonic pitch classes.

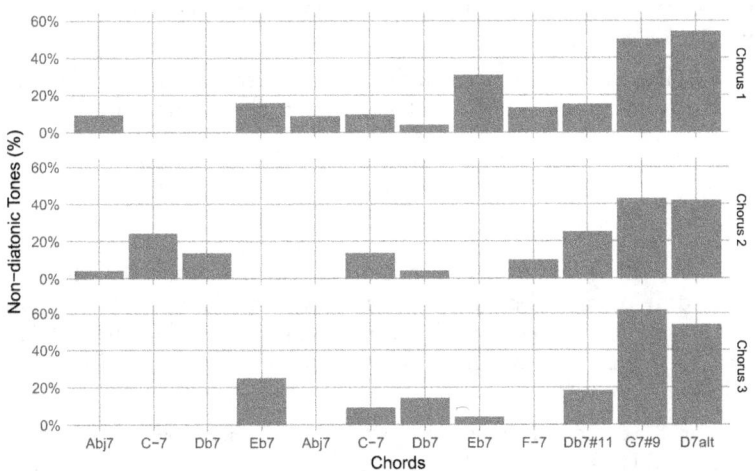

Figure 6: Outside playing in Bob Berg's solo for each chorus. Chords are listed as they appear in the AAB form.

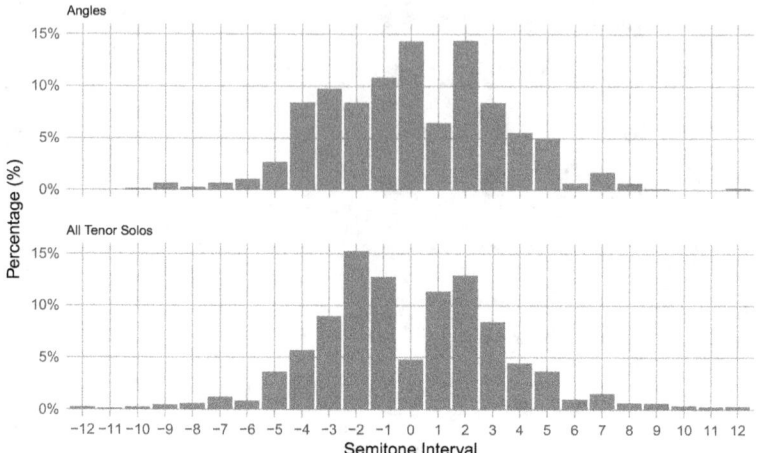

Figure 7: Semitone interval distribution in Bob Berg's solo (top) and in all other tenor sax solos in the Weimar Jazz Database (bottom).

in music due to the lack of denotative meanings. Nevertheless, a certain dramaturgy might be discernible, which might or might not follow narrative prototypes (e.g., the narrative arc).

In the following sections, we will first try a re-narration of the entire solo, based on midlevel units, and then have a look at global dramaturgic shapes.

Midlevel Analysis

Midlevel analysis is a qualitative annotation system for jazz solos which are inspired by playing ideas and called 'midlevel units' (MLU, cf. p. 54 and Frieler et al., 2016a). There are nine main types of midlevel units (MLU) (*line, lick, melody, rhythm, expressive, theme, quote, void, fragment*) with 16 sub- and 38 sub-subcategories.

In Figure 8, a piano roll representation of the solo broken down into the main types of MLUs is depicted. The solo transcription in Figure 17 can be found annotated with full MLU types. Finally, in Table 6 a complete run-down of the sequence of MLUs in this solo is listed.

In this solo, 51 MLUs of only five main types are used: *line* (21), *lick* (11), *melody* (6), *rhythm* (6), *expressive* (6). 13 MLUs are glued together to form

Bob Berg's solo on "Angles"

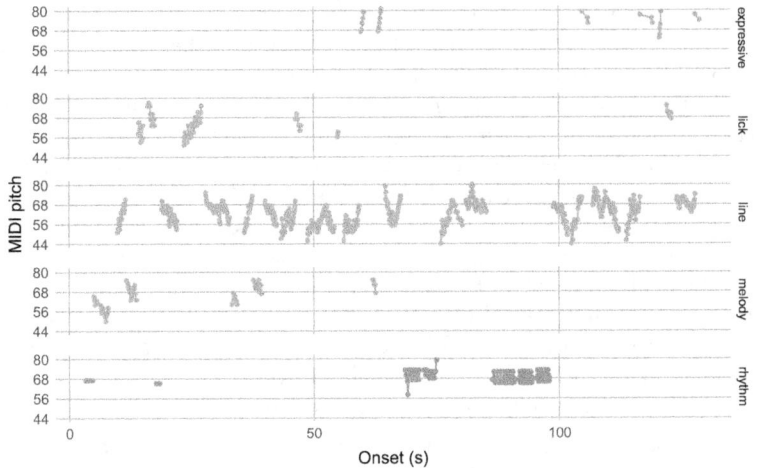

Figure 8: Piano roll of Bob Berg's solo differentiated according to midlevel units. From top to bottom: *expressive* (red), *lick* (olive), *line* (green), *melody* (blue), *rhythm* (purple).

phrases, and 13 MLUs are derived, mostly from the immediately preceding MLU. The mean duration of all MLUs is 2.0 s or 2.75 bars.

One striking aspect about the flow of ideas in this solo is the common combination *line→melody/expressive*, often directly glued to build a phrase. The *line* part is mostly of ascending type, whereas *melody/expressive* parts are mostly very short, just a few tones derived from major and minor triads and with descending contours. The first instance is in mm. 9–13, where a short sequence of four ascending $Fm^{7\flat5}$ arpeggios is followed right away by a simple melody from E♭ mixolydian. The next instance can be found in mm. 30–36, where a long, rather chromatic, wavy line ends in a simple C minor melody in mm. 35–36. Another instance is in mm. 38–42, where an ascending D♭ mixolydian ♯11 line ends in an E♭ mixolydian melody. Shortly after this, in mm. 47–51, a chromatic ascending line (mm. 47–48) is segued into a simple A♭ ionian line—right across the transition from the first to the second chorus and then into another short C minor melody. The next instance is to be found in mm. 63–67. Here, an ascending E♭ mixolydian line is ended by the first *expressive* MLU in the solo, which is constructed from the tones of an $A\flat^{maj7}$ chord and which resembles the melodies in m. 51 and mm. 2–4. It is directly followed by an *expression* variant, with a top tone a whole step up from G5 to A5, which suggests C dorian over the underlying Cm^7. After this instance, which is a first peak moment in the solo, the series of longer oscillations starts. The next instance of the model is then to be found at the beginning of the third chorus (mm. 113–117), introduced here by a long-reaching, arpeggiated ascending line, ending in a C minor triad-based melody. An intensified variant can then be found a few bars later, in mm. 126–132, where the melody at the end is modified a bit to accommodate the Fm^7 chord. Again a few bars later, in mm. 134–136, a shortened and upwardly transposed echo follows, itself immediately succeeded by a *lick*, which resembles the melody in mm. 41–42. Finally, the very last phrase, in mm. 138–144, starts out with a faint echo of the oscillations from the second chorus, and then mutates into a short chromatic passage, segueing into a diatonic ascending arpeggio which ends in a short, two-tone *expressive* MLU. In a way, these very last seven bars contain the whole solo and its main ideas in a nutshell, functioning somewhat as a short conclusion.

The technique of ending a line with a short melodic part, often with longer tone durations, could be dubbed 'piggy tailing'. In many solos, the 'piggy tails' consist of only a few tones, normally one to three, which function as a short deceleration bringing a fast line to halt. One example for a more typical 'piggy tail' can be found in m. 124.

It interesting to look at ideas that occur only once in the solo. First, there is a Parker-sounding lick in m. 14–15 which is glued to a piggy tail melody. Indeed, the interval sequence (−3, −4, −5, +3, −2, +1), starting on the third beat in m. 14, can be found three times in the Charlie Parker Omnibook.

Then, there is a very short *rhythm_single_irregular* in m. 18–19, which functions as an interruption of a longer line, even though the MLU right before it is labeled *lick*. Without this short intermission the whole complex would be just one long wavy line.

Generally, there is a shortage of short licks in this solo. Measures 24–28 present an ascending sequence of licks, which consists of Fm$^{7\flat 5}$ arpeggios, nearly the same as the ones in mm. 9–11, but here extended higher and played in a specific 'choppy' rhythm, which transforms it into a sequence of licks. This is a good example of how the same sequence of pitches can be transformed into something distinctively different by only changing the rhythm—in this case by prolonging some inter-onset intervals. After he reaches the same endpoint (E♭5) as in m. 11, Berg continues with a very short and abridged version of m. 12, which sounds as a descending answer to the ascending arpeggios.

In m. 49, in the first bar of the second chorus, when the rhythm group shifts back from swing to latin, Berg plays his only embellishment figure in the entire solo, which vaguely recalls a pop jazz saxophone lick, but which is fully integrated in a much longer line of mixed character (cf. p. 256).

At the end of the first A section in the second chorus, in m. 60–62, there seems to be a short black-out in the flow of the solo. First, after finishing the long seven-bar line that started in m. 53, Berg continues with a very short lick, which is basically a transposed version of the 'piggy tail' of the line (m. 59). This sounds either as a bold confirmation of the preceding line, a false start of another line, or as a moment to gain time. After a bar-long pause, he embarks in mm. 61 and 62 on a short line, which is basically an $E\flat^9$ arpeggio over the $E\flat^7$ which does not sounds fully convincing, neither tonally nor in regard to phrasing. Next, as if 'upset' about this rather weak passage, he expresses that anger with a short diatonic up-swing (mm. 63 and 64) right into the first *expressive* MLU in the solo, which brings G5, the highest pitch so far, held for over one bar.

The last one-time element in this solo can be found in mm. 86–89, where Berg plays a mixed $E\flat/E\flat^+$ descending arpeggio with a constant eighth/dotted quarter rhythm pattern with tone repetitions (*line_i_dd*) over the $D\flat^{7\sharp 11}$. From that point on, all the remaining material is in one way or another related to some preceding material.

Dramaturgy

The dramaturgy of Berg's solo seems to be well-crafted, either intentionally or as emerging from group interaction. The general tension curve is doubly arched. This can be seen on one hand in the event densities across the course of the solo. In Figure 9, the number of tones of two-bar units shifted bar-wise along the time axis and plotted against the onset of the first tone of the bar unit is depicted, along with a polynomial trend. From the beginning on, the event density increases constantly over a long stretch and then dips down at the beginning of the second chorus to increase even more towards the end of the second chorus, where the highest densities are reached with the sequences of *oscillations*. The third chorus then sees a slow decay, but this does not mean that the intensity decreases, it is merely shifted to another dimension. This can be seen in Figure 10 where pitch and loudness curves of 20 note windows (with a hop-size of 10 tones) are plotted against the onsets of the windows. Both curves show an overall ascending trend—particularly the loudness curve—with some oscillations. One sees that the pitch heights rise quite rapidly in the first chorus but drop towards the beginning of the second chorus, to rise continually towards the end. In the third chorus, a certain saturation is reached, but in fact with strong oscillations, showing a stark contrast (at about 100 s). All in all, a clear peak in global intensity is reached with the sequence of oscillations.

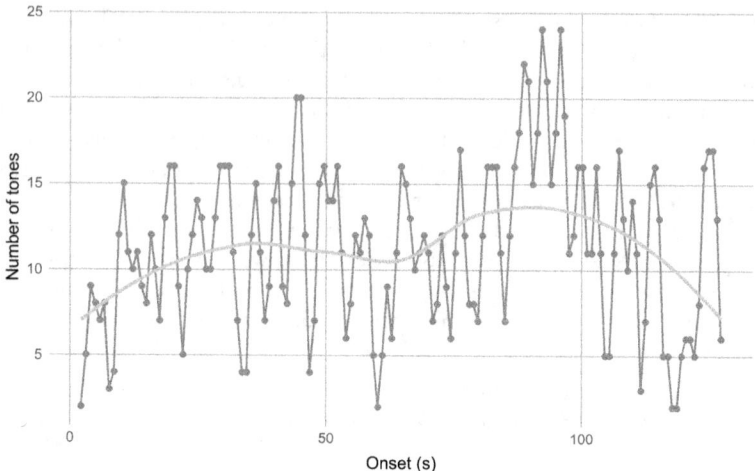

Figure 9: Event densities (number of tones) of Bob Berg's solo for windows of two bars shifted bar-wise along the solo.

This overall dramaturgy is also reflected in Figure 8. The *melody* and *lick* MLUs appear mostly in the first chorus whereas the second chorus is dominated by the sequence of *oscillation*s. The *expressive* MLUs appear for the first time at the beginning of the second chorus, and take over the role of the *melody* afterwards. This has an effect of intensification. The third chorus is then built from the double sequence of *line–expressive* and *line–line–expressive–expressive*, and resolves, finally, in the epitomic phrase *line–expressive* at the very end.

Line construction

The analysis of the MLU content of the solo shows that Berg utilizes different kind of lines in his solo: diatonic lines, arpeggios, chromatic lines, and mixtures thereof. To gain further insights, we manually classified the 21 *line* MLUs using this four-fold classification scheme and found four diatonic, three chromatic, six arpeggiated, and eight mixed lines. They indeed differ with respect to their interval content, as the distributions of frequencies of semitones, whole tones, and thirds show (Figure 11).

Using a similar system, we also classified line segments of seven intervals by moving this window by four elements. Segments always start at the beginning

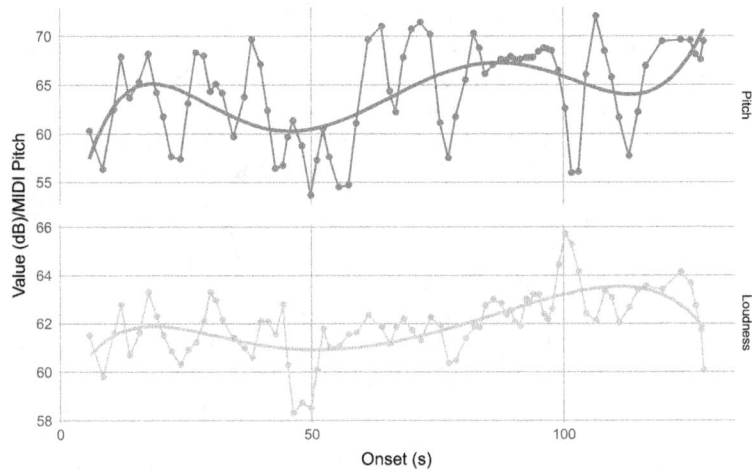

Figure 10: Smoothed pitch and loudness curves for Bob Berg's solo. Smoothing was done with windows of 20 tone events and a hop size of 10 tones. Trend line fitted with a polynomial of 6th degree.

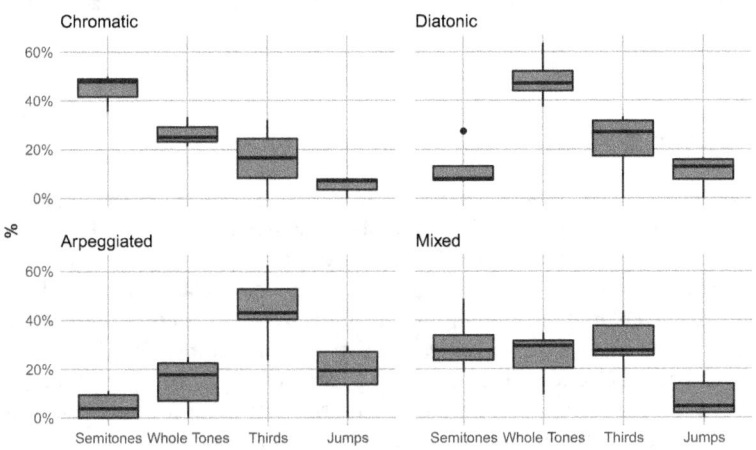

Figure 11: Interval content of the four line types found in Bob Berg's solo.

of *line* MLUs. A segment is classified as 'pentatonic' if thirds and whole tones account for more than two thirds of the intervals (i. e., five or more). It is classified as 'arpeggio' if thirds and larger intervals account for more than two thirds of the intervals. It is classified as 'diatonic' or 'chromatic', if semitones and whole tones account for more than two thirds of the intervals, and then depending on whether there are more semitones ('chromatic') or whole tones ('diatonic'). Finally, segments are classified as 'mixed' if they do not fulfill any of these criteria or if the difference between the first and second most frequent class is less than 0.1. In Figure 12, the sequences of segment classes are plotted for each line in the solo. The first observation is a slight preference for mainly pentatonic lines (e. g., lines 1, 2, 4, 9, 18), although there is an equal share of pentatonic and mixed line segments (30.0 % each). The next common segment type is 'chromatic' (20.8 %), followed by arpeggios (13.3 %), and 'diatonic' 5.8 %. The length of lines ranges from 3 (line 8, 9, 11, 13) to 12 segments (line 7), with a median of 5.5. For the series of segment types, no obvious patterns can be identified, except that a segment type has a strong tendency to be repeated (about 50 %), which is partly due to the construction of our measure. Furthermore, chromatic segments tend to occur earlier in a line (mean normalized position = .45), whereas diatonic and pentatonic segments tend to occur later (mean normalized positions of .68 and .64). With respect to the entire solo, however, pentatonic segments tend to occur earlier, and arpeggios tend to appear later (e. g., in the third chorus, mm. 113ff. and mm. 126ff.). All in all, Berg shows a great variability in his approach to line construction.

Pattern usage

To investigate the usage of patterns in Berg's solo, we used the partition function of the *melpat* module in the MeloSpyGUI with all seven Berg solos in the Weimar Jazz Database as a background corpus. Since the rhythms are rather uniformly based on eighth notes due to the abundance of lines, we only calculated interval and pitch patterns and no rhythmical patterns. For the interval domain, we extracted patterns with at least $N \geq 5$ intervals, which correspond to at least six tones. For the pitch domain, we demanded $N \geq 6$. For both cases, we extracted patterns that occur at least twice, but placed no restriction on the number of solos they should appear in.

We found 147 interval patterns meeting these conditions, with a coverage of 64.8 %, i. e., about two thirds of the tones in Berg's solo are contained in an interval pattern of at least five intervals that occur at least twice somewhere in the seven Berg solos under consideration. This is the highest coverage of all Berg solos, which have a mean coverage of 56 %. But this is partly due to the extensive oscillations in the solo. However, when using all postbop tenor

Bob Berg's solo on "Angles"

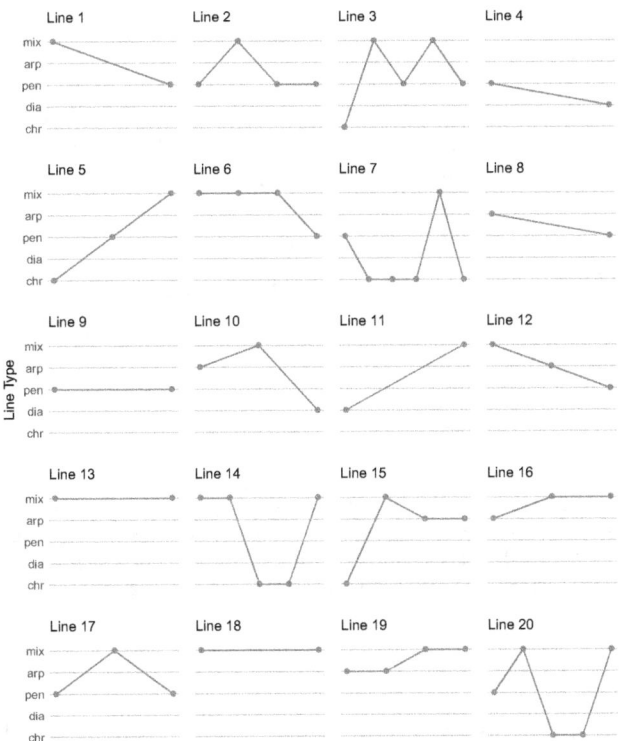

Figure 12: Classification of segments of seven intervals for *line* MLUs in Bob Berg's solo. Hop size is four intervals, i. e., points are separated by four notes each. chr = chromatic, dia = diatonic, pen = pentatonic, arp = arpeggio, mix = mixed.

solos, the coverage rises to 80.7 %, which is close to the mean coverage of 78.3 %.

We found 81 pitch patterns, with a coverage of 46.8 % (mean coverage across all Berg solos: 40.6 %). See Figure 13 for a display of interval and pitch patterns in Berg's solo. The longest patterns are produced by the oscillations and are not shown.

As expected, there are fewer pitch patterns than interval patterns (because a pitch pattern is automatically also an interval pattern, but not vice versa). The shorter patterns are more volatile, whereas the very long interval patterns are also pitch patterns, which shows that they are specifically rehearsed and then

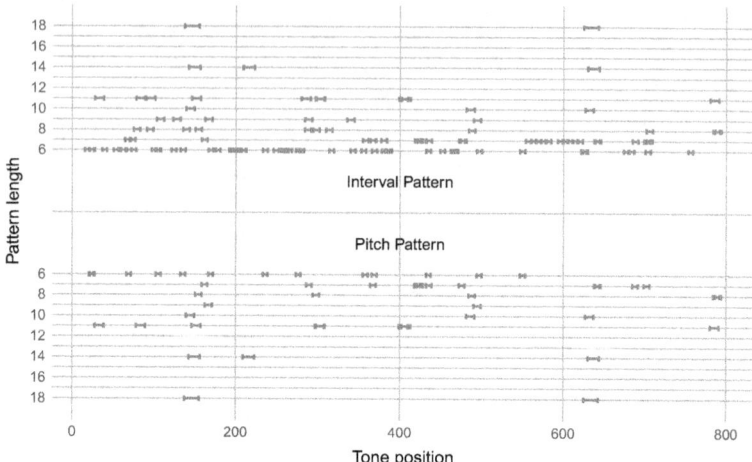

Figure 13: Interval (top) and pitch patterns (bottom) in Bob Berg's solo on "Angles" with an effective length of at least six occurring at least twice in the seven solos by Berg in the Weimar Jazz Database. Only patterns up to an effective length of $N = 18$ are shown, since the longest patterns are due to the oscillations.

reproduced. The shorter patterns are probably rehearsed in many different keys and thus can be used as building blocks, e.g., for line construction in many different harmonic situations. To illustrate the pattern usage by Bob Berg in this particular solo a little further, we produced a network of pattern similarities for the interval patterns. To this end, we calculated edit distances between patterns. The edit or Levenshtein distance (Levenshtein, 1965; Müllensiefen & Frieler, 2004) is defined as the minimum number of editions, deletions, and substitutions required to transform one sequence of symbols (here: intervals) into the other. For two completely different sequences of different length, the maximum number of operations is the length of the longer sequence. This can be used to convert the edit distance into similarity values between 0 and 1. The full matrix of similarities between all interval patterns was then converted into an adjacency matrix using a threshold of 0.5. This means that all similarities lower than .5 were set to 0 and all similarities above .5 were set to 1. These values were used to create a similarity network by feeding them into a graph representation algorithm from the `network` package for R (R Development Core Team, 2008). The result can be seen in Figure 14.

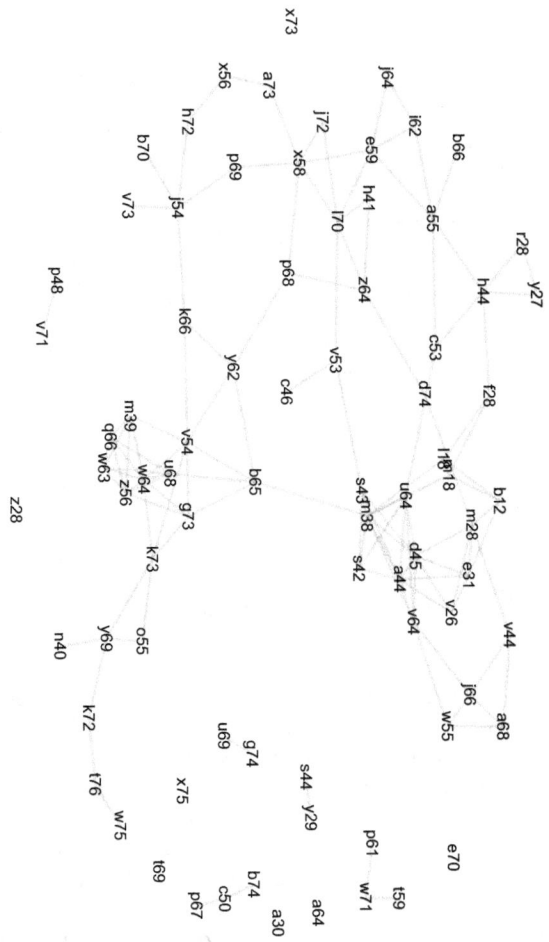

Figure 14: Network representation of all interval patterns in Bob Berg's solo. Edges are drawn according to pattern similarities, which were calculated using edit distance and range from 0 to 1, where a value of 1 means identity. Only connections with similarity greater than 0.5 shown. Node labels are arbitrary tags assigned by the partition algorithm.

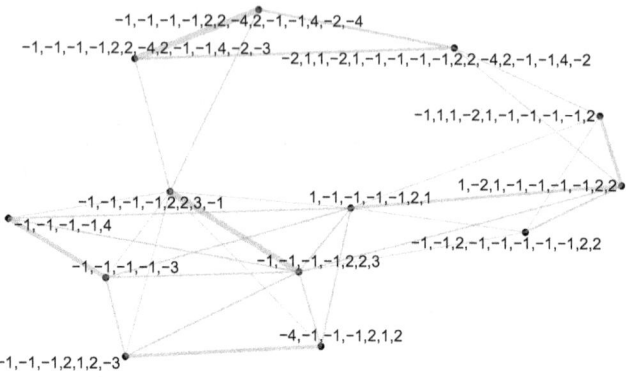

Figure 15: Close-up of the upper middle cluster of the full pattern network. Node labels are pattern values; edge widths are proportional to similarity.

One sees two clusters of strongly interconnected patterns and one rather loose cluster. There are also a few small cluster of only two or three highly similar patterns as well as several singletons. To highlight the cluster structures in more detail, we will have a closer look at the dense cluster in the upper middle of the network plot. It can be seen in Figure 15. A list of the patterns in this cluster can be found in Table 5 and are shown in Figure 16. The pattern b12 is the longest of all with 17 intervals (18 tones). It occurs twice in "Angles" (mm. 30 and 108) at the same metrical position and with identical pitches. It consists of a rather unpredictable sequence of mostly semi- and whole tones. Clearly, this pattern was pre-rehearsed. This is corroborated by the fact that the next two longest patterns, l18 and m18, are, except for their last tones, contained in pattern b12 as a suffix. On the other hand, pattern m28, apart from some slight rhythmical variation, is contained at the beginning of b12, as a prefix. However, it is counted as a separate pattern because it also occurs in another solo by Bob Berg (on "You and the Night and the Music" from the 1997 album *Another Standard*). The same holds true for pattern e31, which is fully contained in b12, but occurs five times in total in three different solos (there only as proper sub-patterns). All other patterns in this cluster are more or less variations of the material from the above mentioned patterns.

The main core of this pattern cluster is the interval pattern -1, -1, -1, -1, 2, 2 of four descending semitones and two ascending whole tones, mostly realized

Table 5: Upper middle interval pattern sub-network.

Tag	MM.	N	F_C	F_A	Value
b12	30, 108	17	2	2	-2, 1, 1, -2, 1, -1, -1, -1, -1, 2, 2, -4, 2, -1, -1, 4, -2
l18	31	13	2	1	-1, -1, -1, -1, 2, 2, -4, 2, -1, -1, 4, -2, -3
m18	43, 110	13	2	2	-1, -1, -1, -1, 2, 2, -4, 2, -1, -1, 4, -2, -4
m28	140	10	2	1	-1, 1, 1, -2, 1, -1, -1, -1, -1, 2
v26	54	10	4	1	-1, -1, 2, -1, -1, -1, -1, -1, 2, 2
e31	30, 92, 109	9	5	3	1, -2, 1, -1, -1, -1, -1, 2, 2
m38	55	8	2	1	-1, -1, -1, -1, 2, 2, 3, -1
a44	55, 92	7	3	2	-1, -1, -1, -1, 2, 2, 3
d45	140	7	2	1	1, -1, -1, -1, -1, 2, 1
s42	141	7	6	1	-1, -1, -1, 2, 1, 2, -3
s43	58	7	4	1	-4, -1, -1, -1, 2, 1, 2
u64	34	5	3	1	-1, -1, -1, -1, -3
v64	93	5	3	1	-1, -1, -1, -1, 4

Note. Tag = pattern name generated by the partition algorithm; MM. = measures in "Angles" where pattern can be found; F_C = frequency of pattern in the entire Bob Berg sub-corpus in the Weimar Jazz Database; F_A = frequency of pattern in the solo on "Angles".

in the middle octave starting from G4 and on a strong metrical position (first or third beat, only exception: v64). Only pattern u64 contains a slightly shorter version (last interval is a descending minor third −3). Notably, this core pattern does not occur as an independent pattern in the pattern partition, because it is always embedded in longer patterns. The most common continuation is a whole tone up (all patterns except s32 and v64), followed either by a descending major third or an ascending minor third.

Taken together, this pattern cluster alone shows clearly that Berg has a pre-rehearsed pattern vocabulary at his disposal, which is stable over time. It is mostly fixed in metrical and pitch position but can be varied by chaining different sub-patterns to longer patterns with contextual adjustments.

Creative Devices

In the foregoing sections, we provided a rich description of Berg's solo on "Angles" using many different perspectives. We would like to summarize here the most important creative devices that are employed by Berg.

Figure 16: Interval pattern of the upper middle cluster of the full pattern network. All instances are the first instances in the solo on "Angles".

First of all, the entire solo seems to follow a rather well-crafted dramaturgy. It shows a double arch shape with overall increasing energy. The dramaturgy seems to develop rather spontaneously and is partially driven by interactions with the band. One characteristic of this solo is the frequent changes of rhythm feel from latin to swing and back, which produce a tension and release pattern on the highest level. Berg nearly always continues his phrases seamlessly over these changes in rhythmic feel, which adds to the flow of his improvisation and the impression of mastery and virtuosity.

On the level of playing ideas, the solo is characterized by an abundance of lines with a conspicuous absence of licks. Rather, the frequently long lines of variable types are contrasted with either pentatonic or diatonic melodies which become more expressive during course of the solo. These melodic licks often occur at the end of a long line, and were dubbed 'piggy tails'. Such small extensions at the end of a longer line, or sometimes also at the beginning, can be frequently observed in jazz solos since bebop, but in this solo, these are rather long and melodious (or expressive). Their general function might be to give a certain form of closure to a line and/or coming to a stop after a fast-moving line. Sometimes, the effect is that the line feels like a mere upturn to its more melodious or expressive piggy tail.

As shown above, Berg constructs his lines very diversely, mixing pentatonic/diatonic sections with (wide) arpeggios and chromaticism. These lines appear to be composed from preconceived patterns that Berg has in his vocabulary. Some of these patterns can be found in solos on the same record but also in solos played years later.

The contrast between pentatonic/diatonic material and chromatic and outside material can be seen as a general feature of this solo. Though it is strictly rooted in A♭ major, the frequent chromaticism as well as the 'trick' of playing the main key over the outside harmonies D^{7alt} and $G^{7\sharp 9}$ at the end of each chorus, i. e., essentially ignoring these chords, create tonal tension and relaxation patterns which propel the solo forward. These parts are contrasted with melodies of ostensible simplicity as well as with expressive outbursts. The construction of lines with inside/outside elements as well as the inside vs. outside contrasts of larger parts can be seen as a kind of self-similarity and might result from deliberate artistic decisions. Berg works by contrasting the simple (e. g., pentatonic, melody) with the complex (e. g., chromaticism, elaborate asymmetric lines) on different levels. This might also be reflected in another important element not only of this solo but also of many other postbop players (e. g., Michael Brecker, Kenny Garrett, Chris Potter), namely the extensive oscillating figures. These normally have an intensifying effect, especially if played in ascending tonal sequences as in this solo. Compared to intricate bebop lines, these oscillations are simple in construction and rather easy to perform, hence early bebop pioneers such as Parker and Gillespie might have shunned them as they were used by Rhythm & Blues 'honkers'. But the need for heightened expressivity in the postbop style, probably starting with Coltrane, (re-)introduced them into modern jazz improvisation, where they serve as energetic counterparts to more sophisticated line constructions.

Finally, Berg frequently uses motivic relationships and tonal sequences to create musical logic and coherence. The use of long and very long patterns (e. g., pattern b12 and m18) and parts thereof might also contribute to a sense of coherence. Apart from a few single ideas, much of the material in this solo is related in one way or another, sometimes subtly transformed and varied, sometime re-contextualized, sometimes re-used verbatim. In this regard, the very last phrase (mm. 139–144) is remarkable as it subsumes the entire solo in a nutshell and is hence also an epitome for Berg's coherent solo design.

Conclusion and outlook

This in-depth case study of a single solo attempts to retrace the underlying creative processes. As a case study, its power for generalizations is of course limited, but a large collection of similar in-depth case studies along with large-scale contextualization in a corpus might finally converge to form a stable and general model of jazz improvisation. We can state for now, however, that the results presented here are compatible with a three-level hierarchical model. The highest level is the overall dramaturgy of the solo, created in interaction with the band, which results in the decisions for certain playing ideas on the middle level, e. g., lines, melodies, expressive moments, oscillations etc., which are then—on the lowest level—realized by combining preconceived material on one hand and spontaneous out-of-the-moment inventions on the other. However, the last point has to actually been proven yet. The sub-corpus of Berg's solos in the Weimar Jazz Database is rather small. For the future, it would be highly desirable to gather a much larger collection to see whether certain elements, such as the melodic 'piggy tails' and the oscillation patterns, were indeed invented on-the-fly or whether pre- or postdecessors can be found in Berg's oeuvre.

Finally, the selection and pre-creation of the material, e. g., their tonal construction, seem to be highly specific for Berg's personal style but are nonetheless shaped by a general stylistic sensitivity.

Table 6: Run-down of MLUs in Bob Berg's solo on "Angles".

Measures	MLU	Scale	Comment
2–3	rhythm-si	G4	
4–5	~melody	C-aeol	
5–7	~#melody	C-aeol	Gm^7 arpeggios.
9–10	line-wavy-asc	D♭-mixo	$Fm^{7♭5}$ arpeggios upwards in zig-zag fashion.
11–13	melody	E♭-mixo	Melody reached after long ascending line ('piggy tail').
14–15	~lick	E♭-mixo	Strong cadential effect.
16–17	lick	E♭-mixo	Jump octave up.
18–19	~rhythm-si	F4	Short thinking pause.
19–23	~line-wavy-desc	E♭-mixo/C-aeol	Mostly diatonic.
24–25	lick	D♭-mixo	Sequence of licks as broken version of the $Fm^{7♭5}$ arps. in m. 9–10.
25	#+lick	D♭-mixo	Three-beat pattern, metric shift.
26	#+lick	D♭-mixo	Last tone of lick is first tone of next.
26–27	#+lick	D♭-mixo	
27–28	#+lick	D♭-mixo	
28	#+lick	D♭-mixo	Last tone missing.
29	#lick	D♭-mixo	Answers last lick, dramatic pause.
30–34	line-wavy-hor	E♭-mixo	Largely chromatic line ('apparatus'). Interesting change to B section (swing feel) in middle of line, accompanied by a register change.
35–36	~melody	C-aeol	Line/melody with piggy tail. Stark contrast.

38–40	`line-wavy-asc`	D♭-mixo	Recalls the D♭⁷ arp. before.
41–42	`~melody`	A♭-ion	Line/melody with piggy tail.
43–46	`line-wavy-desc`	E♭-mixo	Outside.
47–50	`line-wavy-asc`	E♭-WT/A♭-ion	Change to second chorus mid-line.
51–52	`~melody`	C-minpent	Another piggy tail.
53–59	`line-wavy-hor`	chrom → G♭-majpent	Longest line.
60	`#lick`	D♭-mixo	More of a fragment, echoes small piggy tail of last line (cf. m. 29).
61–62	`line-wavy-hor`	E♭-mixo	Unusually short arpeggio line.
75–78	`rhythm-mr`	G♭-majpent	First oscillation. Heating things up a bit.
79–82	`#rhythm-mr`	E♭-mixo/ A♭-ion	Sequencing up first, but then down. Ends with a short piggy tail way up in the sky.
83–86	`line-wavy-asc`	A♭-ion/ D♭-mixo	Zig-zagging upwards.
86–88	`~line-i-dd`	D♭-mixo	Piggy tail after ascending line, between staircase and melody.
89–94	`line-wavy-hor`	A♭-ion	Outside. Mixture of diatonic arps., scales, and chromatic falls.
95–100	`rhythm-mr`	A♭-ion	Three-beat diatonic mordents are shortened to two beats, highest rhythmic energy.
101–104	`#rhythm-mr`	C-dor	Changes only A♭ to A, spicing things up.
105–108	`#rhythm-mr`	G-majpent	Moving a semitone up. Possibly the peak of the solo. Band fires up.

109–112	`line-wavy-desc`	E♭-mixo/ chrom	After a clear mark by the band, Berg is going back to lines, using the apparatus from m. 30.
113–116	`line-wavy-asc`	A♭-majpent	Far-reaching line from A♭2–A♭5.
116–117	`~expressive`	Cm	Again, a piggy tail after a long ascending line, again on a C minor triad.
118–121	`line-wavy-hor`	C-blues	A rather cheesy minor blues line.
122–124	`line-wavy-desc`	D♭-mixo	Continues preceding line after a short stop on C/D♭^{7}. Mistake?
126–129	`line-wavy-asc`	E♭-mixo	Up-swinging diatonic line with large intervals.
129–132	`~expressive`	F-aeol	Longest top tone in the solo. Again, line to expressive piggy tail, with another piggy tail.
134–135	`expressive`	D♭-mixo	Another top tone on #11, a WT higher. Upward sequence of expressive ideas.
135–137	`~##lick`	D♭-mixo#11	Piggy tail of the preceding `expressive`. Extended version of the previous piggy tail.
138–142	`#10line-wavy-hor`	F-minpent/ D-alt	Reminiscence of the last oscillation, but re-mixed into a wavy line.
142–144	`~expressive`	D-alt	Again, expressive piggy tail after a line. Segues into theme after this.

Note. mixo = mixolydian, min/majpent = minor/major pentatonic, aeol = aeolian, blues = blues scale, dor = dorian, WT = whole-tone scale, ion = ionian/major, arp = arpeggio, alt = altered scale, chrom = chromatic scale. See Infobox 5 (Chapter *Computational melody analysis*) for the complete MLU syntax.

Figure 17: Bob Berg's solo on "Angles" with MLA annotations.

Bob Berg's solo on "Angles"

Figure 17: (Continued.)

Figure 17: (Continued.)

Steve Coleman—Balanced improvisation

Friederike Bartel

Steve Coleman is a very productive jazz musician with a very distinctive style of saxophone playing. He can be regarded as one of the less traditional musicians within the Weimar Jazz Database—less traditional in regard to both his compositional work and his approach to improvisation.

After beginning to play jazz in his hometown Chicago, Coleman moved to New York in 1978, where he played in the Thad Jones-Mel Lewis Big Band as well as in other big bands and as a sideman of Dave Holland, Michael Brecker and other prominent musicians of the New York jazz scene (Coleman, n.d.-a; Pfleiderer, 2005, p. 801). Soon he formed his own band, Five Elements, at first to busk on the streets. Since the 1980s, Coleman and Five Elements have produced nearly 30 records. The band still exists today, touring internationally and producing records with various line-ups. Notable members are Cassandra Wilson (voc), Robin Eubanks (trombone), David Gilmore (guitar), Reggie Washington (bass), and Marvin "Smitty" Smith (drums). Many of those band members are also part of M-Base, a collective of musicians with a similar way of thinking about music and improvisation. As they state:

> Within a short time the group began finding a niche in tiny, out-of-the-way clubs in Harlem and Brooklyn where they continued to hone their developing concept of improvisation within nested looping structures. These were ideas based on how to create music from one's experiences, which became the foundation which Coleman and friends call the M-Base concept (Coleman, n.d.-a).

Coleman sometimes expands Five Elements to form a large ensemble with up to 20 musicians, he then changes the name of the band to Council of Balance. This name is a reference to how Coleman thinks about improvisation:

'Balance' is a key concept for his own theoretical approach to music, which is detailed on his homepage and which he calls 'Symmetrical Movement'. Coleman's musical roots in jazz music lie in an early admiration for both Charlie Parker and Maceo Parker. Later on, he learned how to improvise and then played with famous jazz musicians in New York (Coleman, n.d.-a; Pfleiderer, 2005). He combines these roots with an interest in hip hop and funk (e. g., Steve Coleman and Metrics, *The Way of the Cipher*, 1995) as well as in African music and the African diaspora in general. This included research trips to Cuba, Ghana and other places in Africa in the early 1990s. The music of Coleman and the M-Base collective is a mixture of jazz-based styles and forms, such as 12-bar blues, combined with groove- and rhythm-oriented, partly polyrhythmic music (e. g., in "Cross-Fade" on *Black Science*, 1990). Sometimes rhythmical loops are combined with collective improvisation while at other times the standard jazz structure—theme, solos, theme—is maintained. Both of these basic formal structures can also be mixed within a recording.

The aim of this case study is to characterize some aspects of Coleman's personal style of improvisation, which is embedded in his compositions and the input of his band members. So far, there has been almost no analytical research on Coleman's improvisations. There are only a few dictionary entries plus all the information Coleman offers himself on his homepage, where he explains his improvisational concept in a detailed essay (Coleman, n.d.-b), alongside his biography and a discography.

The concept of Symmetrical Movement is based on the terms 'balance' and 'symmetry'. In his essay, Coleman claims that his aim in improvisation is to create a balance in regard to several parameters of the music, e. g., harmony, melody, and rhythm. An overview of this approach will be given in the following. Subsequently, his improvisation on "Pass It On" will be described and analyzed and then compared to the solos of the other soloists on the recording as well as to another, stylistically varying solo by Coleman.

Symmetrical Movement

In the introduction to his concept of Symmetrical Movement, Coleman states that balance can be achieved musically mainly through symmetry:

> We live in a world of immense beauty. [...] I want to speak here about balance and make some comments about how balance can be achieved musically. There are countless ways that architectural balance can be musically achieved from the micro to macro level.

> [...] The most obvious kinds of balance that come to mind are the various forms of symmetry (i. e., bilateral, etc.) that can be applied musically, using intuitive and logical methods (Coleman, n.d.-b).

He uses the terms 'balance' and 'symmetry' more or less as synonyms in his statements. This is although symmetry can be considered as much more mathematically connoted than balance—symmetry generally refers to equidistance in regard to one point or axis, whereas balance rather implies that certain elements should be present in the same amount.

Within the essay, Coleman focuses on how to generate a melody symmetrically through improvisation, although he claims that the concept can also be applied to other parameters of music. The main idea for creating melodic symmetry is to define so-called 'axis tones'. Either one or more tones can function as the center of a constructed, but also improvised melody. The other tones should be symmetrically related to this center or axis. It is important that the axis tone(s) are not regarded as harmonic roots of the music. Coleman does not elaborate on how the axis of the improvisation can be chosen or how often it can change. For a long time, he practiced this method of symmetrical melodic construction by himself without harmonic context, as he writes. In a second step, he was able to bring it into context with the harmonies of a tune.

Coleman establishes rules for how other tones can be symmetrically related to the axis, so-called 'laws of motion'. Symmetry here refers to intervallic equidistance to the axis in both directions, e. g., a minor third above the axis should be balanced by a minor third below the axis. The main process of this symmetrical motion can be described with a simplified example of three consecutive tones: If the first tone is the axis, the second tone is, e. g., a certain interval above the axis and the third tone the same interval below the axis. Therefore, to be able to do this, the musician who follows this concept must be able to know and play all the possible intervals up and down starting from any possible tones.

Depending on whether the intervals derive from a one-tone axis or from an axis consisting of two tones a semitone apart, the arising intervals are divided into symmetrical and non-symmetrical intervals. In the first case, the intervals include the unison, major second, major third, tritone, minor sixth and minor seventh. Non-symmetrical intervals are the minor second, minor third, perfect fourth, perfect fifth, major sixth and major seventh. Additionally, Coleman names a couple of exceptions from this main process:

1. If the first played interval is a symmetrical interval, an additional tone can be played before the interval is balanced in the opposite direction.
2. The axis tones can be played at the end of this construction, as the result of two balanced intervals.
3. The two axis tones can also lie further apart than a minor second.

Coleman introduces a new way of thinking while improvising that differs from the widespread chord-scale approach. The chord-scale approach offers one or more scales fitting each chord by taking into consideration the function of the chord in its harmonic context. It is the most suitable approach to analyzing most traditional jazz improvisations, too. However, Coleman seems to override or at least extend this common approach to improvisation.

Furthermore, if there is no evidence of which tones are the chosen axis tones, it is almost impossible to analyze a solo according to Coleman's concept. Coleman himself specifies that when analyzing improvised material that derives from symmetrical motion, there can always be several solutions, whereas there is no wrong solution. Moreover and significantly, he claims that this is a technique he learned for many years but that it is not his goal to improvise solely in agreement with the rules of the Symmetrical Movement. For him, it is just as boring to simply improvise according to the chord-scale approach as it is to always improvise in a symmetrical fashion. So his concept can be considered as a technique and a way of thinking which Coleman uses to bring up new and uncommon melodic ideas and to shape his own style.

Relating Coleman's improvisations to the concept of Symmetrical Movement is, for several reasons, a rather speculative task. However, the concept obviously leads to more dissonant tones and outside playing than the chord-scale approach. Therefore, the analytical study focuses on Coleman's choice of pitches and gives only tentative examples for the usage of the concept. Another issue is his rhythmical playing, which can be described as characteristic for his distinctive personal style. As an example, Coleman's solo on "Pass It On" will be analyzed and then compared with the solos of Kenny Wheeler and Van Freeman on the same recording, as well as with other improvisations by Coleman.

Analysis: "Pass It On"

"Pass It On" is a title from the record *Rhythm in Mind* that was released in 1991. Besides Coleman on alto saxophone, the line-up includes Von Freeman on tenor saxophone, Kenny Wheeler on trumpet and flugelhorn, Kevin

Eubanks on guitar, Tommy Flanagan on piano, Dave Holland on bass, and Ed Blackwell and Marvin "Smitty" Smith on drums. The rhythmic feel of the piece can be labeled as 'funky' or 'latin', which is underlined by a typical brass section with two saxophone players and a trumpet, the use of percussion instruments, and a bass line that emphasizes the fourth beat of every bar instead of the first. The formal structure of the song is built on recurrent A and B sections. Both form sections have a duration of four bars and the form can be described as 16-bar AABA. The chord changes of the A section consist of bar-wise alternating Cm^7 and $E\flat$, whereby Cm^7 is the relative minor of $E\flat$. The chord changes of the B section are Fm, $D\flat$, Fm, $G\flat^7$. So, the harmonic basis is not very complicated.

Before the wind section starts playing the melody of the theme on top of this form, the rhythm section begins with an intro of eight bars or two A sections, respectively. When the musicians start to improvise after playing the theme, the accompanying musicians keep up that harmonic scheme.

Coleman plays the first solo: He improvises on two choruses, this is 32 bars plus one pick-up bar and one extra bar at the end. Coleman is followed by tenor saxophone player Von Freeman, who plays three choruses, and by trumpet player Kenny Wheeler, who plays two choruses. After one more chorus by bass player Dave Holland, all wind instruments improvise simultaneously for one chorus. Afterwards, the melody of the theme is played again, followed by another collective improvisation and another beginning of the theme. However, the melody is faded out and the rhythm section comes to an ending as well.

Coleman plays his solo continuously on a highly energetic level. A buildup of intensity is noticeable only in regard to the density of the tones he plays. Additionally, the phrases get a little longer during the second chorus of the solo, but the dynamics stay at the same level. Coleman articulates his tones very clearly and precisely in regard to rhythm and by generating a direct and energetic sound. This is remarkable especially compared to the following tenor saxophone solo, which is played by Von Freeman with a less clear and more noisy sound. The impression of a distinct 'sound' in Coleman's solo is corroborated by his choice of pitches. These observations will be detailed in the following description of the succession of phrases and a short re-narration of his solo.

Coleman begins his solo with two rather short phrases, rhythmic statements that both consist of sixteenths and a few eighth notes that derive from $E\flat$ major / C minor pentatonic (Figure 1).

The first A section is then completed with a longer phrase that can be subdivided into a rhythmic idea of sixteenths offbeats and a following line that

Figure 1: Steve Coleman's solo on "Pass It On", mm. 0–1.

combines eighth-note triplets and sixteenth notes (Figure 2). The first idea consists of pitches from the scale E♭ mixolydian over both E♭ and Cm⁷. This means Coleman uses the minor seventh (D♭) instead of the major seventh (D) on E♭ and the minor second (D♭) on Cm⁷ (C phrygian), which can be described as a variation of the scales rather than outside playing. An actual example for outside playing is apparent in the last bar of the first A section.

Figure 2: "Pass It On", m. 4.

Here, Coleman plays a variety of chromatic pitches such as ♯11 (A), ♯9 (F♯) and ♭13 (B) on E♭ major. After this first harmonic outbreak, within the second A section he mainly returns to diatonic pitches. From now on, the phrases consist more and more of sixteenth notes interspersed by a few longer tones. In the third bar of the second A section (Cm⁷) two chromatic four-tone lines can be found (Figure 3).

Figure 3: "Pass It On", m. 7.

Coleman ends this phrase on the major seventh over Cm⁷, a quite dissonant sound. In the last bar of the second A section he picks up the idea of playing both minor and major sevenths on E♭ combined with the use of sixteenth offbeats such as in bar two of the first A section. The B section of the first chorus is played completely harmonically inside with one longer phrase of sixteenths, eighth-triplets and one longer tone (Figure 4).

Figure 4: "Pass It On", m. 14.

The last A section of the first chorus then re-iterates the idea of playing C phrygian / E♭ mixolydian, at least in the first two bars. The second bar is also enriched with chromatic transitions (1, ♭2, 2, ♭2, 1 and 6, ♭6, 5). In contrast to this chromaticism, during the following two bars Coleman strictly uses tones from the C minor pentatonic scale, with frequent large intervals. Again, this section consists of a long line, mainly of sixteenths, with only a few longer tones (Figure 5).

Figure 5: "Pass It On", mm. 15–16.

The second chorus of Coleman's solo mainly consists of longer sixteenth lines, sometimes also using sixteenth offbeats or longer tones as before. In the first A section of the second chorus, Coleman goes back to play E♭ ionian in the second bar, whereas in the fourth bar the chord E♭ is enriched with many chromatic pitches such as ♯9, ♯11, ♭9 and ♭13. On Cm^7, he plays dorian for the first time (Figure 6).

Figure 6: "Pass It On", m. 19.

The chromatic line goes on in the second A section and again he uses the major 7 over Cm^7, as well as ♯11 and ♭13. At the end of the second A section, the idea of playing E♭ mixolydian comes up again, and also ♯9, ♯11 and ♭13. Similar to what he played before, it follows a mainly inside line in reverse, ending on the highest tone of the solo right in the middle of the B section (Figure 7).

Figure 7: "Pass It On", m. 26.

At the transition to the last A section, Coleman plays the major seventh of G♭^{7} (F) which then becomes the fourth of Cm^7 (Figure 8). Finally, the last A section is enriched with chromatic changing tones but there are no longer chromatic passages.

Figure 8: "Pass It On", m. 28.

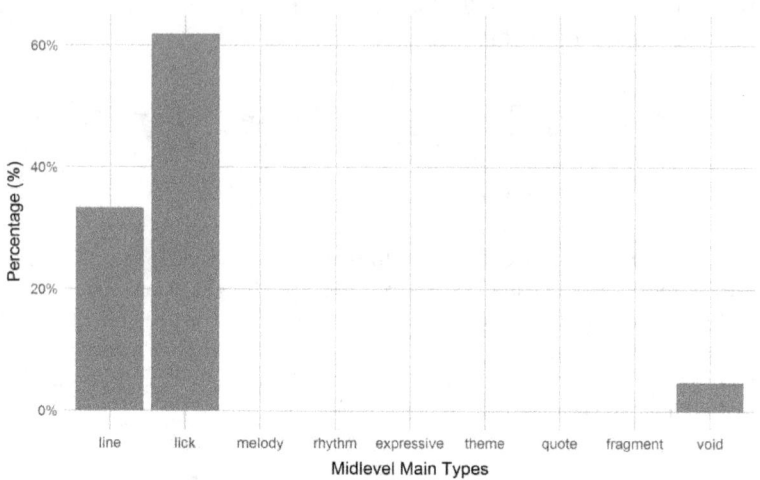

Figure 9: Distribution of midlevel units (MLU) in "Pass It On".

What is remarkable for the whole solo is Coleman's alternation between diatonic and chromatic playing. He repeats certain ideas, such as playing E♭ mixolydian on E♭ and on Cm⁷, which then becomes C phrygian. Rhythmically, the combination of mainly sixteenths with sixteenth offbeats and triple eighths is notable. This examination of the solo provides a first impression and exemplifies Coleman's usage of chromatic pitches—which in turn partly explains the 'special' sound of Coleman's playing. In the following, some of these observations will be enriched and visualized by using tools of the MeloSpyGUI and by giving some examples for possible interpretations according to the rules of Symmetrical Movement. Firstly, on examination of the midlevel annotation (Figure 9, see for an explanation of midlevel units), it is noticeable that there are only *licks* and *lines*, mostly *wavy lines*, as well as one *void*, but no units categorized as *melody*, *rhythm*, *expressive* or as referring to the theme. This observation, in addition to the following analyses, confirms the title of this chapter, for Coleman's playing seems to be mainly concerned with rhythmic and intervallic construction. By listening to Coleman's improvisations, one can get the impression that he builds up an area of tones by compounding certain constant rhythmic and harmonic parameters that follow certain rules. The constructive quality of Coleman's solo may be connected to his concept of Symmetrical Movement, which actually consists of rules for choosing intervals while disregarding chords. Moreover, an ongoing rhythmic grid of sixteenths seems to be underlying his improvisation, like bricks that build the foundation of a building. However, a constant rhythmic grid is contrary to the idea of a rhythmically varied melody.

Figure 10 (top left corner) shows the Metrical Circle Map of Coleman's solo. All the tones are here assigned to 48 rhythmic positions within the $\frac{4}{4}$-bar. The diagram visualizes the frequencies of the different rhythmic placements used by Coleman. Very frequently, Coleman plays on- and offbeat positions concerning the eighth-grid (1, 1+, 2, 2+, 3, 3+, 4, 4+); they all occur between 16 and 21 times. Also very frequently, he plays the sixteenth offbeats in between all the aforementioned positions, whereas tones on sixteenth positions between 3+ and 4, 4 and 4+, 4+ and 1 are as frequent as on eighth positions. So this diagram certainly gives an impression of Coleman's balanced metrical tone placements. Another reference to the terms balance and symmetry is Coleman's preferred use of a binary rhythmic grid rather than a ternary one, as the diagram shows. Eighths and sixteenths form a grid with a symmetric binary division of time intervals which is not possible within a ternary grid. Of course, in this case the rhythmic feel of the music is played in a binary way, but Coleman also plays binary within a ternary rhythmic framework, which will be pointed out later.

The top left corner in Figure 11 pictures Coleman's use of pitch classes with respect to the particular chords played by the rhythm section in percent. The numbers one to seven represent the chord tones (1, 3, 5, 7) and tensions (2, 4, 6), and the numbers and letters on top of that represent the remaining tones that fill up the chromatic scale ($\flat 13$ = minor sixth, $\flat 9$ = minor ninth, $\sharp 11$ = tritone, $\sharp 7$ = major seventh over minor seventh chord, $\sharp 9$ = minor third over major chord, $\sharp 10$ = major third over minor chord, $\flat 7$ = minor seventh over major seventh chord). The diagram shows that Coleman plays primarily diatonic pitch classes while using all of the non-diatonic pitch classes more or less equally. He does not emphasize the chord tones in general, only the fifth and the seventh. Besides, he also uses non-diatonic pitch classes, but with a much lower percentage. So in this case, balance does not mean that Coleman uses all twelve chromatic pitch classes equally often, as in, for example, twelve-tone music. This can also be demonstrated by the diagram in Figure 12 (top left corner), which pictures all absolute pitches Coleman uses. With 45 times, B$\flat$4 is played by Coleman most often, followed by F4 and G4. All three tones

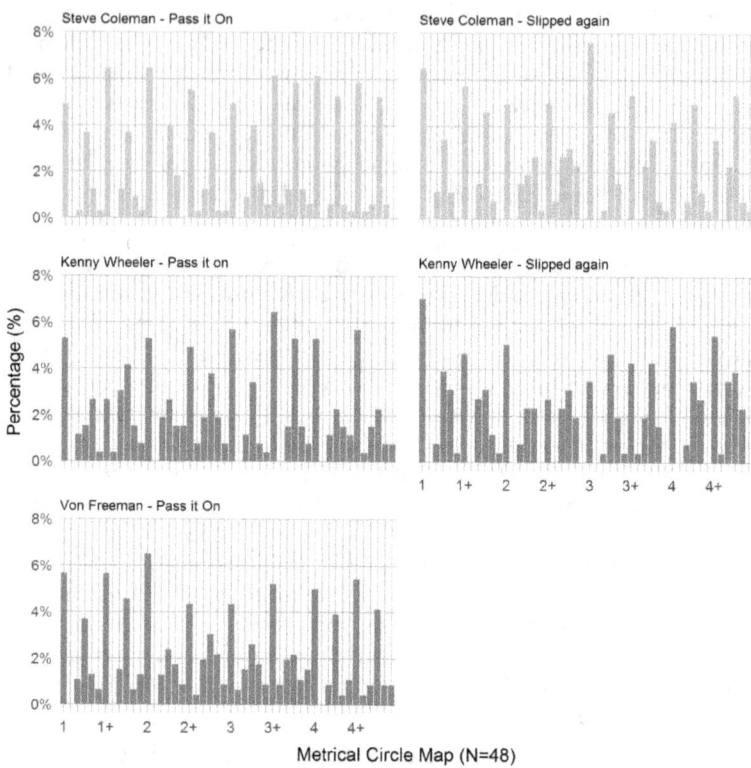

Figure 10: Metrical Circle Maps of Steve Coleman's, Kenny Wheeler's, and Von Freeman's solos on "Pass It On", and Coleman's and Wheeler's solos on "Slipped again".

are consonant with Cm^7 and E♭, the chords of the A section that are played most of the time during the whole piece.

Figure 13 shows the alternating diatonic (or 'inside') and non-diatonic/chromatic (or 'outside') character of successive phrases that were recognized in the re-narration of the solo by picturing pitch classes in relation to the chord(s) within different phrases.

As described before, some phrases are completely diatonic, even pentatonic, such as phrases 2, 4 or 9 (phrase 1, the pick-up bar, is missing because, technically, there was no chord annotation available). Three phrases (7, 8 and 10) emphasize the ♭9 as an extra chromatic pitch. Finally, there are phrases

Steve Coleman—Balanced improvisation

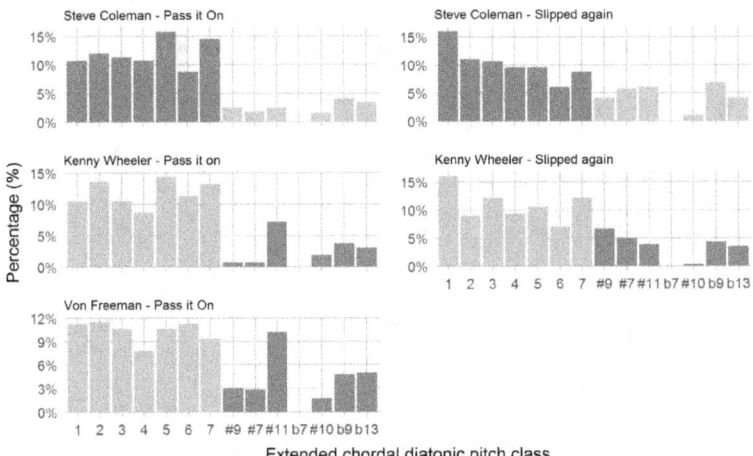

Figure 11: Distribution of extended chordal diatonic pitch classes of Steve Coleman's, Kenny Wheeler's, and Von Freeman's solos on "Pass It On", and Coleman and Wheeler's solos on "Slipped again".

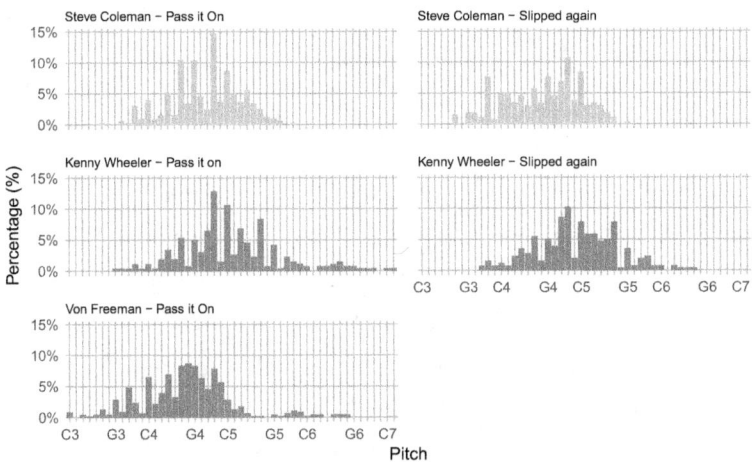

Figure 12: Distribution of pitches of Steve Coleman's, Kenny Wheeler's, and Von Freeman's solos on "Pass It On", and Coleman's and Wheeler's solos on "Slipped again".

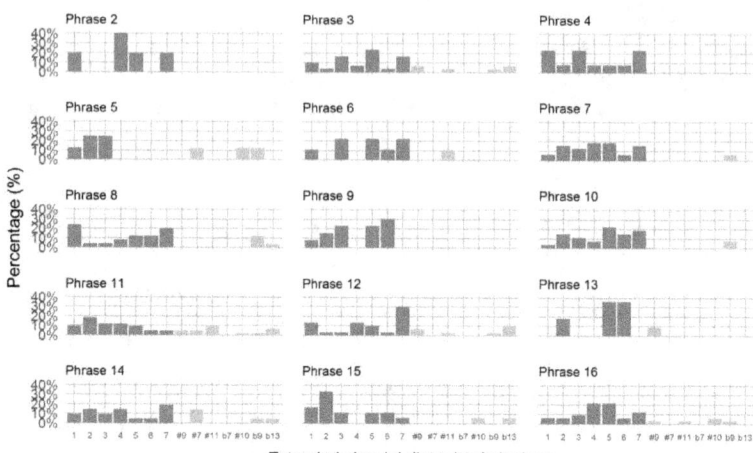

Figure 13: Phrase-wise distribution of extended chordal diatonic pitch classes of Steve Coleman's solos on "Pass It On". Dark blue = 'inside' diatonic tones, light blue = 'outside' non-diatonic tones.

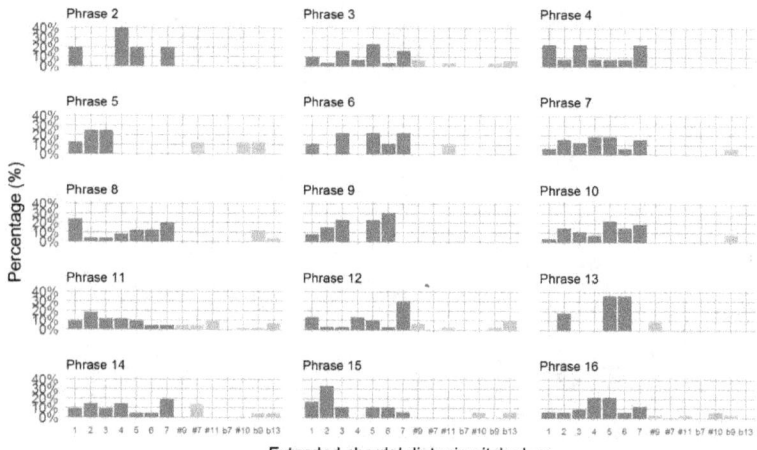

Figure 14: Phrase-wise distribution of extended chordal diatonic pitch classes of Steve Coleman's solos on "Slipped again". Dark blue = 'inside' diatonic tones, light blue = 'outside' non-diatonic tones.

Steve Coleman—Balanced improvisation

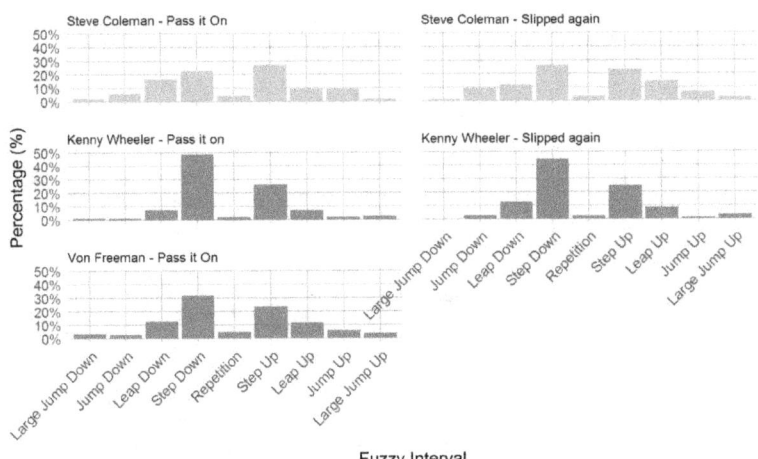

Figure 15: Distribution of interval classes of Steve Coleman's, Kenny Wheeler's, and Von Freeman's solos on "Pass It On", and Coleman and Wheeler's solos on "Slipped again".

that can be described as mainly chromatic, such as phrases 3, 5 or 11. The alternation of diatonic and chromatic phrases is clearly visible. This could be interpreted as a kind of balancing, which means that Coleman doesn't use chromatic tones as a device for building up tension in the course of the solo, but instead starts with a chromatic line right away.

In Figure 15 (top left corner), one can see the percentage of interval classes: steps up and down, leaps (minor and major thirds) up and down, jumps (fourths, tritones, and fifths) up and down, and large jumps (sixths and larger) up and down. The distribution of interval classes can be approximately described as balanced, although Coleman plays slightly more ascending intervals than descending. However, this distribution cannot exactly capture the concept of Symmetrical Movement, because it refers to particular cases in which tones should be played consecutively, not to the occurrence of certain intervals during an entire solo. This is why we will give two typical but rather short examples from the solo.

The first example is taken from m. 10, which is the second bar of the first B section. The eighth triplet on beat three includes the tones A♭, B♭, and G♭. If A♭ is considered to be the axis tone, B♭ and G♭ are equidistant from this axis, either a major second above or below. The same principle can be detected for the tones B♭, C, and G♭ beginning on beat two of the same bar.

Figure 16: Symmetric Movement example ("Pass It On", m. 10).

The second example is part of a more chromatic passage of Coleman's solo in m. 28. On beat three he plays E, F, and E♭, the minor seventh, major

Figure 17: Symmetric Movement example ("Pass It On", m. 28).

seventh and the 13th of the chord G♭^{7} of the last B section. The symmetry here follows the same structure as in the first example, only using minor seconds instead of major seconds. E can be considered the axis tone, followed by the minor second above, F, and the minor second below, E♭. Especially the chromatic passages of the solo offer a good source for more examples like this. There are examples of passages with larger intervals and with more tones which could be related the concept of Symmetric Balance, too. However, in most cases, the relation has a rather speculative character.

Comparative analysis

In the preceding sections, Coleman's style of improvisation was described as individually shaped, originating from his sound, his choice of pitches and intervals, and his alternating usage of diatonic and chromatic pitches resulting in a characteristic style of exact rhythmic and advanced melodic playing. The characterization of personal style can be regarded as one of the main aspects of jazz research as well as highly important for the jazz musicians themselves, since improvisation in jazz involves personal expression and the development of a personal 'sound'. To examine style, comparisons can be of further help.

The first possibility for a comparison is to take other musicians into account. For this case study, it is appropriate to look at the solos of Kenny Wheeler and Von Freeman on "Pass It On". Additionally, Coleman's solo on "Pass It On" will be compared to his improvisation on the blues "Slipped again" whose ternary rhythmic feel contrasts with the binary feel of "Pass It On". "Slipped again" is a piece written by Coleman and recorded on *Rhythm In Mind* (1991). The key is F and the form can be described as a standard blues form enriched with a few II-V progressions. After a tenor saxophone solo by

Von Freeman, a trumpet solo by Kenny Wheeler and a piano solo by Tommy Flanagan, Coleman plays the fourth solo on this recorded version of the song, followed by a bass solo by Dave Holland. Listening to the three solos of Coleman, Wheeler and Freeman, there are clear differences concerning sound, rhythmic attitude, energy, and choice of pitches.

Although the differences between the Metrical Circle Maps of Coleman's, Wheeler's and Freeman's solos (Figure 10) are rather subtle, the distinctive rhythmical playing of Coleman is visibly accessible in "Slipped again", too. Kenny Wheeler mainly emphasizes the downbeats and plays many tones in between the sixteenths, which can indicate a less rhythmically precise or a faster playing (the latter cannot be proved by listening). Freeman, on the other hand, emphasizes the eighth offbeats but not the sixteenth offbeats like Coleman and again, there are more counts in between the sixteenths.

The second comparative diagram (Figure 11) shows the different pitches the three musicians use in their solos. Firstly, it represents the very different pitch ranges, which are partly due to the different instruments being played: alto saxophone, trumpet and tenor saxophone. Wheeler on trumpet therefore uses the highest tones and Freeman on tenor saxophone the lowest. Secondly, the diagram illustrates that Coleman and Wheeler both emphasize B♭4 and a few other tones due to the changes of the A section, whereas Freeman plays very chromatically with nearly uniformly distributed pitches. This corresponds to the listening impression.

To compare sound and dynamics by visualization, different methods would be necessary, for example spectral analysis or other tools the MeloSpyGUI offers. But the analysis so far already proves that many of the previously recognized distinctive aspects of Coleman's improvisational style cannot be found in the same way in the solos of Wheeler and Freeman. These are, for example, a rhythmical exactness based on a clearly played sixteenth-grid and the observation that the goal of reaching musical balance and the training of the Symmetrical Movement don't lead to an entirely chromatic style of playing in Coleman's solos. In fact, Freeman plays more chromatically than Coleman.

Listening to Coleman's solo on "Slipped again" again gives the impression that he switches between blues scale / diatonic playing and outside playing. This is emphasized by a visualization of the pitch classes within the phrases of the solo in Figure 14.

Besides the alternating diatonic and chromatic usage of pitches that was already recognized in Coleman's solo on "Pass It On", some further observations are striking. For example, phrase 14 consists simply of the ♭9 and the root of C^7 followed by the third of the following chord Fm^7. In contrast, in phrase 13, immediately beforehand, there are a variety of diatonic and chromatic pitches with more outside than inside pitches. Yet, this diagram supports the assumption that Coleman uses an alternation of diatonic and chromatic phrases as a stylistic device.

What generates an easily interpreted graphic is the comparison of the Metrical Circle Map of Coleman's solo in "Pass It On" with the one of his solo in "Slipped again" (Figure 7, top row). Arguably, both distributions do not look entirely alike, but they clearly do give an approximative impression. Beat one and three are emphasized more in "Slipped again", and the sixteenth grid is clearly evident. This observation is further supported if one looks at the comparison between the Metrical Circle Map of Wheeler's solo in "Slipped again" and the one of Coleman's solo (Figure 10, left column). Wheeler emphasizes beat one and four, comparable to how Coleman emphasizes beat one and three, but the sixteenth grid is much less visible in Wheeler's solo, probably due to a more ternary style of playing.

All these comparisons underline personal distinctiveness in the improvisational style of Coleman, and also in the styles of Wheeler and Freeman. The examination of stylistic aspects, which in this chapter was focused on rhythmic and harmonic parameters, could be expanded by additional stylistically relevant features.

Conclusion

The aim of this case study was to analyze individual stylistic aspects of Coleman's improvisational style. After outlining Coleman's musical heritage, we had a closer look at one specific solo taken from "Pass It On". Next, we obtained insights from comparative analyses of solos by Kenny Wheeler and Von Freeman on the same tune, on one hand, and of a second solo by Coleman taken from the blues "Slipped again", on the other hand.

The first step disproved the assumption that Coleman plays in a very chromatic way by using all twelve tones equally, due to the melodic approach that was derived from the concept of Symmetrical Movement. It was instead confirmed that Coleman combines intervallic symmetry with the harmonic context of the song rather than ignoring the chord-scale theory altogether, but also that he uses the alternation of inside and outside playing as a stylistic device. Likewise, it came to light that the symmetry he approves in his essay can also be found in prevalent binary subdivisions of the beats, as well as in a rhythmically exact playing.

To make sure that these results of the stylistic analysis are distinctive rather than general occurrences in jazz improvisation, comparisons were made in a second step. The comparative diagrams based on the solos of Wheeler, Freeman and Coleman in the song "Pass It On" result in the findings that neither Wheeler nor Freeman play rhythmically inside a sixteenth grid as Coleman does. This corroborates the assumption that this is an aspect of his individual style.

Finally, the comparison of the first analyzed solo of Coleman in "Pass It On" with his solo in "Slipped again", which are both part of the record *Rhythm In Mind*, again proved the previously made assumptions, e. g., his switching between inside (blues scale) playing and outside passages. As the Symmetrical Movement concept is hard to fully reconstruct, it can only be assumed that the thoughts that go along with it and the training of the intervallic structures lead to the idea of alternating diatonic and chromatic passages, especially in light of Coleman's statement that strictly adhering to either the Symmetrical Movement approach or the chord-scale approach would be equally 'boring'.

Further possibilities for examining Coleman's style would be, for example, in additional timbral studies. Another option would be to analyze the individual phrases or more solos in more detail. In this way, one could draw additional conclusions about how Coleman builds up his improvisations, especially about how fundamental the alternation of inside and outside playing is for his personal style, or how he uses rhythm and certain motives to build up his solos. Possibly, the terms of symmetry and balance might come up again.

Following the red line: Chris Potter's solo on "Pop Tune #1"

Wolf-Georg Zaddach

> A world-class soloist, accomplished composer and formidable bandleader, saxophonist Chris Potter has emerged as a leading light of his generation. Down Beat called him 'one of the most studied (and copied) saxophonists on the planet' while Jazz Times identified him as 'a figure of international renown.' Jazz sax elder statesman Dave Liebman called him simply 'one of the best musicians around,' a sentiment shared by the readers of Down Beat in voting him second only to tenor sax great Sonny Rollins in the magazine's 2008 Readers Poll (Milkowski, 2017).

Going by his biographical article on the saxophonist's homepage, journalist and producer Bill Milkowski is undoubtedly convinced by Potter's accomplishments. By 2017, Potter had recorded 19 albums as a leader and appeared on over 100 albums as a sideman. The list of musicians he worked with reads as a Who's Who of the recent and contemporary American jazz scene: Paul Motian, Dave Holland, Herbie Hancock, John Scofield, Jim Hall, Dave Douglas, and many more. Potter, born in Chicago, Illinois in 1971 and raised in Columbia, South Carolina, has been part of the New York City scene since 1989, when he started studying at the age of 18 and played in the band of Red Rodney, who himself had played alongside Charlie Parker. While Milkowski describes Potter's output in superlatives emphasizing the musician's international success, the attraction of his playing may be rooted in his awareness and mastery of the tradition as well as of contemporary jazz:

> My aesthetic as a saxophonist has always been based in Bird and Lester Young and Sonny Rollins and all the other greats on the

> instrument. What I've learned from them in terms of phrasing, sound, and approach to rhythm I'll never outgrow,

Potter stated, as cited by Milkowski (2017). Nevertheless, even with his solo recordings, Potter displays a diversity that spans from postbop to modern groove and fusion. In fact, Potter shows an openness for diverse musical genres, and reflects artistically on the music he grew up with:

> I've been touched by many forms of music, like funk, hip hop, country, different folk musics, classical music, etc., and for me not to allow these influences into my music would be unnecessarily self-limiting. The difficulty is incorporating these sounds in an organic, unforced way. It helps me to remember I want people to feel the music, even be able to dance, and not think of it as complicated or forbidding (Milkowski, 2017).

His band project Chris Potter's Underground is such an attempt to explore contemporary sounding, groove-based, and rhythmically challenging music. In a setup that includes a modern-sounding electric guitar (Wayne Krantz, later Adam Rogers), a Fender Rhodes (Craig Taborn) that also takes over the function of the bass, and drums (Nate Smith), Potter can connect his education and experience as a postbop saxophonist with groove and funk-oriented music. Since Potter has proved his postbop playing abilities many times with recordings such as *Presenting Chris Potter* (1992), *Unspoken* (1997), or recently *The Dreamer Is the Dream* (2017), it seems worthwhile to analyze his improvisation in a groove context. In the following, I will discuss the solo on "Pop Tune #1" on *Follow the Red Line: Live at the Village Vanguard*, recorded during a three-night appearance from February 15th and 17th 2007 in New York City. At this point, Potter had already been experimenting with this line-up and aesthetic for several years and had released a first studio recording with the highly acclaimed album *Underground* in 2006. One perspective on the music of Potter's Underground could be that it unites funk and groove rhythms and aesthetics with the inventiveness and rhythmic, as well as melodic, versatility of postbop improvisation. "It's an exercise in futility to find a name for the music of *Follow the Red Line*", emphasizes John Kelman in a review of the album. He further states that Potter convincingly

> [...] blurs the lines between jazz, rock, funk and even a little afrobeat in ways that are finally being accepted again two decades after *The New York Times* declared the 'pestilence known as fusion is dead,' the best word to describe this recording is, quite simply, great (Kelman, 2007).

While Kelman is speaking about the music in general, an interesting question is: Does Potter blur the lines during his improvisation, too? And if so, how does he adjust and develop his improvisation in the groove context?

Following the red line: the overall structure of the performance and solo

The hybridization of postbop and modern pop/rock styles is at the core of *Follow the Red Line*. At first sight, most of the tracks follow the conventional structure of postbop music with an introduction, a (sometimes complex) head, solos, and the head again. "Pop Tune #1" is slightly different though. The performance is split into two main parts. The first part (0:00–6:30 min) has a medium slow tempo in a $\frac{6}{8}$-meter, emphasizing a ballad feeling with a constant harmonic rhythm, slightly shifting through different harmonic centers. During the first part, guitarist Adam Rogers plays an intense solo with a repetition of the head at the end. Then, Chris Potter starts an unaccompanied interlude to the second part of the performance (6:30–7:03 min). Following this, Potter improvises for another four and a half minutes, accompanied by the band. The solo culminates in a theme-like passage and ends rather unexpected (11:01–11:38 min). Potter's interlude and solo during the second part will be in the focus of the following analysis.

Setting the groove—Potter's solo interlude

The first main part, at approx. 102 bpm and in a $\frac{6}{8}$-feeling, ends with a slight collective rubato during the last measure and a stop on beat one of the next measure, followed by a slow fade-out by the guitar and keys. Potter uses the stop as a starting point for his improvisation. However, he does not start with the band's emphasis on beat one, but instead installs a new time feeling and meter starting on the next beat. What follows is an improvised 30-second solo of 16 measures without the band, functioning as an interlude to the second part of the performance (see Figure 1). Potter plays in a groovy $\frac{4}{4}$-feeling, emphasizing the beats and off-beats with short, accentuated tones and a harmonically rather stable, static tonal center on G, based on the last chord of part one (Gm). The tempo is marginally faster with approx. 108 bpm, and Potter shifts slightly during his solo interlude. While he starts the phrases on the off-beats, he stabilizes the time feel and meter with the percussive noise of pressing down lower keys without an air stream on the saxophone. However, it is the contrast of accentuation and phrasing as well as the switch

Figure 1: Unaccompanied solo interlude by Potter (6:30–7:02 min).

to a $\frac{4}{4}$-meter with a just slight tempo modification that contributes to the forward propelling character of the second part of the performance.

During these first 16 measures of the improvisation (6:30–7:02 min), Potter emphasizes a general partition into cycles consisting of four measures each. These four-bar cycles become a fundamental structure for the rest of the solo. Each of the four-bar cycles of the solo interlude can be heard as four individual sections. The first two cycles are connected to each other by a slight variation of the first motif at the beginning of the second section; the same happens in the third and fourth section. The first and second section use mainly the G minor pentatonic scale, although Potter adds a major 3rd as well as a flatted 5th as passing tones during mm. 5 and 7, which refer to the usage of the so-called blues scale in G (G–B♭–C–D♭–D–F–G) (Terefenko, 2014, pp. 107ff.). During the first two cycles, Potter demonstrates his ability to develop short and rhythmic motifs which create a certain groove feeling. In fact, the first four measures can be split into three phrases: the introduction of a spontaneous motif in m. 1, which emphasizes the root G and picks up the tonality of the band's playing before the interlude. By starting the phrase in between beats two and three and by placing the other intervals on beat four, Potter creates a certain rhythmic tension due to the new time feel and meter. In measure two, Potter varies the motif, starting with a prelude to the motif between beats one and two, though the G is again placed between beats two and three. The end of the motif is reduced, the F is left out. In measure three and four, Potter plays a fusion of the two previous ideas: The prelude becomes part of the new motif. The G, until now placed on the offbeat, is now placed on beat three, which gives the whole motif a rather stable character. He repeats this variation of motif 1 twice, varying the ending. Both important tones, the G and the following B♭ are repeated now on strong beats with a slightly laid-back feeling. That slight variation in rhythmic placement as well as the limitation to certain repeated tones already prepares the way for the groove feeling to be established by the band.

During mm. 5 to 8, Potter works with the first motif again, varying it in a new way. Sticking with the idea of starting the phrase on the offbeat between beats one and two, he especially mirrors the ending of that motif. Instead of leaping down from the B♭ to the F, he steps up chromatically to the C by adding the major third B (m. 5). By incorporating tones above the B♭ for the first time, he expands his flow of motivic development in a coherent way. The next phrase in m. 6 picks up the idea of preluding the motif again, followed by mirroring the ascending G–B♭–C in m. 5 into a descending C–B♭–G and placing the G on the strong beat one of m. 7, which gives it a certain cadential character. Without a break, he continues to emphasize tones that are built up by a descending line which has a bluesy guide-tone line character (D–D♭–C–B–B♭) as well as a cadential character, too (m. 8). Interestingly, this could be a point where the band enters: So far, Potter has played eight measures and a cadence-like motif at the end of it. Yet Potter leaves the cadence somehow unfulfilled by stopping right between beats three and four, resting on beat four to the next beat one.

The following eight measures work with new motifs and yet are connected to the first eight measures through the usage of and in reference to the G blue scale and the rhythmic placement of accents on beat three as well as on offbeats (mm. 9, 12, 13, 15). In m. 11, he plays natural fourths that leap up but are incorporated in a descending melodic line (G–F–D–C) which gives this part a somehow jumpy, excited feeling (m. 11). During the last four measures, he varies this idea with a rather clear cadence: First he expands the heavily blues-influenced harmonic frame with a descending line that implies a C major pentatonic (G–E–D–C). This is followed by a chromatically descending line (F–E–E♭) varying the motif of fourths into leaps of fifths (mm. 15 and 16). After the A♭ in m. 16, he plays an A♭ arpeggio which could function as a form of cadential closure, interpretable as a tritone substitution of the dominant D or simply a side-stepping from the tonic G turned into major.

At this point, Smith and Taborn enter (7:02 min). They start with hesitant accents on the Fender Rhodes, limited to the higher registers, and quiet rim clicks on the snare drum. They keep the energy low and leave room for the music to grow gradually. In m. 19, a high level of interplay becomes obvious: After the band has entered, Potter stops to play for one and a half measures. Then, he offers a phrase that emphasizes the offbeats with short and concise accents followed by a series of accents on the beats starting with beat two of m. 19. Nate Smith reacts immediately and keeps emphasizing every beat with his bass drum and off-beat accents on the hi-hat. Potter and Smith repeat these accents synchronously for several beats. This spontaneous rhythmic loop enables Smith to stick to a certain groove pattern while still keeping the volume level low. For the rest of the solo, Smith maintains this pattern of a four-to-the-floor disco groove on the bass drum and offbeat phrasing on the hi-hat. After four measures, he adds rim clicks on the snare on beats two and four. At the same time, Taborn starts to play a G in the low register of the Fender Rhodes on beat one of every second measure. It is part of this line-up without a string bass that may enable the feeling and repetition of groove cycles in a certain way: The lower registers of a Fender Rhodes are less prominently audible than the attack of a plucked string bass, therefore lower keys require a strong attack in order to be heard as bass tones, a constant bass line would thus require a lot of muscle strength. However, these strong accents in the lower registers with a certain amount of space in between permit the creation of certain patterns of groove in the context of four-bar cycles as Taborn does. Choosing these regular cycles follows the regular structure of Potter's interlude and yet leaves the opportunity open for developing rather complex rhythmic patterns in the frame of four-bar cycles, e. g., with cross- or superimposed rhythms.

After another four-bar cycle, Adam Rogers adds a funky guitar pattern that at the same time emphasizes the tonal center G and picks up Potter's blues implications during the interlude by sliding into the minor third and fifth of the G minor triad from below. The development of the accompaniment changes in intensity and small chord variations and provides a fundamental groove for another two minutes.

Chris Potter's solo on "Pop Tune #1"

After about two minutes of Potter's solo, Taborn and Rogers split the four-bar cycle harmonically into two parts, beginning in m. 85: Two measures of G minor, occasionally played as G major, are followed by a shift to B♭ minor, accompanied by a switch to the full snare hit on beats two and four. The harmonic rhythm emphasizes the four-bar cycles as well. This section functions as a second part of the solo. The cue happens after exactly 17 four-bar cycles. During this second part of his solo, Potter improvises over another 10 four-bar cycles, followed by a theme-like motif in the high register that spans over four measures and is repeated three times, so that the tune ends with four four-bar cycles—the same length as the interlude at the beginning of Potter's solo.

Distinct features of Potter's solo

As shown, rhythmic motifs especially supporting the strong beats and offbeats are important features since the start of the solo. During his improvisation, Potter balances out complex and fast lines with rhythmic motifs that support the groove established by the drums, Fender Rhodes and guitar. Further, the unaccompanied solo interlude functions as a reference: After the band enters, Potter improvises over two four-bar cycles before he starts repeating the theme-like motif from m. 1 with just a slight variation (mm. 25–28). He contrasts this reminiscence of the beginning of his solo with fast played lines that rise and fall in wave-like contours and span over a length of two measures (mm. 30–41). He mainly uses tones of the G dorian scale, with slight deviations by playing arpeggios that imply a C^{13} (m. 31) and $G^{7\sharp 5}$ (m. 32). In m. 34, he ends a longer line which quotes the distinct motif of m. 1 with its falling interval on beat three.[25]

In m. 39, he begins to introduce another feature of the solo: highly chromatic lines with mainly descending contours. However, Potter organizes these by playing with short ascending motifs of three- or two-tone cells (Figure 2).

Figure 2: Chromatic motif in mm. 39f., starting with an ascending three-tone cell followed by an ascending two-tone cell, built into a line with a descending contour.

---

[25] Potter keeps quoting this motif, e.g. in m. 54.

He frequently gets back to this idea of chromatic descending lines with a clear reference to m. 39 and 40 (Figure 2): in m. 42 and mm. 43f., with variations and extensions in mm. 99ff. He also repeats the idea of two- or three-tone cells, e. g., in m. 56 with tonal material inside the harmonic frame. M. 51 displays a certain variation of this idea: Here, Potter varies the idea of two-tone cells by mirroring and expanding the cell-idea to a sequence of four-tone patterns (Figure 3). He starts with the mirrored cell, so that there is a step downwards by a second. This is answered by the original two-tone cell with a leap upwards by a second so that it expands to a four-tone pattern. The two motifs are connected by a large jump downwards, first by a minor sixth, then by a perfect fifth, a tritone and a minor sixth again. Each four-tone pattern uses tones outside the harmonic center of G. Played in a sequence, the pattern follows the logic of outside-playing called 'constant structure', although the interval structure of the pattern itself is not repeated exactly.

Figure 3: Sequence of four-tone patterns as a motivic variation and extension of previous two-tone cells.

Figure 4: Ascending constant structure of arpeggios (root, fifth, octave) starting on B♭–C–E♭–F–G♭, illustrated by brackets. The arpeggios are played in a wavy contour, however the overall contour with its different roots is ascending.

In mm. 70 and 71, Potter plays a sequence of patterns of upward jumps of a fifth followed by a fourth up and a fourth down. He starts on a B♭ and repeats that exact interval pattern starting on the tone C, then E♭, F, with additional embellishments to the fifth, and G♭ (Figure 4). This stack of fourths and fifths creates another constant structure of a four-tone pattern. Each arpeggio spans over an octave and contains the root, fifth, and octave, e. g., B♭3–F3–B♭4–F3. Due to the rhythmic placement and the speed of the line, the starting tones do not fall on the beats, so that the overall contour consists of wide oscillations over an ascending line.

The fast and complex outside lines are balanced out by harmonically inside and rhythmically clear and rather simple passages. For example, in m. 66, Potter starts with such a passage, which he varies slightly in regard to rhythm (Figure 5). The rather simple character is provided by tone repetition and a rhythmic template of quarter and eighth notes. After the previous dense phrases, this offers a moment of release and supports the groove.

Figure 5: Rhythmic motif with tone repetition and slight rhythmic variations (m. 66–69).

The beginning of the second part of the solo is strongly supported by a rhythmically accentuated passage in mm. 85ff. (Figure 6). Here, Potter plays a rhythmic figure of a dotted quarter note and an eighth note, simply alternating a G and a B♭. Due to its rhythmic and melodic structure, it could be heard as a reference to the solo interlude. However, the funky groove is supported here by rhythmic placements on the beats one and three. Potter reacts to the new chord progression played by Taborn and Rogers immediately. Already at the first appearance of the B♭m^7 in m. 87 he plays the corresponding triad with the tones F–B♭–D♭. In the following measure, he clearly plays the B♭ minor pentatonic.

Figure 6: Rhythmic motif emphasizing beat one and three at the beginning of the second part of the solo (mm. 85ff.).

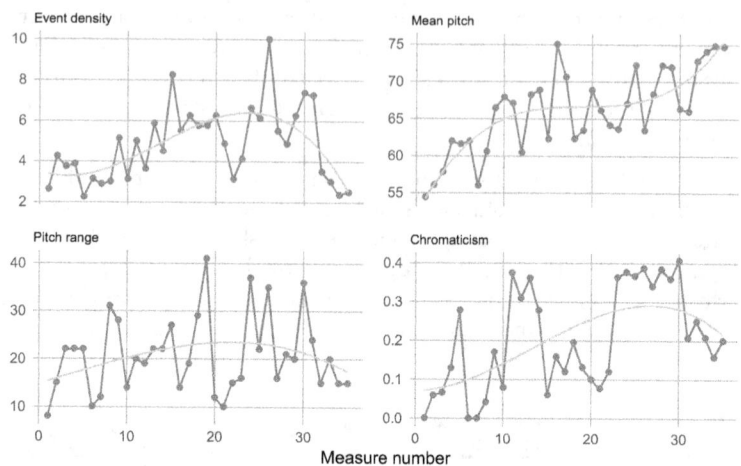

Figure 7: Event density (tones per second), mean pitch (averaged across all MIDI pitches), pitch range (difference between highest and lowest pitch), and chromaticism (percentage of non-diatonic tones) over four-bar segments.

For the rest of the solo, Potter improvises over the chord progression of Gm^7 and B♭m^7 and makes use of high chromaticism and techniques such as side-stepping (m. 95) and constant structure, e. g., of two-tone cells shifted chromatically (m. 114f.). The last 16 measures have the character of a theme again. Potter plays a rhythmically rather simple melody with a characteristic leap up of an octave over the Gm^7 and a twelfth to the B♭ over the B♭m^7. He repeats this motif, which spans over four measures, three times with slight embellishments. The performance ends with a collective stop on the offbeat of beat four in m. 140.

Observations on dramaturgy and the choice of pitches

Up until its theme-like ending, Potter's solo can be described as a discontinuous but still gradual intensification with frequent contrasting passages, supported by the band as well (Figure 7). The event density is at its lowest at the beginning (solo interlude) and at the end (theme-like motif with repetition). In between, Potter intensifies his phrases in general, yet varies the intensity a lot. What is remarkable is that Potter tends to avoid maintaining the event density between the four-bar cycles. However, this is also due to Potter's placement of the phrases. On the one hand, he connects almost

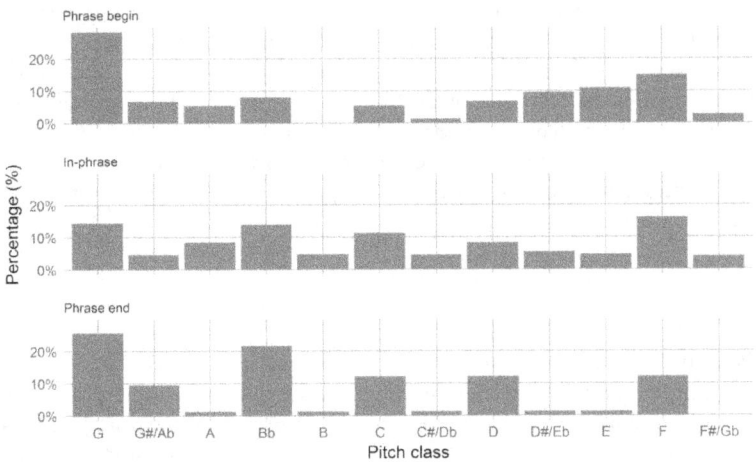

Figure 8: Pitch class distribution over phrase beginnings and endings and within phrases (845 tones in 37 phrases).

all four-bar cycles by playing over the bar-line and ending a phrase at the beginning of the next four-bar cycle. On the other hand, he rests frequently in between the cycles, several times for more than three beats. Due to this, the event density differs from four-bar cycle to four-bar cycle.

A similar observation can be made for the pitch range of every cycle—again, variability and contrast are important aspects for Potter's solo. The most obvious feature of the intensified dramaturgy is the mean pitch: By varying the register and the choice of pitches, Potter creates audible contrasts between the four-bar cycles. Yet the mean pitch rises continuously, with the theme-like ending as one of the highest passages of the solo. The mean pitch rises over one and a half octaves between the beginning and the end.

As described earlier, chromaticism and outside playing are also important features of Potter's solo. Interestingly, Potter plays phrases which are not chromatic at all (e. g., repetition of chord tones, see Figure 5), contrasted by phrases of high chromaticism. It is a distinct feature of the solo that it offers a pronounced contrast between inside and outside tones. Yet even the highly chromatic lines are not completely outside. In more than 80 % of the cases, the ending tones of the phrases are either a G, B♭, D or F, and therefore inside the underlying Gm^7 (Figure 8). The C occurs as often as the D but can be understood as the eleventh and therefore a typical inside upper structure extension for minor chords. The beginnings of the phrases are mostly Gs and

Fs. Potter also starts frequently with an E or D♯ as a chromatic approach or embellishment, which adds a dorian character to the underlying Gm^7. The tonal material within the phrases is dominated by the tones G, B♭, C, and F, which implies the relevance of the G minor pentatonic. By choosing tonal material inside the harmonic frame with a strong emphasis on the G minor pentatonic at the beginnings, endings as well as within the phrases Potter contributes to the less chromatic funk and pop/rock idiom with a static tonal center.

Conclusion

"Pop Tune #1" is one of several revealing testimonials to Chris Potter's musical flexibility and diversity. In the course of the solo, which spans over four minutes, he combines techniques of postbop improvisation within the $\frac{4}{4}$-funk groove and a static tonal center. During his unaccompanied solo interlude, Potter displays his ability to set a new groove feeling and tempo with simple but effective techniques, e. g., offbeat phrasing and accentuation. In the following, he develops his improvisation by using techniques of self-quoting, motivic variation and tonal sequences spiced with a high amount of chromaticism. Especially the latter is the result of postbop improvisation techniques of outside playing and installing constant structures, among others. Yet he embeds these techniques in the musical context of a funk groove by contextualizing his playing in four-bar cycles, emphasizing offbeats and working with rhythmic motifs that support the groove. By doing so, he creates a playful approach to the funk groove—a red line leading through the track.

Head out

Conclusion and outlook

Martin Pfleiderer

The Jazzomat Research Project takes up the challenge of jazz research in the age of digitalization. It intends to open up a new field of analytical exploration by providing computational tools as well as a comprehensive corpus of improvisations with MeloSpyGUI and the Weimar Jazz Database. Following a philosophy of open source, both the solo corpus and the software tools are open for third-party additions and further development. The project aims at initiating collaboration between researchers within the jazz research community as well as researchers from various other fields of research, in particular ethnomusicology, music psychology, and music information retrieval.

How does the computational approach to jazz analysis contribute to jazz research?

This volume presents the concepts and approaches of the ongoing Jazzomat Research Project. Several case studies demonstrate how these concepts can be included in jazz analysis to a varying extent and in different ways. In general, we propose to combine several methods of analysis. A combination of close readings of single improvisations, comparisons, and distant readings of big data corpora could contribute both to a data-rich history of jazz improvisation and a better understanding of the psychology of improvisation. Most of the case studies within the second part of this book start with a close description of single improvisations of an artist followed by either a statistical description of global stylistic features or the dramaturgy of a solo (e. g., Bob Berg, Miles Davis) or are dedicated to more specific research questions such as a comparisons with other improvisations and improvisers (Don Byas, Miles Davis, West Coast jazz, Freddie Hubbard/Woody Shaw, Steve Coleman). For example, Don Byas's solo on "Body and Soul" is compared with Hawkins's famous solo on the same song, and Miles Davis's solo on "Airegin" is contrasted to solos by other bebop trumpet players. Some studies, e. g., of Michael Brecker, Branford Marsalis, and Chris Potter, complement their analytical readings of single solos with certain computational and statistical descriptions. Other chapters aim directly at proving or disproving hypotheses on the improvisational styles of jazz musicians using computational and statistical tools. In doing so, one crucial step is to decide which computational features are particularly well suited. The broad scope of the case studies included here shows that there is no single definite way to use the Weimar Jazz Database and the accompanying analysis software. On the contrary, it is up to the creativity of the researcher to use the possibilities our data and tools offer.

Generally, several musical domains could benefit from complementary statistical approaches. Firstly, they allow both pinning down exact values and frequencies and carrying out statistical tests and modeling, e. g., classification and other machine learning methods. Secondly, pattern usage in a solo or a corpus, which is a central issue for research on improvisation, can be examined using the pattern mining tools of the software. This opens up an area of research on personal style and transmission of musical knowledge within the jazz community as well as on the cognitive foundations of improvisational processes. Last but not least, these issues could be further examined by using the new approach of midlevel annotation that allows to distinguish between several playing ideas which are employed consciously or unconsciously by the musicians.

Are there any specific results that are new and go beyond the findings of previous analytical approaches?

Firstly, there are several clarifications and revisions of previous findings from jazz research. For example, the intensification of Hawkins's solo on "Body and Soul" described by Gunther Schuller is revisited and reformulated. The features that characterize both Miles Davis's personal style of improvisation and the dramaturgy of his solos are examined in detail and contrasted with solos of several bebop trumpet players. The analysis of Davis's solo on "Airegin" shows that the midlevel approach in particular appears to be highly suitable for analyzing jazz improvisations that lack virtuoso parts and instead focus on motivic inventiveness. The 'lyricism' attributed to the improvisations of West Coast musicians Paul Desmond and Chet Baker is tied to certain musical features and compared with solos of other cool and West Coast jazz musicians. Several statistical results make it clear that Desmond and Baker, in terms of tonal and rhythmic details, do not seem to be directly comparable to other musicians generally associated with cool jazz. All these findings point towards the importance of an identification of those musical features that contribute to the overall listening impression of a certain improvisation. Statistical tools could contribute to solving the task of finding the musical

Conclusion and outlook 307

sources for certain stylistic attributions—which are sometimes associated in a rather vague manner. This includes dimensions such as pattern usage and distribution of midlevel units both of which contribute to the dramaturgy and stylistic coherence of a jazz solo.

Six out of nine case studies focus on improvisations by postbop musicians. While the first half of jazz history is well documented and investigated, the second half of its history, starting around 1970, has not received sufficient attention so far. The personal styles of Freddie Hubbard and Woody Shaw are compared, with a focus on specific improvisational details: fast tone chains, intervallic playing, and the usage of long patterns. While Hubbard and Shaw appear to be highly comparable at first sight, the results show that their personal styles, in part, distinctly differ, especially regarding the usage of wide intervals in virtuoso lines and the playing of long interval and pitch patterns. The close analytical descriptions of solos by Michael Brecker, Branford Marsalis and Chris Potter point towards innovative strategies for harmonic and rhythmic playing as well as their vital connection to the jazz tradition. Furthermore, it is demonstrated how the distinctive style of Steve Coleman in regard to melody and rhythm could partly be related to his idiosyncratic system of a 'balanced' or 'symmetrical' approach to improvisation. Probably, the case study on Bob Berg's "Angles" goes furthest in an analytical attempt to reconstruct the formative creative strategies of Berg by analyzing his improvisation in regard to several musical features and dimensions, pattern usage, line construction, and overall dramaturgy.

Additionally, first promising results of using new analytical approaches are presented within the first part of the book. The approach of an automated feature selection enables the identification of those statistically significant features that distinguish certain subsets of improvisations, e. g., the personal style of one jazz musician compared to all other improvisations within the database, to the characteristics of a certain instrument type, or to the improvisations of a certain jazz style. For the first time, relations between harmony and pitch choices within walking bass lines could be investigated on a broad basis using the automatic transcription of bass lines due to an innovative transcription algorithm. A novel algorithm framework for score-informed audio analysis allows us to obtain new insights into expressive properties of solo improvisation such as intonation and the use of pitch modulation techniques and dynamics. As an initial approach to a description of the 'sound' of jazz musicians, several timbre attributes were determined automatically and used to classify the performer of a given jazz solo recording using machine learning techniques.

The Weimar Jazz Database has only a limited corpus of transcriptions in a special data format. Does this restrict its usage for analytical research?

The limitation of a given data corpus is often a problem for statistical and comparative approaches as well as for corpus studies in general. However, we think that the current version of the Weimar Jazz Database gives a more or less representative overview of improvisation within the US jazz canon. Nonetheless, extensions and enhancements are always welcome. Therefore, we have published a short manual for the transcription of new material with the aid of Sonic Visualiser software and with instructions for the correct data format. Following these instructions, anyone can contribute new transcriptions to the Weimar Jazz Database. Furthermore, the explicit data format enables comparisons with other music corpora according to a number of research questions, e. g., the degree of syncopicity or the prevalent melodic contours of jazz lines contrasted to melodies in popular music or folk music.

While the transcriptions within the Weimar Jazz Database have been carefully cross-checked several times, they are unfortunately not free of errors. However, the error rate seems to be very low with only a small impact on statistical explorations. The data format was specifically designed to allow for different directions of research, i.e., for the analysis of syntactical features of a solo on different levels of resolution, from the single-note level to higher levels such as midlevel units, but also for more analysis aiming at performance features such as micro-timing and tone formation. Fundamental to this approach is the realization that there is no best solution when it comes to choosing a representation system or data format for music. Instead, music representations should be open to different functions and analytical applications, e. g., for re-performances or, in our case, for analytical investigations according to several—sometimes conflicting—research issues, as for example in the interplay of micro-timing and syncopicity (Frieler & Pfleiderer, 2017).

Moreover, the data within the Weimar Jazz Database could serve as a ground truth for various MIR tasks especially in regard to the development of innovative algorithms for automatic transcription, annotation, and feature extraction from audio files, as well as for classification tasks. As an example, automatic melody transcription algorithms aim to group a given solo recording into a sequence of tone events with a discrete pitch, onset time, and duration. However, jazz artists frequently use dynamics and pitch modulation techniques such as vibrato or glissandi as an expressive means to alter the pitch and intensity contours of tones, which significantly complicates the transcription task. Hence, the Weimar Jazz Dataset provides a valuable dataset with ground truth for melody annotations and can stimulate further research in this field.

Conclusion and outlook

What are the strengths and weaknesses of the software tools MeloSpyGUI and MeloSpySuite?

In developing the software, we aimed at balancing several criteria: On the one hand, the software should be powerful in covering many aspects and dimensions of melody within the context of jazz improvisation and beyond. On the other hand, it should be intuitive and easy to handle. However, the more functions are included in a software, the higher the risks of loss of usability due to the broad range of possibilities. Moreover, in line with the philosophy of open source and research collaboration, the software should be open to enhancements and further developments. This affords a clear but open concept that allows for extensions by others. We faced these challenges by providing extensive and detailed documentation of the software, with online tutorials as well as several exemplary studies published in journals and proceedings and, last but not least, by publishing this project report.

The main benefits of the software tools are a fast and reliable processing of queries in regard to several musical parameters as well as to pattern usage and midlevel units with a flexible selection of jazz improvisations (or parts of them). There are many features implemented in the software which meet the specific demands of jazz research, e. g., to analyze pitch classes as a function of the accompanying chords (e. g., chordal diatonic pitch classes and extended chordal diatonic pitch classes), swing ratio (micro-timing), or statistical values for syncopicity and the run-length of ascending, descending or chromatic phrases, and many more. This allows for investigations into stylistic features of jazz improvisation, commonalities and differences between different musicians or groups of musicians, into the development of those features over time, into pattern usage and into countless other research issues. The applications are not restricted to jazz improvisation but can be extended to many other areas of musical melody—provided that the melody repertoires are available in one of the usable data formats. Unfortunately, many of the results are given in a data format (spreadsheets with comma separated variables) which requires further processing for exploration and visualization. The main new feature in the upcoming version of the software is to include harmonic concepts of jazz theory which will allow for automatically relating tone sets, as played within phrases or sections, to a harmonic interpretation.

Can sound and timbre, group interaction and other performance qualities be taken into account, too?

Of course, the melodic lines improvised by jazz musicians are only one, albeit very important, aspect of improvisation. Sound, micro-rhythm, and group interaction are indispensable components of jazz performances too, and account for much of the enjoyment jazz listeners experience. In the Jazzomat Research Project so far, we focused on the melodic and rhythmical aspects of jazz improvisation. However, we also indicate new and forthcoming possibilities of including such information as dynamics, intonation, micro-rhythm, or timbre. Information in respect to dynamics and intonation as well as to micro-rhythm is already included in the Weimar Jazz Database and ready to be explored. The aspect of timbre or 'sound' seems to be more complicated, for conceptual as well as computational reasons, but first and promising steps are made in regard to a comparison between the timbres of different jazz musicians.

In regard to group interaction, we have undertaken first attempts to include data of the respective accompanying bass player. The automatically transcribed walking bass lines accompanying most of the solos are already included within the Weimar Jazz Database. Besides examining stylistic traits of walking bass lines by different bassists, one could examine the relation between pitch choices of the soloists and those of the bass player. These observations could lead to hypotheses relating to the mutual exchange of playing ideas in regard to harmony and contour. Another case is the rhythmic interaction between the drummer and the soloist, especially between the micro-rhythm of the ride cymbal figure and the micro-rhythm of the soloist's line. Exploring data taken from the Weimar Jazz Database, Christian Dittmar et al. describe an approach to an automatic estimation of the ride cymbals' swing ratio and relate this 'swingogram' to the micro-timing of the soloist (Dittmar, Pfleiderer, & Müller, 2015; Dittmar, Pfleiderer, Balke, & Müller, 2017). These are promising attempts to include data on tonal or rhythmical interaction which must be further developed in the near future.

How could the approach serve musicians and listeners?

The overall aim of this book, of the Jazzomat Research Project, and of the emerging field of computational music research is to contribute to an understanding of the variety and richness of musical expression. For jazz musicians, both amateurs and professionals, our work on midlevel analysis and on the dramaturgy of jazz solos could serve as a starting point for reflections on principles and strategies for improvisation. At times, these midlevel and high-level dimensions of improvisation are neglected during the training of jazz musicians. Furthermore, the transcriptions could serve as a starting point for working on a repertoire of jazz solos by re-performing canonical solos as well as by absorbing and transforming them in one's own style. Additionally, they offer opportunities to complement the training approach of listening and imitating by reflecting on certain musical dimensions of a given solo,

Conclusion and outlook

whether it be in regard to the choice of tones, or rhythmic design, or many other factors.

These reflections could also inform and enrich the experience of listening to jazz for non-musicians and contribute to the dissemination and discussion of those aspects within an educational or journalistic setting. Additionally, there are several new opportunities for visualizing musical parameters, first and foremost, Stefan Balke's and Meinard Müller's JazzTube application for listening to a solo while watching its piano roll visualization or the visualization of micro-timing provided by the 'swingogram'.

Outro: Appendix

JazzTube: Linking the Weimar Jazz Database with YouTube

Stefan Balke and Meinard Müller

The annotations contained in the Weimar Jazz Database (WJD) start to unfold their full potential in combination with the underlying jazz recordings. Since these are commercial recordings, they cannot be shipped along with the WJD. However, online video platforms such as YouTube^{TM} make billions of videos publicly available to users from all over the world. Many of these videos contain recordings of jazz music performances. The remaining task is to find the relevant YouTube videos which contain the music used for creating the annotations in the WJD and link them together. One way to approach this task is to perform the retrieval based on the audio content. This is also known as audio identification or audio fingerprinting which is an active research subject in the field of Music Information Retrieval (P. Cano, Batlle, Kalker, & Haitsma, 2005; Arzt, 2016; Knees & Schedl, 2016; M. Müller, 2015).

In particular, we follow a two-step retrieval strategy to establish links between the WJD's music recordings and the corresponding YouTube videos using existing retrieval techniques (Balke et al., 2017). Using these links, we are then able to combine the annotations from the WJD with the retrieved YouTube videos in a unifying web-based framework which we call JazzTube. For a hands-on experience, our web-based application can be accessed under the following address:

http://mir.audiolabs.uni-erlangen.de/jazztube

The JazzTube application offers various ways to access the WJD. First, tables of the compositions, soloists, and transcribed solos give an overview of the data contained in the WJD. Furthermore, one can access the data on the record, the track, or at the solo level. The latter is shown in Figure 1 for Clifford Brown's solo on Jordu. At the top of the website, we list some general metadata about the solo (Figure 1a). Many of these entries are hyperlinks and lead to the artist's overview page or the corresponding track. Furthermore, we offer several possibilities for exporting the solo transcription, either as comma-separated values (csv), or as sheet music. The conversion from the annotations to the sheet music is obtained by using the FlexQ algorithm (Frieler & Pfleiderer, 2017). Underneath this basic information, we list the available YouTube videos (Figure 1b). Having more than one match provides alternatives to the user, since the videos might have different recording qualities or may even disappear from YouTube. After pressing the play button, the corresponding YouTube video is automatically retrieved and embedded in our website (Figure 1c). Below the YouTube player, a piano-roll representation of the solo transcription is shown running synchronously when the video is played (Figure 1d). Finally at the bottom, additional statistic about the solo (e. g., pitch histograms) are provided (Figure 1e).

With JazzTube, we offer novel possibilities for interacting with and navigating through the content of the WJD. Furthermore, we believe that the annotations contained in the WJD are a great resource that could help both musicians and researchers in practicing and gaining a deeper understanding of the music.

Acknowledgments

Stefan Balke and Meinard Müller are based at the International Audio Laboratories Erlangen. The International Audio Laboratories Erlangen are a joint institution of the Friedrich-Alexander-Universität Erlangen-Nürnberg (FAU) and the Fraunhofer-Institut für Integrierte Schaltungen IIS. This work was supported by the German Research Foundation (DFG MU 2686/6-1 and DFG MU 2686/12-1).

JazzTube 317

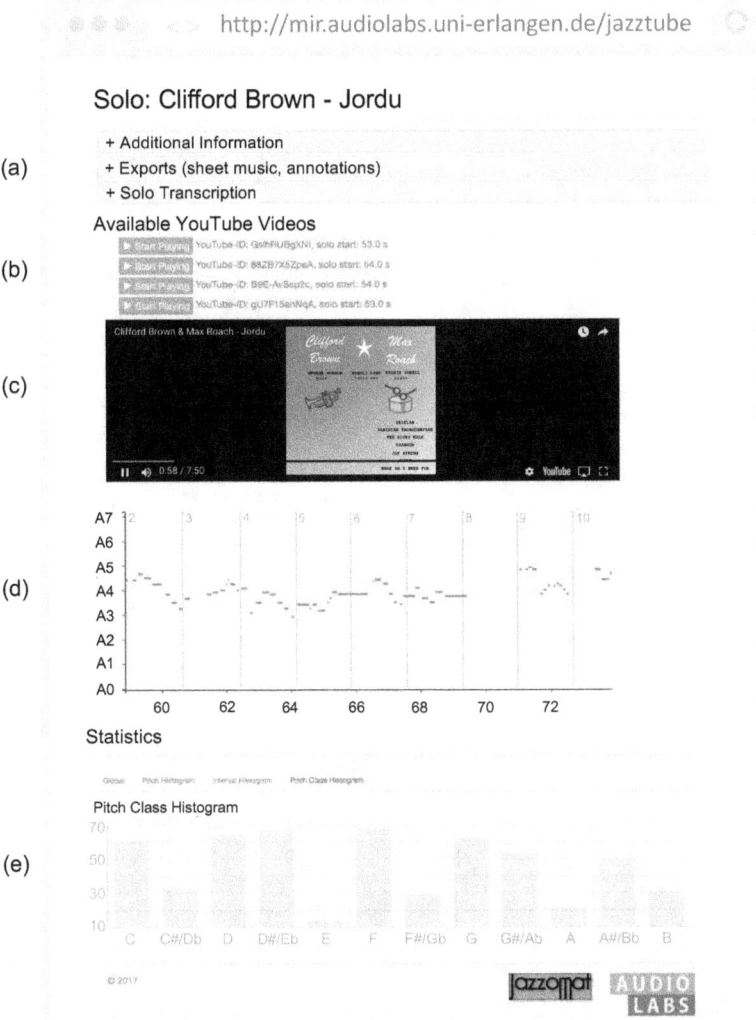

Figure 1: Screenshot of our web-based interface called JazzTube. (a) Metadata and export functionalities. (b) List of linked YouTube videos. (c) Embedded YouTube video. (d) Piano-roll representation of the solo transcription synchronized with the YouTube video. (e) Additional statistics.

The FlexQ algorithm

Klaus Frieler

The FlexQ algorithm uses an optimization approach to find the optimal subdivision for all onsets between two beats. This is achieved by combining certain heuristic principles to construct a suitable loss function for which a subdivision with the least loss can be found by a simple grid search over all admissible subdivisions.

Formally, we consider M onsets $\{t_i\}_{1 \leq i \leq M}$ between two consecutive beats b_L and b_R, i.e., $b_L \leq t_i \leq b_R$ for all i. Without loss of generality, we can rescale all involved onsets by $\frac{t-b_L}{b_R-b_L}$ so that $b_L = 0$ and $b_R = 1$. A tatum K-grid G_K for a subdivision K is then the set of points

$$G_K = \left\{\frac{m}{K}\right\}_{0 \leq m < K} = \left\{0, \frac{1}{K}, \frac{2}{K}, \ldots, \frac{K-1}{K}\right\}.$$

A quantization of the onsets t_i with respect to the grid G_K is defined by the following prescription, if $M \leq K$, else the empty set. For each t_i, the closest grid point is the index

$$m_i = \min_m \arg\min_m \left| t_i - \frac{m}{K} \right|.$$

For the M onsets under consideration we thus obtain a set of closest grid indices. Requiring strict monophony entails that duplicated indices are not allowed. Hence, starting from the leftmost onset, we move all indices successively to the next free position if a duplicated index is found. This might result in new duplicated indices and the process is repeated till all indices occur only once, which might, however, not always be possible. The resulting quantization of the onsets is then either the set of causal grid points, denoted $\{m_i^*\}$, or the empty set.

This might be best illustrated by an example. Set $K = 2$, with grid $\{0, 1/2\}$, and onsets $\{3/8, 5/8\}$. The closest grids points for these onsets are then $m_1 = 1$ and $m_2 = 1$. Since the indices are the same, the second index should be moved, but there is no grid point left to the right, hence the quantization is the empty set. For the 4-grid $\{0, 1/4, 1/2, 3/4\}$, the closest grid points are $m_1 = 1$ and $m_2 = 2$, so no problem arises in this case. But for onsets $\{7/16, 9/16\}$, we have $m_1 = 2$ and $m_2 = 2$, which can be resolved by shifting m_2 one unit to the right with a resulting quantization of $m_1 = 2$ and $m_2 = 3$.

For a non-empty quantization, we can then define the quantization error as the sum of absolute differences between onsets and their modified closest grid points:

$$\Delta q = \sum_i \delta q_i = \sum_i \left| t_i - \frac{m_i^*}{K} \right|.$$

Now we have nearly all the elements for defining the FlexQ algorithm. The last component is the standard deviation of quantization errors:

$$s_q = \sqrt{\frac{1}{N-1} \sum_i \left(\delta q_i - \frac{1}{N} \Delta q \right)^2}$$

The loss function will be built from four preference rules.

1. Prefer smaller subdivisions.

2. Prefer binary and ternary subdivisions.

3. Prefer smaller quantization errors (deviations from the ideal grid points).

4. Prefer homogeneous deviations.

We can now state the loss function:

$$L(K) = \alpha_1 K + \alpha_2 \Omega(K) + \alpha_3 \Delta q + \alpha_4 s_q,$$

where

$$\Omega(K) = \begin{cases} 1, & \text{if K odd and } K > 3, \\ 0.5, & \text{if } K = 1 \text{ or } K = 3, \\ 0, & \text{otherwise.} \end{cases}$$

The function Ω embodies the second preference ("prefer binary and ternary subdivisions") only approximately, but in practice the differences are only marginal because very large grid sizes are not considered. The only practical differences might arise for the (actually) rare case of $K = 9$, which is a ternary subdivision but penalized by Ω. The $\alpha_{1,2,3,4}$ are free parameters.

An optimal grid K for a given set of M onsets $\{t_i\}$ between two beats b_L, b_R can then be found as

$$K_{\text{opt}} = \underset{M \leq K \leq K_{\max}}{\arg\min}\, L(K),$$

where $K_{\max}$ is defined via

$$\frac{b_R - b_L}{K_{\max}} < \alpha_5,$$

with free parameter α_5, which defines the smallest absolute distance between grid points. This parameter should be set in the order of 30 ms to 50 ms which corresponds to the discrimination threshold of two events and to the fastest observed human movement of about 20 Hz $\sim$ 50 ms. For $\alpha_5 = 40$ ms and IBI $b_R - b_L = 1$ s ($\sim$ 60 bpm), an upper bound of $K_{\max} = 25$ can be found.

From the optimal grid size, the optimal tatum positions are then given by the modified closest grid points m_i^*.

The default parameters for $\alpha_1, \ldots, \alpha_5$ were found using manual experimentation. In the current implementation, these are (MeloSpySuite/GUI parameter names in parentheses):

$$\begin{aligned}
\alpha_1 &= 1.0 \quad (\text{mismatchPenalty}) \\
\alpha_2 &= 1.0 \quad (\text{oddDivisionPenalty}) \\
\alpha_3 &= 8.0 \quad (\text{distPenalty}) \\
\alpha_4 &= 10.0 \quad (\text{spreadPenalty}) \\
\alpha_5 &= 0.02 \quad (\text{rhythmThreshold}).
\end{aligned}$$

Brief introduction to circular statistics

Klaus Frieler

In music analysis, so-called circular variables are rather common due to the circular nature of pitch perception, i. e., the phenomenon of octave equivalence, but also due to metrical structures, as used in the metrical circle map. Circular variables require specific treatment if one wants to perform statistical analysis, since the usual formulas do not work in this case.

This can be easily seen in the case of angles, which are also circular variables. Let us assume we have measured two angels 0° and 270°, e. g., by sighting a bird from a bird watch. What is the mean of these two values? Using the standard formula for arithmetic means the answer would be 135°, but one would expect in fact an angle somewhere between 270° and 360° (= 0°), to be specific it should be 315°. One approach to solving this is to use negative angles for angles larger than 180°. In this case the arithmetic mean of 0° and −90° is −45° which is equivalent to 315°. Unfortunately, this does not work in all cases. To illustrate this, consider four angles, 0°, 90°, 180°, and 270° = −90°, with an arithmetic mean of 45°. But intuitively, the mean is somehow undefined, because the four angles point in all four directions, for which no mean direction can be reasonably assigned. Another, related problem is that there is no consistent way to assign a value to 180°.

A solution to this problem lies in actually mapping the angles to points on the unit circle in the x, y-plane. This can be done using polar coordinates, which are defined by

$$
\begin{aligned}
x &= r \cos \phi \\
y &= r \sin \phi,
\end{aligned}
$$

where a vector (x, y) is represented with an angle $\phi = \arctan y/x$ and magnitude/length $r = \sqrt{x^2 + y^2}$. Vectors on the unit circle have by definition a length of $r = 1$, so we map angles (measured in radians[26]) to the vector

$$z = (\cos\phi, \sin\phi).$$

With this embedding of angles into the x,y-plane, the standard formula can now be used for this 2d vectors. The arithmetic mean of a vector is defined by arithmetic means of the coördinates, i.e., for vectors $\{z_i = (x_i, y_i)\}_{1 \leq i \leq N}$ the mean vector is given by

$$\overline{z} = \frac{1}{N}\sum_{i=1}^{N} z_i = \frac{1}{N}\sum_{i=1}^{N} z_i(x_i, y_i) = \left(\frac{1}{N}\sum_{i=1}^{N} x_i, \frac{1}{N}\sum_{i=1}^{N} y_i\right) =: (\overline{x}, \overline{y}).$$

For the embedding of N circular variables ϕ_i this yields the so-called resultant vector

$$\overline{z} = \left(\frac{1}{N}\sum_{i=1}^{N} \cos\phi_i, \frac{1}{N}\sum_{i=1}^{N} \sin\phi_i\right) =: \overline{R}(\cos\overline{\phi}, \sin\overline{\phi},$$

where we defined the resultant length $\overline{R}$ and the resultant angle $\overline{\phi}$, which is possible, because the resultant vector is a normal vector in the x,y-plane, though not necessarily on the unit circle; in fact, one can show that the resultant vector lies generally inside the unit circle, i.e., $\overline{R} \leq 1$.

The resultant angle can interpreted as the mean angle of a sample of angles, the resultant length is a measure for the variance of the sample. Indeed, the circular variance is defined as

$$\overline{s}^2 = 1 - \overline{R},$$

with values between 0 and 1.

The circular standard deviation is, however, defined not as the square root of the circular variance but via

$$\overline{s} = \sqrt{\ln\frac{1}{\overline{R}^2}} = \sqrt{-2\ln\overline{R}},$$

with values between 0 and ∞[27].

---

[26] In radians 360° corresponds to 2π, so every angle α in degree is $2\pi\alpha/360$ in radians.
[27] This definition stems from the observation that this formula is an estimator of the standard deviation of the circular normal distribution.

Circular statistics

Sometimes, the circular dispersion is also used for the analysis of variance it is defined as

$$\delta = \frac{1-\overline{R}^2}{2\overline{R}},$$

also with values between 0 and 1.

Let us consider our four angles example from above. The embedding results in the vectors $z_1 = (1,0), z_2 = (0,1), z_3 = (-1,0), z_4 = (0,-1)$. The resultant vector is thus

$$\overline{z} = \frac{1}{4}(z_1 + z_2 + z_3 + z_4) = (0,0).$$

Since the resultant vector is the origin in the x,y-plane, it has no reasonably defined angle! This corresponds to our intuition that a mean direction is not well-defined in this case. The resultant length is $\overline{R} = 1$, hence the variance is maximal, $s^2 = 1$. This also correspond well to our intuition since all directions are equally present. Accordingly, the circular standard deviation in this case is also maximal $\overline{s} = \infty$. What is the result for our first example with embedding $z_1 = (1,0), z_2 = (0,-1)$? The resultant vector is

$$\overline{z} = \frac{1}{2}(z_1 + z_2) = \left(\frac{1}{2}, -\frac{1}{2}\right),$$

and the resultant length is $\overline{R} = \sqrt{\frac{1}{2}}$, the resultant angle is

$$\overline{\phi} = \arctan \overline{y}/\overline{x} = \arctan(-1) = -\frac{\pi}{4} \equiv -45°,$$

as desired.

Glossary

In the following glossary, several terms used throughout this book are briefly explained. Since readers of this book are expected to come from varying areas of research and to have differing degrees of knowledge, these brief explanations should be of help for quick reference. Included are several terms from jazz practice, jazz theory, and music theory, some statistical terms, as well as several names (and abbreviations) for musical features that are implemented within the MeloSpy software. Some of these features are further detailed in Chapter *Computational melody analysis*; additionally, there are more technical definitions available within the online documentation.[28]

Accent
: emphasis on a particular tone in contrast to its neighboring tones, either by playing it differently (louder, special attack etc.) or by perceptual salience (e.g., highest tone or last tone within a phrase, tones on beats etc.) or both.

Algorithm
: self-contained sequence of actions, e. g., calculation or data processing, to be performed by a computer.

Arpeggio
: a chord broken into a sequence of tones.

Bend
: the effect of bending and releasing the pitch of a tone upwards (in the case of the guitar) or downwards (in the case of brass and reed instruments).

---

[28] See especially http://jazzomat.hfm-weimar.de/commandline_tools/melfeature/melfeature_features.html.

CDPC
→Chordal Diatonic Pitch Class.

CDPCX
→Extended Chordal Diatonic Pitch Class.

Chord changes
succession of musical chords.

Chordal Diatonic Pitch Class (cdpc)
→diatonic pitch classes in relation to the root pitch of a given chord (based on major and dorian scales) plus additional symbols for the non-diatonic pitches.

Chordal Pitch Class (cpc)
→pitch class of a tone in relation to the root pitch of a given chord which has pitch class 0.

Chorus
one round within the cyclical form of a jazz piece, given that within pieces of chorus-form the →chord changes are repeated again and again during a performance. The term originated from the final chorus parts (sung by a chorus) of American popular songs which follow the opening verse(s) sung by one singer only; in jazz those verses are omitted in most cases and one or several improvised solos are played, lasting one or several choruses.

Chromatic
with several pitches each a semitone above or below the other.

Chromaticity
percentage of semitone intervals in proportion to all intervals.

Constant structures
a technique to achieve coherence while improvising →outside which mostly relies on the repetition or transposition of certain interval structures.

Contour
a curve that tracks the absolute pitches over time.

Glossary

CPC
→Chordal Pitch Class.

Density
a function whose values at any given point can be interpreted as providing a relative likelihood of the variable (in percentage).

Diatonic
with seven pitches within an octave but with varying intervals (heptatonic scale), in contrast to →chromatic scales and →pentatonic scales.

Entropy
the degree of predictability (or information content) within a system or structure subject to random processes; measured normally in bits (i. e., the mean number of yes-no-questions one has to ask to identify any result from such a random process). Entropy is maximal for uniformly distributed random variables, i. e., where each event has the same probability. Normalized entropy is entropy divide by the maximal possible entropy for this process and attains values between 0 (perfect order or redundancy) and 1 (high complexity or chaos).

Extended Chordal Diatonic Pitch Class (cdpcx)
variant of →Chordal Diatonic Pitch Class with additional symbols for the non-diatonic pitches.

Fall-off
effect caused by the pitch gliding downwards at the end of a tone.

Fundamental Frequency
the lowest frequency of a periodic waveform; in music and speech often correlated to the perceived pitch of a sound.

Fuzzy Duration Class
classification of durations (very short, short, long, very long) in regard to meter (relative) or time (absolute).

Fuzzy Interval Class
classification of intervals (big jump, jump, leap, step—up and down, resp.—and repetition).

Guide-tone line
: a melodic line that guides through a chord progression. Guide-tone lines consist of different chord tones and mostly progress by interval steps.

Histogram
: a graphical representation of the distribution of data by representing the frequency or overall percentage of a certain category or class. For continuous numerical data, classes have to be defined beforehand.

Intensity
: 1) a metaphor to describe the strength, magnitude, density, vehemence, or level of music;

2) in an acoustical sense: a relative measure for the momentary degree of dynamics; normally correlated with the degree of perceived loudness.

Inter-onset interval (IOI)
: time interval between the onsets of two successive tones.

Intonation
: the pitch accuracy of a musical instrument or of a musician's or singer's realization of pitches according to a certain →tuning system.

IOI
: →Inter-onset interval.

Laid back
: playing 'behind the beat', i.e., with a tendency to place tones later than the nominal metrical position in a given metrical frame, e.g., as provided by the rhythm section. Cf. →Micro-rhythm.

Lick
: 1) a colloquial term for a succession of tones that are played regularly by a musician;

2) a category for →midlevel units with a certain rhythmic and melodic conciseness—in contrast to an uniform line–, but less singable than a melody.

MCM
: →Metrical circle map.

Mean
: a value for the central tendency (or average) of a metric data sample or distribution.

Median
: measure for the central tendency of a data sample or distribution that separates the higher half from the lower one, i.e., above and below the median 50 % of the data can be found. More robust to outliers than the →Mean.

Metrical Circle Map (mcm)
: a representation of meter by dividing a bar in N equal time spans; in this publication mostly $N = 48$ is used (cf. Frieler, 2007, 2008).

Micro-rhythm
: timing nuances in the placement of tones; slight deviations from idealized metronomic time frames or time frames provided by other players.

Midlevel annotation
: an annotation technique encompassing the segmentation of a melody into →midlevel units, the categorization of those units, and the annotation of references back to previous midlevel units (see Frieler et al., 2016a and Chapter *Computational melody analysis* for more details).

Midlevel unit
: a musical unit on a middle level, i.e., between the level of form sections and that of musical cells or motives. Since a midlevel unit is conceived to represent a musical decision or idea, it is often as long as a musical →phrase, but could also be shorter, i.e., phrases can consist of several midlevel units.

N-gram
: a contiguous sequence of N items taken from a given sequence of tones or other musical elements.

Offbeat
: points in time or tones positioned on these points that do not fall on a beat.

Outside
: tones or lines contrasting to or deviating from a given harmony, chord, or mode.

Parsons code
: a simple notation of melodic motion, basically: interval up, interval down and pitch repetition (proposed by Denys Parsons in his book *The Directory of Tunes and Musical Themes*, 1975).

Pattern
: a succession of elements—e. g., tones, intervals, durations—which is repeated or occurs several times.

Pentatonic
: scales with five →pitch classes.

Phrase
: a melodic unit or perceptional chunk of the melodic stream; phrases have a complete musical sense of their own, or are separated before and after by rests, or can be sung or played using a single breath.

Pitch Class (pc)
: a set of all pitches of the same chroma, i. e., lying a whole number of octaves apart; e. g., the pitch class C consists of the Cs in all octaves.

Pitch Waviness
: percentage of tones within a melody that are preceded and followed by changes of intervallic direction, i. e., local maxima and minima of a pitch contour.

Postbop
: a rather vague umbrella term for a style of jazz emerging in the 1960s that developed from hardbop and bebop and contrasts to avant-garde jazz and fusion music.

Scatter plot
: a graphical representation that is used to display the paired values for two variables for a set of data units.

Self-similarity matrix
: a graphical representation of similar sequences in a data series.

Glossary

Side-stepping (side-slipping)
: technique of improvising →outside by shifting chords or lines one semitone upwards or downwards.

Significance
: statistical measure for the likelihood that a statistical result is not purely due to chance. Statistical significance is computed by one of various significance tests and is expressed as the probability ('p value') that the result could have been generated by chance; by convention, if that probability is lower than 5 % ($p < .05$), the result is termed "significant", if it is lower than 1 % ($p < .01$), "highly significant".

Slide
: effect caused by the pitch gliding up at the beginning of a tone.

Source separation
: procedures in digital signal processing with the objective of recovering the original component signals of a certain sound source from a combined or complex signal.

Standard deviation
: a measure for the amount of variation or dispersion of a set of data values in regard to their →mean.

Swing ratio
: ratio of the longer to the shorter eighth in a line played with swing feeling.

Syncopation
: in general, the temporary displacement of an accent from a strong to a weak metrical position; in a narrower sense (as often used in this publication), the shifting of a tone from a beat to an →offbeat position immediately before the beat, while leaving the beat empty ('anticipation').

Syncopicity
: measure for the degree of →syncopation within a given musical unit; percentage of syncopated tones.

Timbre
: perceived sound quality of a sound or tone, often in relation to the

composition of its harmonics and noise over time; quality that differs between two different tones of equal loudness and pitch.

Tonal Diatonic Pitch Class (tdpc)
→pitch class in relation to the overall tonal center of a piece and to its →diatonic scale; only pitch classes of the diatonic scale of the tonality are considered.

Tonal Pitch Class (tpc)
→pitch class in relation to the overall tonal center of a piece of music.

Tuning (system)
the practice of adjusting musical instruments or devices according to a specific system of pitches, often in relation to a fixed reference pitch. The most common tuning in contemporary Western Music is 12-tone equal temperament (12-TET), i.e., an octave is divided in twelve equal intervals, with a reference pitch A4 of 440 Hz.

Variance
a measure for the amount of variation or dispersion within a set of data values; the square of the →standard deviation.

Vector
a geometrical object that has a magnitude (or length) and a direction in several (N) dimensions. Often used in a more abstract sense for a ordered collection of N values.

Vibrato
a more or less regular modulation of a tone; pulsating change of its pitch and/or dynamics.

Walking bass
a style of bass accompaniment with a regular quarter note movement similar to the regular alternation of feet while walking. Walking bass accompaniment was developed during the swing era and is very common among various modern jazz styles.

References

Abeßer, J., Balke, S., Frieler, K., Pfleiderer, M., & Müller, M. (2017). Deep learning for jazz walking bass transcription. In *Proceedings of the AES International Conference on Semantic Audio*. Erlangen, Germany. Retrieved from https://www.audiolabs-erlangen.de/resources/MIR/2017-AES-WalkingBassTranscription/

Abeßer, J., Cano, E., Frieler, K., & Pfleiderer, M. (2014). Dynamics in jazz improvisation – score-informed estimation and contextual analysis of tone intensities in trumpet and saxophone solos. In *Proceedings of the 9th Conference on Interdisciplinary Musicology (CIM)* (pp. 156–161). Berlin, Germany.

Abeßer, J., Cano, E., Frieler, K., Pfleiderer, M., & Zaddach, W.-G. (2015). Score-informed analysis of intonation and pitch modulation in jazz solos. In *Proceedings of the 16th International Society for Music Information Retrieval Conference (ISMIR)*. Málaga, Spain.

Abeßer, J., Frieler, K., Cano, E., Pfleiderer, M., & Zaddach, W.-G. (2017). Score-informed analysis of tuning, intonation, pitch modulation, and dynamics in jazz solos. *IEEE/ACM Transactions on Audio, Speech, and Language Processing*, 25(1), 168–177.

Abeßer, J., Pfleiderer, M., Frieler, K., & Zaddach, W.-G. (2014). Score-informed tracking and contextual analysis of fundamental frequency contours in trumpet and saxophone jazz solos. In *Proceedings of the 17th International Conference on Digital Audio Effects (DAFx-14)*. Erlangen, Germany.

Abeßer, J., & Schuller, G. (2017). Instrument-centered music transcription of solo bass guitar recordings. *IEEE/ACM Transactions on Audio, Speech, and Language Processing*, 25(9), 1741–1750.

Arzt, A. (2016). *Flexible and robust music tracking*. Universität Linz.

Atkins, E. T. (Ed.). (2003). *Jazz planet*. Jackson: University Press of Mississippi.

Baker, D. (1985). *How to play bebop* (Vol. 1). Bloomington: Frangipani Press.

Balke, S., Dittmar, C., Abeßer, J., Frieler, K., Pfleiderer, M., & Müller, M. (2017). Bridging the gap. Enriching YouTube videos with jazz music annotations. *Frontiers in Digital Humanities (accepted)*.

Ballou, G. (2008). *Handbook for sound engineers* (4th ed.). Taylor & Francis.

Barnhart, S. (2005). *The world of jazz trumpet. A comprehensive history & practical philosophy*. Milwaukee, WI: Hal Leonard.

Barrett, S. (2006). Kind of Blue and the economy of modal jazz. *Popular Music, 25*(2), 185–200.

Berliner, P. F. (1994). *Thinking in jazz. The infinite art of improvisation*. Chicago: University of Chicago Press.

Bickl, G. (2000). *Chorus und Linie. Zur harmonischen Flexibilität in der Bebop-Improvisation (= Jazzforschung / Jazz Research, Vol. 32)*. Graz: Akademische Druck- und Verlagsanstalt.

Bjerstedt, S. (2014). *Storytelling in jazz improvisation. Implications of a rich intermedial metaphor*. Lund: Lund University Publications.

Bohlman, P. V., & Plastino, G. (2016). *Jazz worlds, world jazz*. Chicago: University of Chicago Press.

Bowen, J. A. (2011). Recordings as sources in jazz. A performance history of "Body and Soul". In *Five Perspectives on "Body and Soul" and Other Contributions to Music Performance Research. Proceedings of the "International Conference on Music Performance Analysis"* (pp. 15–27). Zürich: Chronos.

Bregman, A. S. (1990). *Auditory scene analysis. The perceptual organization of sound* (2nd ed.). Cambridge: MIT-Press.

Breiman, L. (2001). Random forests. *Machine Learning, 45*(1), 5–32.

Brogan, D. (1985, September). Branford Marsalis feels the zing and the sting of instant pop. *Chicago Tribune*. Retrieved from http://articles.chicagotribune.com/1985-09-05/features/8502280144_1_branford-marsalis-wynton-marsalis-live-aid

Bronson, B. H. (1949). Mechanical help in the study of folk song. *Journal of American Folklore, 62*, 81–90.

Brownell, J. (1994). Analytical models of jazz improvisation. *Jazzforschung / Jazz Research, 26*, 9–29.

Cano, E., Schuller, G., & Dittmar, C. (2014). Pitch-informed solo and accompaniment separation: towards its use in music education applications. *EURASIP Journal on Advances in Signal Processing*, 1–19.

Cano, P., Batlle, E., Kalker, T., & Haitsma, J. (2005). A review of audio fingerprinting. *The Journal of VLSI Signal Processing, 41*(3), 271–284.

Chilton, J., & Kernfeld, B. (2002). Hinton, Milt. In *The New Grove Dictionary of Jazz* (2nd ed., Vol. 2, pp. 245–246). New York: Grove.

Cohen, J. (1988). *Statistical power analysis for the behavioral sciences* (2nd ed.). New York: Lawrence Erlbaum Associates.

Cole, G. (2006). *The last Miles. The music of Miles Davis, 1980–1991* (repr. in paperback ed.). London: Equinox.

Coleman, S. (n.d.-a). *Biography*. Retrieved 2017-08-15, from http://m-base.com/biography/

Coleman, S. (n.d.-b). *Symmetrical Movement Concept*. Retrieved 2017-08-15, from http://m-base.com/essays/symmetrical-movement-concept/

Cook, N. (2004). Computational and comparative musicology. In E. Clarke & N. Cook (Eds.), *Empirical musicology. Aims, methods, prospects*, (pp. 103–126). Oxford: Oxford University Press.

Cuthbert, M. S., & Ariza, C. (2010). music21. A toolkit for computer-aided musicology and symbolic music data. In *Proceedings of the International Symposium on Music Information Retrieval 11* (pp. 637–642).

D'Agostino, R. B. (1971, August). An omnibus test of normality for moderate and large size samples. *Biometrika*, *58*(2), 341–348.

DeClercq, T., & Temperley, D. (2011). A corpus analysis of rock harmony. *Popular Music*, *30*, 47–70.

DeVeaux, S. (1991). Constructing the jazz tradition. Jazz historiography. *Black American Literature Forum*, *25*, 525–560.

DeVeaux, S. (1997). *The birth of bebop. A social and musical history*. Berkeley: University of California Press.

DeVeaux, S., & Giddins, G. (2009). *Jazz*. New York: Norton.

Dittmar, C., Pfleiderer, M., Balke, S., & Müller, M. (2017). A swingogram representation for tracking micro-rhythmic variation in jazz performances. *Journal of New Music Research*, *46*.

Dittmar, C., Pfleiderer, M., & Müller, M. (2015). Automated estimation of ride cymbal swing ratio in jazz recordings. In M. Müller & F. Wiering (Eds.), *Proceedings of the 16th ISMIR Conference, Málaga, Spain, October 26–30, 2015* (pp. 271–277).

Dowling, W. J., & Fujitani, D. (1971). Contour, interval, and pitch recognition in memory for melodies. *The Journal of the Acoustical Society of America*, *49*(2, Suppl. 2), 524–531.

Eerola, T., & Toiviainen, P. (2004). *MIDI toolbox: MATLAB tools for music research*. University of Jyväskylä.

Finkelman, J. (1997). Charlie Christian and the role of formulas in jazz improvisation. *Jazzforschung / Jazz Research*, *29*, 159–188.

Fletcher, N. H., & Rossing, T. D. (1998). *The physics of musical instruments* (2nd ed.). New York: Springer.

Forte, A. (1973). *The structure of atonal music*. New Haven: Yale University Press.

Fraisse, P. (1982). Rhythm and tempo. In D. Deutsch (Ed.), *The psychology of music* (pp. 149–180). New York: Academic Press.

Friberg, A., & Sundström, A. (2002). Swing ratios and ensemble timing in jazz performance. evidence for a common rhythmic pattern. *Music Perception, 19*, 333–349.

Frieler, K. (2007). Visualizing music on the metrical circle. In *Proceedings of the 8th International Symposium on Music Information Retrieval, ISMIR 2007.* Wien: OCG.

Frieler, K. (2008). Metrical circle map and metrical Markov Chains. In A. Schneider (Ed.), *Systematic and comparative musicology.* Frankfurt/M., Bern: P. Lang.

Frieler, K. (2009). *Mathematik und kognitive Melodieforschung. Grundlagen für quantitative Modelle.* Hamburg: Dr. Kovač.

Frieler, K., & Lothwesen, K. (2012). Gestaltungsmuster und Ideenfluss in Jazzpiano-Improvisationen. Eine Pilotstudie zum Einfluss von Tempo, Tonalität und Expertise. In A. C. Lehmann, A. Jeßulat, & C. Wünsch (Eds.), *Kreativität – Struktur und Emotion* (pp. 256–265). Würzburg: Königshausen & Neumann.

Frieler, K., & Pfleiderer, M. (2017). Onbeat oder offbeat? Überlegungen zur symbolischen Darstellung von Musik am Beispiel der metrischen Quantisierung. In M. Eibl & M. Gaedke (Eds.), *INFORMATIK 2017* (pp. 111–125). Bonn: Gesellschaft für Informatik.

Frieler, K., Pfleiderer, M., Abeßer, J., & Zaddach, W.-G. (2016a). Midlevel analysis of monophonic jazz solos. A new approach to the study of improvisation. *Musicae Scientiae, 20*(2), 143–162.

Frieler, K., Pfleiderer, M., Abeßer, J., & Zaddach, W.-G. (2016b). "Telling a story". On the dramaturgy of monophonic jazz solos. *Empirical Musicology Review, 11*(1). Retrieved from http://emusicology.org/article/view/4959

Gabbard, K. (Ed.). (1995a). *Jazz among the discourses.* Durham: Duke University Press.

Gabbard, K. (Ed.). (1995b). *Representing jazz.* Durham: Duke University Press.

Gabbard, K. (1996). *Jammin' at the margins. Jazz and the American cinema.* Chicago: University of Chicago Press.

Gans, C. J. (2017). *Saxophonist completes final pilgrimage.* Retrieved from http://www.michaelbreckerliverecordings.com/Reviews/Pilgrimage%20review%20by%20Charles%20Gans%20Associared%20Press.pdf

Gioia, T. (1992). *West Coast jazz: modern jazz in California, 1945–1960.* New York: Oxford University Press.

Givan, B. (2016). Rethinking interaction in jazz improvisation. *Music Theory Online*, 22(3).

Gliesche, G. (2006). *Paul Desmond. Der Poet auf dem Altsaxophon*. Heidenau: PD-Verl.

Goldsher, A. (2002). *Hard bop academy: the sidemen of Art Blakey and the Jazz Messengers* (1st ed.). Milwaukee: Hal Leonard.

Goodrick, M. (1987). *The advancing guitarist. Applying guitar concepts & techniques*. Milkwaukee: Hal Leonard.

Goodwin, J. D. (2015, January). Branford Marsalis, taking the long view. *Boston Globe*. Retrieved from https://www.bostonglobe.com/arts/music/2015/01/24/branford-marsalis-taking-long-view/v61yiNOgm1dbZuQCfWDsDK/story.html

Gordon, R. (1986). *Jazz West Coast. The Los Angeles jazz scene of the 1950s*. London, New York: Quartet Books.

Grella, G. (2015). *Bitches brew*. New York: Bloomsbury Academic.

Gridley, M. C. (1978). *Jazz styles. History and analysis*. Englewood Cliffs: Prentice Hall.

Harrison, M., & Kernfeld, B. (2001). Desmond, Paul. In B. Kernfeld (Ed.), *The New Grove Dictionary of Jazz* (2nd ed., Vol. 1, pp. 605–606). New York: Grove.

Harte, Christopher, Sandler, M., Samer, A., & Gómez, E. (2005). Symbolic representation of musical chords. A proposed syntax for text annotations. In *Proceedings of the 6th International Conference on Music Information Retrieval (ISMIR)* (pp. 66–71). Queen Mary, London. Retrieved from http://ismir2005.ismir.net/proceedings/1080.pdf

Hellhund, H. (1985). *Cool Jazz. Grundzüge seiner Entstehung und Entwicklung*. Mainz: Schott.

Hodeir, A. (1956). *Hommes et problèmes du jazz. Suivi de la religion du jazz*. Paris: Portulan.

Hodson, R. (2007). *Interaction, improvisation, and interplay in jazz*. New York/London: Routledge.

Huron, D. (1996). The melodic arch in western folksongs. *Computing in Musicology*, 10, 3–23.

Huron, D. (1999). *The Humdrum toolkit. Software for music research*. Retrieved 2016-01-02, from http://dactyl.som.ohio-state.edu/Humdrum (Published Online Manual)

ISO16:1975. (1975). *Acoustics – Standard tuning frequency (standard musical pitch)* (Standard Specification). International Organization for Standardization.

Jackson, T. A. (2012). *Blowin' the blues away. Performance and meaning on the New York jazz scene*. Berkeley: University of California Press.

Jost, E. (1975). *Free Jazz. Stilkritische Untersuchungen zum Jazz der 60er Jahre*. Mainz: Schott.

Jost, E. (1987). *Europas Jazz 1960-80*. Frankfurt: Fischer.

Jost, E. (2003). *Sozialgeschichte des Jazz* (1st ed.). Frankfurt: Zweitausendeins.

Kelman, J. (2007, September). *Chris Potter Underground: Follow the Red Line: Live at the Village Vanguard*. Retrieved from https://www.allaboutjazz.com/follow-the-red-line-live-at-the-village-vanguard-chris-potter-sunnyside-records-review-by-john-kelman.php

Kernfeld, B. (1995). *What to listen for in jazz*. New Haven and London: Yale University Press.

Kernfeld, B. (2002a). Hubbard, Freddie. In *The New Grove Dictionary of Jazz* (2nd ed., Vol. 2, pp. 288–289). New York: Grove.

Kernfeld, B. (2002b). Improvisation. In B. Kernfeld (Ed.), *The New Grove Dictionary of Jazz* (2nd ed., Vol. 2, pp. 313–322). New York: Grove.

Kernfeld, B. (2002c). Shaw, Woody. In *The New Grove Dictionary of Jazz* (2nd ed., Vol. 3, pp. 557–558). New York: Grove.

Kerschbaumer, F. (1971). Zum Personalstil von Miles Davis. *Jazzforschung / Jazz Research*, 3/4, 225–232.

Kerschbaumer, F. (1978). *Miles Davis. Stilkritische. Untersuchungen zur musikalischen Entwicklung seines Personalstils*. Graz: Akademische Druck- und Verlags-Anstalt.

Kerschbaumer, F. (2003). Hubbard, Freddie. In *Die Musik in Geschichte und Gegenwart. Personenteil* (2nd ed., Vol. 9, pp. 435–437). Kassel: Bärenreiter.

Kerschbaumer, F. (2006). Shaw, Woody Herman II. In *Die Musik in Geschichte und Gegenwart. Personenteil* (2nd ed., Vol. 15, pp. 685–686). Kassel: Bärenreiter.

Kipperman, J. P. (2016). *Milt 'The Judge' Hinton. A musical analysis* (Unpublished doctoral dissertation). University of Miami.

Kissenbeck, A. (2007). *Jazztheorie*. Kassel: Bärenreiter.

Knees, P., & Schedl, M. (2016). *Music similarity and retrieval*. Heidelberg: Springer.

Krieger, F. (1995). *Jazz-Solopiano. Zum Stilwandel am Beispiel ausgewählter "'Body and Soul'"-Aufnahmen von 1938--1992 (= Jazzforschung/Jazz Research, Vol. 27)*. Graz: Akademische Druck- und Verlagsanstalt.

Kunzler, M. (2002). Desmond, Paul. In M. Kunzler (Ed.), *Jazz-Lexikon* (2nd ed., pp. 292–293). Reinbek bei Hamburg: Rohwolt.

Kunzler, M. (2004a). Hubbard, Frederick Dewyne ("Freddie"). In *Jazz-Lexikon* (2nd ed., Vol. 2, pp. 581–583). Reinbek bei Hamburg: Rohwolt.

Kunzler, M. (2004b). Shaw, Woody Herman II. In *Jazz-Lexikon* (2nd ed., Vol. 2, pp. 1205–1206). Reinbek bei Hamburg: Rohwolt.

Langner, J., & Goebel, W. (2003). Visualizing expressive performance in tempo–loudness space. *Computer Music Journal*, 27(4), 69–83.

Lee, C.-H., Shih, J.-L., Yu, K.-M., & Lin, H.-S. (2009). Automatic music genre classification based on modulation spectral analysis of spectral and cepstral features. *IEEE Transactions on Multimedia*, 11(4), 670–682.

Lee, D. D., & Seung, H. S. (2001). Algorithms for non-negative matrix factorization. *Advances in Neural Information Processing Systems*, 556–562.

Lerdahl, F., & Jackendoff, R. (1983). *A generative theory of tonal music*. Cambridge, MA: The MIT press.

Levenshtein, V. I. (1965). Binary codes capable of correcting deletions, insertions, and reversals. *Doklady Akademii Nauk SSSR*, 163(4), 845–848. (English translation in: Soviet Physics Doklady, 10(8), pp. 707–710, 1966)

Levine, M. (1995). *Jazz theory book*. Petaluma: Sher Music.

Liebman, D. (2006). *A chromatic approach to jazz harmony and melody*. Rottenburg: Advance Music.

Lomax, A. (1976). *Cantometrics. An approach to the anthropology of music*. Berkeley: University of California Extension Media Center.

Mauch, M. (2010). *Automatic chord transcription from audio using computational models of musical context* (Unpublished doctoral dissertation). Queen Mary University of London, London.

Mauch, M., & Dixon, S. (2014). PYIN: A fundamental frequency estimator using probabilistic threshold distributions. In *Proceedings of the 39th IEEE International Conference on Acoustics, Speech and Signal Processing (ICASSP)* (pp. 659–663). Florence, Italy.

Meyers, J. P. (2015). Standards and signification between jazz and fusion: Miles Davis and "I Fall in Love Too Easily," 1963–1970. *Jazz Perspectives*, 9(2), 113–136.

Milkowski, B. (2012). *Like it is: The Branford Marsalis interview. Bill Milkowski's extended conversation from the october issue*. Retrieved from https://jazztimes.com/features/like-it-is-the-branford-marsalis-interview/

Milkowski, B. (2017). *Chris Potter – Bio*. Retrieved from http://chrispotter.net/home/biography

Monson, I. (1996). *Saying something. Jazz improvisation and interaction*. Chicago: University of Chicago Press.

Müllensiefen, D., & Frieler, K. (2004). Cognitive adequacy in the measurement of melodic similarity. Algorithmic vs. human judgments. *Computing in Musicology, 13,* 147–176.

Müllensiefen, D., Frieler, K., & Pfleiderer, M. (2009). The perception of accents in pop music melodies. *Journal of New Music Research, 38*(1), 19–44.

Müllensiefen, D., Wiggins, G., & Lewis, D. (2008). High-level feature descriptors and corpus-based musicology. Techniques for modelling music cognition. In A. Schneider (Ed.), *Systematic and Comparative Musicology (= Hamburger Jahrbuch für Musikwissenschaft, Vol. 25)* (pp. 133–156). Frankfurt/M., Bern: P. Lang.

Müller, C. (2017). *Doing Jazz. Zur Konstitution einer kulturellen Praxis.* Weilerstwist: Velbrück.

Müller, M. (2015). *Fundamentals of music processing: Audio, analysis, algorithms, applications.* Heidelberg: Springer.

Müller, M., & Ewert, S. (2011). Chroma Toolbox: MATLAB implementations for extracting variants of chroma-based audio features. In *Proceedings of the 12th International Society for Music Information Retrieval Conference (ISMIR)* (pp. 215–220). Miami, USA.

Nicholson, S. (2005). *Is jazz dead? (Or has it moved to a new address).* New York: Routledge.

Nicholson, S. (2014). *Jazz and culture in a global age.* Boston: Northeastern.

Norgaard, M. (2008). *Descriptions of improvisational thinking by artist-level jazz musicians* (Unpublished doctoral dissertation). University of Texas, Austin.

Norgaard, M. (2014). How jazz musicians improvise. The central role of auditory and motor patterns. *Music Perception: An Interdisciplinary Journal, 31*(3), 271–287.

O'Meally, R. G. (Ed.). (2007). *The jazz cadence of American culture.* New York: Columbia University Press.

O'Meally, R. G., Edwards, B. H., & Griffin, F. J. (Eds.). (2004). *Uptown conversations. The new jazz studies.* New York: Columbia University Press.

Owens, T. (1974). *Charlie Parker. Techniques of improvisation* (Unpublished doctoral dissertation). University of California, Los Angeles.

Owens, T. (1995). *Bebop. The music and its players.* New York: Oxford University Press.

Owens, T. (2002). Analysing jazz. In M. Cooke & D. Horn (Eds.), *The Cambridge companion to jazz* (pp. 286–297). New York: Cambridge University Press.

Painter, T., & Spanias, A. (2000). Perceptual coding of digital audio. *Proceedings of the IEEE*, *88*(4), 451–515.

Panken, T. (2016). *For Harry Connick's 49th birthday, a jazziz feature article from 2002.* Retrieved from https://tedpanken.wordpress.com/2016/09/11/for-harry-connicks-49th-birthday-a-jazziz-feature-article-from-2002/

Parsons, D. (1975). *The directory of tunes and musical themes.* London: British Library.

Peeters, G. (2004). *A large set of audio features for sound description (similarity and classification) in the CUIDADO project.* IRCAM.

Pfleiderer, M. (2005). Steve Coleman. In P. N. Wilson (Ed.), *Jazz Klassiker* (pp. 801–807). Stuttgart: Reclam.

Pfleiderer, M. (2006). *Rhythmus. Psychologische, theoretische und stilanalytische Aspekte populärer Musik.* Bielefeld: transcript.

Pfleiderer, M. (2011). "Body and Soul" and the mastery of the jazz tenor saxophone. In *Five perspectives on "Body and Soul" and other contributions to music performance research. Proceedings of the "International Conference on Music Performance Analysis"* (pp. 29–43). Zürich: Chronos.

Pfleiderer, M., Frieler, K., & Zaddach, W.-G. (2016). Pitch class hierarchies in Miles Davis's "So What". Reconsidering modal jazz improvisation with computer-based analysis tools. In W. Auhagen & W. Hirschmann (Eds.), *Beitragsarchiv zur Jahrestagung der Gesellschaft für Musikforschung Halle/Saale 2015 – Musikwissenschaft: die Teildisziplinen im Dialog.* Mainz: Schott-Campus.

Polkow, D. (1989, August). Jazz vs. Pop. For Branford Marsalis, it doesn't pay to be a purist. *Chicago Tribune.* Retrieved from http://articles.chicagotribune.com/1989-08-07/features/8901030105_1_branford-marsalis-kenny-kirkland-wynton

Porter, L. (1985). *Lester Young.* Boston: Twayne.

Porter, L. (1998). *John Coltrane, his life and music.* Ann Arbor: University of Michigan Press.

Porter, L., Ullman, M., & Hazell, E. (Eds.). (1993). *Jazz. From its origins to its present.* Englewood Cliffs: Prentice Hall.

Poutiainen, A. (1999). *Brecker and patterns. An analysis of Michael Brecker's melodic and instrumental devices.* (Unpublished doctoral dissertation). Sibelius Academy Helsinki, Helsinki.

Prouty, K. E. (2010). Toward jazz's "official" history. The debates and discourses of jazz history textbooks. *Journal of Music History Pedagogy*, *1*(2), 19–43.

Putschögl, G. (1993). *John Coltrane und die afroamerikanische Oraltradition (=Jazzforschung / Jazz Research, Vol. 25)*. Graz: Akademische Druck- und Verlags-Anstalt.

R Development Core Team. (2008). *R: A language and environment for statistical computing*. Vienna.

Ramsey, D., Brubeck, D., Brubeck, I., & Caulfield, P. (2005). *Take five. The public and private lives of Paul Desmond*. Seattle: Parkside Publications.

Rawlings, D. F. (2003). *Brecker's blues. Transcription and theoretical analysis of six selected improvised blues solos by jazz saxophonist Michael Brecker* (Unpublished doctoral dissertation). Ohio State University.

Raz, G. (2012). *Branford Marsalis on sensitive musicians and the first family of jazz*. Retrieved from http://www.npr.org/sections/ablogsupreme/2012/08/11/158525752/branford-marsalis-on-sensitive-musicians-and-the-first-family-of-jazz

Reid, G. (2010, June). *Branford Marsalis interviewed (1988). Family matters.* Retrieved from https://www.elsewhere.co.nz/jazz/3196/branford-marsalis-interviewed-1988-family-matters/

Richardson, E. R. (2006). *Structural elegance and harmonic disparity in selected solos by jazz trumpeters Freddie Hubbard and Woody Shaw*. Retrieved from http://digitalcommons.lsu.edu/cgi/viewcontent.cgi?article=1028&context=gradschool_majorpapers

Rusch, R., Salley, K., & Stover, C. (2016). Capturing the ineffable. Three transcriptions of a jazz solo by Sonny Rollins. *Music Theory Online*, 22(3). Retrieved from http://mtosmt.org/issues/mto.16.22.3/mto.16.22.3.rusch.html

Sagee, A. (2003). Miles Davis's improvised solos in recordings of "Walkin'{}": 1954–67. *Annual Review of Jazz Studies, 13*, 27–47.

Sandke, R. (2000). The trumpet in jazz. In B. Kirchner (Ed.), *The Oxford companion to jazz*. Oxford, New York: Oxford University Press.

Schuller, G. (1958). Sonny Rollins and the challenge of thematic improvisation. *Jazz Review, November 58*, 6–11.

Schuller, G. (1968). *Early jazz. Its roots and musical development*. Oxford, New York: Oxford University Press.

Schuller, G. (1989). *The swing era. The development of jazz 1930–45*. Oxford, New York: Oxford University Press.

Schütz, M. (2015). *Improvisation im Jazz. Eine empirische Untersuchung bei Jazzpianisten auf der Basis der Ideenflussanalyse*. Hamburg: Dr. Kovač.

Seeger, C. (1958). Prescriptive and descriptive music writing. *The Musical Quaterly, 44*(2), 184–195.

Selfridge-Field, E. (Ed.). (1997). *Beyond MIDI. The handbook of musical codes*. Cambridge: The MIT Press.

Shannon, C. E. (1948). A mathematical theory of communication. *Bell System Technical Journal*, *27*(3), 379-423 and 623-656.

Shipton, A. (2007). *A new history of jazz* (Rev. and updated ed.). New York: Continuum.

Smith, G. E. (1991). In quest of a new perspective on improvised jazz: A view from the Balkans. *The World of Music*, *33*(3), 29-52.

Sudnow, D. (1999). *Ways of the hand. The organization of improvised conduct.* Cambridge, MA: MIT Press.

Sugg, A. (2014). *The influence of John Coltrane's music on improvising saxophonists. Comparing selected improvisations of Coltrane, Jerry Bergonzi, and David Liebman.* Lewiston: The Edwin Mellen Press.

Sullivan, L. T. (n.d.). *Don Byas. Legendary jazz saxophonist.* Retrieved from http://donbyas.jazzgiants.net

Svorinich, V. (2015). *Listen to this: Miles Davis and Bitches Brew.* Jackson: University Press of Mississippi.

Temperley, D., & DeClercq, T. (2013). Statistical analysis of harmony and melody in rock music. *Journal of New Music Research*, *42*, 187-204.

Tercinet, A. (1986). *West Coast jazz.* Marseille: Parenthèses.

Terefenko, D. (2014). *Jazz theory. From basic to advanced study.* New York: Routledge.

Tingen, P. (2001). *Miles beyond. The electric explorations of Miles Davis, 1967-1991.* New York: Billboard Books.

Tirro, F. (1974). Constructive elements in jazz improvisation. *Journal of the American Musicological Society*, *27*, 285-305.

Tirro, F. (1977). *Jazz. A history.* New York: W.W. Norton.

Tjao, S. K., & Liu, K. J. R. (2010). Musical instrument recognition using biologically inspired filtering of temporal dictionary atoms. In *Proceedings of the 11th International Society for Music Information Retrieval Conference (ISMIR)* (pp. 435-440).

Tomlinson, G. (1991). Cultural dialogics and jazz. A white historian signifies. *Black Music Research Jounal*, *11*(2), 229-264.

Valk, J. d. (1991). *Chet Baker.* Schaftlach: Oreos.

Waters, K. (2011). *The studio recordings of the Miles Davis Quintet, 1965-68.* New York: Oxford University Press.

Weiskopf, W., & Ricker, R. (1993). *The augmented scale in jazz.* New Albany: Jamey Aebersold Jazz.

Williams, M. (1973). *The Smithsonian collection of classic jazz.* Smithsonian Collection – P6 11891.

Wilson, P. N. (2001). *Miles Davis. Sein Leben, seine Musik, seine Schallplatten.* Waakirchen: Oreos.

Winkler, P. (1997). Writing ghost notes. The poetics and politics of transcription. In D. Schwarz, A. Kassabian, & L. Siegel (Eds.), *Keeping score. Music, disciplinarity, culture* (pp. 169–203). Charlottsville: University Press of Virginia.

Yanow, S. (2017). *Branford Marsalis, Trio Jeepy.* Retrieved from http://www.allmusic.com/album/trio-jeepy-mw0000200678

Zanette, D. H. (2006). Zipf's law and the creation of musical context. *Musicae Scientiae, 10*, 3–18.

www.ingramcontent.com/pod-product-compliance
Lightning Source LLC
Chambersburg PA
CBHW051557230426
43668CB00013B/1880